Mapping Civilizations Across Eurasia

H. K. Chang

Mapping Civilizations Across Eurasia

Translated by Bruce Humes in collaboration with the author

palgrave
macmillan

H. K. Chang
Hong Kong, China

ISBN 978-981-99-7640-9   ISBN 978-981-99-7641-6 (eBook)
https://doi.org/10.1007/978-981-99-7641-6

Jointly published with Foreign Language Teaching and Research Publishing Co., Ltd
The print edition is not for sale in the mainland of China. Customers from the mainland of China please order the print book from: Foreign Language Teaching and Research Publishing Co., Ltd

© Foreign Language Teaching and Research Publishing Co., Ltd 2023

This work is subject to copyright. All rights are solely and exclusively licensed by the Publisher, whether the whole or part of the material is concerned, specifically the rights of translation, reprinting, reuse of illustrations, recitation, broadcasting, reproduction on microfilms or in any other physical way, and transmission or information storage and retrieval, electronic adaptation, computer software, or by similar or dissimilar methodology now known or hereafter developed.
The use of general descriptive names, registered names, trademarks, service marks, etc. in this publication does not imply, even in the absence of a specific statement, that such names are exempt from the relevant protective laws and regulations and therefore free for general use.
The publishers, the authors, and the editors are safe to assume that the advice and information in this book are believed to be true and accurate at the date of publication. Neither the publishers nor the authors or the editors give a warranty, expressed or implied, with respect to the material contained herein or for any errors or omissions that may have been made. The publishers remain neutral with regard to jurisdictional claims in published maps and institutional affiliations.

Cover illustration: funkyfood London-Paul Williams/Alamy Stock Photo

This Palgrave Macmillan imprint is published by the registered company Springer Nature Singapore Pte Ltd.
The registered company address is: 152 Beach Road, #21-01/04 Gateway East, Singapore 189721, Singapore

Paper in this product is recyclable.

Contents

Part I Introduction

1 **Mapping Civilizations** — 3
   The Genes Behind Civilization — 3
   The Course of Civilization's Development — 8
   Modules of Civilization — 13
   Interactions Between Civilizations — 16
   Current Dilemmas — 24
   The Outlook for Civilization — 26

Part II Studies on Civilization

2 **From Movable Type to the World Wide Web** — 35
   Recollections in the Long River of Time — 35
   An Advanced Society — 39
   The Meteoric Rise of Arabian Civilization — 42
   Civilizations that Influenced the World — 48
   Super-Stable Structure — 50
   Western Science Migrates East — 54
   The I Ching *and Microelectronics* — 55
   The C++ Project — 57
   In Today's World — 59

3	**Speaking of Mesopotamia**	63
	The Cradle of Civilization	63
	Heirs to Ancient Civilizations	65
	Complex Role of the British	65
	Iraq and Syria Today	67
4	**My Take on the Middle East**	69
	What Is the "Greater Middle East"?	70
	Decoding the Region's History of Violent Conflict	72
	Islamic Tradition	74
	The Development Dilemma and Democracy's Double-Edged Sword	77
5	**Cultural Conflict and Integration Throughout History**	81
	Cultural Integration: From Nomadic Society to Agrarian Society	81
	Inclusiveness: The Root of the Chinese Nation's Vitality	82
	Years: Paper's Long March to the West	84
	Kaifeng and Baghdad: Concurrent Global Cultural Centers	85
6	**Tracing the Footsteps and Influence of Xuanzang and Ibn Battuta**	89
7	**My Views on Orientology, Area Studies and Silk Road Research**	99
	Orientology: A Retrospective	100
	Overview of Area Studies	106
	Placing Our Hopes in Silk Road Exploration and Research	111

Part III Silk Road

8	**Cultural Interaction Along the Silk Road**	119
	Five Silk Road Trailblazers	120
	Faith and Worship	128
9	**The New Silk Road: Strategic Thinking**	135
	Sea Power, Terrestrial Power and Geopolitics	135
	New Era, New Power, New Reasoning	137
	Silk Road Rules of Conduct	140

10	Frankincense, Oil and Geopolitics	145
	The 2015 Doha Forum	145
	Frankincense and Oil	147
	Actions of the Colonialists	147
	Relations Between Middle Eastern Oil-Producing Countries	149
	The War in Iraq and Oil Prices	150
	Pax Americana and New Geopolitics	151
	Future Energy Demands	153
	Whither the Middle East?	154
11	China and Pakistan: A Historical View	157
	The Indus Valley Figurines: Who Are We?	158
	The Gandhara Statues: We Belong to Everyone	158
	Cheng He and Chen Cheng: We Are Friends from Afar	159
	Babur and Akbar: We Bestow Order and Harmony	160
	Karakoram Mountains: We Are Not Your Barriers	161
	The China–Pakistan Economic Corridor: We Bring Prosperity	162
12	Tempest in Eurasia: Russia, Ukraine and Georgia	163
	Prelude to the Russo-Ukrainian War	163
	Shared Roots	165
	Turkic, Norman, Slavic and Mongolian Peoples	167
	The Grand Principality of Moscow and the Kipchak, Crimean and Kazan Khanates	167
	Proud but Isolated Georgia	169
	Ukraine's Destiny	171
	Pawns in a Strategic Game: Ukraine and Georgia	173
	Tough but Vulnerable	174

Part IV Survey of Greater Central Asia

13	Greater Central Asia and the New Silk Road	179
	What Constitutes "Greater Central Asia"?	180
	Three Environments, Three Cultures	181
	Turbulent Times Along the Silk Road	182
14	Migration of Populations Within Greater Central Asia	185
	Clues to Understanding Greater Central Asia	185
	The Warp and Weft of History	187
	4,500–2,300 Years Ago: Indo-European Tribes Migrate Eastward in Four Waves	187

	Second Century BCE to Eighth Century CE: Altaic Tribes Migrate from East to West in Three Waves	189
	Eighth–Twentieth Centuries: Successive Invasions by Arabs, Mongols, and Russians	192
15	**Greater Central Asia: A Cultural Mosaic**	197
	Herding Sheep by Lake Baikal	197
	History of Lake Baikal	198
	Greater Central Asia as Seen from Southern Gansu and the Hexi Corridor	199
	Scientists and "Father of Algebra"	200
	Lahore: Sights and Thoughts	202
	Central and Southern Asia: Like "Lips and Teeth"	203
	The Sogdian Homeland	204
	Tradition and Modern: Kazakhstan's Old and New Capital	205
16	**My Journeys to Xinjiang: From Dream to Reality**	209
	Hami Wheat and "Hami Melon"	210
	Turpan: Ancient Documents, Origins of Its People	211
	Urumqi's Erdaoqiao and an Elderly Turkic Language Scholar	213
	Korla's Hong Konger	214
	Kucha's Murals and Pipa Tunes	215
	Khotan: Gangzi Rou and Donkey-Powered Cart	217
	Kashgar: Cultural and Religious Status	218
	Yining: Nomads and Border Town	221
	Altay: Tuva and an Eight-Year-Old Girl	222

Part V Portrait of India

17	**Experiencing Emerging India**	227
	Indian Affinities	228
	Bangalore and Soft Power	229
	Closed-Door Brainstorming Session in Goa	231
	Calcutta and Vestiges of the British Raj	234
18	**Getting Acquainted with the Indian Elephant**	239
	Ethnicities and Tongues	239
	Rebellion, Independence, Constitution	241
	Religious Society, Secular Nation	243
	Democracy, Rule of Law, Corruption and Electoral Bribery	245
	Great Wealth, Extreme Poverty and Tardy Justice	247
	Tradition vs. Westernization: The Sole Option?	249

19	**India's "Special Administrative Region"—Pondicherry**	253
	Tamil Nadu's Ancient Tongue	253
	Snapshot of Chennai	255
	Britain and France Battle for India	256
	India's Union Territory	258
	Culture and Customs of Pondicherry	259
20	**India's Take on "Belt and Road"**	263
	Ancient Civilization, Massive Population, Advantageous Geography	263
	India's Early Maritime Navigation	265
	The Indian Ocean: An Inland Arab Sea	267
	Maritime and Land-Based Trade Under the Mongols	267
	The Indian Ocean After the Sixteenth Century	268
	Belt and Road: But How Do the Indians See It?	269
	Three Sorts of Reactions	271
	Tenor of Sino-Indian Relations	272
	May Each Party's Beauty Shine Forth	273

Part VI Persian Cultural Sphere

21	**Early Civilizations on the Iranian Plateau**	277
	Geography and Human Environment	277
	Three Early Civilizations	278
	Aryans: Masters of Iran	279
	The Median and Persian Kingdoms	280
	The Achaemenid Empire	281
	Grecian Influence	283
22	**Renascence of Persian Culture**	287
	Hellenization and Persianization	287
	The Prophet Born Smiling	289
	Parthian Empire: Founded on Horseback	290
	Persia Pushes Back Against the Romans	291
	Zoroastrianism and Manichaeism Under the Sassanids	292
	Anushirvan and the Sassanian Renascence	295
23	**Islam and the Invaders**	299
	Persia: Islamization and Arabization	300
	Persianization of Islam	302
	Islamic Civilization: The Perso-Arabic Version	303

	The Persians Establish Regional Regimes	305
	Invasion by Turkic Peoples and Mongols	307
	The Timurid Empire and Islamic Renaissance	310
24	**Persian Poetry and Painting**	315
	Persian Cultural Awareness: Inspired by Invaders	315
	Hallmarks and Evolution of Persian Four-line Verse	316
	Sufi Poetry: Intoxicated by Romance	318
	From Bas-Reliefs to Persian Miniatures	321
	Miniature Painting Guide: My Name Is Red	322
25	**Shia Islam and the Safavid Dynasty**	327
	Sufism and Sufi Orders	332
	Turkmen Military Alliances and the Safavids' "Red Heads"	334
	Shah Abbas the Great	335
26	**Persian Civilization and Iran's Modernization**	339
	The Qajar Dynasty Reforms	340
	The Pahlavi Dynasty	343
	The White Revolution	346
	Revolution and Modernization, Cleric-Style	347

Part VII Caucasus

27	**Ethnographic Museum on the Border Between Europe and Asia**	355
	The Caucasus: Geography and Culture with a Difference	356
	A Virtual Museum of Peoples and Tongues	359
28	**Musical Chairs in the Caucasus**	365
	The Tujüe Make Their Entrance	365
	The Persian Renaissance	367
	The Russian Long-term Strategy	369
29	**North Caucasus: Russia's Southern Frontier**	373
	Unique Peoples of the North Caucasus	374
	Circassian Traumas	375
	Crimean War: Causes and Consequences	378
	Soviet Era: Policy Toward North Caucasus	379
	The North Caucasus after the Second Chechen War	380

30	The Post-Soviet South Caucasus	383
	Georgia and its "European Complex"	384
	Azerbaijan and Black Gold	386
	Armenia and a Twentieth-Century Massacre	388
	Awkward Transcaucasia	389
31	South Caucasus: International Machinations	391
	Maneuvers of the Turks, Iranians and Russians	392
	What the United States, EU and Russia May Envision	395

Part VIII Turkish March

32	Westward Migration of the Turkic-speaking People	401
	From the Yenisei River to the Danube (552–1529)	402
	From Principality to Empire (1299–1566)	404
	From Brave Armies to Conniving Courtiers (1566–1699)	408
33	The Road to Republicanism	411
	From "Study the Barbarians" to "Reform and Adjustment" (1699–1839)	412
	From Reform to Revolution (1839–1908)	415
	Constitutional Monarchy to Republic (1908–1923)	418
34	Toward a Modern Republic	423
	A Fitting Hero for His Era (1919–1938)	423
	The Atatürk Era—without Kemal Atatürk (1938–1980)	429
	Geopolitics and Changes in Social Structure (1980–2014)	431
35	European Turkey: The Bosphorus and Edirne	435
	Living in Both Europe and Asia	435
	A Visit to Architect Sinan's Chef-d'oeuvre	439
36	Anatolian Turkey: Trabzon and Konya	441
	Greek Church, Tea Plants and a Wedding Party	441
	Checking out Rumi's Roots	444
37	Emergence of Neo-Ottomanism	449

Part IX Conclusions

38	The Ancient Silk Road: "Geography as Destiny"	459
	Emerging from Africa, Surveying the World	459
	West Asia: Cradle of the Agricultural Revolution	461

	Nomadic Commerce and the Spread of Civilization	463
	Silk, Spices and Empire Building	465
	Linking Europe and Asia by Land and Sea	468
	Pax Mongolica: The Ultimate Land-based Power	469
39	**The New Silk Road: Eurasia's Historical Destiny**	473
	Maritime Power and the Rise of Western Europe	473
	The Industrial Revolution and Colonial Empires	477
	World War I and the American Surge	479
	World War II and American Hegemony	481
	The New Silk Road: Reliant Upon the East	483

Index 487

PART I

Introduction

CHAPTER 1

Mapping Civilizations

By way of introducing this book, I shall take the reader on a journey that spans 7.5 million years of the history of human civilization. What I will say about "civilization" can be divided into six parts:

- The Genes Behind Civilization
- Early Development
- Core "Modules" of Civilization
- Impact of Interactivity
- Current Dilemmas
- Future Outlook

THE GENES BEHIND CIVILIZATION

"Genes" is a popular term nowadays, and everyone is familiar with the older concept of "civilization." But where did the genes of our civilization originate? Here's the picture that initially piqued my interest in human civilization as a whole, and made me consciously seek to comprehend it.

This is a photo I shot in the Ethiopian National Museum. Anthropologists have dubbed this character "Lucy." She lived 3.2 million years ago. As you can see, she could walk upright on two legs and her front limbs were shorter than her hind limbs.

"Lucy" from the Ethiopian National Museum

Her descendants gradually emerged from Ethiopia and trekked to the corners of the world. According to the great majority of paleoanthropologists, Lucy is the common ancestor of mankind. But her cranial capacity was still largely inferior to that of modern man, so scientists classify her as a *Hominid*, not a "human" in the modern sense.

Based on fossils discovered to date, scientists believe that mankind started to differentiate itself from the ape approximately 7.5 million years ago; about 3 million years ago lived the Australopithecus africanus, bipedal hominids who possessed about one-third the cranial volume of modern man; 2 million years ago *Homo habilis*—capable of creating tools—appeared; and about 1.5 million years ago *Homo erectus* emerged, *Hominids* who could not only stand erect but may also have been able to make use of fire.

Homo erectus came out of East Africa and, via the Middle East, arrived in Asia—the "Java Man" and "Peking Man" are both their descendants— and made it to Europe too. About 200,000–500,000 years ago the *Homo erectus* who had remained in Africa evolved into *Homo sapiens*, although the distinction between the two is not perfectly clear.

About 200,000 years ago these *Homo sapiens* also departed from Africa. Their descendants, known as *Homo neanderthalensis*, left behind many remains, tools and traces of human burials throughout the Middle East and Europe. In terms of anatomy, the *Homo sapiens sapiens*—also known as "modern humans"—who emerged about 100,000 years ago were anatomically similar to humans today, and we should be considered their direct descendants.

Some 100,000 years ago, mankind basically consisted of two branches: the more ancient *Homo neanderthalensis* in the Middle East and Europe, and modern humans who spread from Africa throughout the Middle East and Asia, and later reached Europe. The modern humans in Europe both bred with and eventually wiped out *Homo neanderthalensis*. But the shapes of the forehead, brow and chin differed between these two branches, indicating that they underwent distinct evolutionary processes.

Approximately 40,000 years ago, when the earth was in the midst of the Ice Age and the waterway between Indonesia, Australia and New Guinea was still narrow, some modern humans migrated by sea from Indonesia to Australia and New Guinea, becoming the earliest humans in these two places.

Due to warming, the earth later entered the current Fourth Interglacial Period. The oceans rose, landmass receded and Australia became further isolated from adjacent islands and Eurasia. Thus, the modern humans of Australia were deprived of contact with those of other regions for several tens of thousands of years, resulting in very different developments between humans there and continental Eurasia.

Approximately 20,000 years ago, mankind's ability to resist cold was heightened by the use of animal fur, and some modern humans migrated from East Asia to Siberia. Before the glaciers receded, around 15,000 years ago, they crossed the Bering Strait and entered Alaska. These people were the forerunners of the native peoples of the Americas.

Based on archaeological evidence, we know that within less than a millennium after crossing the Bering Strait, they had reached the tip of South America, migrating 15 kilometers southward annually on average. The indigenous peoples of the Americas strongly resemble Northeast Asians, and their shared roots are borne out by DNA research.

Since modern humans share a common ancestor, what makes man different from other animals, and what are man's most intrinsic characteristics? These are questions to be explored by philosophers; I cannot offer a thorough explanation. As a scientist, I will simply enumerate these four points:

1. Humans possess a more complex throat structure than animals which gives us the ability to use sound to communicate, i.e., language;
2. Humans possess emotions such as remorse, envy and yearning, and the depth of these sentiments is unmatched by other animals;
3. Humans can apply rational thought according to certain rules in order to make sense of things and events. Besides experiencing via our senses, we can also make certain inferences based on reasoning;
4. Humans tend to cluster and live in groups, and society's organizational ability and complexity are much greater than those of other animals.

Interestingly, due to evolution the human eye comprises a sclera—the white of the eye—that neither the monkey nor ape possesses. Due to the contrast between the sclera and the colored iris, the human eye can display emotion, and can glare and even convey distrust, facilities that reveal one's thoughts and feelings to others.

Curiously, among animals only man can "flirt" with his eyes. As clever and attuned to people's moods as dogs and monkeys can be, they don't possess this ability.

The first humans to discuss or write "the history of civilization" were members of agrarian societies. Therefore, the starting point of civilization is usually defined as the period when mankind began to consciously cultivate crops for food. If we follow this definition, then the first regions to produce foodstuffs independently should be the sites of the origins of civilization.

Let's first look at the Americas that were isolated geographically from Africa, Europe and Asia, because the Americas formed a separate ecosystem. In Central America, the earliest evidence of food production and storage is mainly of crops such as corn and beans. Later in the Andes Mountains in South America food production appeared, the main types being beans and potatoes.

Now let's look at Africa, Europe and Asia. These three continents hosted four regions of ancient food production, each with its own special crops, and these crops were naturally associated with indigenous wild plants. The earliest agricultural region was in West Asia's Mesopotamia, where farming and animal husbandry were both practiced. Wheat and barley, first planted there, eventually spread throughout Europe, North Africa, South Asia and East Asia. Africa practiced agriculture quite early, the primordial crop being the yam.

India's Indus River Valley had an independently developed agriculture very early, but we do not know which were its main crops. Use of wild rice as food was first experimented some 10,000 years ago along the middle and lower reaches of the Yangtse River, and East and Southeast Asia later emerged as prominent regions for rice production. China's Yellow River Basin developed its own agriculture based mainly on millet. Wheat was introduced later from the Middle East.

I've enumerated a number of crops, but agriculture is not confined to plants—right from the start there was livestock too. Thus the origin of civilization should also be defined as the beginning of animal domestication.

Man's best friend is the dog, and over the last 12,000 years among the animals exploited by man, the dog was the earliest, and the only one that was not raised specifically to be eaten. Sheep and goats were first domesticated in Southwest Asia, about 10,000 years ago, and the pig was also domesticated at that time in China.

The pig is an extremely important creature to the Chinese! The Chinese character for house or home, "*jia*," is a pictograph of a roof with a pig underneath. In ancient China, "*jia*," the family, was the primary social unit and source of power.

The ox, water buffalo, horse and donkey are also worth a mention. The ox was domesticated about 8,000 years ago in India. Water buffalo was tamed 6,000 years ago in China, and so was the horse at about the same time on the grasslands of what is today north of the Black Sea and Caspian Sea, Ukraine.

At first, horses were raised for their meat, and then to transport goods. But later it was discovered that they could be mounted. With their long necks, ability to see into the distance, good memory for the paths they trod, and their intelligence and sensitivity, they were ideal for riding, herding livestock, seasonal migration and use in warfare. Thus was born the lifestyle of the nomadic peoples.

As for the shorter donkey, it should not be underestimated. First domesticated in Egypt 6,000 years ago, it has proven very useful to mankind as a beast of burden. And if they mate, a male donkey and female horse will create a (sterile) mule. The single-hump and double-hump forms of camel were domesticated 3,000–3,500 years ago in Yemen and Central Asia, respectively.

Once mankind and animals bonded, naturally there were innumerable benefits. But they also brought us some deadly "gifts" along the way, for like us, animals are germ carriers. Smallpox, measles, whooping cough and the flu all came to us via animals that we have domesticated—like the "avian influenza H7N9" of our day that was passed to us by poultry. The novel coronavirus that caused the global pandemic in 2019 may have originated from the bat.

THE COURSE OF CIVILIZATION'S DEVELOPMENT

Our knowledge of early human civilization comes primarily from archaeology. Since the nineteenth century, European and American scholars have attached great importance to the disciplines of archaeology and ancient philology. As a result of large-scale excavations conducted worldwide, scholars have discovered large numbers of precious relics such as pottery, bronzes and ancient manuscripts.

From those relics, archaeologists speculated about the lifestyles of peoples inhabiting different regions and during different time periods, as well as the relations between them. For instance, those between Semitic and Mediterranean civilizations. Later, drawing on the findings of those archaeologists, historians dubbed "civilization" the relatively fixed material way of life within a specific but fairly large geographic area, while employing the word "culture" to describe more abstract phenomena such as religious beliefs and social values.

In fact, both are new words coined by eighteenth-century Europeans based on Latin roots: "Civilization" comes from *civilis* (related to or befitting a citizen), and "culture" from *cultura* (agricultural cultivation).

Scholars frequently endow these terms with new shades of meaning, and they are regarded as close synonyms and often used interchangeably.

Approximately 12,000 years ago when the earth entered the current Interglacial Period, the globe was already inhabited by distinct groups of humans. As the earth warmed, more edible species of plant life and animals became available, and man could migrate to previously uninhabitable frigid zones and hunt large animals that had adapted to the cold environment, such as reindeer. At that time, agriculture had either not commenced or was just about to emerge. This is to say, the human beings on the five continents—or six, if Oceania is included—were all poised at the same starting line.

If we fast forward to some 6,000 years ago, agriculture-based societies in the Middle East, South Asia and East Asia were then leading in the development race, while the Americas and southern Africa were far behind. Yet today, it is largely the countries of Western Europe and countries in North America, Oceania and South Africa founded by European colonizers that have taken the lead in establishing the advanced industrialized and post-industrialized societies.

Most of East Asia and Eastern Europe are in hot pursuit but still lagging. Furthest behind are sub-Saharan Africa, and countries in South America's interior and the mountainous regions of Southeast Asia.

It was in the middle of the nineteenth century when European colonial empires ruled the world that Darwin's Theory of Evolution came onto the scene. It provided the Europeans, already infused with a sense of racial superiority, with a timely excuse to argue that the Caucasian race was indeed innately superior, and that persons of brown and black complexion were inherently simple-minded and lazy.

On the one hand, these racists believed in a Christian God and professed to "Love thy Neighbor." Yet on the other hand, they erroneously interpreted the Theory of Evolution. They transformed it into a "social Darwinism" that fostered belief in "survival of the fittest" among different ethnicities and races. It advocated that based on the laws of natural selection, survival itself was proof of superiority—even that "inferior" groups of human beings should be pro-actively eliminated—and thus rationalized genocide.

These ideas were widely circulated by advocates of colonialism, racism and Nazism, to the point where even many of their victims accepted their validity. In recent Chinese history, not a few people have also been subconsciously persuaded by these fallacies. Put simply, they attributed the relative underdevelopment of material culture among certain races or peoples to low IQ or indolence.

But these beliefs do not explain this conundrum: Despite the lack of major changes to the gene pools of the Han Chinese and peoples of Europe over the last millennium, why did Chinese society's development clearly outpace Europe's during the seventh–fifteenth centuries, only to lose leadership to Europe from the eighteenth century onward? Any person influenced by racism and Social Darwinism would inadvertently find himself behaving very courteously to Europeans and Americans, while looking down his nose at the impoverished peoples of underdeveloped countries and ethnic minorities in his own country.

I'd like to spend a few lines here addressing the issues noted above, and speak a bit about the scientific interpretation of the theory of evolution and the impact of geography on human history.

It is common knowledge that humans in cold regions are typically tall and fair-skinned, Lapps and Inuits whose ancestors first arrived near the North Pole 12,000 to 15,000 years ago being notable exceptions. However, their body stature is not shorter than the residents in northern Europe before the fifteenth century, when nutritional improvement began to make the Europeans grow taller than their forefathers.

On the other hand, humans in tropical zones are shorter and their skin color darker.

Seen from the angle of gene mutation, this can be easily explained.

I'll first address skin color and "natural selection." It is widely recognized that exposure to strong ultraviolet radiation leads to skin cancer, while pigmentation can block it and lower the likelihood of cancer. In the tropics, due to a greater likelihood of developing cancer, fair-skinned persons have a lower survival rate and thus reproduce less. Thanks to gene mutation, those possessing darker skin are more likely to live longer and produce more offspring.

Skin color and synthesis of vitamin D are also related. Ultraviolet radiation facilitates the human body's synthesis of vitamin D, which is very important to fortifying bones. In high-latitude frigid regions, there is less sunlight and weaker ultraviolet radiation. If one's skin color is too dark it lacks the means to synthesize vitamin D, and this is deleterious to bone health. If humans in cold regions have lighter skin color, however, their bones will be healthier and this in turn increases reproductive potential.

Therefore, whether from the point of view of avoiding cancer or the state of one's bones, people living near the equator will naturally have relatively darker skin, while those near the North Pole will have fairer skin.

Now let's talk about body height. Any animal, including man, suffers ill effects if its body loses heat too quickly in the winter, or cannot release sufficient body heat in the summer. In order to slow heat release, ideally the ratio of surface area to body volume should be lower; to speed heat dissipation, ideally the ratio of surface area to body volume would be higher.

Imagine two squares, one measuring 1 centimeter on each side, and the other 2 centimeters on each side. Their surface area to volume ratios are, respectively, 6:1 and 24:8—that is, 3:1. So a tall person dissipates heat more slowly, and survives more readily in a cold climate; that he will also lose heat more slowly in the summer doesn't matter, because it doesn't get too hot in a cold region. Conversely, a short person survives more readily in a warm climate, and while he will lose heat more quickly in the winter, this matters little since it doesn't get very cold in the tropics. Therefore, using the Theory of Evolution, it can be clearly explained why some people are dark-skinned and others fair-skinned, and why some are tall and others are short.

Furthermore, according to gene research conducted in recent years, differences among humans in terms of every sort of body shape, skin color, hair, nose and eyes could all have occurred via gene mutations over a 50,000-year period. This signifies that everyone alive today possibly—though not necessarily—descended from a small group of humans who lived 50,000 years ago or earlier. Since all mankind possesses similar genes and potential, theories of superiority or inferiority of a given race based on its genetics are totally untenable.

But how to explain that people of certain regions possessed a glorious civilization several thousand years ago, while people in other regions had not until recently entered the Agricultural Age, and were still stuck in a primitive mode of life, materially speaking?

First of all, let's take a look at the map of the earth's continents. Eurasia is the world's largest landmass. It is located entirely within the northern hemisphere and mainly in a temperate zone. The east–west axis that extends through Eurasia runs between 40- and 50-degrees N latitude. If you were to proceed from the west all the way east, you would not need to pass through regions where temperatures vary greatly, and would find that a grand stretch of grassland—the Eurasian Steppe—extends unbroken from the Danube River to the Greater Khingan Mountains in northeast China.

Then look at Africa. Its widest points are near the equator near which the tropical rain forests impede human movement. Its axis is mainly north–south oriented and passes through bands of different climates. South America is the same. It is a long, narrow shape that extends on either side of the equator, and it features the Andes Mountain Range that runs north–south, dividing the continent into three large parts: the Pacific region, the Atlantic region and the Amazon River Basin that is dominated by tropical rain forests.

Just based on the terrain we know that in Asia and Europe, the movement of man and livestock and the transport of goods are fairly convenient. Hence, different cultures can easily interact and civilization's spread is facilitated. By comparison, such movements are relatively more difficult in South America and Africa.

The primary pre-condition for civilization is agriculture. This requires an appropriate indigenous crop that will grow if cultivated, is adaptable to seasonal change, and doesn't take too long to mature for harvest. Early man could not wait several years for a plant to bear fruit, because he did not have surplus foodstuffs to eat in the meantime.

Wheat, barley, millet and rice are all crops that mature once or even twice yearly. That is why man chose to cultivate them. Of course, without wild wheat there was no domesticated version, and without wild rice there would not have been any rice seeds for human cultivation. Africa and South America didn't have wild wheat, so people couldn't plant it. Originally, neither did Europe nor Asia. But because land-based travel was more feasible, West Asia's wheat spread through Europe, South Asia and East Asia. The development of civilization in Africa and South America, however, was hindered by this inherent lacuna.

The condition required to most directly power early civilization was the availability of large-bodied animals that could be domesticated for transport and farming. I noted earlier that large mammals such as the ox, horse, donkey and camel were domesticated in Asia or Europe. Once domesticated, these animals propagated rapidly. They plowed fields and transported people and goods. And their flesh could be eaten too.

Reflecting on the past, people have often queried: Within one or two centuries of the arrival of the Europeans, why did the US and Australia transform into two of the world's most important granaries and production sites for cotton and sheep's wool, when the native inhabitants had left these same fertile lands undeveloped for ages? The answer is simple: Because the Europeans colonized those continents *after* the commencement of the Industrial Revolution, when they already had modern agricultural technology and tools at their disposal.

As I mentioned earlier, the indigenous people of Australia migrated there by sea from Indonesia some 40,000 years ago, but later sea levels rose and the waterway widened, hindering further migrations. So prior to the eighteenth-century arrival of the Europeans, they had no contact with other peoples, leaving the first inhabitants of Australia with few companions... besides the kangaroo.

Given Australia's and New Guinea's terrain of towering mountains, deserts and ocean shores, eco-systems and species distribution, the indigenous peoples could only reproduce within those limitations. There was little they could do, so they did not develop agriculture. In terms of agricultural output, California is America's leading producer today. But California's aboriginal peoples had no seeds appropriate for cultivation. Even if they had had any, they lacked water for irrigation, because much of California is an arid region. The water now used is transported from the Rocky Mountains via canals stretching 1,500 kilometers.

Based on the above, just one point needs to be remembered: Ten thousand years ago, none of the inhabitants of any continent had attained a "civilized state." Everyone was at the same starting line. But some civilizations got off to a rapid start while others seemed to run in place.

The blame shouldn't be placed entirely on the latter peoples. Or at least we shouldn't simplify things by blaming it on a lack of innate ability, because the earth beneath their feet was not the same; some of it was straight and flat, while other peoples faced rugged, vertical terrain. That's why the pace of civilization's progress differed across the globe.

Modules of Civilization

Because people in different regions faced different environments, distinct "modules" of civilization emerged.

The first module of human civilization was that of Mesopotamia. Early on, the two river basins of West Asia—the Tigris and Euphrates—achieved results that are startling even from our perspective today. For example, the casting of bronze statues some 4,000 years ago, correct calculation of the cube root, and in astronomy, the discovery of the Zodiac that led to the division of the year into 12 months, one day into 24 hours, etc.

In reality, no culture anywhere is entirely "self-invented." Interaction with and borrowing from others is extremely important. For 40,000 years, the Australian continent had no opportunity for contact with other regions, and as a result its inhabitants lived by hunting and foraging.

The "Code of Hammurabi," expressly promulgated about 3,800 years ago, includes details such as the basic principle that the "user" is responsible for payment. For instance, in a transaction between a buyer and a seller, unlike in modern times, there was no "after-sales service"— the seller's responsibility ended once money switched hands. This stipulation and the principle of "eye for an eye, tooth for a tooth," were later incorporated in the Jewish Talmud. The Jews, as well as the Babylonians before and the Assyrians afterward, all spoke a Semitic tongue.

The ancestor of the Jews, Abraham, a shepherd, brought his clan along with their religious philosophy to the Land of Canaan, in territory that is south of today's Syria, Palestine. They merged with Canaanites, earlier residents of this land, to form a mixed culture of the Israelite.

The second module of civilization was located in the Nile Valley. Egypt was not a primordial birthplace of civilization per se, for it spread there from Mesopotamia and flourished mightily thanks to the Nile. The Nile Delta was the recipient of silt left behind in the wake of the river's once yearly downstream floods, rendering the soil remarkably fertile. The Upper Nile has several waterfalls that hinder navigation between it and the Lower Nile. The two constitute separate geographic and cultural regions, the former sparsely peopled, while the latter is rich and heavily populated.

Egypt has always been influenced by the Nile. Some 95% of Egyptians today live by its banks which account for just 5% of the country's territory. The remaining 5% of the people are scattered throughout the other 95% of Egyptian territory that is desert. So this is a highly centralized civilization and the river is its lifeline. The Upper Nile does not generate much production, and historically it has been dominated by the Lower Nile.

The third module of civilization was the Indus Valley. But today's Indians are not the direct heirs of this civilization. Genetically speaking, they may be related, but not in cultural terms. The Indus Valley refers to the five river basins of Punjab. The British discovered the remains of ancient Indus civilization before and after World War I. They excavated several cities, including Mohenjo Daro, which already had bathrooms, drains and devices to warm bathing water some 6,000 years ago. Group burial sites were exhumed there as well. In Harappa, a city with neatly aligned streets, the torso of a male statue was unearthed. He was likely a black-skinned indigene, and not an ancestor of today's Indus Valley inhabitants.

We don't know why, but this civilization later disappeared. When the Aryans invaded India 3,500 years ago, they did not encounter strong resistance from the locals.

Mesopotamia and ancient India were similar in many respects, so they must have interacted. For example, cylindrical rolling seals have been unearthed in both places. Later, the usage of scripts to write Sanskrit and other Indian languages may also have been inspired by the use of cuneiform script in Mesopotamia.

The fourth module of civilization was China's Yellow River civilization. It is known that it fabricated silk more than 5,000 years ago, fine bronzes 3,500 years ago and horse-drawn carriages 2,300 years ago. I assume that the latter were not independently developed by the Chinese, however. Some 4,500 years ago, the Mesopotamians were already using chariots in battle, and they had wheels and spokes as well. Two millennia later King Wu of Zhou used horses to pull his army's chariots, and that shouldn't be a mere coincidence. The horse was domesticated about 6,000 years ago in modern-day Ukraine, and the spokes used in Zhou Dynasty chariots may have originated in the West.

Personally, I find the order of China's "four great inventions" fascinating. The beautiful and highly detailed banner discovered in the Mawangdui Tombs, which dates from 2,100 years ago during the Han Dynasty, was made of silk. This and other relics underline the fact that silk, used for writing and for dress, was created first, while more than two millennia passed before a simpler and more important invention—paper— occurred in China.

Ancient Indic civilization existed very early, and it disappeared mysteriously. More than three thousand years ago the Aryans invaded India from Afghanistan, and their fusion with the erstwhile inhabitants of India created (as it is dubbed in the West) "Hindu" civilization.

From the perspective of physical anthropology, people in the north and west of India are typically a bit taller, and have somewhat more pointed noses and lighter skin, while those in the south tend to be a bit shorter, with darker skin and flatter noses. That is to say, more than 3,000 years after the entry of the Aryans into India, due to reasons of geography, the level of genetic mixing between the Aryans and peoples in the south remains relatively low.

The main languages of India today, classified as Indo-European, share the same roots as those of Europe and Iran. Just which languages the creators of ancient Indian civilization actually spoke remains unclear. The country has 14 legally recognized scripts and 29 official languages. Today's Indian civilization represents the coexistence of several, mainly Hindu and Islamic.

There were several successors to Mesopotamian civilization. One is the Canaanite civilization built by Jews in Palestine; the other successor, the Hittite civilization, is located in modern-day Turkey's central and eastern regions. Hittite civilization reached a very high level during 1,900–1,500 BC, but today's Turks are not descendants of the Hittites.

The third successor to Mesopotamian civilization—though also influenced by Egyptian culture—was the Minoan civilization on the island of Crete. Much fine pottery has been found on the island, as well as vivid rock paintings and an ancient script that has not been decoded because few examples of it have been recovered.

The fusion of Canaanite and Hittite cultures gave birth to the so-called Mediterranean civilization, of which both Greek and Roman civilizations are sub-sets.

The Mediterranean and Canaanite civilizations have two shared descendants: Christianity and Islam. And there is one more—Eastern Orthodox—which first appeared after Roman Empire was split into two parts in the late fifth century and was consolidated around the year 1,000 when the Slavs converted to Eastern Orthodox Christianity, a religion created by the Russians (and the Ukrainians and Serbians) based on the Greek Orthodox variety.

INTERACTIONS BETWEEN CIVILIZATIONS

In this section, I intend to use some concrete examples to illustrate how civilizations interact. Many of them are photos I took when I felt I'd discovered something during my travels.

Over many centuries, the main conduit for exchanges between East Asia and Europe was the "Silk Road." This appellation, a very fitting one, was coined by a nineteenth-century German geographer. Strictly speaking, there are actually three routes: one further north, one to the south and one in between.

North of the Mongolian Plateau and south of the conifer forests of Siberia lies the Eurasian Steppe that extends from Hungary to the Greater Khingan Mountains, and constitutes a "Steppe Silk Road." Historically speaking, it was via this route that the Tocharians and Scythians came from Europe to East Asia, while the Huns and Turkic peoples, and later the Mongols, traversed it in the opposite direction on their way to the West. These migrations are the most obvious examples of interaction between civilizations.

The southern route consists of the land and the sea. Moving from central China southwards via Sichuan and Yunnan, one arrives at modern-day Myanmar and the Indian Ocean, and then onward by sea to the Persian Gulf and, finally, overland to the eastern Mediterranean. Alternatively, one can set out to sea from Guangzhou, follow the Vietnamese coast, bypass the Malay Peninsula, enter the Indian Ocean and then proceed to the Mediterranean. This latter route is the so-called "Maritime Silk Road." Archaeological discoveries prove that goods from Egypt had already reached Guangzhou during the transition between the Qin and Han Dynasties in third century BC.

Between the northern and southern routes is the main route of exchange on the Eurasian landmass for many centuries. If you mention the Silk Road to a Chinese, they are most familiar with this middle route. It covers the areas of Central Asia traversed by Zhang Qian, the Han Dynasty imperial envoy to the exotic "Western Regions," and Faxian and Xuanzang, both pilgrims to India who brought Buddhist canons back to China. Departing from Chang'an, through the Hexi Corridor and desert, over high mountains, this is the famous land-based Silk Road comprising a network of oases, often called "Oasis Silk Road."

It is true that trade was the initial force driving the development of the Silk Road. But it actually promoted relations between different regions and also illustrates interaction between civilizations. Beyond the trade in silk and other goods, the exchange of faiths and lifestyles had a longer-term impact on future generations. The entry of Buddhism into China, for example, was a major event in human history.

In the spring of 2006, I took a month's sabbatical at the Sorbonne, primarily to research ancient European history. Early one morning as I strolled near the campus, I came upon a church that had previously not caught my attention. A brass plaque in French and Arabic at the entrance explains that this place of worship belongs to the Syriac Catholic Church, and mass is conducted in ancient Syriac supplemented by Arabic.

The Syriac Catholic Church differs from the Syrian Orthodox Church (which is independent from the Vatican), and it is also distinct from the Latin Church whose bishops are directly appointed by the Pope. According to an eighteenth-century agreement with the Vatican, the Syriac Catholic Church recognizes papal leadership, but elects its own Patriarch and retains its own Syro-Arabic-based rituals.

I'd like to point out that the earliest Christian churches were, of course, not in Rome. They were in areas such as Palestine, Syria, Asia Minor and Egypt. Each of these places had their own traditions, ceremonies and faithful, and there was no question of who was subordinate to whom. It was only after the Roman Empire designated Christianity as its state religion that the thorny issue of orthodoxy arose.

After several centuries of political and social change, two main branches of Christianity emerged: One formed under the leadership of the Diocese of Rome (with Latin rites), commonly known as the "Roman Catholic Church," and the Eastern Orthodox Church, led by the Patriarch of Constantinople, which follows Greek rites. Apart from these two branches, there are also several fairly large ones in Egypt, Armenia and Ethiopia, and many smaller sects.

During the fifth century, in the wake of the demise of the Western Roman Empire, and the lack of an emperor and the resulting chaos, the Roman Catholic (Latin) Church became a stabilizing force in the societies of Western Europe. This gradually distanced them from the Eastern Orthodox (Greek) Church based in Constantinople. In the seventh century, Muslim armies occupied several territories of the Byzantine Empire, including Egypt, Palestine and Syria. Although their churches were protected under Islamic law, their relations with Constantinople were also greatly diluted as a result.

In the eleventh century, relations between the Roman Catholic and Greek Orthodox churches formally ruptured. Each "ex-communicated" the followers of the other. But some small sects maintained their independence. When the Crusaders occupied Palestine and Syria, a few local Christian sects wished to merge with the Roman Catholic Church. However, due to differences in language, rites and organizational structure, little came of it.

In the fifteenth century the Ottomans destroyed the remnants of the Byzantine Empire, and less than one hundred years later, it won control over Egypt, Palestine, Syria and Iraq. The Ottoman rulers exhibited bias in their treatment of different branches of Christianity: Those close to the Roman Catholic Church were suppressed, while those close to the Greek Orthodox Church fared somewhat better. But more than a century later, the power of the Roman Catholic Church grew stronger thanks to Europe's rise, and the Greek Orthodox Church grew more autonomous due to the increasing vulnerability of the Ottoman Empire.

In the eighteenth century, Western Europe grew increasingly powerful in the Middle East. Under these conditions, the newly appointed Syriac Orthodox Patriarch suddenly announced his conversion to Roman Catholicism, causing a split in the Syriac Church. He led a portion of followers to Lebanon where he established his new headquarters. There, he signed an agreement that merged his church with the Roman Catholics, but allowed it to retain the use of Syriac and Eastern Orthodox rites.

Beginning in the eleventh century, Central Asian Turkic Muslims frequently went south to loot Delhi and later established a foothold there. By the closing years of the century, they had gradually occupied and ruled northern India. During this period the Central Asian Turks from the north not only fortified the administration they had in Delhi, but various leaders also founded local governments in north and central India.

From the twelfth to fifteenth centuries, the northern and central parts of India ruled by Muslims were known as the Delhi Sultanate. In fact, a large portion of the inhabitants were devotees of Hinduism, and many Hindu kings ruled principalities of various sizes within the Sultanate. These interlocking Hindu and Muslim states frequently forged fast-shifting political and military alliances, irrespective of religious differences. Interreligious alliances and those uniting military men and scholars who gave allegiance to a Hindu ruler or a Muslim ruler were not uncommon.

One of India's—if not the world's—most elegant and beautiful structures is the Qutb Minar, located in the south of Delhi. Built by the Muslim rulers to commemorate the eradication of the Hindu state, construction began in the thirteenth century and took more than a century to complete.

The 73-meter-high tower, which uses decorative stones of various colors, has a wide base that gradually slims toward the top. The guide for my visit to the Qutb Minar was a passionate Hindu devotee. He pointed out that throughout the tower are interspersed five balconies in the shape of lotus petals, a symbol of Hinduism (and Buddhism), and he opined that the craftsmen who designed and constructed the tower for their conquerors were actually loyal Hindu followers like himself. At the bottom of the high tower there is an explanation stating that the tower's stones were taken from several demolished Hindu temples elsewhere in Delhi.

During almost the same era (twelfth–fifteenth centuries), what is now Turkey was ruled by different Muslim and Greek Orthodox states. The former was dominated by the Seljuk Turks, and known as the Seljuk Sultanate, while the latter were states formed by Greeks who came to prominence after the Fourth Crusade (1202–1204).

Among them was the Empire of Trebizond, centered in modern-day Turkey's Trabzon on the Black Sea. I've been to its remains, and visited the Byzantine architectural masterpiece, the Hagia Sophia—sharing the same name as the early Byzantine structure in Istanbul—that still stands. It was built in the fourteenth century when the Seljuks had surrounded the remnants of the "empire" and were in the process of eating away at it. Some of the stone carvings in the Hagia Sophia of Trabzon are obviously in the Seljuk Islamic style, suggesting that their craftsmen were Turks employed by the Greek patron.

From these examples of India and Turkey, we can see that civilizations borrow from one another in both directions. Powerful ones can borrow from those on the wane. Those in decline typically seek to learn from stronger ones, and may even tap into their talent pools.

Next are two photos I shot while traveling in the Mekong River Basin. I took this one after my guide pointed it out to me. It is a relief, carved in the ruins of Cambodia's Angkor Wat. Based on the hair bun and decorative head-ware, and the weapon he is holding, we can deduce that this is a Southern Song soldier. Or perhaps a soldier from the early years of the Yuan Dynasty that succeeded it.

Cambodia's Angkor Wat is a royal mausoleum built during the reign of King Suryavarman II. First Hindu, then Buddhist, it required more than three decades to complete. It is today one of the largest religious monuments in the world. Chinese history books note that Zhou Daguan, a diplomat who resided in the Khmer Empire's capital, penned *The Customs of Cambodia* upon his return to Mongol-ruled China. I don't claim to know how the soldiers who accompanied him were accoutered. Nonetheless, the fact that a soldier of twelfth–thirteenth-century China appears in a relief carved in a Cambodian ritual building, itself deeply influenced by Indian religions, is indeed a telling manifestation of the interaction of civilizations.

The next example of interaction is even more concrete. But it hasn't been recorded in any history book. As I was strolling through the streets of Vientiane, the Laotian capital, I noticed a sign, "Liaoning Dumpling Restaurant." I entered, chatted for a moment... and ended up getting a free meal from a fellow Liaoning native!

The earliest writing methods were all rather problematic, and the invention and usage of phonetic symbols represented a major improvement. Some 3,000 to 4,000 years ago, the Phoenicians invented 20 letters—but they were all consonants. For the Semitic language, which has only three vowels whose order follows clear rules, this was not a big problem; even today, the Arabic script in newspapers does not indicate vowel sounds.

The Phoenician alphabet spread widely, and its successor, the Aramaic script, was employed by the Aramaic-speaking Babylonians. In the sixth century BCE, the Persians defeated the Babylonians to become the new masters of the Middle East, but Aramaic remained the region's lingua franca.

The Babylonians oversaw the relocation of the Jewish elite to Babylon, referred to as the "Babylonian exile" in Jewish history. But when the Persians destroyed Babylon, they allowed the Jews to return to Israel. For several centuries thereafter, the Jews continued to speak Aramaic, the language Jesus of Nazareth grew up speaking. After his crucifixion, the earliest Christians inhabited Syria and Turkey. Later, the Syrian Christians translated the Bible from Greek into Syriac. Thanks to the translation of this sacred text, a connection was established between the second-century Syrians and Jews, Babylonians and Phoenicians.

After Syriac became popular, Christians in the Middle East, Manicheans and Nestorians all wrote texts in the script, altering it only slightly. Because the Nestorians were persecuted by Orthodox Christians, their followers ended up in Persia and modern-day Uzbekistan, where they converted many Sogdians who formerly believed in Zoroastrianism.

Between the fourth and tenth centuries, the Sogdians were the most active traders along the Silk Road. The "Hu" of the Tang Dynasty era, a catchall term for foreigners from the Western Regions, were principally Sogdians. Perhaps the best-known Sogdian—among the Chinese, at least—was An Lushan, who was born in Liaodong in northeast China into a Sogdian family originally from Bukhara in Central Asia. He eventually became the military governor of the Liaodong garrison, but started a prolonged rebellion in 755 against the Tang emperor and occupied the capital city Chang'an, causing the Tang Dynasty to decline thereafter.

In the early twentieth century, seven letters were discovered in a beacon tower of the Great Wall in China. Early fourth-century Sogdian traders in Gansu and Xinjiang apparently wrote these letters to their relatives back home, but for some reason, they weren't dispatched and instead remained under the ruins of the tower for 1,700 years! They are the oldest extant examples of Sogdian script, and they clearly reflect the situation of Sogdian merchants doing business in China. One relates the tragic story of a Sogdian wife abandoned by her husband.

These letters and many other extant Sogdian documents were written in the phonetic Sogdian script. Sogdian is an eastern Iranian language whose written form is a revised version of the Syriac script. Because the Sogdians did business in many regions, their religion won some local converts, particularly among the Uyghurs, descendants of Turkic peoples. Prior to conversion, some believed in Buddhism, and some were Manichaeans, while many were Nestorian Christians.

Under the dual influence of the Chinese and the Sogdians, the Uyghurs adopted the Sogdian alphabet while altering it somewhat and "rotating" it 90 degrees, so that it reads vertically from the top—like the *hanzi* of the Chinese. Later, Genghis Khan ordered a Uyghur scholar to adapt the Uyghur alphabet to Mongolian, and the vertical Mongolian script he invented is still used today, with some alterations, in places such as Inner Mongolia.

An important and unusual document in Mongolian is a letter written in 1289 to France's King Philippe IV from Arghun Khan, ruler of the Mongol Ilkhanate mainly in today's Iran. To paraphrase: "I want to attack Egypt, and if you want to take possession of Jerusalem, you'd best send your troops with mine. You get Jerusalem. But we split the booty." The letter carries the imprint of the Ilkhanate's seal bestowed upon it by Kublai Khan, which is engraved with six Chinese characters in the *Zhuan Shu* seal script, "*fuguo anmin zhi bao*" ("Treasure for Assisting the Empire and Pacifying the Subjects").

Arghun Khan chose a Genoese merchant residing in Persia to deliver the letter, but by the time it reached Paris, the French were no longer keen to attack Jerusalem, so they politely declined in writing. This letter from the French entrusted to the Genoese merchant also took a long time in getting to the Ilkhanate, by which time Arghun Khan was dead. But the original letter sent to the French monarch by the Mongol ruler has become a precious artifact reflecting Eurasian diplomacy, and is now housed in the National Library of France.

We can summarize as follows: The Phoenician alphabet spread northwesterly to Greece. Greek is an Indo-European language with vowels whose usage is quite complex, while the Phoenician alphabet did not include vowels. The first and second letters of the Greek alphabet are a vowel, α, and a consonant, β. These combined sounds have been shortened into our familiar word, "alphabet." The Greek alphabet later transformed into the Latin alphabet that is used in all European countries once under the cultural domination of the Latin Church. The Greek alphabet also spread northward to the Slavs in the tenth century, becoming Cyrillic letters, and all Slavic peoples (such as the Serbs) and countries later influenced by them (such as Kazakhstan) use the Cyrillic alphabet.

Meanwhile, the Phoenician alphabet moved south, morphing into the Hebrew alphabet. From there the alphabet entered Ethiopia, becoming the Amharic alphabet (Amharic is also a Semitic language). The Phoenician phonetic symbols traveled easterly to Babylon, becoming the Aramaic alphabet. Aramaic moved southwesterly to the Arabian Peninsula, where the Nabataen consonantal letters first emerged, and were subsequently revised to form today's Arabic alphabet.

Aramaic also spread northwesterly to become the Syriac script (that includes the Manichean and Nestorian alphabets), and then the Sogdian alphabet. With some changes Sogdian became Uyghur letters, and eventually the Uyghur script when written vertically. Afterward, the Uyghur script inspired the Mongol alphabet, which in turn transmogrified into written Manchu.

Coincidentally, many of the scripts used in South and Southeast Asia originate in Sanskrit, and use cursive Brahmi letters. Brahmi letters did not evolve directly from the shape of Phoenician letters. However, due to the early historical contacts between the Aryans and peoples of the Middle East, the concept of a phonetic alphabet may well have been introduced from there, while the shape of the letters and the sounds they represent were a product of India.

Writing systems of various languages worldwide are numerous and jumbled, but there is a common strand running throughout. And there is no better illustration of the interaction between civilizations than this.

Current Dilemmas

Today, humanity faces many problems. Firstly is the issue of water resources that are very unevenly distributed worldwide. If calculated on a per capita basis, China is badly lacking, in contrast to two large countries in the boreal zone, Canada and Russia, which are blessed with an abundance. North America's Great Lakes region is the world's largest freshwater system, and Siberia's Lake Baikal is the world's deepest and largest freshwater reservoir.

The second problem is that of uneven and rapidly disappearing forest coverage. Some have been replaced by farmland, some occupied by buildings, and some even transformed into golf courses. Brazil's Amazon River Basin hosts the world's largest tropical forest, and Malaysia and Indonesia also possess large tropical tracts.

The status of forests cannot be separated, of course, from the issues of fossil fuels and other hydrocarbons. Since their consumption generates carbon dioxide, which in turn feeds global warming, this is not a matter for any single society; it is a dilemma facing all mankind. China now leads the world in carbon emissions. Although they are not necessarily alarming when calculated on a per capita basis, carbon dioxide emission levels are dangerously high in many Chinese metropolises.

If temperatures rise 4–6 degrees due to the greenhouse effect, the world's glaciers melt and sea levels will rise, many places on land will be submerged, and many river waterways will be invaded by alkaline seawater that will render farmland uncultivable. Even if ensuing problems of food and housing can be resolved, the areas in which bacteria and viruses can propagate will expand massively, and human civilization as we know it will face unprecedented crises.

Different societies govern themselves in different manners. Be it the pharaohs of Egypt or agricultural-based civilizations such as that of China's Yellow River Basin, the basic method of rule was autocracy. In other words, "what I say goes," regardless of the matter in question. Since the Industrial Revolution, however, many modern governments have played a role with certain built-in restrictions, such as collecting taxes, allocating revenues, handling diplomacy and defense affairs according to the law.

Awareness of the concept of "citizenship" is undoubtedly on the rise. Modes of interaction are progressing, so in today's society besides government departments there are also NGOs such as the International

Red Cross and Red Crescent Society. Not all these bodies are simply "non-governmental." Some such as Green Peace frequently oppose the powers-that-be and lodge protests against governments.

How to effectively handle relations between NGOs and governments is a very thorny issue. No government to date has come up with a genuinely satisfactory system to deal with the challenges of taxation, land acquisition, construction of public facilities, environmental protection and other issues impacting the public.

In terms of understanding and exploiting Nature, mankind is many times smarter than just a few centuries ago. However, despite the popularization of education and very convenient transportation, no political system has shown itself capable of effectively handling conflicts between people. This is a problem worthwhile contemplating.

The United Nations "one country, one vote" was borrowed from the League of Nations. It is based on the concept of a world consisting of nation-states—a concept that did not exist in earlier times—with clearly defined administrative boundaries of each state. Yet cross-border problems such as piracy, refugees, contagious diseases and environmental damage continue to occur.

These problems cannot be resolved within the nation-state framework, and even less so by relying solely on a vote at the United Nations. In fact, they continue to spread among many countries, and as difficult to handle as they are, they cannot be ignored.

Thus, while the concept of the nation-state is under attack, there is no handy substitute. After World War I and the disintegration of the Ottoman Empire, US President Woodrow Wilson proposed his "Fourteen Points." Among them was "national self-determination," for example, that the Arab people should manage the affairs of Arab countries. But once national boundaries had been demarcated, there were innumerable instances where a single ethnic group was effectively split among two or more countries. This was especially the case in Africa. Clearly, relying on "national self-determination" to resolve problems that arise between different peoples and ethnicities has proven itself less than practical.

Wilson probably never imagined that someone like me—who has no need for "national self-determination"—would still be thinking about this issue a century after his death.

The concept of the "development of civilization" assumes that humanity has a fixed direction and goals; when we move toward them, we are "progressing," otherwise we are "lagging behind." But there is no such premise or consensus. If we want to clarify in which direction humanity should go, we cannot ignore the following three essential questions:

1. Each human being must eventually face illness and death, inescapable facts that lead any thoughtful person to wonder: What is the ultimate purpose of life and what do "personal fulfillment" and "happiness" signify?
2. In terms of the relationship between man's inner world and external behavior, an individual's interaction with others, and interaction between man and Nature, what should the individual do in order to orient society in the direction of realizing his or her sense of personal fulfillment and happiness, rather than moving in the opposite direction?
3. What kind of people should society choose to maximize each individual's happiness and sense of personal fulfillment, and what form of "management" should they employ to achieve these goals?

These questions may not have trapped all of humanity in a dilemma, but they are weighty questions likely to perplex each of us.

The Outlook for Civilization

I wouldn't claim to have definitive answers to the questions posed above. Nor do I believe that there are many people in contemporary society who truly care about these somewhat abstract issues. So I'll end this essay with a macroscopic and hopefully realistic vision of the world as it is today.

First of all, information technology will continue to impact heavily on the progress of the human civilizations. Everyone can bear witness to the mass and speed of information generated by computerization, as well as changes in lifestyle and values. But this is just a sign of things to come.

Computer operating programs require a simple and pragmatic kind of logic. In order to adapt to computer operations, more and more people apply computer "thinking" to real life, and the social effects can be very far-reaching. But for now, there is no way to foresee just how far. The application of big data, the power of artificial intelligence, the concept of metaverse, etc., all hover over our horizon.

Secondly, the impact of biotechnology on human society will also be massive. Some say that in the future, the human life span may reach 200 hundred years. Isn't that incredible?

There are also biotechnology issues concerning genetically modified food, stem cells and health care resource allocation, which will naturally affect human ethics.

Thirdly, space technology can help mankind obtain much new information, new materials and new methods of energy extraction. Synthesis can be undertaken in outer space, where molecular crystallization in a gravity- and pollution-free environment can generate many novel composites.

It may also be possible to obtain new energy resources from beyond our planet. For instance, by collecting solar energy in outer space and then using a special directional microwave to transport the solar energy to a location on earth. Once converted, it could serve as a form of ready-to-use energy, and one that would represent an almost inexhaustible source.

The power of technology's impact on the civilizations has been unquestionably massive, but during the process of industrialization, especially in today's emerging economies, environmental pollution has become extremely serious and worrying. Air, water and soil pollution cannot be undone overnight.

Everyone is familiar with air and water pollution, but soil pollution is actually more frightening. Air and water can flow and be refreshed, but soil cannot be replaced in the short term, nor can contamination be easily eradicated. Such pollution seriously damages human health and can deal a heavy blow to agriculture.

I'd like to cite a story from history. Long ago Rome and North Africa's Carthage were at war. Rome triumphed. To ensure that Carthage could no longer produce its own foodstuffs, the victors spread salt on their farmland. Predictably, the Carthaginians could no longer raise an army to threaten the Romans. This saga is being repeated in today's industrial societies. What's different is that the land area we are ruining is many times greater than that laid to waste by the Romans.

Language, entertainment and media are very important for the direction of our future world's cultural development. Today, and for the foreseeable future, English will certainly remain the world's dominant language. Because the two most powerful countries over the last three centuries have been Anglophone, therefore in today's world English is the undisputed *lingua franca* of diplomacy, commerce and technology.

In the media and entertainment industry, English is the most popular language and this also increases its supremacy. In 1980, prior to the dissolution of the Soviet Union, I went to Hungary to take part in an international academic conference. I heard East German and Polish scientists address one another in English. "One falling leaf heralds the autumn," as we say. If Russian couldn't compete with English even behind the Iron Curtain, then how could it do so in the world at large?

I dearly love my mother tongue, particularly Chinese characters, and I'm very pleased to see the language gradually win international respect. But I do not expect that Chinese will take place beside English as the world's second *lingua franca* in the foreseeable future. My prediction is based on three facts: (1) Chinese characters are very difficult to learn and memorize; (2) written and even oral Chinese contains a much larger set of proverbs, historical allusions and allegories than any other major language, and (3) its current use is confined to China and some parts of Southeast Asia.

Another very important factor in the development of civilizations is, of course, the earth's human population. The demographic explosion of the past few decades, attracting so much attention, has actually slowed. Improved living standards and access to medical treatment has stimulated a sharp rise in the number of elder people worldwide, while changing lifestyles and values among the young in relatively well-to-do societies means they are rearing less children or none at all.

Future competition between countries will not just focus on resources and markets. Those countries that can attract large numbers of well-educated young immigrants will obtain a twenty-first-century "demographic dividend."

Now let's turn to major world trends. I'd like to take a look at several countries and regions, which feature distinct civilizations, and compare them in terms of overall "national strength." From a global perspective, transatlantic trade was most important in the nineteenth century, and transatlantic and transpacific trade were almost equally important in the twentieth. But in the new century, transpacific trade will dominate.

The global economic center of gravity is gradually shifting to the two sides of the Pacific, and, barring a new world war and simultaneous devastation by natural forces on both sides of the Pacific, this is unstoppable. The only three countries that face both the Atlantic and the Pacific are in North America, so this shift will not adversely affect them. To the contrary, since the US, Canada and Mexico face vast bodies of water to the east and west, they are unlikely to face hostile adversaries from those directions, and actually enjoy an advantage as a result.

The US arguably possesses the highest "coefficient of national security," thanks to its population of some 330 million that is aging fairly slowly, the lack of any threat from its land-based neighbors to the north and south, and the fact that it borders on oceans to the east and west.

In terms of hi-tech strength, the US created cutting-edge technologies—and continues to lead—in areas such as the Internet, satellite remote sensing, wireless telecoms, genetic engineering, stem cell research, nanotechnology and new energy sources. American society strongly encourages innovation, emphasizes attracting immigrants (particularly scientific talent), and its society has shown itself to be very adaptable.

These are the areas of America's core competitiveness. Competition from other countries cannot reduce its overall national strength; subcultures that flourish within it may do so, however. These include a significant portion of the population that is discontented with its current status, declining effectiveness of its primary and secondary schools, and a disinclination for plain hard work. Lately, there has also been a trend to balk at the multi-ethnic, multi-religious society and push the salient immigration issue to the national political discourse. Overall, however, I believe the US will continue to lead the world over the next 50 years.

Now for Russia. Many ethnic and territorial issues are left over from the Soviet era, and because the buffer territory between Russia and both Iran and Turkey ceased to exist with the dissolution of the Soviet Union, Russia's room for maneuver around its "new" southern borders have been reduced. The spread of radical Islam to the North Caucasus has certainly generated security concerns.

Russia's population is not just aging. It is also declining. Its "Far East" was already fairly sparsely populated, and recently inhabitants have begun migrating westward to "European" Russia. Meanwhile, due to perceptions that the EU and NATO seek to bring the Baltic Countries and Ukraine more fully into their embrace, Russia's ability to focus single-mindedly on improving its own economy has been diluted. But based on its vast territory with rich resources, its scientific and technical strengths and indomitable cultural traditions, Russia should remain a big and powerful country over the next 50 years.

However, the recent war launched by Russia against Ukraine has made two possible long-term prospects much less likely. The first is for Russia (at least the European part of Russia) to integrate with Europe as Peter the Great envisioned three centuries ago. The second is for a large and energy-rich Russia to live alongside and trade peacefully with a Europe which will become less dependent on the United States as General De Gaule of France once hoped. Hence the Czarist Russian nationalism of Vladimir Putin and his supporters has obscured their view of Russia's future.

Now let's take a look at China. Over the past four decades, the process of China's modernization surely figures as a phenomenon of the greatest consequence. And its progress over the coming 50 years is a factor equally likely to influence major world trends. Today's China is big but not really strong, but its eventual ranking among the most powerful nations of the world is not mere talk.

China possesses an abundance of human resources that are unmatched by any other country; the Chinese people's will to see the country modernize and society progress is very intense; cultural cohesion is very solid; and urbanization of the rural population is an unstoppable trend—all these factors are massive and long-term drivers of social and economic development. A yet unknown factor in China's development is how to govern such a large population over such an immense territory under the overall principles of democracy and rule of law that were advocated by its early modernizers and that will satisfy the better educated and more affluent populace.

After enjoying "demographic benefit A" that has come from three decades of tightly restrained population growth, if it can gradually reverse the one-child family trend, China should be able to enjoy a twenty-first-century "demographic benefit B" without further dependence on the "foreign aid" that has come in the form of huge investment from abroad. On the other hand, like Japan and Russia, China is also moving toward becoming an aging society. Overall, the potentially negative demographic trends notwithstanding, providing that there is no outbreak of a devastating, large-scale war with other countries and no protracted social turmoil, China's revitalization is to be expected.

In the coming decades, China and the US will be the world's most dynamic economies. If they cooperate, it will be a win–win situation; if they oppose one another, both will incur injury. Leaders in Beijing and Washington are generally not foolish, and will adopt rational approaches that take national and international conditions into account as they set policy.

Over the next 30 to 40 years, technological developments and demographic changes will unleash huge changes in lifestyle, social structure and values. Turmoil may well occur in some regions, but large-scale, protracted war should be avoidable.

Finally, unless mankind is somehow driven to self-annihilation, which I don't see at all, the double threats of global warming and world war should be mitigated and human being's survival instinct will prevail.

PART II

Studies on Civilization

CHAPTER 2

From Movable Type to the World Wide Web

The title of the lead chapter of this book is one I view with some reverence. I served as President of City University of Hong Kong for eleven years, and not long after taking up the post, I formally proposed that the university establish the "Chinese Civilization Center." It was officially founded in 1998, and we invited a US-based graduate of China's Taiwan University, Pei-kai Cheng, to serve as director and organize a series of lectures on Chinese culture.

As founder and promoter of the center, I had the honor of giving the first lecture in October 1998. The topic of my presentation was *From Movable Type to the World Wide Web*. The fact that I am once again using this topic doesn't signify that I haven't progressed; indeed, I feel that revisiting it after some 20 years has special significance.

Recollections in the Long River of Time

Of course, human civilization originated in material civilization, i.e., when mankind began to consciously cultivate plants and domesticate animals for food. Hunting and gathering activities do not qualify. One can say that pre-historical rock art marks the beginnings of spiritual civilization. But I think it is easier to distinguish a starting point when man began to deliberately employ fixed symbols to leave his thoughts behind in the long river of time—specifically, in the form of a script.

The pictographs that appeared in Mesopotamia more than 6,000 years ago should be considered mankind's earliest writing. Soon thereafter, easier-to-write cuneiform scripts emerged. These were comprised of wedge-shaped strokes impressed on a clay tablet. There are numerous types of cuneiform, and scholars have decrypted several that were used during various time periods by peoples who spoke different languages.

The next earliest form of writing to emerge was the hieroglyphs of the Egyptians, about 5,200 years ago. They may well have been inspired by the Mesopotamian script. Some consisted of drawings, while others comprised phonetic elements. Due to differences in the environment of Mesopotamia and Egypt, the Egyptians wrote on wood or papyrus rather than carving on a clay tablet. It was only in the nineteenth century that they were deciphered, for once Western scholarship had progressed to a certain level, there were the desire and the means to seek examples of ancient writing, and to apply scientific methods such as parallelism to "decode" them.

Around the time that Mesopotamian civilization was 2,500 years old, and nearly 2,000 years after Egyptian hieroglyphs had appeared, the forerunner to the modern Chinese character, "oracle bone script"—inscriptions on tortoise shells or ox bones used for divination—also emerged. The script does not require too much effort for today's scholars to recognize. After all, Chinese characters, or *hanzi*, are the direct successors of the former.

This is quite different from the historical development and changes undergone by Egyptian hieroglyphs. Egyptians invented hieroglyphs and then simplified them into the so-called Demotic (popular) script. Following Alexander the Great's conquest in fourth century BCE, Greek rule in Egypt introduced Coptic letters of Greek inspiration that were used concurrently with Demotic symbols over a long period of time. After the seventh century, the Egyptians gradually began to speak and write Arabic, as did Coptic Christians and Jews. But some continued to use Coptic and Hebrew letters to transliterate Arabic.

West Asia is where human civilization first made its appearance. Whether it was the cultivation of crops, domestication of animals or the invention of a written script, all occurred earlier here than elsewhere.

China is located at the eastern end of the Eurasian continent. For humans in the ancient world, the Atlantic and Pacific Oceans were uncrossable barriers, so until 500 years ago, virtually all exchanges of human thought and consciousness took place on Eurasian pathways. It is possible that some artifacts, crops, ideas and concepts found throughout Eurasia initially spread from West Asia. At present, we do not have the means to ascertain whether the Chinese developed *hanzi* while ignorant of systems of writing that had been invented two thousand years previously in West Asia, or whether they knew of them, but elected to create a new set of symbols based on their own language.

Much writing on bones and tortoise shells has been unearthed in Shangqiu, Henan Province. At about the same time as oracle bone script appeared in China, another set of written symbols, the Phoenician consonantal alphabet, emerged in the eastern Mediterranean in the region of modern-day Syria and Lebanon, where the ancient Phoenicians were active.

Phoenician belongs to the Semitic language family. Similarly to Arabic and Hebrew, it can easily be expressed with letters. But China in East Asia is separated from West Asia by the Himalayas and the Pamir Plateau, and as a monosyllabic, tonal language, Chinese is not easily adapted to the use of letters. So even if they had been aware of another people's alphabet, the Chinese would still have found it inconvenient to use.

Whatever the script, it must be written on some sort of material, be it a tablet of clay or stone. But for writing a lot of text, a large supply of such a medium is necessary. From very early times, the Egyptians used papyrus fabricated from reeds. Since both sides of the Nile are arid desert, ancient papyrus was easily preserved, and much can be found in today's museums. Clay tablets were easily preserved, and writing on stone even more so.

When Napoleon led his army to attack Egypt in 1798, it marked the first invasion of the land by Westerners since the Crusades. But one very significant result of this campaign was recorded in the domain of human civilization, *not* in the annals of military history. After all, as Napoleon returned to France via the Mediterranean, he met defeat at the hands of Nelson's British fleet, so France did not attain true hegemony over Egypt.

But in a small village in the Nile Delta, the French forces discovered a stone slab inscribed with three different scripts. One was Greek. The second was a Demotic script used in the Late Period of ancient Egypt. The third was not recognized by anyone, but featured a pictographic script widely found on tablets throughout Egypt. A French army officer spent more than two decades and eventually deciphered the ancient Egyptian writing on this stele. If today we have a good grasp of ancient Egyptian history, especially dynastic history, it is thanks to this Frenchman.

After World War II, many handwritten scrolls were discovered near Israel's Dead Sea. These are the earliest Jewish scriptures extant, probably written around the first century. The Hebrew letters in them had first appeared more than four thousand years previously, earlier than China's oracle writing.

At the turn of the twentieth century, in a place called Juyanhai (formerly a lake) located in China's Inner Mongolia, and very near to Gansu Province, Swedish scholars discovered a cache of bamboo strips inscribed with *hanzi*. They did not require deciphering, as the script has evolved relatively little over the centuries. Based on their content, we can obtain an understanding of the region's lifestyle, ecology and commercial activities.

It was the Chinese who invented silk. In ancient China people wrote on silk, later referred to as "silk strips." Beginning about 2000 years ago, Central Asians also used silk as a medium for writing. Many Manichean scriptures discovered in various parts of China's Xinjiang applied Syriac letters to the cloth. And of course, some Nestorian documents have come down to us via silk.

Several millennia ago, our ancestors first invented this material dubbed "silk," with a very complex production process that they eventually simplified and applied to other fibers in order to fabricate "paper." Archaeological evidence shows that silk existed five thousand years ago, but the earliest paper did not come into being until 2,100 years ago, during the Western Han Dynasty. We can see this from the composition of the *hanzi* for paper: 纸. The left half of this character—the space often used to "categorize" a word—contains one-half the radical for silk, "丝." It follows that silk came first, then paper. Otherwise, the Chinese word for silk would contain an element referring to "paper."

It's easy and economical to write on paper. One sheet at a time, that is. But if you engrave a block of wood, and press it onto one sheet of paper after another, that's printing. Xylographic printing probably began during the early years of the Tang Dynasty. The desired characters and images were engraved backward on a woodblock, ink smeared on it, and then paper placed atop the board to effect printing. This method was widely used, especially for Buddhist scriptures and images of the Buddha. The earliest ones still extant are the Wuzhou Period (690–705) Tripitaka woodblocks.

The Tang Dynasty reigned almost three centuries from 618 to 907 CE. During the century and a half prior to the Lu Anshan Rebellion (755–63), society enjoyed widespread prosperity and stability. At the height of the Tang Dynasty, troops were stationed in Qiuci (now Kucha, Xinjiang, China), and its domain extended to parts of the so-called Western Regions, including a part of Uzbekistan and Kyrgyzstan today. In terms of governance, the imperial examination system gradually improved. On the spiritual front, Confucianism, Taoism and Buddhism began to merge, becoming the key elements guiding social development and the concepts of life and death among ordinary Chinese.

An Advanced Society

Song Dynasty China (960–1279) was a fairly mature society possessing a straightforward imperial examination system and a population with quite a number of formally educated people. Of course, the Song also faced problems defending itself against the threat of the Tanguts' Western Xia, the Liao Dynasty of the Khitan, and the Jurchen's Jin Dynasty. Nonetheless, the maturity of civilization under the Song ranked it as a leader worldwide. Only Islamic civilization, which I'll cover later, could possibly compare.

A special characteristic of Chinese culture is its search for *yijing*—a term for an intangible, heightened spiritual state of being for which there is no satisfying English equivalent—in literature and art. The pursuit of *yijing* is most obvious in landscape painting, but there were also paintings of beautiful court ladies, and many Song tableaux also captured joyous scenes of song and dance in times of peace and prosperity. Mastery of the qin, a seven-stringed zither, was another expression of the *yijing* quest among the literati. During the Song appreciation of qin music reached unheard of heights. "Listening to the Qin," a famous painting of an al fresco zither concert, was reportedly rendered by Emperor Huizong himself.

Although the imperial examination system supplanted the hereditary aristocracy, it did make considerable economic demands on the family. Unless the successful candidate was unusually clever or had a benefactor, a young man had to spend ten years studying hard, and typically came from a very well-to-do family.

Among Song scholar-officials, whatever one's administrative ability or achievements, each seemingly had his own inner life. The renowned poet

Fan Zhongyan expressed his political philosophy and concern for the common people most clearly in a line in his *Memorial to Yueyang Tower*. It reads:

> Feel concern for others under Heaven before others
>   and rejoice after others under Heaven have rejoiced.

But in his poetry, we also find more personal verse such as:

> White clouds against a blue sky
>   Yellow leaves cover the ground ...
>   Liquor feeds the belly of sadness
>   and turns into tears of yearning.

Therefore, we can see that literati often possessed two realms: one public, one private. Ouyang Xiu, Sima Guang, Su Dongpo and Wang Anshi—all famous men of letters who served the Song state at one time—are examples of such a dichotomy.

Song philosophy was also quite advanced. For example, the neo-Confucian school of rational philosophy was espoused by Zhou Dunyi, Cheng Yi, Cheng Hao and Zhang Zai. The latter wrote:

> Define society's values, set down the meaning of life for the people, revive the neglected teachings of earlier sages, and establish the foundation for peaceful existence of generations to come.

The contribution of the Tang and Song Dynasties in radiating Chinese culture in all directions is evidenced in several domains.

In Japan, after the Nara Period (710–794) which imported all sorts of "Things Chinese," particularly Buddhism and concepts of governance, the Heian Period (794–1185) ruled by the Fujiwara clan was more inward looking, relatively speaking. At the beginning of the eleventh century, the first novel authored by a Japanese female appeared—in fact, you could say it was the first literary work in the form of a novel to appear *anywhere*. While undeniably a work of great creativity, the *Tale of Genji* by Lady Murasaki Shikibu also showed the continued influence of Chinese culture. One example: the novel is littered with references to Chinese poems, particularly those of renowned Tang poet Bai Juyi, whose works she quotes in several places.

In addition to Han culture and thought, even the structure of *hanzi* exercised a huge influence on neighboring peoples. For example, the Tangut of Western Xia studied Chinese characters and promoted Sinification. They even used the basic structure of *hanzi* to create their own Xia script, and printed classics such as *The Analects of Confucius* in the latter.

Like Chinese, the Khitan script was square-shaped, i.e., each stroke remained inside the borders of an imagined square. The Jurchen, forerunners of the Manchu, also employed square-shaped characters. The Koreans used *hanzi* as did the Japanese. But Japanese scholars also invented two syllabaries, *hiragana* and *katakana*, for words with Japanese and foreign origins, respectively.

Yijing, poetry and neo-Confucianist philosophy—in reality, all must be founded on a society's economic wealth. On the material level, three of ancient China's four great inventions, including gunpowder in 1041 CE, occurred during the Northern Song. Someone once said that the Chinese love peace, and we used gunpowder just for firecrackers and fireworks, while Westerners transformed it into a weapon. This is erroneous. In fact, gunpowder was used to wage war during the Northern Song. The *Military Annals of the Song Dynasty* clearly records:

> In the third year of the reign of Song Emperor Zhenzong (1000 CE), Tang Fu, leader of the water-borne troops on the downstream Yangtse, revealed the rockets, fireballs and grenades that he had fabricated.

The Europeans learned of gunpowder via the Mongols who used it in battle, and that is how it passed to the West.

I mentioned earlier that printing dates from the Tang, while movable type was invented during the Song and marked a new era in civilization history. Chinese characters are not strictly phonetic, and consist of many thousands of square *hanzi*. The benefits of printing Chinese with movable type are considerable, but they are not as evident as for a phonetic script. For a script that employs letters to spell a word, movable type printing requires only a limited number of molds, but the resulting improvement in efficiency and cost savings are enormous, and its role in propagating culture undeniable.

Under the Northern Song, both in terms of its economic capacity and legal system, and in terms of its ability to create material goods, China was also very mature and technically advanced.

In addition, Song merchant ships were equipped with multiple masts and as tall as four decks, and could sail to the distant Arabian Sea and Persian Gulf to engage in trade. Material and intellectual civilization advance in tandem, and it is impossible for a society that lacks material wealth to create a splendid intellectual civilization.

Indian civilization is also an ancient one, and its "civilization circle" encompassed Bangladesh, Myanmar, Thailand, Cambodia, Malaysia and Indonesia.

Tu Weiming, a professor of philosophy and a "New Confucian," is an old friend of mine, and once over dinner we touched on the diffusion of the "Confucian civilization circle." At one point I blurted out that it and the "chopstick civilization circle" overlap. This assertion left my old friend—just then putting his own pair to good use—momentarily speechless. But this is indeed the case. Those countries where one eats with chopsticks are all within the Confucian circle: China, South Korea, Japan and Vietnam. Although this was just a dinner chat, my "chopsticks thesis" illustrates that material and spiritual civilization are related and interdependent.

THE METEORIC RISE OF ARABIAN CIVILIZATION

After continuous attacks by "barbarians" from the northeast, Rome fell, and the Greek-speaking Byzantine Empire, with its capital in Constantinople, became the successor to the Latin-dominated "Western" Roman Empire. During China's Northern Song (960–1127), Russia embraced Christianity and with it the written word, whereupon the Russians entered the ranks of the civilized world. Italy was the heart of the old Roman Empire and had long possessed a high degree of civilization. The Catholic pope was then regarded as the center of European power, but his sphere of power was quite narrow. Germany was the center of the Teutonic or Germanic peoples, and in order to appease them, the Pope occasionally bestowed the title of Holy Roman Emperor upon a German Duke.

In the early Northern Song which began in 960, Spain and Portugal were still ruled by the Moors of North Africa, and it was only 500 years later that the Spanish and Portuguese Catholics were able to expel the Muslims from the Iberian Peninsula; meanwhile, Britain and France were not yet independent countries. In 1066, the Grand Duke of Normandy, better known as William the Conqueror, set out from his base in northwest France, crossed the channel and vanquished southeastern England, thereby establishing himself as the founding ancestor of today's royal family.

Prior to the seventh century, the Arabian Peninsula was primarily inhabited by culturally backward Arab tribes. But there were also many Jews, Christians and Arab traders who settled in oasis towns. When the Persian Sassanid Dynasty was facing off against the Eastern Roman Empire, most Arabs were still living in a state of semi-ignorance.

But as the ancient Chinese adage relates, when a long-billed snipe busies itself snagging a recalcitrant clam, it is the fisherman looking on who stands to benefit. In the middle of the seventh century, the Arabs burst forth to occupy a vital part of the Eastern Roman Empire and then vanquished Persia. By the mid-tenth century, Arabo-Islamic civilization was experiencing vigorous development, surpassing East and South Asia, as well as Europe, in several areas.

In 622 CE, when Xuanzang had not yet commenced his journey to retrieve the Buddhist canons from India, Muhammad was leading the Muslims from Mecca to Medina, where he would establish the beginnings of an Islamic state. When the prophet passed away a decade later, Xuanzang was in India poring over Buddhist scrolls in Nalanda Temple, and Islam's power had grown very strong throughout the Arabian Peninsula. Within 30 years, Muhammad's three "Caliph" (successors) had not only united the peninsula, they had also captured the key Byzantine territories of Syria, Palestine, Egypt, Tunisia and Libya, and even taken Persia—something neither the Roman legions nor the Byzantine forces had accomplished.

Within less than a century after Muhammad's passing, the Islamic forces had transformed into an unprecedented empire: east to the Indus, and west to the Atlantic. In 750, due to civil war and a coup, the Umayyad Caliphate that had united this great Damascus-based empire was wiped out by the Abbas family, relatives of the Prophet. The Persians had contributed very energetically to this struggle, so the Abbasids chose a spot in southern Iraq near their Persian allies at which to establish their new capital, Baghdad.

By the eleventh century, Chinese civilization had already progressed to a fairly mature phase. Meanwhile, contemporary Baghdad was very advanced and prosperous, and was already a metropolis in terms of the scale and dynamism of its religious, cultural, political and commercial life.

In 751 during the last years of the high Tang Dynasty, an encounter between the armies of the Tang and the Arabs (Abbasid forces) at Talas in the Chu River Basin, on the border of present-day Kyrgyzstan and Kazakhstan, ended in a devastating defeat for the Tang. Over 10,000 troops were wounded or killed, and several thousands taken prisoner—including a number of papermaking craftsmen. It was this battle that saw the art of paper fabrication pass from Chinese into Arabian hands.

The Arabs commanded the Chinese craftsmen to set up a paper workshop at Samarkand. The art of papermaking passed westward from this point, emerging in Europe in 1250 when the first atelier was established in France. After paper spread throughout Muslim lands and into Europe, it greatly reduced the costs of book fabrication. It not only facilitated the transmission of Islam and Christianity and the popularization of education, it also laid the material and cultural foundations for Europe's future Renaissance.

Here I'd like to share a few thoughts I had while in Damascus' Umayyad Mosque. Muslims occupied Damascus in the late seventh century, and it became the capital of the Islamic state. The Umayyad Caliphate constructed this Byzantine-style mosque, one of the first mosques anywhere. Many people erroneously believe that nomadic peoples founded Islamic civilization. But in reality, as in China, the foundations of their civilization were also laid by sedentary populations. Where they differ is that Chinese rulers emphasized agriculture at the expense of commerce, while Islamic rulers heavily favored the latter.

I believe that geography determines history. Located at the junction of Europe, Asia and Africa, early on the emerging Islamic states controlled the trade routes between the three. This facilitated tax collection and absorption of new know-how. Although the Arabs initially did not possess a high degree of sophistication, thanks to this location they were able to absorb alien culture and import foreign talent. For example, after the Persian Sassanids were vanquished by the Arabs, most Persians converted to Islam within one hundred years, thereafter the Persians made a weighty contribution to the creation of new Islamic civilization.

The Arab Empire followed the Byzantine system of taxation and management, and borrowed greatly from the Persian Sassanid Empire's personnel and financial systems. By the early ninth century, the construction of Baghdad was complete, and the Arab Muslims had commenced their "Century of Translation" campaign. They commissioned scholars to translate Greek, Roman, Persian and Indian works—be they scientific, medical or philosophical in nature—into Arabic. They did so inspired by a phrase attributed to the Prophet Muhammad: "Seek knowledge even as far as China." Therefore, beginning with the eleventh century, the world's most significant scientific works could basically all be found in Arabic.

Sitting in that Damascus mosque, I couldn't help but ponder how keen the Arabs must have been to learn from foreign civilizations, and in a way that inspired them to obtain knowledge of their own along with the ability to innovate. They Islamicized and Arabized the peoples they vanquished; solely Persian speakers managed to accept Islam while resisting Arabization. The Egyptians are an ancient people, but prior to being conquered by the Arabs, they had already been ruled by the Greeks and the Roman and Byzantine Empires, so their will to resist had been weakened. Because Islamic law protects the Jewish and Christian faiths, Egypt's Coptic Christians have survived to our day; like Cordoba and Baghdad, during the eleventh–thirteenth centuries Cairo was a center for Jews, and a center of Jewish law.

Baghdad became the political and religious center of the Sunni Muslim world. The empire ruled by the Abbasids lasted from 750 to 1258. Why 1258? Because that's the year Hulagu Khan, Kublai Khan's younger brother, captured Baghdad, and executed the Caliph who refused to surrender his city. This marked the end of the centralized state within the Islamic world.

At this point, I'd like to briefly describe contributions of Arabo-Islamic civilization to mankind. After all, modern mathematics, astronomy, physics, chemistry and medicine have all directly benefited from works written in Arabic.

The algebra of our day was basically developed by the Arabs. Arabic numerals, including the concept and symbol of "zero," passed from India to Persia, and then to the Arabs. Without zero, mathematical calculations are indeed difficult. In the ninth century, a mathematician of Persian extraction wrote a book in Arabic on algebra in which he demonstrated how to solve linear and quadratic equations by performing repetitive operations using Indo-Arabic numerals. He lived in an area of greater Persia named Khwarezm (modern-day Uzbekistan), and is therefore known as al-Khwarizmi. Today's mathematic operations, particularly computer-based computations known as "algorithms," are named after him.

Muslims pray five times daily and fast during Ramadan, the ninth month of the Muslim calendar. This requires ascertaining the precise positions of the moon and the earth relative to one another, so medieval Arabian astronomy was cutting-edge.

The modern western word "chemistry" derives from the medieval term "alchemy," itself a transliteration of the Arabic word "al-kimia."

The Canon of Medicine, written in Arabic by Ibn Sina (aka Avicenna, born in what is now Uzbekistan), was not just a classic within societies where Arabic culture dominated. Its Latin translation was a standard medical text for Europe right up until the fourteenth century.

In the area of philosophy, the Arabs pioneered Neo-Platonism and Neo-Aristotelian thought, and essayed applying these theories to explain God's nature. They also used logic to explore certain theological issues. For instance, was the Quran a creation of Allah, or His actual words? Since Allah is omniscient and omnipotent and all that occurs is arranged by Him, does this signify that everything is pre-determined? Since man is a creation of Allah, why does he sin? If man has free will and should take responsibility for his actions, then what was Allah's true intent?

These questions are quite similar to those explored by medieval Catholic theologians, but Muslims had raised them two hundred years earlier. In fact, the school of Scholasticism during Europe's late Middle Ages, as represented by Thomas Aquinas, drew on the philosophical works of Ibn Rushd, better known in the West as Averroes.

The expansion of the Islamic world can be divided into several stages. By the end of the eleventh century, Islam tended toward conservatism, and social vitality declined markedly. But in territorial terms, within a century of Muhammad's death it had transformed into an Arabo-Islamic empire, the core of the Islamic civilization circle. Once a majority of a region's population had embraced Islam, it no longer re-entered the sphere of influence of another faith. Even though the circle long ago lost its dynamism, it continued to expand slowly, and today is no exception.

Indonesia, Malaysia and Central Asia (including China's Xinjiang) are not within the "core" area of Islam. It was Arab and Persian traders who brought Islam to Southeast Asia, and itinerant Sufi who converted the nomads of Central Asia. Who were these Sufi? They were the mystics within Islam who attach less importance to doctrine and philosophical questions, but emphasize religious experience. They employ meditation, contemplation, music and dance to obtain this experience. Once a person feels that he has experienced God directly, that sort of experience will serve to anchor his faith, a faith born of vivid sensation rather than rigid, difficult-to-fathom dogma.

Originally, the Turkic nomads of the Eurasian Steppe believed in Shamanism and the experience of divine possession. The largely Persian-speaking Sufi roaming the vast grasslands reinterpreted and adapted the Shamanistic rituals practiced by the nomadic peoples in terms of Islamic teachings, thereby making it possible for nomads to convert to Islam in large numbers.

In Southeast Asia and sub-Saharan Africa, Islam also partially integrated the local faiths or religious traditions of indigenous tribes, and thereby aided these regions to enter the Islamic civilization circle. In other words, new entrants to the circle were first influenced by Sufism, and in turn, they influenced the rituals of Islam, even impacting the content of that faith.

One example is the Republic of Turkey. One century ago, Turkey was the core territory of the Ottoman Empire. For 500 years the Ottoman Empire was the political, economic and cultural center of the Islamic world, and the ancestors of the Ottomans were Turkic nomads who migrated west from Central Asia. Therefore, Turkey's Islam is quite distinct from that of Saudi Arabia. The latter's official faith emphasizes compliance with classical doctrine and adherence to fundamentalism, while Turkish beliefs and customs are much more lenient. In Turkish society, despite attacks on Sufi orders and even their banning, Sufism has a considerable number of devotees and exercises influence even today.

Traditionally Sufi disciples expressed their religious zeal via poetry, and wine and beautiful women often appear in their verse. But in Saudi Arabia, alcohol is forbidden, and Sufism is also not permitted.

After the Arab Empire turned conservative, it gradually lost momentum. The Crusaders penetrated the heartland of Islam in the twelfth century. Then the Mongols destroyed the Arab Empire in the thirteenth. But as the forces of these enemies gradually departed in the fourteenth century, the plague took the lives of many in the Arab world.

There was an Arab scholar born in North Africa who settled in Egypt after traveling widely. This was Ibn Khaldun (1332–1406), the founder of sociology and the science of statistics. He sought to understand the changes wrought on society by the plague. He also witnessed the rise and fall of dynasties, and therefore he began to research the "natural laws" that govern history. Prior to Ibn Khaldun, history mainly recorded personalities and events; it did not treat the study of history itself as an object of inquiry.

Likewise, China's scholars and official historians typically recorded and researched historical events via documents. They did not seek to define the laws of historical development. Ibn Khaldun's famous *Introduction* (*Muqaddimah*, 1377), a work that records an early view of universal history, pioneered the field of macro historical research. The famous twentieth-century British historian Arnold Toynbee, who held a somewhat pessimistic view of history as cyclic, was deeply influenced by Ibn Khaldun and praised him highly.

Civilizations that Influenced the World

We just discussed a precocious Arabo-Islamic civilization that emerged suddenly on the scene. Now I want to examine one with which everyone is fairly familiar: Europe's Christian civilization.

Let me begin with Dante Alighieri. He was born in Florence to a moderately wealthy feudal family whose fortune was diminishing. At the time Italian feudal lords had begun their decline. It was an era of transition when the merchant class, beneficiary of handsome profits from external trade, was increasingly prosperous. Due to his educational and cultural background, experience in society and powers of observation, coupled with his literary talent, Dante penned his immortal *Divine Comedy*. And therewith sounded the clarion call of Europe's Renaissance. His descriptions of Hell, Purgatory and Heaven and the post-death ordeals of certain personalities were truly vivid. This won him much admiration.

Readers may assume that the entire plot was the figment of Dante's imagination. But those who are familiar with the Quran and Islamic tradition will easily see that much of the storyline of *Divina Commedia* was inspired by Islamic culture. This should hardly surprise, because it was during the twelfth–thirteenth centuries that Italy was in contact with large numbers of Muslims in Spain, Sicily, North Africa and the Middle East. Many Arabic tomes were translated into Latin.

Leonardo da Vinci was a master at the height of the Renaissance. He was the first person to study biomechanics. A look at his sketches of the human body confirms that the Renaissance brought Europeans a fresh sense of self-awareness and confidence.

I'd like to backtrack a bit here to mention that during China's Northern Song (960–1127), new metallurgic techniques had spread to Europe. With stronger blades, deeper plowing became possible. As new iron blades on plows made their appearance in Europe during the eleventh and twelfth centuries, large swaths of virgin land were cultivated, agricultural output skyrocketed and the population increased. Despite the reduction wrought by the Black Death during the thirteenth and fourteenth centuries, population growth soon resumed and continued steadily. Meanwhile, the lives of the common people improved, and this helped build confidence and engendered humanist thought.

The Renaissance heightened awareness of mankind's rational nature. Although the Europeans still believed in God, now they recognized the important role of rationality in one's life. It followed that people no longer blindly followed the Pope. Successive Popes wanted to build majestic, sumptuously furnished cathedrals in Vatican City. In order to raise funds, they sold *Letters of Indulgence* everywhere that guaranteed the purchaser entrance to Heaven. But many Catholics no longer believed in those *indulgentia*. They were unwilling to treat such "royal edicts" (equivalent to God's command) on the part of the Pope as part of their religious faith.

Those who were relatively distant from the Pope, such as the Germanic high-ranking nobles and the priests they frequented, openly debated the rights and wrongs of those *Letters of Indulgence*. In 1521, Martin Luther set off a religious revolution with his courageous defense of his writings before the Diet of Worms. He took papal-centric Roman Catholicism (Western Europe's "old religion"), with its idol worship, verbose and elaborate rites, purified and improved upon it, transforming it into a "new religion" (Protestantism)—one that stressed God's authority and opposed idolatry, in which every believer was free to read the Bible, and each church managed its own affairs.

The first to come out in support of Martin Luther were the princes north of the Rhine. In geographical terms, this was very significant, for the Roman Empire's power had always terminated south of the river. In order to prevent invasion by the Germanic peoples, the Roman Empire built a great wall near the Rhine, part of which still stands today. In the Middle Ages, the Roman Catholic Church was also powerless to control those regions not formerly within the Roman Empire. So in the sixteenth century, Norway, Sweden, Denmark and Germany were the first to leave the sway of the Catholic Church and establish the Lutheran Church.

The theological proposition of John Calvin, a Swiss francophone priest, was even simpler. Later, a group of Puritans, who primarily followed Calvin's doctrine, left Britain for North America and established the American Puritan tradition. Although they believed firmly in God, they also believed in a man's own efforts, and advocated industriousness and frugality.

In the midst of the Reformation and the 150-year-long contest between Catholicism and Protestantism, the Holy Roman Emperor did not, of course, approve of the latter. Within the Holy Emperor's dominion, the princes of Austria, Spain and Italy remained resolutely opposed to reform. Therefore, these three areas remain core areas of Roman Catholicism to our day.

SUPER-STABLE STRUCTURE

Some historians call the Chinese social system a "super-stable structure."

What constitutes a "super-stable" social structure? I assume many people have a sense of what this means, but can't express it clearly. I'm not too clear about it either. But I'd nonetheless like to cite three examples of how cultural continuity and reinforcement of the social structure contributed to stability in pre-twentieth-century China.

Here's the first: the Catholic priest Matteo Ricci was dispatched to China as a missionary during the late Ming Dynasty, arriving in Macao in 1582. Initially, he assumed China was a predominantly Buddhist country, so he shaved his head, wore prayer beads, and dressed himself up like a Buddhist monk, intending to use this identity to get closer to the Chinese. Later, when he discovered that the typical Chinese didn't respect monks, and only esteemed Confucianists, he donned a Confucian cap of his own design, studied the Confucian classics, and claimed to a be Confucianist from the West. In so doing, he managed to win the esteem of officials and local worthies in Guangdong and Jiangsu. He eventually even made it to Beijing, winning over not a few scholars to Catholicism.

Based on more than two decades of experience as a scholar and missionary, Ricci proposed a "special dispensation" for Chinese Catholics. He explained that the "God" in whom he believed was the "Heavenly Emperor" (*shangdi*) of China in their ancient canons. Therefore, the Chinese need only reacquaint themselves with this primordial Emperor. He also agreed that Chinese Catholics could worship their ancestors and Confucius, for this was reverence for the ancients, not worship of a god. From Ricci's experience, it appears that Western churches were free to evangelize in China. But if they wished to achieve real results they could not infringe upon Chinese traditions; in other words, Confucianism was capable of coexisting with other schools of thought, but would not tolerate one that subverted it.

My second example: Ricci and Li Zhi were contemporaries. The latter was a Chinese Muslim and a scholar who opposed Confucianism. He felt that seeking advantage while avoiding the disadvantageous—looking after one's self first and foremost—was a normal state of affairs. "Eliminate human desire and what remains is heavenly reason," as advocated by the neo-Confucians, was either hypocrisy or an unattainable truth, in his eyes. But he was tolerated neither by other literati nor the emperor, and ended up committing suicide in prison. Even though different religions coexisted in China, an idea that contradicts the orthodox Confucianism could not be tolerated in this case.

My third example: When Islamic civilization entered China, the emperor did not interfere, but the Muslim elaboration of Islam could not help but undergo changes in order to accommodate Chinese culture and Confucian orthodoxy, because only by doing so could it take root in Chinese society. Two years after the birth of Li Zhi, the chief Imam of Jinan South Temple (*Friday Mosque*) in Shandong Province, Chen Si—a Muslim scholar deeply versed in Confucianism and fluent in both Chinese and Arabic scripts—wrote an inscription on a stele for the mosque over which he presided, entitled *"lai fuming."*

From the text of the inscription, it appears that the teachings of Islam had already penetrated and fused with Confucian culture.

Today the inscription on the stele, which are extremely difficult to translate, remain in front of Jinan South Mosque. Although the inscription did not skip the basic Islamic teaching—"There is no God but God" and made it clear that men should submit themselves to God—the words and reasoning come from the neo-Confucianism of the Song and Ming periods.

The above three examples illustrate the "super-stable structure."

As for the causes of the "super-stable structure" there is no consensus among scholars. In my view, three facts offer a partial explanation to this phenomenon in Chinese history.

First, from the Warring States period (475–221 BC) until very recently, the predominant economic activity in China was agricultural production, usually by independent small farmers; wealth came mainly through repetition and augmentation of agricultural output. Second, since the

Qin dynasty (221–206 BCE), China—often unified though divided into regional regimes at times—has been ruled by centralizing authoritarian governments, almost all of which deliberately favored agriculture over commerce. Third, the education method as well as the examination system for the selection of officials have remained largely unchanged since Tang dynasty, with the overall effect of emphasizing Confucianism. These three factors were intertwined and worked together to promote stability rather than induce change. Of course, these factors themselves were probably the result of China's geography.

One saying has it that because China's population density is so high, arable land is lacking and the distance between people so small that Chinese society must take human relationships into account; it is virtually impossible to escape from the network of personal ties.

I had an epiphany once in flight. When you fly over a farming area in the United States, about every two kilometers you will see a family home, each with its own grain silo. But if you fly over a farming region in China, there is more than one village per kilometer, and each village comprises a cluster of farmhouses.

America is indeed rich in natural resources, but this isn't the case for Europe. Traditionally, land could not be freely bought and sold there, because it belonged to the nobility that practiced primogeniture, so farms tended to be fairly large. But according to Chinese custom, each male offspring has a claim to the family's assets, so lots grew smaller and smaller, and there were basically no large landowners. Everyone was a small-lot farmer living in densely packed housing, with lots of neighbors, many of whom were relatives. Seen in that light, the interpersonal networks and kinship relations of the Chinese and Americans are utterly different. Even today when China has embarked on the road of industrialization, respect for parents and elders, and the obligation to obey them, has not disappeared.

I'd like to mention a conversation I overheard in an elevator in Hong Kong. Two middle-aged women, obviously from the mainland, were chatting.

> One woman asked: "How old's your child?"
> "Twenty-six," replied the other.
> "You'll be holding a grandson in your arms soon, eh?"
> "I won't let him start a family yet! No marriage before thirty."

You probably won't hear this sort of conversation in the United States. Even though most young people in China are economically independent, many in the upper-middle class or upper class still depend on their parents for housing as well as employment opportunities. In other words, traditional human relations continue to operate, and mutual reliance among family members is much greater than in the United States or Europe.

Let me tell another story. When I first went to the United States, I learned to play "Monopoly." This board game is quite similar to "Moving up the Civil Service Ladder," a game I learned back in Taiwan, China. The starting point for "Monopoly" is a small amount of cash, while the player in the latter starts out as an undistinguished man-in-the-street.

The incentive for the "Ladder" player is to obtain honors and public office, climbing higher one post at a time, via virtuous actions, ability or even bribery. In "Monopoly," the incentives are the cash, stocks and real estate that obviously illustrate the workings of capitalism. From the Ming and Qing Dynasties down to the Republican Era, "Moving up the Civil Service Ladder" has always been popular. And I hear that it has been adapted now into a computer game too.

The major aspect of the super-stable social structure since the Song Dynasty was that, under the imperial examination system, official position, wealth and social standing transformed the literati into a "scholar-official" class that monopolized power and controlled every sort of resource. Regardless of where the scholar was in the sea of officialdom—floating or sinking—his sons and grandsons were duty-bound to study and seek official position, wealth and social standing too.

Merchants who possessed only great wealth also hoped their sons would be studious so that they could become civil servants and be held in high esteem in their hometown, bring honor to the family and protect family property. Merchants didn't take the money they earned and invest it in industry; they used it to buy land, thereby participating in an ancient form of agricultural "recycling."

Under such conditions, social stability was easily maintained. But as for social development, that's another matter.

Western Science Migrates East

Matteo Ricci was born into an aristocratic family and received the best sixteenth-century European education. That means he studied both rhetoric and logic, was familiar with Euclidian geometry and well versed in Aristotelian philosophy. He could even draw maps. It was he who first introduced Chinese scholars to the knowledge that European had accumulated over the last three centuries. For instance, his good friend Xu Guangqi was surprised to discover that Chinese culture lacked detailed analysis; instead, it excelled at providing a comprehensive overview of principles. I'd put it like this: geometry doesn't just lead us to an understanding of the form of things—it should train us to apply logical thought to things.

In physics, besides describing the temporal and physical status of things, the spatial element is also very important. Take the spread and movement of fog, for instance. If the description is not "three-dimensional"—with details about time, space and density—and simply informs us tonight will be "foggy," or Tianjin will experience a "big" fog, then this is insufficient.

People say that eating wood ear fungus can reduce cholesterol. Even restaurant menus claim so. But how much should one eat daily to achieve such an effect, and how much may cause side effects?

Traditional Chinese culture does not emphasize scientific methodology and lacks logical analysis and the means to quantify. Perhaps Ricci's friend Xu Guangqi had some inkling of this. Two hundred years later, even the emperor realized that if Western methods of fabrication were not applied to ships and cannons, then the ships wouldn't be rugged and the cannons wouldn't be deadly.

By the end of the nineteenth century, China's understanding of biology took a giant step forward, one that included Darwin's theory of evolution. Huxley was more audacious than Darwin, who had a bit of the country gentleman about him. The latter merely put forward his ideas. He was unwilling to enter into direct conflict with others.

But Huxley was different. Once he met an Anglican Bishop at the annual meeting of the Royal Society of Biology. The bishop, predictably, was opposed to the theory of evolution. At the time, based on the Bible, the Anglican Church speculated that God had created mankind more than 4,000 years ago, and completely dismissed any talk of "evolution."

"I hear that you and the apes are related," said the bishop, mocking Huxley.

Retorted Huxley, "If I had a choice, I'd prefer to be related to apes rather than a blatantly ignorant bishop who imagines himself a gentleman."

The famous late Qing and early republican era translator Yan Fu rendered Huxley's *Evolution and Ethics* in Chinese.

THE *I CHING* AND MICROELECTRONICS

There are Chinese who argue that *The Book of Changes* (*I Ching*) is the ancestor of atomic physics because it contains these words:

> The universe moves energetically. The superior man steels himself for ceaseless activity.

In other words, the world of objects is mightily in flux. Electrons revolve around nuclei, the planets circle the sun, all the universe's material things are in motion—the *I Ching* pointed this out very early. But putting aside the question of whether this interpretation of one line of text is meaningful, mankind must have some understanding of an electron's trajectory and energy in order to invent and manufacture today's microelectronics products.

It isn't disputed that Newton and Leibniz invented infinitesimal calculus at roughly the same time. They did correspond about this topic, but never met, and did not show each other their theses prior to publication. At any rate, who first invented calculus is not terribly important, because over the last three centuries most scientific experiments and engineering calculations have been carried out based on this mathematical foundation. Just getting half the credit makes each of them a colossus in the history of modern science.

From a practical standpoint, the calculus notation invented by Leibniz is very simple and easy to use, and therefore more efficient. This is to say, differentiation (d/dx) of a function (f) begets its derivative (df/dx); integration ($\int$) of this derivative returns to the original function (f), thus one can write $\int [df/dx] \, dx = f$. Recognizing the utility of this simple notation system and its conceptual power, I think Leibniz contributed more than Newton in the popularization of calculus.

Why mention Leibniz? Because Leibniz once resided in Paris where he came into contact with a few Jesuits who had been in China. One Jesuit told him that the *I Ching* was based on *yin* and *yang*—from which the Eight Trigrams or can be deduced—and their interpretation can explain many phenomena in Nature. This might have prompted him to think more about a binary system in mathematics.

Why must numbers be expressed via the decimal system? Because primitive man used his fingers to count, naturally enough. But what if one doesn't use one's fingers? Leibniz reckoned that 0 and 1—or *yin* and *yang*—could be used as a basis for calculation instead. Here's the binary system he invented out of sheer interest:

$0 + 1 = 1; 1 + 1 = 10; 10 + 1 = 11; 11 + 1 = 100; 100 + 1 = 101; 100 + 10 = 110; 110 + 1 = 111; 111 + 1 = 1000$, and so forth.

We can say that there was a linkage between Leibniz's binary system and the *I Ching*. If we use a binary mathematical description of things to perform digital calculations, we would employ a long string of 0 and 1.

From quantum physics and solid-state physics, we know that there are elements of nature that conduct electricity under certain conditions, but are non-conductive under others, e.g., a semiconductor. We can use 1 to represent a conductive state, and 0 for a non-conductive one. If we place a series of semiconductor components together, link them via an electric circuit, and instruct them to conduct or not conduct electricity according to binary algorithms using a long string of 0 and 1—and employ these semiconductors to compute and store the digital data—then what takes place is the basic task of microelectronic engineering in action.

This innovation began at Stanford University in the United States, so Silicon Valley is located near the university.

Leibniz lived at the same time as two emperors whose reigns largely coincided. They were aware of one another but did not correspond: France's Louis XIV, and China's Kangxi. One of Louis XIV's descendants was hung and lost the throne in 1789, but later France became a colonial empire (and even today has a few overseas territories). It still qualifies as a rich and strong country. One of Kangxi's descendants was forced to abdicate in 1911, but survived. The territory he ruled between the ages of three and six is now without an emperor; and we are discussing the development prospects of the huge country ruled by the child emperor.

But before delving into this theme, I'd like to briefly switch topics. Around 1985, I once wanted to learn "C," a new programming language, because I'd already mastered an upgraded version of Fortran, an earlier language. I reckoned I had a decent foundation, since the calculations in my PhD thesis used Fortran IV. At the time I was using a CDC3600 computer. CDC was an abbreviation for "Control Data Corporation," the computer maker's name; 3600 signified that the computer memory storage was 3600 bytes. In other words, a massive 3.6 K!

When it occurred to me to study C Language, I had just taken up the post of department head at the University of Southern California, and due to lack of time, I didn't master it. Soon thereafter, C was found to be less than user-friendly, so some people improved upon it and dubbed the new version C++. Shortly thereafter I went to the Hong Kong University of Science and Technology in order to serve as Founding Dean of the School of Engineering (1990–1994). The first two departments we established were the Computer Department and the Electronic Engineering Department. Everything is hard in the beginning, and a pile of trifling chores required my attention, so even though I remained keen on mastering C, in the end, it just didn't happen.

THE C++ PROJECT

During my speech in 1998 on the same topic as this essay, I mentioned a "C++ Project." In this, "C" represents "Chinese Culture." And like the programming language, the original "C" doesn't suffice. It needs to be altered to "C++" in order to be useful. But in order to create Chinese culture for a new era, we must use quintessential Chinese culture as a foundation. So "C" is the foundation, and that's important. The first "+" signifies that we have to reflect upon Chinese history and culture, in order to add value; the second "+" means we need to open our minds, see things from an international perspective, absorb new nutrients and promote new culture.

But what is "quintessential" Chinese culture?

I consider one distinctive feature is the written Chinese character. Mandarin is monosyllabic and *hanzi* are square in shape, something truly unique in the world. China's primary school students can even read most of the characters originally used in a fourth-century text like Wang Xizhi's "Orchid Pavilion Preface." The script with the longest continuous usage on the face of the earth, and the language spoken by most people worldwide—these facts are indisputable.

Furthermore, I feel that another trait of Chinese culture is a certain "reserve." One's talent, feelings and intentions are not to be easily visible to others. Another characteristic is moderation, an unwillingness to be too aggressive toward others or push people into a corner. Also, one's thinking and behavior ought to seek balance and avoid extremes.

These are the qualities of Chinese people in general. Given this, it is hard to find a person to take the lead, someone who won't quit until he has proven himself right. This sense of reserve has good points when it comes to politics and personal relations. But in science—where the pursuit of truth is the basic goal—one must not lack tenaciousness. In this sort of cultural environment, it's hard to predict if one can cultivate a Newton, Leibniz, Darwin or Huxley.

That's (almost) all I will say about Chinese characters. But there is a famous couplet I'd like to cite:

寄寓客家牢守寒窗空寂寞，
远避迷途退还莲迳返逍遥

As even those unfamiliar with *hanzi* will note, in the first line each character has a roof-like structure over it, while in the second line, each character sits atop an "L" shape of sorts (a radical which suggests movement). Additionally, in a couplet the two lines must be symmetrical in length, tonality and parts of speech. What other script can match this sort of linguistic—and visual—game-play?

In the first half of the twentieth century, the famous author Lu Xün advocated Romanizing Chinese. But today, no one calls for their abolition. Why? I think the answer lies in the electron that circles the nucleus.

In comparison with phonetic scripts, Chinese characters are hard to memorize. In earlier times, typesetting and printing books with *hanzi* was difficult and literate people were few, so the dissemination of knowledge was very slow, and this negatively impacted the level of culture among Chinese as a whole. But *hanzi* have their advantages. Although learning characters requires great effort, once they are memorized, the function of both auditory and visual senses are enriched. So the characters have pros and cons. The downside is the long time spent putting them to memory, but the upside is that they stimulate the brain in different ways, and enhance its potential. If a literate Chinese undergoes a stroke that impacts his hearing, he can still use his visual memory to recall the characters; if the visual part of the brain is injured, he can still identify words via hearing.

It was quantum physics that made us aware of the microscopic world and led us to invent the microcomputer by exploiting semiconductors. Nowadays people use PCs for text input and to carry out laser typesetting and printing; in terms of speed and accuracy, the processing of Chinese characters is not inferior to any other script. Therefore in the twenty-first century, it is not spoken or written language where Chinese culture needs to compete. It is in the domains of scientific and technical innovation.

In Today's World

I authored an article in the 2006 issue of *Peking University* magazine in which I declared that for China to function as the world's factory is not enough. We must develop the brainpower and creativity of our large population. But this is a new challenge for the East Asian civilization circle, which traditionally strives for social order and ethical behavior. China's most prestigious scientific awards are often given to someone in his or her eighties. Stressing ethics is a good thing, but it can be a negative incentive when it comes to technical innovation. As I noted earlier, East Asian culture emphasizes the need to obey the collective, one's elders and one's superiors. Parents want well-behaved children, and the government wants the masses to do as they are told.

Under these conditions, it won't be easy for another Steve Jobs to emerge. As president of City University of Hong Kong, I proposed to the Hong Kong government—and it agreed—the establishment of a School of Creative Media. With a few years of hard work, the funds arrived, we got the land, the buildings went up and people already occupied them. My worry now is that after the Hong Kong government spent so much on land and financing, will it resemble what I envisioned two decades ago: to serve as an incubator nursing batch after batch of human talent, and exploit new media to renew Chinese culture? I suppose it depends on how the C++ Project is progressing.

When I was studying for my PhD at Northwestern University outside Chicago, I often came into contact with Professor Xu Langguang, then head of the department of anthropology there. He later wrote a book comparing the social cultures of China and the United States. There are things in the book with which I don't necessarily agree, but right now I'd like to focus on things he argues in Chapter 13, "Shortcomings of the Chinese." He mentions the way in which tradition acts to inhibit the

Chinese. Chinese generally only oppose, but lack a sense of how to renew, so they often change emperors…instead of changing the system itself.

He also believes that Chinese lack a sense of science and music. I'd like to speak about music for a moment. Han Chinese often say that a certain ethnic group is comprised of "born singers and dancers," meaning they know how to let their hair down, and aren't so bashful or inhibited.

In the minds of many Chinese, this description applies to most of China's ethnicities as well as the peoples of many countries. This is equivalent to saying that the only people who *cannot* "sing and dance" are the Han. It may be due to the constraints engendered by Confucianism, particularly during several recent centuries when girls from well to-do families bound their feet. How could they dance? It was over a century ago that foreign missionaries first opposed foot-binding ("lotus feet"), and then the Chinese who were influenced by Westerners also opposed it. Even though many women found foot-binding extremely painful, at first no one was willing to grapple with this problem. Perhaps everyone was totally unwilling to alter the status quo.

Regardless, I am very keen to promote Chinese culture. But the Chinese culture I want to promote is modern—a work-in-progress—a new culture that comprises diverse elements with potential for progress. This kind of culture is not a recreation of Confucian culture, nor is it merely a revival of Han and Tang culture. We should respect the achievements of those who came before us. We should also put more emphasis on the circumstances of those who are alive now. We are proud of our own people's culture, but we are even keener to draw on the excellent cultures of others. Our starting point is today, but our eyes are on the future.

This essay is entitled *From Movable Type to the World Wide Web*. I speak of the World Wide Web because we can find *hanzi* on the Internet throughout the world. The importance of Chinese on the web is arguably second only to English. The World Wide Web is like a network of highways, and we can say that the Chinese-language web sites are vehicles for *hanzi*-literate passengers. This public roadway wasn't invented by the Chinese, nor was it laid using Chinese technology, and only a few of the vehicles on it were made by Chinese—in fact, many were copied straight from someone else's blueprints.

Internet domain name classifications are currently proposed mainly by Americans, and are managed mainly by US-based servers. With China's new knowledge and new techniques, the people of China have the requisite conditions for rejuvenation. But *daring* to innovate, and *excelling* at it, are necessary for optimizing that potential. When Chinese can create something superior to the World Wide Web on the level of the "Four Great Inventions" of yore, truly make our influence felt on global civilization, become the trend-setters of the era, and guide the whole world's domain name classification into a new realm, then that will mark the renaissance of Chinese culture.

To paraphrase a famous line by Tang Dynasty literary genius Luo Binwang:

Look about you at the virtual world today: who will pioneer this new domain in the decades ahead?

Only time will tell.

CHAPTER 3

Speaking of Mesopotamia

After the 2013 Lunar New Year, I visited the Hong Kong Museum of History to check out an exhibition, "The Wonders of Ancient Mesopotamia." Once wasn't enough; I went back a second time. It was both general and focused, with marvelously complementary physical and virtual displays, and informative text and audio explanations. I recommended it to many friends, even though it was crowded on both occasions.

In April of the same year, I taught "Mapping Civilizations: Retrospect and Prospects" at Peking University, and naturally I touched upon Mesopotamia. Queried one student: How is it that the heirs of this glorious civilization—today's Iraqis and Syrians—are living amidst the chaos of war and suffering when Mesopotamian civilization was so ahead of its time?

Readers who are interested in Mesopotamian civilization may be asking themselves the same question.

THE CRADLE OF CIVILIZATION

Scientists generally agree that after hundreds of millions of years of evolution, "homo habilis" could walk upright and exploit tools appeared in Africa more than two million years ago, and later spread to the Middle East, Southeast Asia, and East Asia. "Java Man" and "Peking Man" are presumably their descendants. Modern humans (with skeletons and brain capacity no longer distinct from ours) also appeared in Africa about 300,000 years ago. About 100,000 years ago, Homo sapiens came out of Africa, proceeding first to the Middle East, and then to the rest of the world.

About 10,000 years ago, some people living in the fertile valleys between the lower and middle Tigris and Euphrates rivers roughly in present-day Iraq and northeastern Syria—i.e., Mesopotamia, which is formed from the ancient words "meso," meaning between, and "potamos," meaning river—began to raise animals and grow crops as alternatives to hunting and fruit-gathering. This was the beginning of humankind's conscious transformation of its environment, and the very origin of civilization. Since the beginning of agricultural production to the present day, human life has been transformed by social rather than biological evolution.

The development of civilizations has been very uneven: Modes of production, social organization, and ideology have varied greatly. Generally speaking, geography has been the decisive factor. There should be no difference in intelligence between people who lived 10,000 years ago (or even 100,000 years ago) and those who live today; there is arguably no difference in the intelligence quotients between people who live today in cities in a post-industrial society versus those who live in the jungle in a clan-based society.

The Sumerians, Akkadians, and Assyrians of Mesopotamia created marvelous material and spiritual cultures. The Sumerians first made pottery with a hand-wheel and then invented the chariot wheel. They founded some of the world's first city-states, and evolved from worshiping natural phenomena to honoring anthropomorphic deities. The Akkadians, who founded the ancient kingdom of Babylon, were skilled in astronomy and mathematics, used multiplication and division tables, and knew how to obtain square roots and cubic roots 4,800 years ago. They divised the 60-minute system, and divided the day into two 12-hour periods of 60 minutes each. The Assyrians conquered Babylon with chariots, established a vast empire, constructed ornate palaces, composed extraordinary epics and developed medicine.

Heirs to Ancient Civilizations

Heirs of these ancient civilizations were not just the Iraqis and Syrians of today, nor were they limited to peoples in the Middle East and the Mediterranean, but should have included the Chinese as well! Wheat and chariots were imported from Mesopotamia, and ancient Chinese astronomy was clearly inspired and influenced by the Babylonians. In the Hong Kong museum exhibition, there were several cylindrical rolling seals, with very delicate and vivid designs.

The cylinder seals from the Indus Valley that I saw at the National Museum of India in New Delhi are also exquisite. It is unlikely that such seals were independent discoveries, but rather are evidence of early Mesopotamian and Indus Valley interactions. There are many examples of considerable borrowing between ancient cultures, even in less developed antiquity.

From the sixth century BCE onwards, Mesopotamia was ruled successively by the Persians, Greeks and Romans. From the second century BCE to the seventh century CE, Mesopotamia was governed by the Persian Parthians and then the Sassanids (224–651).

In the seventh century, the Arabs occupied the region. For the next 500 years, Mesopotamia became the political and cultural center of a flourishing Islamic civilization. The Islamic Abbasids built Baghdad as their new capital at the end of the eighth century, not far from the city of ancient Babylon.

During the twelfth to the fifteenth centuries, Mesopotamia was ruled successively by the Turkic Seljuk dynasty that originated on the Mongolian Plateau, the Ilkhanate inherited by Genghis Khan's grandson Hulagu, and then the Timurid dynasty (1370–1507), founded by Turkified Mongols in Central Asia.

From the first half of the sixteenth century to 1918, Syria and Iraq belonged to the Ottoman Empire which was founded by a branch of the Seljuk Turks who settled in Anatolia (Asia Minor).

Complex Role of the British

After gaining dominance in India, Britain began to covet territories within the Ottoman Empire, including Mesopotamia, the western Persian Gulf and Palestine. During this period the British were present in the Middle East in large numbers, including diplomats, soldiers, merchants and scholars. The first three were colonialists who aimed to gain material profit; the scholars were there to accumulate knowledge, but were protected and supported by the first three, and thus enjoyed certain advantages.

It was, of course, no accident that Britain became a colonial empire. Since the eighteenth century, the British government was able to gain insight into—and thus impact—situations around the globe, thanks, of course, to the careful study of the world by British scholars and officials.

Over the past three centuries, Britain has been blessed with a wealth of talent: Isaac Newton, Michael Faraday, James Maxwell and Charles Darwin were giants in science; Adam Smith, John Stuart Mill and John Mayard Keynes influenced the world with their ideas about the economy and philosophy, and the work of the British "Orientalists" also made a remarkable contribution to the understanding and preservation of early civilizations.

British archaeological research on Mesopotamia recorded some very important achievements, especially the decipherment of cuneiform scripts and excavation of the ancient Assyrian city of Nimrud. Of course, British scholars whisked away many excavated treasures, including huge statues and even city ramparts, to the British Museum in London.

In the second half of the nineteenth century, the British Empire under Queen Victoria was known as the "Empire on which the sun never sets." It is no exaggeration to say that she was the most prominent person in the world of her era. Even though the Queen possessed the world's most famous Koh-i-noor diamond—"ceded" to Britain after it annexed Punjab in 1849—she could not help but envy the jewelry worn by Lady Enid Layard, with whom she once dined: A necklace comprising eleven ancient Mesopotamian cylinder seals and four square seals, with a pair of earrings and a bracelet inset with seals too. Need it be noted that the Lady's spouse, Sir Henry Layard, headed the excavation of the remains at Nimrud?

During World War I in 1916, Britain and France secretly negotiated the Sykes–Picot agreement that effectively divided the Ottoman Empire's Middle Eastern territories into two spheres of influence. After the war, Britain was to take over Iraq and Palestine, while Syria would go to the French.

France made several Sunni Muslim areas originally in southern Syria a separate country called Lebanon and then transformed Lebanon into a republic, but this caused discontent in the Syrian kingdom that was under French trusteeship.

For its part, Britain separated Kuwait—where oil had been newly discovered—from Iraq and designated it as a protectorate, and also carved out a Jordanian sheikhdom (now the Kingdom of Jordan) from Palestine.

In addition, in their role as "trustee" the British appointed two brothers of the Hashemite family—that claims descent from the family of the Prophet Muhammad—who formerly served the Ottomans in administering the Islamic holy land of Mecca, as the King of Iraq and the Emir of Transjordan, respectively.

Both Britain and France used the divide-and-rule tactic of elevating minority religious sects to help rule the majority. After World War II, the British and French ended their rule in the Middle East. But conflicts between Syria and Lebanon, Iraq and Kuwait, and decades of ethnic and sectarian conflict in Lebanon, Syria and Iraq can be traced back to the British and French administrations.

From the perspective of preserving the traces of ancient cultures, however, the British mandate also had its positive aspects. In 1933–1934, British archaeologists excavated many ancient Mesopotamian sites. The British government and "Mandatory Iraq" agreed that half of the unearthed relics would accrue to the British; due to the disparity in knowledge and power between the two sides, this inevitably meant the most prized ended up in Britain. Additionally, using the best technology available, facsimiles of the half that remained in Iraq were made by British scholars, and played an important role in the future study of ancient Mesopotamia.

Iraq and Syria Today

In March 2003, the so-called Multi-National Force—Iraq (MNF–I)—mainly peopled by US and British soldiers, with a smattering of other troops from Europe and Australia—invaded Iraq with the stated aim of uncovering and neutralizing Saddam Hussein's purported "weapons of mass destruction." Subsequently, none were found.

Shortly after the fall of Baghdad, organized thieves entered the National Museum of Iraq and looted almost all of its precious collections despite the valiant efforts of some museum staff to protect the treasures. Fortunately, some of the stolen items had previously been reproduced and their facsimiles are in the British Museum, but many monuments were destroyed or severely damaged during the war.

Sunni–Shia tensions have become more pronounced since the war that officially ended with the departure of the US occupiers in 2011, and Kurdish–Arab friction has not abated either. Iraq is currently in a precarious political and social situation.

In March 2011, inspired by the "Arab Spring" uprisings across the Middle East, anti-government demonstrations also broke out in Syria. Within two years, the Sunni armed insurgency—Sunni Arabs dominate Syria number-wise—had grown stronger thanks to foreign support. Meanwhile, the central government dominated by the Alawite, a small Shiite sect that constitutes only 12% of the population of 23 million, had lost control of large swathes of territory outside of its stronghold in the provinces of Tartous and Latakia on Syria's mountainous western coast.

Soon, several armed groups supported by Western countries and Turkey literally carved up Syria. The Islamic State infiltrated Syria from its base in Iraq, and the United States, Russia, France, Turkey, and Iran each stationed considerable numbers of armed personnel inside Syria.

After a decade of complex and difficult diplomatic and military confrontations, the Syrian government is now—amazingly—in a position to emerge victorious, due in no small part to the military support from Russia and Iran. But most cities have been reduced to rubble, at least 400,000 Syrians have died in the civil war, more than 6 million are internally displaced, and another 6-million-plus refugees have fled Syria, mainly for Turkey. Whether or not President Bashar Hafez al-Assad and his supporters retain power, a long period of suffering yet awaits the people of Syria.

I visited the Damascus National Museum's exquisite and copious items on exhibit in November 2010. And I wonder: What fate awaits them?

CHAPTER 4

My Take on the Middle East

The "Greater Middle East" is the region where human civilization first emerged, where the clash and fusion of civilizations have been most evident over the course of world history, and where various conflicts manifest in today's world are concentrated.

Even for those persons who are habitually unconcerned with world affairs, over the past decade they are bound to have noticed certain buzzwords and topics that frequently popped up in print, on TV and the Internet: "Arab Spring"; regime changes in Egypt; cantonization of Libya after "Strongman" Gaddafi took a bullet to the head; internal conflicts in Syria that transformed nearly half the population into refugees; Islamic State's expansion followed by collapse; the democratically elected president of Tunisia's preference for ruling by decree; Saudi bombing of an already divided Yemen; Iraqi masses taking to the street in protest; terrorist bombings in Somalia, Lebanon's faltering to become a failed state, and so on.

More recently, oscillating war and peace between Ethiopia and Eritrean in the Horn of Africa, Turkey's intervention in the Libyan civil war; Egypt and Ethiopia, the two oldest countries in Africa, fighting over damming the Nile; an American drone terminated Iran's star military strategist Qasem Suleimani, and Iran's shooting down a Ukrainian airliner, killing 176.

Since the "Arab Spring" blossomed in 2011, many countries in the Greater Middle East have rejigged their constitutions, regimes have changed several times, and not a few leaders have fallen from power, fled, or been executed. The political scene in each country is relatively unstable, and meanwhile, the daily lives of the people have seen little amelioration.

What Is the "Greater Middle East"?

These dramatic events have inevitably led us to focus our attention on a single region, the meeting points of the continents of Asia, Africa and Europe, which I have dubbed the "Greater Middle East." In fact, the term "Middle East" was coined by Western Europeans, who were prone to proceed east to find places of greater interest. Those lands close to Europe they called the "Near East," those a bit further away they termed the "Middle East," and most remote was the "Far East," home to China and Japan. The earth being round, such terminology was an expression of Eurocentrism.

Of course, in ancient times, the Chinese people—*Huaxia*—called their homeland "Middle Kingdom." Today's Xinjiang Uygur Autonomous Region and uncharted territory toward Central Asia were labeled somewhat mysteriously as "*Xi Yu*" or "Western Regions," while to China's east lay Japan, formerly referred to as "*Dongying*," or "Eastern Sea."

In fact, the term "Middle East" is hardly ancient, as it was first used by some Orientalists a century or so ago.

In our minds, the lands occupied by Egypt, Turkey, Israel, Iraq and eastward to Iran is referred to as the Middle East because of their relatively concentrated location at the confluence of three continents: Asia, Africa and Europe. This "traditional" Middle East comprises 16 countries: Egypt, Israel, Palestine, Turkey, Jordan, Lebanon, Syria, Iraq, Saudi Arabia, Yemen, Oman, the United Arab Emirates (UAE), Qatar, Bahrain, Kuwait and Iran.

But my concept of the Greater Middle East is much broader. For example, from Libya westward to Morocco, people in these countries speak Arabic and mainly believe in Islam, and they are culturally similar, so these places can be considered part of the "Cultural Middle East," and I also classify them within my Greater Middle East.

When change occurs in the Middle East, it is impossible for the Greater Middle East to stay out of it. For example, if something happens in Tunisia or Libya, the island nation of Malta in the Mediterranean will inevitably be affected, though its population is Catholic. Cyprus, where sixty percent of the population are Greek-speaking Orthodox believers, is also part of the picture. Greece, of course, is the birthplace of European civilization and Western civilization as a whole, but due to its location and historical origins, its fate is largely inseparable from that of Turkey and Egypt. Even after Greece freed itself of Ottoman tutelage in 1830, the Greeks remained surrounded by the Balkan Peninsula comprising Serbia, Albania, Bulgaria and so forth, so it could not insulate itself from the Ottoman Empire and the Middle Eastern ambiance.

Situated between the Ottoman and Persian Empires, there were also three countries in the Eastern world that were historically influenced by them: Armenia, Georgia and Azerbaijan. In addition, several countries in the Horn of Africa—Ethiopia, Eritrea, Djibouti and Somalia—are also closely linked to the traditional Middle East.

The Middle East "periphery" therefore consists of fifteen countries: Morocco, Tunisia, Algeria, and Libya on the northern coast of Africa; East Africa's Ethiopia, Eritrea, Djibouti, Somalia and Sudan (newly independent South Sudan is part of Central Africa, not the Greater Middle East); the Mediterranean's Greece, Cyprus, Malta; and the countries of the Southern Caucasus, Armenia, Georgia, and Azerbaijan.

Altogether there are 31 countries in the Greater Middle East as I define it; 23 have Muslim populations as a major component, and 20 are mainly Arabic-speaking. Therefore, it can be said that almost all the Arabophone countries are in the Greater Middle East, and furthermore, Arabic and Islam are the principal characteristics of this entity.

But the cultural landscape of the Greater Middle East is diverse and complex precisely because some societies do not fit this mold. Some countries, such as Ethiopia and Armenia—both founded prior to the Roman Church—are predominantly Christian, and about ten percent of Egyptians identify as members of the Coptic Orthodox Church. And the establishment of Israel in 1948 as a Jewish-majority state represents a historical first and a political breakthrough in the Greater Middle East.

In fact, a key characteristic of the Greater Middle East is that within almost every country there are distinct regional cultures and different religions, ethnicities, tribes, classes and languages, so that almost every Middle Easterner can claim "multiple identities."

To the average Chinese, this is very difficult to grasp. Nearly ninety-two percent of the Chinese population is Han Chinese, and there are only dialectal differences among the Han Chinese, not differences in religion, ethnicity, writing or cultural background, so there is a high degree of homogeneity among them.

Decoding the Region's History of Violent Conflict

The Greater Middle East is the region where human civilization first emerged, where the intermingling—and clash—of civilizations has been most pronounced throughout history, and where the conflicts of today's world are concentrated.

From ancient to modern times, the more powerful empires have established trade routes and collected taxes in this region. The wealthy Persian empire was founded by Darius the Great 2,500 years ago and located its royal palace in Persepolis not far from the eastern shore of today's Persian Gulf. Alexander destroyed the Persian empire in 330 BCE, and then continued his conquests to the banks of the Indus. Cleopatra VII Philopator, the last of the Greek Ptolemies to rule Egypt and the last queen of the kingdom, married the Roman general Antony, an act—rendered famous by Shakespeare and Hollywood as well—that did not alter the looming extinction of her kingdom.

At the time, in the east there was the Parthian Empire of Persia whose territory extended as far as Iraq and Syria. Directly facing the Persians were the Romans, who governed Palestine and Asia Minor. In the fourth century, the Roman Emperor Constantine I added a new capital to the eastern part of the empire, Constantinople, now known as Istanbul. In ancient Greek times, it was a village named "Byzantium." After the western part of the Roman Empire was destroyed by the northern "barbarians" (Visigoths), the eastern part of the empire became what historians have labeled the "Byzantine Empire."

The Persian Sassanid Empire lay to the east of the Christian Byzantines, and the two subsequently had a continual struggle for almost two to three hundred years, with both sides suffering from the conflict.

In contrast, the late-blooming peoples of the Middle East were the Arabs who used Islam to give them new strength and Islamic methods of warfare and governance to quickly wipe out the ancient nations of Persia and Egypt. Later, the Tujüe or Turkic peoples emerged from the Mongolian Plateau, slowly migrated westward to the Persian region and established the Seljuq Empire, and then occupied Byzantine territory. This triggered panic in Western Europe, inspiring Christians to launch the Crusades.

The Seljuq Empire was defeated by another group of later invaders from the East, the Mongols. The thirteenth–fourteenth centuries marked an era of great accessibility for Eurasia, featuring unimpeded land-based travel between the eastern coast of the Adriatic and the Korean Peninsula. Prior to the era of global sea navigation, land transportation was already very well developed.

In modern times, it was the Ottoman Empire that dominated this region. They governed Egypt and the Arabian Peninsula after the sixteenth century, but before that they had already ruled the bulk of the vanquished Byzantine Empire for more than two centuries.

There was also the Safavid dynasty of Persia. The Ottomans and Safavids sometimes fought over their territories. For example, Tabriz (now capital of Iran's East Azerbaijan Province) changed hands several times.

Later, Britain and Russia also debuted in the Greater Middle East. France occupied Algeria in 1830, and having declared it a French province, after World War II they resisted strident calls for independence. It was only after Algerian guerrillas pinned down the bulk of the French army that President Charles de Gaulle decided to give up this "province" across the Mediterranean.

Italy, belatedly unified, had also colonized parts of the Greater Middle East such as Eritrea and Libya by the late nineteenth and early twentieth centuries. Today's Somalia was separately colonized by three European countries: France, Britain and Italy.

After World War II, both the Soviet Union and the United States expanded their influence in the Greater Middle East, with the latter forming the Baghdad Pact, a Cold War military alliance that included Turkey, Iran and Iraq, in 1958.

Since Israel's founding in 1948, it has fought four major wars with neighboring Arab countries—all resulting in resounding Israeli victories—which generated immense frustration in the Arab world.

Arab nationalism was galvanized by Europe's imperialism and colonialism, and many Arabs dreamt of uniting the Arab nation and restoring its past glory, power and influence, so both Christian and Islamic Arabs supported Arab nationalism. In fact, many of the pioneers of Arab nationalism were Christian Arabs. For example, many of the early leaders of Iraq's Baath Party were Christians; the last Minister of Foreign Affairs during Saddam's lifetime, Tariq Aziz—the regime's well-spoken apologist for Sadaam's regime often seen on western TV screens in the lead-up to the Persian Gulf War—was a Chaldean Catholic. But since the American invasion, it has become very difficult to imagine a Christian Minister of Foreign Affairs in a future Iraq, no matter who holds power.

At the same time, because Islam had been very powerful during the eighth–twelfth centuries and many people still longed for their past grandeur, Muslims of all denominations sought to restore the glory of the Middle Ages—specifically the eighth–twelfth centuries—now that they were under attack by imperialism and colonialism.

The moderates wish to restore Islamic society's self-respect and influence, while extremists such as the Salafists reckon that any custom that is not in accordance with the Qur'an, such as women not wearing a veil, should be eradicated.

In the last hundred years or so, Arab nationalism has crossed swords with imperialism and Zionism. Meanwhile, the competing ideologies of the Islamic revival movement, socialism, and democracy have all rubbed shoulders in societies throughout the region. Recent political turmoil reflects social contradictions within each country, ongoing machinations of the great powers, and the desire of people everywhere to achieve a better life through change.

Looking back at 2011, I fear that so many people continuously gathered in Cairo's Tahrir Square not for ideological reasons, but out of dissatisfaction with their own lives, and loathing of the hegemony of those in power and the illegitimate accumulation of wealth by the powerful. Of course, when people are burdened with unemployment, they cannot afford to buy a house or get married. In the Islamic world in general, relations between men and women are relatively strict, i.e., if unmarried, the two genders can hardly enjoy sex life. A normal person who has reached a certain age and wishes to marry, or is inclined to marry and raise a family—but does not possess the means to do so—is bound to resent their long-time rulers.

Islamic Tradition

At the end of the nineteenth century, Britain and Egypt together nominally governed Sudan which lies to the south of Egypt, but of course, it was Britain that ruled both. The people of northern Sudan are fairly dark-skinned, but speak Arabic and identify as Arabs. More darkly pigmented, the southern Sudanese speak a different tongue, and many are Christian or practitioners of fetishism. In the summer of 2011, Sudan officially split into two countries, followed by a civil war in the newly founded South

Sudan. Relations between the two remain tense. I do not classify South Sudan as part of the Greater Middle East.

Many people may have a misunderstanding of the Middle East or the Greater Middle East, assuming that the Middle East is strictly Islamic, which is incorrect. The Greater Middle East includes one Jewish and seven Christian states. If this weren't the case, the question of the Middle East might be much simpler. Ironically, Israel is also the most developed state in the entire region, and its location is so strategic that it cannot be excluded from the Middle East in any way. Despite a large number of Muslims within its borders, it is unquestionably a Jewish state, and Judaism and modern Hebrew are the official religion and language of Israel.

That said, there are 23 Muslim-majority countries in the Greater Middle East. From the historical point of view, no matter how much Islam has evolved or how many regimes arose, from its genesis it was agreed that all Muslims belonged to one community (Umma) under a single leader. The first was Muhammad, in whose hands were concentrated responsibility for religion, administration, education, economy, and military affairs. Later on, regional chiefs gradually emerged, and there were Persian regimes in Central Asia as well as independent regimes in the Iberian Peninsula, but most of these regimes did not dare augustly proclaim that they were the supreme ruler, nor did they issue money in their own name, but only borrowed the name of the caliphate.

Nowadays there are those who wish to return to the era when the Messenger of God, Muhammad, ruled directly in Medina, and they aim to establish a global "Islamic Emirate." Arguably, this is a delusion, but there are also historical reasons for it, namely, the fact that in Islamic tradition, there has never been a real separation between political and religious power.

During the Middle Ages, the Islamic world indubitably led the world in science, especially astronomy and medicine. So Muslims today, especially scholars, are aware that there was a significant period of human history in which Muslims made significant contributions to human knowledge. For example, the subject of "algebra" and many terms in chemistry, now used in Western languages, originated in Arabic.

Traditionally, Islamic rulers have been autocrats who centralized power in themselves. Many were diligent in their governance, regularly inviting their subjects to the palace to voice their concerns, and thereby exhibiting sensitivity to them; they were not necessarily arrogant sovereigns who rarely held court.

According to Islamic custom, every Friday at noon all Muslims should try to gather in a public place for congregational prayer (*Ṣalāt al-Jumuʿah*). At this time, there will be an imam present in the mosque who not only reads from the Qur'an, but also links its verses to the events of the day. Although there is no hierarchy in Sunni Islam, the influence of clerics who can deliver such a talk (*khutbah*) is significant.

In Shi'ite areas such as Iran, there is a hierarchy, and each Friday a senior cleric gives an important discourse during which he explicates the Sharia-based interpretation (fatwa) of a given topic. This was a very important phenomenon in Islamic society, and remains so. In Cairo, I attended such a talk citing a passage from the Qur'an that was used to comment on a current event. Actually, this is similar to the role of a sermon in Catholic or Protestant worship.

Islamic religious beliefs and rituals are uniformly monotheistic, and manifest absolute reverence for the Prophet Muhammad, the Chosen One of God. For the majority of Muslims, however, such doctrine and rituals are relatively dry, and do not easily facilitate a deeply religious experience that touches them to the soul.

Therefore, a group of believers seeking their own direct religious experience naturally emerged in the Islamic community. They sought to get closer to God through prayer and meditation. Since many of the thriving Muslim regimes of recent times were founded by Turkic-speaking peoples who entered the Islamic world only in the tenth century, many Muslims in Central Asia have retained traces of the Shamanism inherent to Turkic culture. They recite the Qur'an, which speaks of the 99 names of God, but borrow the rituals of the Turkic-speaking peoples of the steppe to chant, whisper, meditate or dance, as if they were in a trance and at one with God. Although these rituals have been condemned as heretical by some strict religious scholars, such religious experiences are difficult to prohibit. That is why Sufi Orders can be found within various Islamic denominations everywhere.

Sufis generally have a spiritual guide who instructs them how to unite with God, the so-called "Sheikh" or "Pir" (Persian, literally "elder"). Sufi Orders feature distinct strengths in different Islamic communities, but they are interconnected, with members often sharing common political views and looking after one another in society.

Lastly, some people consider that Islam is a religion of nomads, but it is not. It was born along the commercial routes of the Arabian Peninsula, and its earliest followers were merchants. Therefore, Islamic rulers have generally been supportive of industry and commerce, but prohibit usury as per Sharia.

The Development Dilemma and Democracy's Double-Edged Sword

Now back to the contemporary era. For the Greater Middle East countries of the present-day world, especially Muslim-majority ones, it is clear since the "Arab Spring" that the democratization of the Middle East has functioned as a double-edged sword for them, as well as for outsiders—including Israel and the West.

Basically, political participation by the masses in these Islamic countries has been relatively lacking. Their economies are relatively uncompetitive, and their glorious cultural traditions of the past have been greatly challenged, and this in turn makes both the international and domestic environments of the entire Middle East region vulnerable to instability.

Lack of democracy in politics breeds "family (dynastic) rule." For example, in recent years, leaders who have stepped down in Islamic countries in the Middle East were all "family-style rulers" whose offspring soared to great heights. There has been a tendency for a son to follow in his father's footsteps and inherit his progenitor's "enterprise"—while the average citizen's life did not improve but even got worse.

At the same time, traditional tribal thinking has lived on, and state power often depends upon coordination among tribal or clan leaders. This was the case when Gaddafi was alive, for example.

Some people have the misconception that most Islamic countries have adopted Sharia as the law of the land, but this is not the case; only Iran and Saudi Arabia have done so. According to my observation and reading, despite widespread belief in Sharia, although a romantic couple holding hands in the street is liable to prohibition and punishment by the "Morality Police," privileged persons are often exempt from such treatment. The elite have the chance to go abroad to places like London, New York or Paris, and such romantic behavior while overseas is not considered problematic. This also engenders resentment among the general public.

"Family-style rule" has its historical roots, however. It is not necessarily that these "Strongmen" insisted on "dynastic" rule, but in Islamic society, divine and patriarchal authority have been conflated and adopted based on past practice. Divine and patriarchal power have often been merged, and military power was a means of manifesting divine power.

The economies of the Middle East are generally uncompetitive, and with the exception of Israel, all other countries (including even Greece) are "developing" countries. Countries possessing fossil fuel reserves are somewhat better off, but these richer countries have not really broken away from the "single-source economy" model so far, i.e., they cannot survive without exporting their oil and natural gas. Furthermore, the real workers in energy-rich countries are foreigners.

Their societies are roughly divided into five classes: The top class is the royal family and their cronies; technicians and managers of large Western companies are the second; local civil servants form the third; professionals from other Arab lands, especially Egypt and Palestine, such as engineers and professors, are the fourth; and the fifth class is the majority of persons who are engaged in physical work at the bottom of the pyramid, mostly Bangladeshis, Indonesians and Filipinos. So far, these Middle Eastern countries have not adequately trained their own personnel, and thus import staff from outside as needed.

Even worse off are impoverished countries such as Yemen and Eritrea, which have no such energy reserves.

My travels have taken me to countries in Europe, Asia and the United States, North Africa and East Africa, including almost all of the countries in the Greater Middle East. The changes around the world over the past few decades have been tremendous. Change in East Asia has been the greatest, among which those in China are particularly striking. Southeast Asian countries such as Malaysia, Thailand, and Vietnam have also changed a lot, so too certain countries in Central and South America, such as Mexico, Costa Rica and Brazil.

However, in Ethiopia, Lebanon and Egypt, the transformations have been less pronounced. When you look at the rural villages of Ethiopia today, it would not be too much of an exaggeration to say that they mirror those of half a century ago. Djibouti, which has retained a French garrison of several thousand troops since independence in 1976 and leases its seaport to Dubai, the United States and China, has not applied its revenue to improve the people's livelihood; local consumption by the French garrison, rental income from the seaport, and railroad fees paid by Ethiopia have not kept most of the people of this small country of less than a million people out of poverty.

Middle Eastern traditional culture is being contested. In 2005, I spent one month at Cairo University in Egypt. My assistant was a young woman then studying for an MA in English literature. One day I asked her, "You have three identities: Egyptian, Arab, and Muslim. Which is the most important to you?".

"Muslim, of course," she responded. Apparently her Egyptian and Arab identities were secondary. Her choice illustrates that the Arab nationalism of Gamal Abdel Nasser's era is no longer in vogue among Egyptian youth.

The potential of women's intelligence has also not been adequately cultivated in the Middle East. In Islamic society, women's rights seem to be a hot cultural issue, but in fact it is key for economic development: If 50% of a country's intellectual resources are not tapped, how can society's potential be optimized? I learned that in the anti-government demonstrations in countries such as Yemen in recent years, some women did take part, but they were roundly scolded by men, who insisted a woman's place is in the home. "What are you doing here—this is a man's business!".

Even in westernized Turkish society, it is still traditional for women to be separated from male devotees in a compartment at the back of the mosque, and if there are many female attendees, then they can only pray outside.

Without the "Arab Spring" and the removal of some presidents who ruled thanks to their "family dynasty," it would have been very difficult for society to progress and government-sponsored reforms to take place. But is it evident that forcing the latter to stand down would succeed in altering a society's shortcomings? Civil wars or sharp internal divisions still exist in Iraq and Libya. Although the Assad regime in Syria has not experienced "regime change" as desired by the West, the entire country has lost a third of its population, and the remaining towns are strewn with rubble.

Collaboration among the Syrian opposition is difficult to bring about because each faction has a different ethnic, religious and class consciousness, and foreign powers that back them with money and material resources. This is similar to China's chaotic Warlord Era (1916–1928), but the situation is much more complicated than the latter.

I wasn't optimistic at the start of the "Arab Spring," but I held the well-intentioned hope that the countries experiencing it would gradually achieve success. In my 2011 book, *Greater Middle East: Travelogue and Reflections*, I wrote, "I hope these are the labor pains prior to an infant's birth, not the spasm foreshadowing a chronic malaise." Taking the long view of history, I still hold this attitude today.

CHAPTER 5

Cultural Conflict and Integration Throughout History

Cultural Integration: From Nomadic Society to Agrarian Society

> Mere dust and dirt now my accomplishments over thirty years, Beneath cloud and moon I had journeyed eight thousand *li*.

General Yue Fei (1103–1142), the author of these lines, was haunted by the invasion of the Jurchen-ruled Jin dynasty that destroyed the Northern Song in 1127, and he later led the battle against the Jurchens during the Southern Song. They express his frustration when, having achieved some success in his campaign against the Jin in 1140, the emperor suddenly ordered him to withdraw in order to facilitate peace negotiations.

More than a century later when Yue Fei had long since passed away, it was no longer possible for the Southern Song to counterattack. In the north, meanwhile, the Jin adopted the imperial examination system to identify and install loyal civil servants, following the Han method of rule.

Shortly afterward, however, the Mongols attacked the Jin from the north and the latter retreated. Yuan Haowen, a Jin Dynasty minister, fled the capital for Lianyungang. Deeply perturbed, he penned a poem containing these lines of verse:

> Leaning against my sword, wine cup in hand, I sing a long lament for our divine territory is obscured by shifting clouds.

Looking back from safety in Lianyungang, Yuan realized that *Shenzhou*—the entire divine territory to the northwest of Lianyungang—was the very foundation of his culture and home to his soul. His ancestors were the proto-Mongolic Xianbei people who had migrated southward. In the Northern Wei Dynasty (386–535 BCE), Emperor Xiaowen (r. 471–499), born "Tuoba Hong," took Yuan as surname in order to Sinicize himself, and his descendants followed suit.

What does this tell us? It illustrates the difference between nomadic and agriculture-based societies. From west of the Greater Khingan Range to the Ural Mountains, and even as far as what is now Hungary, lay a great swathe of grassland. On this steppe, there were peoples who lived as nomads and herders, and they made their entry into "civilization" at about the same time as those who lived in agrarian societies.

The latter are sedentary, i.e., they reside in a fixed location, while nomadic people roam. In ancient times, the Great Wall was built to guard against the Hu from proceeding south with their grazing horse herds. They were all northerners who had entered the Central Plains. After they arrived in the south, they naturally tended to adapt to the agrarian lifestyle. Both Yue Fei and Yuan Haowen, nearly a century later, were witnesses to this process of cultural friction and integration.

Wrote the Southern Song Dynasty poet Lei Zhen:

> Sideways atop an ox the shepherd lad homeward bound His picccolo's notes willy-nilly at random sound.

Since the first Chinese character in my given name is "Hsin," which principally means "faith," but could also mean "random" or "as one wishes" that occurs in this idyllic verse above, I pray the reader grant me a bit of latitude regarding the essay that follows …

INCLUSIVENESS: THE ROOT OF THE CHINESE NATION'S VITALITY

In the previous section, we talked about the different ways of life of various ethnicities. The Chinese people are very inclusive, not only because they incorporated the characteristics of many nomadic peoples in the north, but also by introducing very significant Buddhist concepts from India that have influenced us for centuries. In my understanding, the

Chinese are not xenophobic; the main reason for the outstanding vitality of the Chinese people is our great inclusiveness.

In fact, as early as the Warring States period, King Wu Ling of Zhao (r. 325–299) advocated "riding and shooting in Hu garb," yet no one denied he was Chinese simply because he donned the clothing of these nomads.

"If it weren't for Guan Zhong, we would all be letting our hair hang free and folding the right lapel over the left, like a nomad on the steppes," said Confucius of the philosopher-statesman two centuries before his time. This was one way to call attention to the distinction between the Chinese and non-Chinese, but at the time when King Wuling's adopted Hu attire and rode on horseback, he was recognized as wise.

Clothes worn by Chinese emperors and ministers more than a century ago differ greatly from those of Chinese presidents and premiers of our day—but there is no doubt all qualify as "Chinese."

After Buddhism was introduced to China, it merged with Taoism and Confucianism, giving rise to new religious schools such as Chan Buddhism (better known in the West as Zen). It is precisely because the Chinese people are inclusive and do not insist that "I am the only one" or "I am unchangeable" that we have such great continuity. This continuity is based on concrete facts. Today, in what other country can elementary school students recognize a script written 1,600 years ago?

The French pride themselves on their lengthy cultural history, but the average French person can't read French from 500 years ago fluently because its spelling and vocabulary have greatly altered. Meanwhile, Chinese elementary school students now can recognize the characters of Wang Xizhi, the fourth-century general and master calligrapher, and can read many of his works.

Today, even if we went to a remote place in China where education lags, we could visit most any secondary school where students would be able to recite a few lines from the *Book of Songs* (*Shi Jing*), such as:

> Guan! Guan! whistle the ospreys
> on the river islet.
> The graceful, virtuous maiden
> Is a fine match for the gentleman.

The *Book of Songs* was compiled at about the same time as Homer's the *Iliad* and the *Odyssey*. Although these eighth-century-BCE epics are still extant, a typical twenty-first-century Greek cannot read them. Yet in today's China, almost all secondary school students know snippets of ancient verse like this from the *Book of Songs*:

> Willow and poplar leaves sway like silk in the breeze

Patriots like Yue Fei and Yuan Haowen, whom I mentioned above, certainly couldn't bear to see their people vanquished. But today, no one would maintain that you are "not Chinese" just because your ancestors were Khitan. This is due to inclusiveness, and integration of different ethnicities in terms of attitudes and customs is eminently acceptable.

YEARS: PAPER'S LONG MARCH TO THE WEST

Wang Changling was a famous poet residing in the empire's borderlands. I like one of his poems very much:

> Same bright moon as in Qin times,
> same majestic passes as under the Han.
> Men trekked ten thousand *li* to secure the borders
> yet failed to return home.
> Were the Flying General of Longcheng here,
> Hu horses dare not cross Yin Shan.

Wang Changling (698–765), who lived during the Tang, wrote of the moon during the Qin (221–206 BCE), mountain passes during the Han (206 BCE to 220 CE), and even of the Tang's far-reaching military campaigns. In his writing, time and space are shuffled in a manner that highlights the tension inherent in literature and expands one's imagination.

Wang Changling died in 757. In the last years of his life, two major events occurred within China and on its far western frontier. In 755, the An Lushan Rebellion began, nearly overthrowing the Tang Dynasty. A few years earlier, the Battle of Talas broke out between the Tang and Arab armies in Central Asia, and the defeat of the Chinese had a great impact on the world, although its significance is not recognized by most people today.

In 751, when the Tang Dynasty was in its prime, the "Western Regions" or *Xi Yu*—the Chinese term for remote territories west of the

Great Wall's Jade Pass—were under administrative control of the Tang, which had stationed the Four Anxi Garrisons there. Military Commissioner Gao Xianzhi (son of a Goguryeo military commander who served in the Tang Army) realized that the Arab army had arrived in Central Asia and might invade the Western Regions, so he decided to lead a force to destroy it. However, he may have underestimated his foe, and did not bring sufficient soldiers.

When Gao's army reached Talas, near modern Uzbekistan's Tashkent, the Turkic Karluk army—supposedly allies—turned against him. Of his 20,000-strong forces, more than 10,000 were taken prisoner and less than 2,000 returned to their base in Qiuci (present-day Kuche in Xinjiang, China).

It so happened that among the captured soldiers were clerks and paper makers. When the Arabs discovered this, they said, "It's very costly and troublesome for us to copy the Qur'an on sheepskin, but it's much easier for you to do so on paper!" Taking advantage of their skilled prisoners, the Abbasids set up a papermaking workshop in present-day Samarkand, and after they started making paper, this know-how continued to spread westward from Samarkand to Baghdad, then to Damascus, Cairo, Morocco and across the Strait of Gibraltar to Moorish Spain.

The westward spread of paper can be summarized as follows: In 751 it was introduced in Talas, in 1150 it spread to al-Andalus (most of the Iberian Peninsula under the Moors), and in 1250 it appeared in France.

New historical data show that paper was actually invented in China during the Western Han (202 BCE–9 CE). The paper made by a court eunuch, Cai Lun, during the Eastern Han around 100 was not the earliest, but his technique improved quality, reduced cost and paved the way for mass fabrication. From the first century to the middle of the thirteenth century, it thus took 1,200 years for paper to complete its journey from China to Western Europe. This "8,000-mile journey" was quite a long one.

Kaifeng and Baghdad: Concurrent Global Cultural Centers

The Arab world underwent a transformation in the middle of the eighth century. It germinated in Mecca, and then the Umayyad Dynasty (known in China as the "White-robed Dashi") took Damascus as its capital. After

750 CE, the Abbasid dynasty—i.e., the "Black-robed Dashi"—built a new city, Baghdad, as its capital. Baghdad absorbed Greek, Persian, Indian, Hebrew and Byzantine cultures, while retaining the culture inherent to the Arabs.

The Arabs spent more than 100 years actively engaged in a campaign aimed at translating a large number of Greek, Persian and Indian works into Arabic. Thus, in Baghdad at that time, there was great intellectual activity, and religious doctrine, jurisprudence, philosophy, medicine and astronomy were all very developed. Baghdadis compiled folklore from India and Persia in the famous *One Thousand and One Nights*. In the ninth century, the city hosted the House of Wisdom—also known as the Grand Library of Baghdad—which was said to contain 400,000 tomes.

In the same era, Kaifeng, the capital of China during the Tang and Song Dynasties, was also very advanced. Although it is not known whether there were 400,000 books in the Imperial Academy (Guozijian) located in Kaifeng, the Chinese nation became more culturally prosperous and more vital with the commencement of the Northern Song (960–1127). At that time, Kaifeng boasted a population of one million, while residents of Constantinople, the capital of the Eastern Roman Empire, the largest city in Europe, numbered just 100,000.

It is not difficult to imagine that to provide for the daily needs of a population of one million, to maintain security and so forth, requires a highly capable society. So, there were two cultural centers in the world: One in Baghdad and one in Kaifeng.

> Feel concern for others under Heaven before others
> And rejoice after others have rejoiced.
> (Fan Zhongyan)

> Helpless before the blossoms falling
> I see familiar swallows returning.
> (Yan Shu)

> For drink cares naught the Old Tippler
> But for what lies within the landscape.
> (Ou Yangxiu)

> I pray our lives be long
> And share moonlight tho' leagues apart.

(Su Dongpo)

All the iconic verses above—and Sima Guang's *Zizhi Tongjian* chronicling 16 dynasties—were authored in this era. Cheng Hao and Cheng Yi, architects of Neo-Confucian cosmology, were also contemporaries of these men of letters.

It seems that there was a surfeit of talented people in those days! Not only were they concurrent peers, but they also frequented one another and sometimes disagreed heartily. Moreover, of China's four great inventions, three—printing, the compass and gunpowder—were all initiated then as documented in the *Dream Pool Essays* (*Meng Xi Bi Tan*) by the polymath and statesman Shen Kuo, and published in 1088 during the Song.

The creativity and culture of the Chinese people were at their peak during that period. We often talk about material creativity and intellectual imagination, and it was during this era that the Chan Buddhist aesthetic was embodied in paintings of the period. Of course, there were also many renowned calligraphers as well.

We Chinese tend to recall the Han and Tang Dynasties nostalgically. The Han and Tang were certainly prosperous, but the Northern Song wasn't bad either. It is just that the nomads in the north were more robust warriors and thus able to vanquish farming folk. But soon after conquest, nomads tended to gradually adapt to their new geographical environment and adopt the agrarian system and way of life. This was the case in China, in Central Asia and further west in Persia.

CHAPTER 6

Tracing the Footsteps and Influence of Xuanzang and Ibn Battuta

The celebrated French historian Fernand Braudel famously argued that geography determines history. When we speak of the Silk Road, we are thinking of both history and geography. Of course, the "geography" here is not just a narrow road. If we do not know yesterday, we cannot understand today; if we do not understand today, how can we talk about constructing the New Silk Road? With this in mind, I would like to look back at two historical figures and the geography associated with them.

As emphasized in China's Belt and Road Initiative, there are two Silk Road routes—terrestrial and marine. The traditional Silk Road ran from present-day Xi'an (formerly Chang'an) to the eastern coast of the Mediterranean Sea. The sea route began in Guangdong, China, and passed through Southeast Asia and the Straits of Malacca to southern India, then reached Yemen, and traveled north along the Sea to finally reach Alexandria or Antioch on the eastern Mediterranean Sea.

Here, I'd like to tell two short stories. The first one is about Cleopatra, the last ruler of the Ptolemaic Dynasty of Egypt (305–330 BCE). She was fond of wearing silk robes, and at that time, she had to pay one tael of gold in exchange for one tael of silk. The high price she forked out was not earned by the Chinese silkworm farmers, but by intermediate merchants on the Silk Road—mainly Central Asian Sogdian traders and the Persian traders of Western Asia.

The second tale is set in the time of the Parthian Dynasty of Persia (247 BCE–224 CE). Two armies were at war. At the head of the army from the east, the standard-bearer waved a scintillating banner. When their foes from the west caught sight of this glittering, eye-catching streamer, they believed it must be a work of God. Fearful that the Almighty favored the opposing army, they were defeated first in their hearts and thus in battle. Of what magical material was that ensign woven? Silk, of course!

Merchants trafficking silk were not the only ones who traversed the Silk Road. What follows below recounts two persons who journeyed long distances on it, but did not engage in business and were not motivated by profit.

The first part of the seventh century coincided with the emergence of Islam. By this time, many people in China had already converted to Buddhism. Although many Buddhist scriptures had been copied and translated by Faxian (Fa-hsien), An Shigao and Kumarajiva—the latter two natives of the Western Regions—the total number of scriptures transmitted to China was still not large enough to allow Chinese Buddhists to grasp the full scope of Indian Buddhism.

At this time, a Chinese monk named Xuanzang went to India on a one-man pilgrimage in search of the genuine Buddhist canon. Here is the route he took: Through the northern foothills of the Tianshan Mountains to Samarkand (also visited by Zhang Qian of the Han Dynasty and Faxian during the Jin); southward through the Hindu Kush Mountains to North India, and then from North India (Taxila in today's Pakistan) to Nalanda, a Buddhist shrine in the then central Indian state of Magadha.

In fact at that time, Indian Buddhism had already begun to decline and was gradually incorporated by the more ancient Brahmanism (Hinduism).

Today, India is no longer a Buddhist country at all, but there is a College of Buddhist Studies at Nalanda University, claimed by some to be the oldest university in the world.

While at Nalanda, Xuanzang was not an ordinary student. He was a disciple who excelled in his studies and was therefore invited to stay and instruct others in the Dharma right there in the holy land of Buddhism. For a period of time, he was recognized as the leading light of Buddhist doctrine in North India. Many an Indian scholar debated him only to face defeat.

On one occasion, his elderly teacher sent Xuanzang to debate the scriptures on his behalf on account of the former's advanced age, with the result that his disciple's arguments were so brilliant and eloquent that he proved invincible.

After studying and living in India for more than a decade, Xuanzang followed the southern portion of the Silk Road through the Tarim Basin and returned to China proper in 645. Thus in his round-trip he experienced both the northern and southern portions of the Silk Road that diverge at the Tianshan Mountains.

Although India also has a lengthy history, unlike in China, detailed official historical records were not kept, or if there were any, they were destroyed or lost in the flames of war as dynasties rose and fell. Until the mid-nineteenth century, when India came under direct colonial rule, i.e., the British Raj (1858–1947), India comprised many large and small states. Never a fully unified country, it did not have a national set of state-sponsored chronicles. For this reason, many contemporary experts in Indian and Central Asian history today rely on two books authored by Chinese monks: Faxian's *A Record of Buddhist Kingdoms* and Xuanzang's *The Great Tang Records on the Western Regions*.

When Xuanzang was in India, the local monarch heard tell of a Chinese religion called Taoism and asked Xuanzang to introduce it to him. Although Xuanzang was a Buddhist monk, he translated and annotated Lao Tzu's *Tao Te Ching (Book of the Dao)* into Sanskrit, which was probably the first foreign transmission of Taoist thought. During his stay in India, he was supported and respected by several Indian kings and senior monks who believed in Buddhism. When he was about to return to India after living there for more than ten years, one king gifted him with thousands of Buddhist scriptures and some sturdy horses to facilitate his journey homeward. After his return to China, Xuanzang established the Yogācāra school of Mahayana Buddhism based upon his own study of the sutras.

Before Xuanzang set out for the Western Regions in 629, Emperor Taizong of Tang was already aware of him. Because the Tang were at war with the First Turkic Khanate at the time, however, Chinese subjects were forbidden to leave the empire. Perhaps moved by Xuanzang's adventurous spirit, "If you leave clandestinely," confided a border garrison general, "I'll look the other way!"

Upon Xuanzang's return, Emperor Taizong held a grand welcome ceremony for him and offered him a high official position. Xuanzang declined, instead requesting a site to translate the scriptures he had brought back. His wish was granted and the site of his translation institute in Chang'an was known as Hongfu Monastery. As instructed by the emperor, Xuanzang also dictated his *The Great Tang Records on the*

Western Regions, describing his travels between 626 and 645, and it constitutes a highly detailed report on the geography, history and folk customs of Central Asia and India.

Thanks to this ancient travelogue, 19th-century archaeologists discovered many Indian relics. For example, when the Mauryan (Peacock) Dynasty's Ashoka the Great ruled India (268–232 BCE), he vigorously promoted Buddhism and erected stone pillars with Sanskrit texts in many places to immortalize his achievements. Following clues in Xuanzang's travelogue, British archaeologists found stone pillars in good condition near Nalanda that had been obscured by jungle growth. In addition, also thanks to Xuanzang's account, archaeologists found a casket containing Buddha's relics that was left by King Kanishka I of the second-century Kushan Empire beneath stupa ruins near modern-day Peshawar, Pakistan.

Now, let's turn our attention to the small town of Tangier in the northwest corner of the African continent, some seven hundred years later. It is located opposite Spain, which is visible across the Strait of Gibraltar. In Tangier, there was a man named Ibn Battuta, born into a wealthy local family in 1304, a devout Muslim and a believer in Sufism. In Central, South, Southeast Asia and Africa, Sufis often traveled to spread the Sufi creed.

Ibn Battuta left his family in his early twenties with a sum of money and set out on a pilgrimage to Mecca. Little did he know that it would be nearly 30 years before he would see his family again.

In all, Ibn Battuta made four pilgrimages to Mecca. He first arrived in Tunisia along the southern Mediterranean, where he took a wife and lived briefly, but soon divorced and continued on to Mecca. After the pilgrimage, he proceeded to the area of Jerusalem and then south again to Mecca. Later, he went to Baghdad, then to the Mongol Ilkhanate, and then further east to Samarkand and further north to the Golden Horde.

Once by chance he arrived in Yemen, from where he took a boat to South India, and then to the Delhi Sultanate founded by Central Asian Muslims. In Delhi, he won the sultan's favor and served as a *Qadi* (Muslim judge) for nine years, where he was well treated and saved a fortune.

At the time, the Delhi Sultan received a shipment of gifts from the emperor of the Yuan Dynasty. Believing that lack of reciprocity in one's relationship is poor etiquette, the sultan wished to dispatch in return someone bearing gifts and accompanied by dancers, acrobats and the like, so he appointed Ibn Battuta as his envoy to the Yuan.

However, when the Delhi Sultan's ship sailed to the south of the Indian Ocean, some valuable gifts were washed away due to the wind and waves, and Ibn Battuta drifted to the present-day Maldives. The sultan of the Maldives also appreciated him and invited him to stay as a judge. Ibn Battuta served as a judge there, but he still often contemplated continuing on to China.

So, he eventually went to China even though no longer laden with gifts. The first Chinese city that Ibn Battuta visited was Quanzhou, beside the Taiwan Strait. He spoke very highly of Quanzhou in his book, *The Travels*. Whenever he wanted to convey that a given seaport was a world-leader in some aspect—e.g., Alexandria was the largest—he would not fail to add: *Except* for China's Quanzhou.

When Ibn Battuta arrived in Cairo, Egypt was governed by the Mamluk Dynasty (1250–1517). The most famous mosque in Cairo, the Al-Azhar Mosque, was built in the tenth century by the Shiite Fatimid Caliphate, and later expanded by the Mamluks.

In addition, Cairo has a long-established mosque that served as a madrasa or center of Islamic learning, now called Al-Azhar University. In the early twentieth century, many renowned Chinese Islamic scholars studied there. For example, Ma Jian (1906–1978), a professor of Arabic at Peking University who rendered the Qur'an into Chinese, and Na Zhong (1909–2008), a famous Arabic scholar from Beijing Foreign Studies University, also studied there and obtained the highest traditional degree, called the "Scholar's Certificate," from the university.

The Wailing Wall in Jerusalem, with the Dome of the Rock behind it

Crossing the Sinai Peninsula you arrive in Jerusalem. From above, you can see the Western Wall, known to many as the "Wailing Wall," which remained after the destruction of the Second Jewish Temple by the Romans in 70 CE. Many Jews come to the wall every day to pray and weep, confessing their sins. The Al-Aqsa Mosque in Jerusalem is one of the first two mosques in the Islamic world (the other is in Damascus), and was built in Greek style around 700.

On one occasion, Ibn Battuta journeyed from Lebanon to Turkey, and after making a great circle in Turkey, he traveled along the northern coast of the Black Sea, north of the Caspian Sea, to the territory of several countries in present-day Central Asia, including Uzbekistan's Bukhara and Samarkand. Around Bukhara, Ibn Battuta should have been able to see the remains of ancient Persia's Zoroastrianism. Before Islam penetrated Central Asia, Zoroastrianism was the dominant religion in the Persian-speaking world.

In the tenth century, a large swathe of Central Asia and the eastern part of present-day Iran belonged to the Samanid Empire (819–999), founded by Persian-speaking nobles. A memorial hall from the Samanid era still stands and bears the traces of Zoroastrianism—a round dome with a representation of the sun shining in all directions. The Zoroastrian religion worships light, so this building features both Islamic and pre-Islamic Zoroastrian styles, a manifestation of the mingling of these two religions in Central Asia.

In the Middle Ages, in all Muslim-ruled societies there were roadside inns for itinerant merchants, known as caravanserai. They could eat and lodge there, board livestock, replenish their supplies, and engage in trade. Ibn Battuta's traveling companions were often merchants, so he stayed at many of these inns.

In 1349, he finally returned to what was then capital of his homeland, present-day Fes, Morocco. Upon his return, the ruler of the Marinid Sultanate there took him seriously and requested that Ibn Battuta write about what he had seen and heard. So, the explorer duly dictated his travelogue, and the sultan's secretary took it down for him. *The Travels*—full title: *A Masterpiece to those Who Contemplate the Wonders of Cities and the Marvels of Travelling*—has since been translated into 100-plus languages.

A centuries-old caravanserai in Azerbaijan

An old caravanserai in Azerbaijan, newly decorated with miniatures

Fes, Morocco: Erstwhile capital of Ibn Battuta's homeland

The time lag between Xuanzang and Ibn Battuta is about 700 years, with one born at the easternmost point of the continents of Europe, Asia and Africa, and the other at their northwest corner. Far apart in space and time, what were the similarities between them?

First, they both traveled long distances on the Silk Road, but they did so out of religious devotion, not for financial gain.

Second, although Xuanzang knew some Sanskrit and Ibn Battuta spoke Arabic, the important point is that they were both able to deal with people who were different from themselves and to understand and trust one another. Although they remained true to their own faiths, they were able to respect others, communicate and associate with people of different cultures and ethnicities.

Thirdly, at times of difficulty both had benefactors who proffered material or administrative support. At the very least, both of them were born in the right era and happened upon wise patrons. After returning to their home countries, they were both encouraged by their monarchs, which led to the popularization of their legendary works—*The Great Tang Records on the Western Regions* and *The Travels*—that were recognized even during their lifetimes. Their influence on future generations, especially in promoting mutual understanding between people of different regions and cultures, was even greater. Cultural exchange promoted commercial interaction, and economic development in turn promoted further cultural exchange.

I'd like to conclude this chapter by citing Wang Bo (649–676), a famous literary genius:

> *Wenhua yu jingji qifei* (Culture and economy together in flight)
> *Senglü gong shangren yi se.* (Merchant and monk are but one form.)

The first verse needs no explanation. In the second, the word "form" is found in the Buddhist *Heart Sutra*, and refers to the mundane material world:

> Form is no different to emptiness
> Emptiness is no different to form.

My own (slightly tweaked) translation of Wang Bo's lines:

> Economy and culture soar side-by-side,
> Merchants and monks share a common world.

It is my hope that this vision will once again be realized via the twenty-first-century New Silk Road.

CHAPTER 7

My Views on Orientology, Area Studies and Silk Road Research

The launch of the Belt and Road Initiative has garnered a great deal of attention both within China and internationally. Discussion of the initiative and writing about the Silk Road are ubiquitous, and related video products can be measured by the truckload. From this mass of materials, the careful observer can discern that familiarity with land and maritime silk routes among the Chinese is actually still quite limited. China possesses first-rate experts in many domains, but overall academic understanding of the regions and individual countries that comprise the Belt and Road are still relatively weak, especially in terms of systematic knowledge and pioneering theory. Given these shortcomings, it will be difficult to meet current and future needs for expertise in the fields of society, economy, politics, geography, history, religion, linguistics, literature and art as development of the Belt and Road is promoted.

With the encouragement of China's Ministry of Education, many universities have recently established "Silk Road Research Institutes" or similar bodies. As someone with a longtime interest in the various silk routes—and who has visited nearly all the countries along their pathways—I am encouraged by this trend, and hope that China will be able to train a large number of persons who know those countries well and can generate a rich body of groundbreaking scholarship about them.

As Silk Road research moves ahead, perhaps it would be meaningful and advantageous to review experiences in the early days of "Orientology" in Europe, as well as the late twentieth-century origins of "Area Studies" in the United States.

Orientology: A Retrospective

European studies of the Near and Far East originated with the fifth-century-BCE Greco-Persian Wars. But the concept of Orientology emerged after the birth of Islam (seventh–eighth centuries CE), developed during the Crusades (twelfth–thirteenth), took on a fixed meaning during the Renaissance (fifteenth–sixteenth), flourished at the height of European colonialism (eighteenth–nineteenth) and waned during the twentieth century's Cold War.

Among Western Europeans, Orientology was long regarded as the study of the "Other." It was not the study of any specific domain of knowledge. Rather, it treated the "Orient" as an object of cognition that was defined by its distinctness from the "West," geographically speaking. An "Orientalist" could be someone with a specialist's knowledge of the Middle East or Asia, including language, literature, history, ethnicity, religions, philosophy, folklore, art, astronomy and medicine. But a general knowledge of a region in the Middle East or Asia did not suffice; even if a scholar specialized in researching several of these domains, such a person could not be considered an "Orientalist" *unless* he or she concentrated on applying this knowledge to the perception of the "East" that already existed in the minds of Western Europeans.

After Islam's birth in the seventh century, it rapidly occupied territories such as Palestine, Syria and Egypt, previously ruled by the Eastern Roman Empire (Byzantine Empire). This inspired Byzantine officials and scholars to strive for an understanding of Islam as well as the language and customs of the Arabs. But at that time Western Europeans who had the opportunity to observe Islamic society and Arab territories in depth were very limited in number, or if they did, their chronicles have not survived to our day.

But in distant China, someone did leave behind his own record. In 751, a Tang dynasty soldier named Du Huan was captured by the Arab army at the Battle of Talas in Central Asia. Incorporated into their forces, he subsequently traveled with them to Muslim regions such as Iraq, Syria, Egypt and North Africa. He spent a decade in various parts of the Eastern

Roman Empire, and finally returned to Guangzhou on a boat via the Persian Gulf.

Upon his return to China, he penned his memoir entitled *Jingxingji* (lit., record of places passed through), describing the region's peoples, languages, religions and customs. Therefore, in the eyes of Europeans, Du Huan should be considered an early and important Orientalist. Of course, had anyone in China advocated such a field of study, he would certainly not have been known by this Eurocentric etiquette; he would have been classified as an expert in the remote and exotic "Western Regions."

But if that were the case, then Du Huan would hardly qualify as an early authority on the Western Regions. The progenitor of this branch of knowledge was unquestionably Western Han Dynasty's Zhang Qian (second century BCE), while early experts were widely traveled officials such as Gan Ying (Eastern Han) and Pei Ju (Sui), and India-bound Buddhist monks such as Fa Xian (Eastern Jin), Song Yun (Northern Wei) and Xuan Zang (early Tang).

We Chinese are proud of our ancient and great nation but we should not be arrogant, for one cannot rely upon ancestral glory to win respect in the present. The Belt and Road Initiative, which aims to facilitate mutual development with the countries in its path, is a welcome modern-day addition to China's list of pioneering ventures.

In the late eleventh century, large numbers of Turkic Muslims penetrated Asia Minor (modern-day Turkey), hinterland of the Eastern Roman Empire. To resist encroachment, the emperor requested help from Western Europe's Roman Catholic Church. Pope Urban II initiated a call to Christians in the West for the formation of the First Crusade in 1095, whose raison d'être was to retake the Holy City of Jerusalem, occupied by Muslims for more than four centuries.

Flush with religious fervor, keen to obtain the church's promised absolution for all previous sins, and coveting the wealth of the Orient, major and minor members of nobility from throughout Western Europe—mainly Franks, including France's canonized Louis IX—undertook seven crusades to the Levant during the twelfth–thirteenth centuries, in which the peasantry and petit-bourgeois also participated. They occupied Jerusalem, ransacked Constantinople, and even established a number of "Crusader States" or Latin kingdoms along the east Mediterranean coast that ruled for more than a century. Nearly two hundred years later, however, the Crusaders gradually lost their zeal for their holy mission, and in the middle of the thirteenth century, they gradually retreated to Rhodes, Malta, Sicily and various sites within Western Europe.

As they interacted with Muslims, Western Europeans discovered that medicine, astronomy, mathematics and navigation techniques in the Islamic world were more advanced than their own. Based in Palestine, the Knights of St John who were dedicated to the treatment of injuries, adopted Arabic medical techniques. The enmity with which Western Europeans viewed the Muslims actually transformed into imitation of some of their cultural practices. Beginning in the thirteenth century, Jews in Spain and Christians in Sicily began translating Arabic texts into Latin, and this proved very useful later on during the Renaissance in Italy, and in opening up new maritime routes by the Spanish and Portuguese.

In the fifteenth–sixteenth centuries, the Ottomans captured Constantinople and the Eastern Roman Empire was destroyed. Large numbers of Greeks fled to Italy and throughout Western Europe where they taught Greek for a living, which also nurtured the ability of Western European scholars to study the Middle East. The term "Orientology" was therefore coined in Western Europe, and its study attracted large numbers of learned people.

Perhaps the best-known achievement of Orientology was the deciphering of the Rosetta Stone. In 1799, when Napoleon led his army to invade Egypt, a stele dating from 196 BCE was discovered in a Nile Delta village named Rosetta (Arabic: Rashid). Three different scripts were engraved upon it: Ancient Egyptian hieroglyphics at the top, which no one recognized; in the middle, a 4th-century BCE demotic script that no one could read; and at the bottom, classical Greek dating from the era when the Greek Ptolemy family ruled Egypt, which many European scholars could understand. After several decades of effort, the French scholars who initially possessed the stone, and later British ones who won access to it after Napoleon's defeat, eventually decoded the demotic and hieroglyphic scripts, and thereby pioneered the "Egyptology" that swept Europe. By the close of the twentieth century, Egyptologists could read the ancient writing engraved on buildings within Egypt, and were thus able to reconstruct ancient Egyptian history.

At the height of European colonialism, Orientology saw progress in leaps and bounds. One reason was that colonizing countries required a group of administrative and military personnel familiar with the Near and Far East; another was because the Christian church required missionaries willing to live in the colonies; and thirdly, a group of scholars specializing in studies of the East emerged among European academics. By exploiting the privileges available to them in various colonial or semi-colonial territories, these three categories of Europeans did indeed make quite a few exemplary contributions to scholarship.

Egyptology aside, the nineteenth and twentieth centuries also witnessed several other outstanding achievements in Orientology.

The first was the role of archaeological research in Mesopotamia (mainly modern-day Iraq) that resulted in the reconstruction of six thousand years of history and the deciphering of several cuneiform-based scripts. Excavations of many ancient sites in this region by Western scholars uncovered some thirty thousand clay tables engraved with cuneiform, the great majority of which are now in the collections of European museums. Only one-tenth have been translated to date, but they have given us an exceedingly clear grasp of the succession of ideas that led to civilization's evolution and dissemination.

In the process of an excavation in Mesopotamia, one Briton—Henry Austin Layard—achieved both fame and fortune. During his youth he traveled throughout the Middle East on horseback, and even undertook special assignments for Great Britain on Ottoman soil. He was later commissioned by the British Ambassador to undertake archaeological work in Mesopotamia, then ruled by the Ottoman Empire. He believed that Nimrud, which he had previously observed, was in fact Nineveh, the most ancient city of the Assyrian Empire, and therefore he undertook large-scale excavations there. Though his instincts proved mistaken, by accident he stumbled upon a priceless treasure. He claimed a portion of the jade cylinder seals he had discovered for himself, and after his return to Great Britain, he was elected to Parliament, served briefly as Under-Secretary for Foreign Affairs, and was subsequently designated Ambassador to the Ottoman Empire. After he had been knighted, his wife Lady Layard once wore a necklace featuring faux Assyrian cylinder seals (made of jade) while dining with Queen Victoria, allegedly eliciting the latter's envy.

The second noteworthy achievement of the Orientologists was the discovery of Indo-European languages—the most widely distributed language family worldwide—that enabled linguists to identify the evolution of several other large language families.

In 1783, the Briton William Jones arrived in India, then ruled by the East India Company, where he served as a judge. He had long been interested in languages of the East, and before his arrival had already mastered Arabic and Persian. While studying Sanskrit in India, he realized that Sanskrit shared many characteristics with Greek, Latin and German and hypothesized that these languages could have been different branches of an ancient Indio-European language. Through the work by many scholars in the past two centuries, it is certain that the distribution of various Indo-European languages stretching from the Atlantic Ocean in the west to the Bay of Bengal in the east signifies that today's two-billion strong multi-ethnic population may once—six thousand years ago—have spoken a proto-Indio-European language, and may be the direct or indirect descendants of a people who resided in the Pontic steppes of southern Europe.

The third occurred in the early twentieth century when British archaeologists conducted digs in the Indus Valley (now located within Pakistan), where they discovered the ruins of two cities (Harappa and Mohenjo Daro) that were more than five thousand years old, as well as excavating several other sites and uncovering many cultural relics. This now-vanished civilization did not belong to the Indo-European speaking Aryans who invaded Central Asia more than three thousand years ago. Most scholars believe that the originators of this ancient civilization were probably related by blood to India's current Dravidian population, and therefore contemporary Indians are composed mainly of a hybrid people of mixed Aryan and Dravidian descent.

Another of Orientology's important contributions was the rigorous examination of Silk Road data, including renewed exploration of the Steppe Silk Road and the Oasis Silk Road, numerous excavations, and appraisal of large numbers of related books and works of art. Thanks to the efforts of these scholars, we are now generally familiar with the various ethnicities who were active in the grasslands of Northern and Central Asia over thousands of years, as well as their interactions. We also have a clearer understanding of the peoples residing between the Hexi Corridor and the Mediterranean, as well as their spoken and written languages, religions and commerce.

As far as China is concerned, the most noteworthy was research into the dissemination of Buddhism, particularly the study of Gandhara art, Buddhist rock-cut Kizil Caves, Turfan documents, Dunhuang frescoes and religious scriptures. Of course, the topics studied also included the territorial reach of each Chinese dynasty, beacon towers and armies stationed along the Silk Road, and the status of trading activities.

Among the Europeans who specialized in Silk Road research, the names of those such as Sven Hedin, Aurel Stein and Paul Pelliot are quite familiar to Chinese ears.

An explorer without a colonial background, Hedin was a Swedish explorer. He led a team into the Taklamaklan Desert in search of the source of the Hotan River, and when their drinking water ran out, he refused to quit, and continued trekking on his own in the dry riverbed for five nights and six days until he had located the source.

Aurel Stein was a Hungarian-born archaeologist in the service of the British Raj in India. He was sharp-eyed and incredibly lucky, and his methods of purloining ancient relics were also highly sophisticated.

Paul Pelliot was proficient in Chinese and worked at length for the French government. When France's Beijing embassy was surrounded by the Boxers in 1900, he emerged alone and negotiated with them. Armed with his mastery of written Chinese, he was able to select and abscond with many important documents that had escaped Stein's notice. He also personally surveyed other sites in Central Asia, and after his return to France, he founded and served as editor-in-chief of a highly respected academic journal, and became a leading twentieth-century orientologist and sinologist.

After World War II, colonialism went into retreat, and the practice of Orientology that had concurrently flourished, also waned. Several literary and artistic works that exhibited bias and condescension toward non-European peoples, as well as patently absurd, nonsensical statements about them, came under fire. In 1978, Edward Saïd, a Palestinian-American professor at Columbia University, penned *Orientalism*, a work featuring many concrete examples that critiqued the prejudices of several Orientalists.

Like any field of academic study, undertaking Orientology required certain external conditions and material resources, as well as scholarly attitude and abilities. The European Renaissance, Enlightenment and Industrial Revolution provided the Europeans with a highly advantageous position throughout the world that led to colonialism and imperialism. These were the external conditions that allowed Orientology to flourish, and they comprise the indispensable backdrop to its era.

No one can deny the exploitation and humiliation of Asians and Africans by Europeans during this period, or the arrogance and prejudices of the latter. But there were distinctions among Orientalists. Many of them genuinely did not fear hardship when carrying out fieldwork, and strove to uncover the truth; many devoted a lifetime of professional study to researching a specific topic in detail, and showed great perseverance. Many others read extensively, excelled at drawing inferences, and pioneered new knowledge and theories. Regardless of the circumstances of the time and their motivations, the overall achievements of these scholars should be obvious to all. In short, while Orientalism is not worthy of emulation, Orientology was not a bad thing.

Overview of Area Studies

Area Studies originated in the United States during the Cold War, and can be seen as a modern-day modified version of Orientology. Except within Latin America—effectively posited as their "backyard" by the Monroe Doctrine—the United States did not actively participate in overseas colonization during the nineteenth century. Therefore, while American academia was very familiar with Europe and Latin America, it had no domestic tradition of Orientology.

Beginning with the Berlin blockade and the Korean War, the American and Soviet camps became sharply opposed. Both parties were keen to understand one another, and both wanted to win over the Asian and African countries, be they newly independent nations or those soon to achieve independence.

At this time, the American elite recognized that the US government and business community urgently required people proficient in the languages and cultures of various countries. In 1951, the Ford Foundation and Rockefeller Foundation invited twenty or so leading universities to a conference where they recommended establishing a new field of interdisciplinary specialization that encompassed a region, such as East European Studies, Middle East Studies and East Asian Studies. This proposal was incompatible with the traditional structure of the American university, because there were separate faculties for each discipline, and each department's focus was on knowledge relating to just one or two fields, such as history, language and literature, economics, sociology, etc. In the past, research into the Near and Far East were carried out under a specific discipline, i.e., scholars of Chinese politics were located in the Department of Political Science, and those studying Chinese economics were to be found in the Economics Department.

Some scholars initially resisted the method of training students by drawing on disparate areas of specialization, fearful that this would result in students whose grasp of their "major" would be superficial. But the Ford Foundation believed that the United States needed many people with a general knowledge of a given region's history, society, economy and politics, and therefore it invested large amounts of money in these universities to establish scholarships for Area Studies. Not long after, the US government also implemented the National Defense Education Act, which offered funding to subsidize students willing to study the language or culture of a specific country. At the time, one exasperated academic coined this adage: "The Golden Rule of Science is he who has the gold makes the rule!".

After 1965, the Orientology that originated in Europe had transmogrified into "Area Studies" in North America. The goal was to train persons who possessed general knowledge about a certain region (or country). Money talks! By 1975, just about all top-notch universities in North America had established majors in the study of this or that region.

Stanford University, where I earned my MS, and Northwestern University, where I completed my PhD, both moved early to establish centers for Area Studies. Stanford is located on the west coast of the United States, and ever since one of its first graduates, President Herbert Hoover, had once worked for Kaiping Mines as a coal mine engineer in modern-day Hebei Province, the school strongly emphasized East Asian studies.

I often went to read Chinese books in the Hoover Institute that was rich in resources, including *China Pictorial*. Because of our acquaintance, my roommate became interested in the country and took an elective course in Chinese. He went on to carry out considerable field research in Taiwan and Guangdong's Pearl River Delta, and became an authority on Chinese folk religions.

Northwestern University outside Chicago features a strong program in African Studies, and has an exchange program with Sudan, and therefore many a member of the Sudanese elite received an education at Northwestern. One Sudanese classmate in my department returned to his home country with a PhD in engineering, and was appointed Minister of Defense not long after.

During 1969–1976, when I taught at the State University of New York, I came to know a scholar who was studying Chinese politics. He had learned a few years of Chinese and could speak simple Mandarin. One time he mentioned a Mr. Chen (陈), and when I asked how to write the full name of Mr Chen, he gave me a slip of paper with three Chinese characters, the first was supposed to be the surname of this Mr Chen. But he reversed the two elements comprising the character, placing the so-called "ear" radical (阝) to the right, and the word for "east" (东) to the left, effectively making it unreadable! When I saw how even this "China expert" had miswritten this common character, I realized how difficult the Chinese script really is. Other surnames such as Zheng (郑) and Guo (郭) are written with the so-called "ear" radical to the right, so why is it located on the left in Chen (陈)? And then there is a character like *gou*, that also consists of just two elements—多 and 句—and they can each be placed either to the left or right, i.e., 够 or 夠, and both versions are acceptable!

In 1976 I began teaching at McGill University in Montreal, Canada, which has an Institute of Islamic Studies. During 1981–1982 I was a visiting professor at the University of Paris, and it was during this period that I became interested in Islamic studies. It was after I returned to McGill that I learned that this prestigious institute was founded in 1952. Funded by the Ford Foundation and Rockefeller Foundation, it was probably a product of the transition from Orientology to Area Studies.

During 1984–90, I served as professor and department chairman at University of Southern California in Los Angeles. I was elected to the University Tenure and Promotions Committee for three years, and participated in the review of faculty members engaged in Area Studies, a process that touched upon the academic value and standards of such research.

At the time, there were two opposing views of Area Studies in American academia.

One held that while Area Studies was nominally interdisciplinary, in fact it formed students who often had a bit of knowledge about everything, but were not experts in anything in particular. If such a person later became a teacher, this person was unlikely to undertake genuinely innovative scholarship. I well understood this criticism, because my own profession, biomedical engineering, is itself interdisciplinary. In 1988, when I served as president of Biomedical Engineering Society of the US, I emphasized that we should be specialized in some form of engineering (e.g., instrument design) but also familiar with some subjects in bio-medicine (e.g., the cardiovascular system). As university faculty, our research papers must be eligible for publication in academic journals for engineers or biomedical professionals; otherwise, we could only stand outside these two disciplines looking in, and could not serve as a bridge between the two. Based on this viewpoint, my stand on the committee when reviewing applications for tenure was that any Area

Studies instructor should possess mastery of at least one field of academic study. Candidates must not fall into the "Jack of all trades, master of none" category.

The second viewpoint held that since Area Studies were fairly new, it was not yet possible to formulate a set of academic standards for each area/region. But academia would inevitably inject sufficient knowledge content into this new-fangled phenomenon that had been ushered into campuses by external forces. As for research topics that were overly pragmatic and lacked academic content, they should be handled by governmental and commercial bodies, including think tanks. Before reaching this point, screening of faculty for tenure should not be too harsh, or it would result in premature elimination of potentially excellent scholars.

After the disintegration of the Soviet Union and the end of the Cold War, the United States and other Western countries strongly advocated economic globalization and the parliamentary democracy that was developed in modern times by Western Europe. Optimistic expectations of a united world were widespread, as exemplified by the predictions of Francis Fukuyama in his *The End of History and the Last Man* (1992). But after 9/11, the tone changed to talk of inevitable conflict due to competition between Christianity, Islam and Confucianism, as foreseen by Samuel Huntingdon in *The Clash of Civilizations and the Remaking of World Order* (1996).

Just then, I was recruited to join the University of Pittsburgh—a seat of learning boasting nearly three hundred years of history—to serve both as dean of the Swanson School of Engineering and professor at the School of Medicine, with the goal of using biomedical engineering to help revitalize this old industrial base located in America's rustbelt. At the time, the two big strengths of the university happened to be medical studies and area studies, both of which I happened to be acquainted with.

During my leisure time, I often communicate with two history department colleagues: Professor Cho-yun Hsu, an overseas Chinese who is a member of Academia Sinica, and Professor Evelyn Rawski, a Hawaiian-born, fourth-generation Japanese-American who is proficient in Mandarin and Manchu. The latter's husband is Thomas Rawski, the economics professor. I held several conversations with them in 1995–1996, during which Evelyn Rawski elaborated on her "New Qing History" concept that was soon to shock Chinese history scholars. The Qing Dynasty rulers had not been truly assimilated by Han culture, she asserted; rather, the Manchu exploited various identities and methods to dominate an empire comprising many peoples and cultures, and China, with its mainly Han population, was but one part of that empire.

This is a very challenging academic argument. Intuitively, I disagree with this viewpoint, but I have not researched this aspect, and could not refute her psychological assessment of the mindset of Qing royal family members. But she told me that this viewpoint was based upon her reading of a large amount of files in the Manchu Military Bureau and records of activities within the palace. This demonstrates that if a scholar wishes to advance a fresh discourse about Chinese history, she must possess considerable skill and be well prepared.

While I did not have any evidence to rebut Professor Rawski's main argument about the Manchu, I did once refute her viewpoint that Mongolia, Xinjiang and Tibet do not belong to China.

My reasoning is as follows: After the defeat of the Boxer Rebellion and occupation of Beijing by the Eight-nation Alliance in 1901, the Qing government was forced to pay an indemnity of 400 million silver taels. This figure was based upon an estimate of China's entire population, including Xinjiang, Mongolia and Tibet—400 million—and a portion of this huge compensation was to be paid by each region, including Xinjiang, Mongolia and Tibet. These are concrete historical facts. After the 1911 Xinhai Revolution, the foreign powers demanded that the newly established republic recognize the international treaties signed by the Qing Empire. Since the Republic of China had to bear all the treaty obligations of the Qing Empire, why should it not inherit all the territory of this empire? This case shows that practitioners of area studies need to specialize (e.g., be able to read Manchu historical materials systematically), and also must be capable of looking at an issue from multiple perspectives (e.g., know diplomatic history and international law).

While I was busy debating the concept of New Qing History with Professor Rawski in Pittsburgh, however, a bigger debate was taking place across North America—should "Area Studies" continue to evolve?

After half a century of development, America possesses a considerable pool of talent in Area Studies. With the Cold War behind us, however, some scholars have turned their energies to global issues rather than regional ones. They reckon that global issues of modernization and democratization should be paid more attention, and that problems such as global warming exceed the natural limits of Area Studies, and so forth. As a result, regional research is less valued than it was thirty years ago. But I believe that as long as distinctive regional characteristics continue to exist, then Area Studies will not lose its relevance. The larger question is, what kind of research results are academically rigorous and possess long-term value?

Placing Our Hopes in Silk Road Exploration and Research

More than forty years ago, in accordance with China's international situation at that time, Mao Zedong proposed his "Three Worlds Theory": The two superpowers, the United States and the Soviet Union, constituted the First World; the lesser powers, Japan and the countries of Europe comprised the Second; and the Third World consisted of the exploited nations of Asia, Africa and South America. The countries of the Third World should unite and resist the superpowers. When Deng Xiaoping advocated this theory to the full session of the United Nations General Assembly in 1974, I was seated in the gallery. At the time, all of the Third World countries were underdeveloped, the great majority were suffering from internal ethnic and religious conflicts, and many also had intractable mutual enmities and territorial disputes with their neighbors. Just how these countries could join forces to seek development has never been clear.

In the autumn of 2013, in Kazakhstan and then Indonesia, respectively, Chinese President Xi Jinping proposed two initiatives: Construction of the "Silk Road Economic Belt" and the "21st Century Maritime Silk Road." Belt and Road, as it has come to be known, reflects a fresh international configuration, and conveys China's future-oriented vision of international relations. It is inspired by English geographer Halford Mackinder's so-called "Heartland Theory," which envisaged promoting links among different regions within Asia, as well as between Europe and Asia, and between Africa and Asia, in order to strengthen land and sea travel. To further develop the economies of these lands new infrastructure should be put in place, and for this purpose Mackinder strongly advocated sharing resources, and jointly undertaking commerce and construction.

To this end, the Asian Infrastructure Investment Bank (AIIB) proposed by China will finance construction projects in countries with diverse political and social systems. In terms of the rise of China's national power, China's advocacy of Belt and Road and AIIB both have similarities with the Marshall Plan proposed by the United States, and the establishment of the World Bank, at the end of the 1940s. From the perspective of promoting new international relations, Belt and Road can be seen as a revised version and an attempt to bring Mao's "Three Worlds Theory" to realization.

Forty years ago, only a tiny portion of Chinese had ever ventured abroad. In the wake of more than three decades of rapid development, however, in just 2016 alone 122,000,000 Chinese went outside of the mainland of China, and several million now reside outside the PRC. But when we attempt to quantify the number of citizens familiar with the countries along the various silk routes beyond China's borders—and the amount of knowledge they possess about those lands—then the situation is far from satisfactory.

Peking University hosted an event, "Regional and Country Studies Syposium" in 2017. This school is home to a rich pool of talent and many scholars there possess a profound understanding of the history, cultures and languages (including ancient scripts) of countries along the Silk Road. I was designated as the keynote speaker. I will briefly relate my presentation below.

It was in 1877 that Baron von Richthofen, the German geographer, coined the terms "Seidenstraße" and "Seidenstraßen" (lit., Silk Road and Silk Routes). Commissioned by the German government to recommend a railway route connecting Germany and China, he traveled throughout Central Asia, East Asia and Southeast Asia, and selected a route through Eurasia that was consistent with his understanding of what comprised the ancient Silk Road.

A century and a half later, the railway connecting China and Germany has become a reality. This is just in order to promote mutual aid and cooperation among Silk Road countries, and an initial achievement in furthering the development of their economic and cultural ties. To truly realize the Belt and Road Initiative, even more capital, technology and international cooperation are required—as well as Silk Road "savvy" human resources.

For China, first of all, there is a need for a large group of persons who possess general knowledge of the geography, history, politics and economy of each Silk Road country, and who also have expertise in a particular discipline. This can generally be attained via an undergraduate degree; the key lies in guaranteeing good quality curriculum design and instruction. Secondly, there is a need for a very large number of people capable of researching a specific region or country in a specific academic field. This should be achievable at the MA stage. By means of visits, internships or actual work on the ground, they should have the experience of interacting smoothly with local people and governments of a given region, and be capable of working with them. The greatest challenge will be to form a group of people who possess specialized expertise and can produce innovative research that serves the diverse needs of government bodies, think tanks, business enterprises and institutions of higher learning. These people are likely to require a doctorate, and ideally, would undergo a period of postdoctoral training too.

As the country that launched the Belt and Road Initiative—and the ancient homeland and starting point of the Silk Road—China must utilize knowledge and goodwill to win the trust and respect of the peoples along the length of the Silk Road. In this respect, China's institutions of higher learning are indeed duty-bound.

China's institutions of higher learning still mainly teach knowledge accumulated by European and American scholars during the eighteenth–twentieth centuries. But in recent decades, archaeological and textual research carried out within China's borders has given us a clearer understanding of the multiple origins and melding of the peoples who comprised ancient *Huaxia* civilization, thereby clarifying the positioning of China's multi-ethnic *Zhonghua* culture. With this as a foundation, Chinese scholars can continue their efforts to forge ahead in deeper Silk Road research on the ground in the countries through which the ancient routes once passed.

Asia and Africa have longer histories of civilization than Europe. It follows that West, Central, North, East, South and Southeast Asia, as well as East, Central and Southern Africa surely possess a large amount of yet undiscovered archaeological resources and historical and cultural data. For instance, ancient ruins often accidentally come to light during modern-day construction of roads, etc. In the coming years, in the course of infrastructure construction and geological prospecting in Silk Road countries, further ruins worthy of archaeological study will certainly emerge, and Chinese scholars should participate in the protection and development of such cultural heritage. In addition, Silk Road language, customs, religious rituals and folk bodies also await analysis and interpretation by experts and scholars.

In the social sciences, there is no universally applicable political economy, nor is there a single developmental model that is suitable for the specific situation of each country. The development and modernization of any region is impacted by a unique set of geographical, historical and cultural factors. If Chinese scholars wish to seriously undertake Silk Road research, then they should seek inspiration from the construction of the Belt and Road to pioneer new topics of study and author innovative scholarship.

In my opinion, the greatest challenge facing China's intellectual community is how, by means of in-depth observation and analysis of land and maritime silk routes, and by referencing the experiences of the developed world, to construct a political economy in which developing countries join forces to drive mutual growth, and elucidate a development methodology that is feasible given contemporary levels of technology and the emerging international order.

Faced with this challenge, China's institutions of higher learning will naturally need to strengthen cooperation. But perhaps more direct and pressing is the need for cooperation between different faculties within a given university. At present, the organizational structure and resource allocation in major tertiary institutions tend to push different faculties to engage in vicious competition, each taking its own path and refusing to interact with others. Hopefully, Silk Road research will not take this oft-trodden path. The methodology and organizational structure required for Silk Road scholarship will certainly be rather different from those of traditional branches of learning within a university. Based on my years of experience at various schools worldwide, the most rational choice would be the establishment of an interdisciplinary "Silk Road Research Center/Institute/School" with its own student quota and a separate budget.

The relevant departments can refer to the experience of the United States in the 1950s as regards the Ford Foundation and Rockefeller Foundation: Investing new resources that can be put to practical use is an effective incentive for stimulating universities to restructure their framework, and for faculty members to adjust their attitudes. Therefore, the Ministry of Education and other official institutions, as well as large enterprises preparing to expand their overseas business, should help China's tertiary institutions to complete the dual mission of training new talent and generating knowledge.

One other crucial point: Institutions of higher learning should not be treated as "Royal Warrant Holders," i.e., think tanks exclusively at the service of enterprises or government bodies. There is no denying that today's Silk Road studies have both mercantile and practical significance. But if scholars at tertiary institutions merely express support for existing government policy, or confine themselves to penning the formulaic "eight-legged" essays once used to pass the Imperial Exams, or busy themselves crafting memorials to the Emperor, then this will amount to wasting years of specialized knowledge and abandoning an opportunity to make a contribution to the Silk Road countries and mankind as a whole.

PART III

Silk Road

CHAPTER 8

Cultural Interaction Along the Silk Road

The term "Silk Road" was first used by nineteenth-century Europeans in reference to the transportation network between Europe and Asia that took shape after the Han Dynasty's diplomat-explorer Zhang Qian pioneered passage to the "Western Regions" in the second century BCE. In fact, interactions between Europe and East Asia were underway 4,500 years ago, and three different routes emerged over time.

Along the northern steppes of the Eurasian continent was the "Steppe Silk Road," which was pioneered mainly by nomads on horseback and horse-drawn wagons. The Scythians, who appeared there in the seventh century BCE, were the best-known steppe people. They promoted trade on the Eurasian continent, amassed considerable wealth, and built tombs only discovered in the twentieth century. However, the steppes were sparsely populated and lacked cities as a venue for trade and provisions, so the total scale of trade was small.

The Oasis Silk Road—a string of fertile desert towns watered by mountain rainfall—linked East Asia and Europe, passing through Central and West Asia, as well as a branch destined for South Asia, and effectively encompassed the world's major agricultural civilizations prior to the fifteenth century. The camel provided the main means of transportation along this route. The sound of camel bells on the Silk Road symbolizes the trade in goods on the Eurasian continent, but also symbolizes the interaction of civilizations and large-scale cultural exchanges over a long period of time.

© Foreign Language Teaching and Research Publishing Co., Ltd 2023 119
H. K. Chang, *Mapping Civilizations Across Eurasia*,
https://doi.org/10.1007/978-981-99-7641-6_8

The Silk Road can be roughly divided into four sections from east to west: The first was from Chang'an to the Jade Pass west of Dunhuang, beyond which lay the Western Regions outside the Han cultural sphere; the second section stretched from Dunhuang (home to the Buddhist-themed Mogao Caves) through Xinjiang to Samarkand in present-day Uzbekistan, a long and arduous journey for the itinerant merchant; the third section ran from Samarkand across the southern shore of the Caspian Sea to the eastern Mediterranean Sea, or across the northern shore of the Caspian to present-day Istanbul. The fourth section extended between the eastern shore of the Mediterranean or from Istanbul into the Balkans, the Italian Peninsula, the Danube Valley and the Rhine Valley.

FIVE SILK ROAD TRAILBLAZERS

Myriad persons left their footprints on the Silk Road. Here below, we'll discuss just five of those who proved themselves most historically influential.

Zhang Qian (c. 164–114 BCE): A native of Shaanxi's Hanzhong region, he was one of the first people from the Central Plain—the cradle of Chinese civilization located in the lower reaches of the Yellow River—to acquire first-hand knowledge of the deserts, the Pamir Plateau, and the culture specific to these remote lands far west of China's heartland.

The immediate impetus for Zhang Qian's diplomatic mission to the Western Regions (the Chinese term for then-uncharted Central Asia) was the confrontation between the Han and Xiongnu Empires. Emperor Wu of Han wished to forge an alliance with the Great Yuezhi people, nomads who had been bullied by the Xiongnu and driven out of the Hexi Corridor, in order to outflank the Xiongnu and effectively "break their right arm," so he was keen to recruit warriors. Zhang Qian applied for the job and was selected to undertake this risky and formidable task.

Shortly after his departure, he was captured by the Xiongnu and placed under house arrest near the residence of the Chanyu, the Xiongnu ruler, where Zhang Qian married and had two children. Eleven years later he took advantage of internal turmoil among the Xiongnu to escape from surveillance and flee with his wife, children and a loyal Xiongnu servant. He didn't return to the Han capital Chang'an, instead continuing his journey westward to Dayuan (Ferghana Basin), where he learned that the Great Yuezhi had migrated south to Daxia, i.e., Bactria, south of the Oxus

River or Amu Darya River, in present-day northern Afghanistan. Thus he proceeded to Daxia, attempting to complete his original mission.

Already settled in their new land, the Great Yuezhi did not wish to make enemies of the Xiongnu, and this meant Zhang Qian's diplomatic mission could not be achieved.

However, upon his return to China, he provided the Han court with invaluable intelligence about the Western Regions, which played an important role in the later Han Dynasty's strategy regarding parts of Central Asia.

Zhang Qian's second mission took him to the Kingdom of Wusun in the Ili River Basin. He brought with him a large number of people and goods from China's Central Plain, such as silk, and dispatched his deputy commanders to travel throughout the Western Regions and genuinely pioneer a trade network along what would become the Silk Road.

The imperial envoy's second foray was not successful on the diplomatic front either. The Xiongnu were very strong at this end of Central Asia, and the King of Wusun was not keen to choose between them and the Western Han; he preferred fence-sitting, as it were.

That said, without Zhang Qian, there would have been no cultural exchange on the Oasis Silk Road. He brought back to the court excellent horse breeds (the famed "blood-sweating" horses of Ferghana) and introduced many crops and fruits such as alfalfa, grapes, pomegranates, walnuts and melons, as well as the *pipa* and *huqin* now widely considered to be traditional Chinese musical instruments (Map 8.1).

Kumarajiva (344–413): His father was an Indian nobleman exiled to the Kingdom of Qiuci (now Kucha, Xinjiang), and his mother was a Qiuci princess. Because of her devotion to Buddhism, Kumarajiva studied Buddhist texts from an early age, and traveled to India to learn from famous masters. He became proficient in both Mahayana and Theravada scriptures, and this highly cultivated young acolyte became known throughout the Western Regions.

The ruler of Former Qin (351–394), Fu Jian, wished to invite Kumarajiva to Chang'an to preach, but the monk was reluctant, whereupon Fu ordered his general Lü Guang to invade Qiuci and forcefully bring Kumarajiva to China's Central Plain where he would be married. But Fu was killed in a military-led coup before Lü's troops could return, and Lü proclaimed himself the ruler of Liangzhou (now Wuwei, Gansu), where Kumarajiva stayed for 16 years and mastered Chinese.

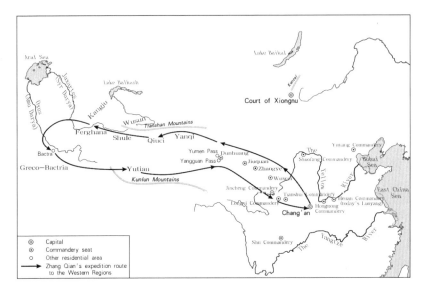

Map 8.1 Zhang Qian's first diplomatic mission to the Western Regions (139–126 BC)

Yao Chang subsequently established the Later Qin in Chang'an and Lü surrendered. Yao's son Yao Xing also admired Kumarajiva and had him brought to Chang'an and forced him to take ten concubines so that his intelligence could be passed on via his offspring.

Having left the monkhood, Kumarajiva resided twelve years in Chang'an, often lecturing to Yao Xing and others, and introducing several important schools of Buddhism to China, including Madhyamaka, a tradition of Buddhist philosophy and practice founded by the Indian philosopher Nagarjuna.

Kumarajiva also led his disciples to translate 74 Buddhist sutras in 384 volumes, including the *Amitabha Sutra*, *Perfection of Wisdom*, the *Lotus Sutra*, as well as the *Heart Sutra* and the *Diamond Sutra*, the last two of which are very important in Mahayana Buddhism. His translations are simple, free of error and fluent, and instrumental in getting Buddhism to take root in China. It was he who rendered thusly a renowned verse from the *Heart Sutra*:

Form is emptiness, (se ji shi kong)
emptiness is form. (kong ji shi se)

Xuanzang (602–664): Under the Tang, comprehension of Buddhism became more and more profound, and conflicting views emerged among the various sects. Therefore, Xuanzang decided to go to India to study and bring back Buddhist scriptures for his own translation (see Chapter 6 for the route of his westward journey). After arriving at Nalanda, the center of Buddhism in India, he studied Sanskrit and the local language, intensely contemplating the Dharma and attaining a high level of mastery.

The abbot of Nalanda once asked Xuanzang to head a debate about the Buddhist scriptures in his stead, and senior monks from all over India interrogated Xuanzang for eighteen days without catching him out. The elderly abbot wanted Xuanzang to succeed him, but Xuanzang refused, insisting on returning to his homeland. But before doing so, he spent another five years traveling through India to learn about the local people and their customs.

Xuanzang came from a family of officials and was familiar with court etiquette and the machinations of officialdom. In fact, at the time when he left Chinese territory, he was actually violating an imperial edict forbidding travel outside the Middle Kingdom. Therefore, upon his return eighteen years later, he paused at Hotan, an oasis town in southeastern Xinjiang, and tested the waters by submitting a missive to the court. Learning of this, Emperor Taizong of Tang immediately dispatched cavalry to welcome him and commanded him to proceed to Luoyang for an audience. The emperor tried several times to appoint him to various offices, but Xuanzang declined, opining that he wished to find a quiet place to translate scriptures and the Tripitaka.

So, the emperor arranged for him to reside in Hongfu Temple at first and later in the newly completed Daci'en Temple in Chang'an and provided him with some 200 learned monks with various skills to form a large-scale atelier, whereupon Xuanzang began to lead this team to translate the scriptures he had brought back from India; this translation project lasted 19 years.

Emperor Taizong also commanded Xuanzang to write down what he had seen and heard during his eighteen years abroad, and his *Great Tang Records on the Western Regions* has been translated into many languages. More than two centuries before Xuanzang's pilgrimage, Jin Dynasty monk Faxian (334–422) traveled to India at the age of 60 or so and returned home at the age of 75, authoring *A Record of Buddhist Kingdoms*. Faxian was devoted to praising the Buddha and did not expect support from his government. By beginning the title of his book with the words "Great Tang," Xuanzang essentially defined the Western Regions as part of the magnificent Tang Dynasty's territory, and thus won the emperor's favor.

As an early Buddhist monk once said, "If a nation's laws are not followed, Buddha's Dharma can hardly be established." How right it is!

The rich and detailed *Great Tang Records on the Western Regions* provides valuable information for scholars of medieval India and Central Asia. Prior to independence in 1947, India had no central government and therefore no tradition of official chroniclers of history, so to write about ancient Indian history nowadays, one must rely on Xuanzang's recollections. Murals portraying Xuanzang hang in the Indian Parliament today to show gratitude for his contributions to Indian history and culture.

In fact, many nineteenth-century European archaeologists also based their archaeological excavations in India on details found in the *Great Tang Records*. For example, the reproduction of the site of the Nalanda monastic university and discovery of the stone pillar erected by King Ashoka (269–232 BCE) at the birthplace of the Buddha were entirely dependent on information provided by Xuanzang.

When Xuanzang was in India, he translated the *Tao Te Ching* (*Book of the Tao*) into Sanskrit and wrote a commentary on it, which possibly represents the premier foreign transmission of Taoist thought.

After his return to China, Xuanzang led his disciples in translating a large number of sutras that were elegantly and fluently written, far surpassing those of his predecessors, and the most popular Chinese-language version of the *Heart Sutra* today is Xuanzang's rendition. In addition to translating sutras, Xuanzang also authored many treatises and founded the Yogacara school of Buddhism. If the translation of the sutras by Kumarajiva led to the penetration of Buddhism into Chinese people's hearts and minds, it was Xuanzang who began the Sinification of Buddhism by endowing Buddhist thought with Chinese characteristics.

Genghis Khan (1162–1227): It is purely historical coincidence that Genghis Khan and his descendants penetrated the western section of the Silk Road. After the unification of Mongolia, Genghis Khan attacked Tangut-ruled Western Xia four times and conquered the neighboring areas of Hami and Turpan.

The largest power on the western Silk Road at the time was Khwarazm. In 1219, Genghis Khan sent a huge trade mission there consisting mainly of Muslim merchants. Keen to get his hands on the caravan's goods, the governor of the border city of Otrar claimed that there were Mongol spies among the merchants. In the end, all 500 people were slaughtered, and only one camel driver escaped to report the news.

Genghis Khan dispatched an ambassador to the capital of Khwarazm to negotiate. The Shah of Khwarazm humiliated the envoy and sent him back, but only after severing his ear. This incident infuriated Genghis Khan and he decided to cease warring with Western Xia, and instead plan a western expedition against the Khwarazmians. This not only reoriented Genghis Khan's strategy, but also altered the history of the entire Eurasian continent, and thus the history of all humankind.

Genghis Khan and his descendants undertook three Westward Expeditions over a period of 40 years.

The first, commanded by Genghis Khan himself, conquered most of present-day Central Asia, as far west as the Caucasus on the western shore of the Caspian Sea, and southeast to the Indus River. The route taken for this campaign and the scope of its conquests were located mainly along the Oasis Silk Road. After the khan's death, his second son, Chaghatai, ruled these lands, which included present-day Xinjiang in China, Uzbekistan, Tajikistan and eastern Afghanistan.

The second expedition, led by Genghis Khan's grandson, Batu, pushed westward mainly along the Steppe Silk Road, defeating the Khitans in Central Asia after they had been laid low by the Jin Dynasty; crossed the Urals and the Volga River to take Kiev, the early Slavic heartland, and Moscow, vanquishing the Russians. His troops then exited the Steppe Silk Road to penetrate Hungary and approach Venice.

When Batu returned east, he stopped at the Volga River and founded the Kipchak Khanate (Golden Horde), which ruled Europe east of the Danube and the entire Kipchak Steppe. It took more than 200 years for the Russians to win independence after Mongolian rule, and another 200 years to build up their strength before they would cross the Volga, conquer the Turkic-speaking Tatars, and expand eastward.

The third expedition was led by Hulagu, son of Genghis Khan's fourth son Tolui, and targeted Persia and the Arab world. The Mongol army first pacified the "Assassins" belonging to the Shi'ite sect's Ismaili branch and occupying many mountain strongholds in what is now Iran. After stabilizing all of Persia, it moved westward to capture Baghdad in 1258.

Hulagu ordered the execution of the caliph, destroying the political and spiritual center of Sunni Islam. By this time, the Mongol army had occupied all of Iraq, most of Syria, and a small part of Asia Minor, and was approaching Jerusalem. But this was as far east as the Mongols would go.

Founded by Hulagu in West Asia, the Mongol Ilkhanate (1256–1335) was the meeting point of the Steppe, Oasis and Maritime Silk Roads. The Mongols established the largest empire in the history of humankind on the Eurasian continent, facilitating the unimpeded flow of people, goods, ideas and the arts. Today's globalization can be said to have begun in the Mongol era, and the concept of the Silk Road Economic Belt (aka the Belt and Road Initiative) seems to echo that of the past.

Timur (1336–1405): Timur was born in Transoxiana near the city of Kesh, south of present-day Samarkand in Uzbekistan, and was a Turkic-speaking Mongol of the Barlas Confederation. His father was the feudal lord of Kesh and a vassal of the Chaghatai Khan of Ili. Through his powers of observation, personal ambition, adventurous character, political savvy and ability to seize opportunities that came his way, Timur established the largest state in Central and Western Asia since the Mongol Empire, and the strongest Islamic regime in the world at the time.

As a young man, Timur rebelled against Mongol rule, for which he was wounded and crippled for life. Later, as a Mongol nobleman, he married the princess of the Western Chaghatai Khanate and preferred to be addressed as Lord Fu-ma, "royal son-in-law," because his wife was a member of the Golden Family, i.e., descendants of Genghis Khan. He claimed to have restored the ancient Mongol Empire (and therefore often attacked areas ruled by other Mongol princes), and was a purveyor of Islam. He labeled himself the "Shadow of Allah," but frequently killed other Muslims.

In his later years, he invaded India, vanquished the Ottomans and captured their sultan, and defeated the remnants of the Christian crusaders. His last aspiration was to attack the Ming Dynasty and reestablish the Yuan Dynasty.

But in 1405, Timur died of illness while leading his expedition against the Ming at Otrar—the very site where Genghis Khan's trade mission had been slaughtered nearly two centuries earlier.

Timur and Ming founder Emperor Zhu Yuanzhang (1328–1398) were contemporaries. During his struggle against the Eastern Chaghatai Khanate, Timur offered tribute to the Ming several times and requested an alliance, but later turned against it. In his 40 years of warring, he never lost a battle, and he built an empire that included almost all of the Western Chaghatai Khanate and the Ilkhanate, as well as the southern part of the Kipchak Khanate. This empire, like the Mongol empire of 200 years ago, was built by rapid and brutal plundering, burning and killing over a period of decades. Nonetheless, like the Mongol empire, its existence did facilitate long-distance trade and the integration of the Steppe, Oasis and Maritime Silk Roads.

Zheng He (1371–1433): The famed Muslim admiral commanded expeditionary voyages to Southeast Asia, the Indian subcontinent, Western Asia and East Africa, and his first voyage took place in 1405, the year that Timur died.

I have always suspected that these expeditions were related to the Ming Emperor Yongle's desire to join forces with the Timurids against the Northern Yuan. Since the primary sources at the time were deliberately burned, and I have not seriously studied other historical sources, I am not sure about this conjecture. However, the integration of the maritime and land-based Silk Roads, and friendship between the Ming and the Timurids, would not have been bad things for the Chinese, which had both land and sea frontiers. In other words, although the Timurid Empire and the Ming Dynasty were separated by mountains, they did not lack common concerns. This was the case six hundred years ago. And the geopolitical considerations concerning the land-based and maritime silk roads are not different today!

Despite his own illiteracy, Timur was passionate about education and culture, and was keen to promote Islam, admittedly perhaps for image building purposes. The Timurid Empire was in fact an important base for the Persian Renaissance: Mystical poet Jami (1414–1492), known for his collection of Persian poetry, and Bihzad (1450–1535), a master Persian painter, both grew up in Herat (in present-day western Afghanistan), the second capital of the Timurid Empire.

When Timur's grandson Ulugh Beg ruled Samarkand in the fifteenth century, he built a magnificent mosque and a madrassa and taught classes himself. Ulugh also loved literature, philosophy, mathematics, and especially astronomy. He ordered the Ulugh Beg Observatory to be constructed in Samarkand, the world's most advanced astronomical observatory of its time, and personally charted over 1,000 planets, making him the world's most accomplished astronomer before Copernicus.

Timur's sixth-generation grandson Babur (r. 1526–1530), whose mother was a direct descendant of Genghis Khan, briefly succeeded to the throne, but he was expelled by Muhammad Shaybani, a patrilineal relative of Genghis Khan's eldest son, Jochi, who had proceeded southward from the Kipchak Steppe, an event which marked the launch of the Shaybanid Dynasty in Uzbekistan.

After wandering for some years in southern Afghanistan, Babur entered northwestern India and established the Mughal Dynasty (1526–1857), which ruled India for more than three centuries. Like his predecessor, the poet Ali-Shir Nava'i (1441–1501), Babur wrote first in Persian and then in his native Turkic language. Based upon Chaghatai Turkic and containing some Arabic and Persian vocabulary—transliterated via Latin letters—his memoir is of high literary value. The Chagatai script, a literary language, was widely used in Uzbek and China's Xinjiang region before the twentieth century and was one of the distinct cultural features of the Oasis Silk Road over the last few centuries.

Faith and Worship

Every tribe has its own view of the universe, life and death, and worship of gods and spirits. The Silk Road crossed the borders of many different ethnicities and countries and naturally featured many distinct religious beliefs and rituals, so interaction between different faiths was inevitable. The native Chinese religions believed in *Tian* (the Heavens), worshiped various gods and spirits, and offered sacrifices to their mortal ancestors.

Through the introduction of merchants and monks who came to China via the Silk Road, at least five religions spread and took root in the Han cultural area:

The earliest was Buddhism. Some of the processes by which Buddhism penetrated Chinese society have been mentioned above. It entered China during the Eastern Han Dynasty in the first century and spread around the same time as the native Taoism, resulting in mutual influencing and borrowing. Because Buddhism already comprised a fairly complete system of thought and worship when it entered China, it had considerable influence on the belief system and rituals of Taoism—the folk religion, that is, not the philosophy.

The interaction of Buddhist and Confucian thought has also influenced the mores of the Chinese people for more than a millennium. The evolution of Buddhist thought in China (especially Chan Buddhism) resulted from the fusion of Buddhism and Confucianism, while the Neo-Confucianism popular during the Song (960–1279) and Ming (1368–1644) was the product of a new-fangled Confucianism influenced by Buddhism.

This Gandhara Buddha in the National Museum of Pakistan portrays similar artistic techniques as found in statues of Greek and Roman Gods of the Pantheon (see Chapter 11 for details)

The Buddhism that traveled via the Silk Road also included music, art and architecture. The stupa—a mound-like structure containing relics—is an Indian architectural form that was introduced to China as a result of

Buddhism, and stupa, meaning "heap," is borrowed from Sanskrit. Also noteworthy were the paintings and sculptures of Buddha.

In the early days of Buddhism in the Ganges Valley, there were no images of the Buddha, and even statues were not permitted. However, the Kushan Empire, founded by the Great Yuezhi in first century, was peopled by many descendants of Alexander the Great's army. Although these Greek-Bactrians were Buddhists, they were nostalgic for the Greek manner of worship and felt that the Buddha required a concrete image.

Thus, from the Gandhara region where the Greek-Bactrians were concentrated—i.e., the area where southern Afghanistan and western Pakistan meet, such as Peshawar—images of Buddha became popular and were sculpted in the same manner as the Greek-Roman Pantheon of deities. As with Greek gods, Buddha's nose was sculpted as high-bridged and straight, his hair curly, and his robe pleated. This unique fusion of Greco-Roman and Indian art is known to scholars as Gandhara art.

Gandhara art was introduced to China through Central Asia and became generally accepted, but over time the Buddha's nose has flattened and the look of his eyes has grown more Chinese; his hair, however, remains curly to this day.

The second religion to arrive via the Silk Road was Zoroastrianism (Mazdayasna). The Persian Zoroaster (c. 628–551 BCE) founded the religion based on Aryan legend, which has the same origins as Indian Brahminism. However, the teachings of Zoroaster highlight one god, Ahura Mazda, who is the Master of Light and Darkness, so unlike Brahminism, which is a polytheistic religion, the former has a distinctly monotheistic orientation. Zoroastrianism predates Buddhism, and still has many followers in India and Iran. Since Zoroastrians use fire as an altar at which to pray to their god, in China it was also referred to as "fire worship."

Under Persia's Sassanids (220–644), Zoroastrianism was adopted as the state religion and spread throughout the Persian cultural sphere. The most active merchants on the Silk Road were the Sogdians, who spoke an Eastern Iranian tongue, and the great majority practiced Zoroastrianism (see Chapter 23).

The Sogdians formed a large international commercial network. Many dwelled in Xinjiang, the Hexi Corridor, the southern edge of the Erdos Steppe (now Inner Mongolia), and Chang'an (now Xi'an). During the Tang, the main inhabitants of the capital Chang'an's western district were the Hu people, a term generally applied to Sogdians. In one of Li Bai's two poems, jointly titled *Youthful Adventures (shaonian xing)*, he writes:

> Trampling the capital's fallen petals
> At length—but to what destination?
> Grinning, he enters a pub for exotic Hu entertainment.

This referred to a pub where Sogdian maidens, devotees of Zoroastrianism, regaled the customers.

There were many intermarriages between the Sogdians and the local Chinese, and most of the former took Chinese surnames and gradually Sinicised. The "Nine Surnames of Zhaowu," as they are denominated in Chinese chronicles, refer to the Chinese surnames given to the Sogdians according to their place of origin. An Lushan, born in Liaoning and the instigator of the An Lushan Rebellion in 755, is a famous example: His ancestors came from the Kingdom of Anxi (then Parthia, and Bukhara in modern Uzbekistan), hence the surname An.

The ancestors of the Cao family, who ruled the Dunhuang region for seven generations in the eleventh century, originated in the Cao Kingdom (present-day eastern Uzbekistan). The Sogdians formed communities with their own religious societies throughout China, and Zoroastrianism was maintained by these societies and developed through intermarriage with the Han Chinese.

Zoroastrianism was followed by Manichaeism. The Persian Mani (216–276) founded Manichaeism, a syncretic, dualistic faith that borrowed elements from both Zoroastrianism and Christianity. The religion professed that there were two forces in the universe, Light and Darkness; in the Upper Ages (the past), the pair coexisted while struggling; Darkness had the upper hand in the Middle Ages (present), but Light eventually defeated its inverse in the Lower Ages (future). Manichaeism was considered heretic during the Sassanid period, but it attracted many followers nonetheless, and there were many Manichaeans among the Sogdians. During the Tang Dynasty, the Turkophone Uyghurs adopted Manichaeism as their state religion, and Manichaeism remained active on the Silk Road for a long time (see Chapter 23).

In the Han Chinese society of the Central Plain, Manichaeism was more influential than Zoroastrianism because of its doctrine asserting the ultimate victory of Light over Darkness, which was why the former was also known in China as Mingjiao ("Religion of Light"). The Manichaen community did not submit to the imperial court, and was repeatedly banned beginning with the campaign to eradicate Buddhism led by Emperor Wuzong of Tang (840–846). He considered Manichaeans as comparable to Buddhist monks and nuns and slaughtered the lot, while formally interdicting both Zoroastrianism and Nestorianism somewhat later.

However, folk bodies banned by the imperial court traditionally went underground, and Manichaeism was periodically—but ineffectively—proscribed.

During the Northern Song, there were simultaneous peasant uprisings popularly described as "Song Jiang in the north and Fang La in the south," and the latter exploited the teachings of the Mingjiao as a rallying cry. Zhu Yuanzhang, founder of the Ming Dynasty (1368–1644), had contact with this religion during his struggle to overthrow the Yuan Dynasty, and he called the regime he established the "Great Ming"—which suggests an association with the Mingjiao faith.

There was also Nestorian Christianity, which was recognized by the Tang court. In the fifth century, the Archbishop of Constantinople Nestorius (386–451) rejected the doctrine of the duality of Jesus as both mortal and divine; he believed that Jesus was human, linked to God only in spirit, and not in both body and spirit. Therefore, Mary was simply the mother of Jesus, not Mother of the son of God.

For this reason, Nestorius and his followers were not accepted by the orthodox church or the Byzantine emperor and were persecuted as heretics. They fled to Iraq and Iran, where they joined forces and developed the local Church of the East (not to be confused with Eastern Orthodox Christianity, e.g., the Greek Orthodox Church).

Some of the Nestorians migrated to the middle and eastern sections of the Silk Road where they proselytized, attracting a large number of converts among Sogdians and Turkic tribes. In the early Tang Dynasty, the sect was welcomed by the Chinese imperial court and designated as *Jingjiao* or Nestorianism. In 781, the court allowed the erection of the "Memorial of the Propagation within China of the Luminous Religion from Daqin." Inscribed in Syriac, it documents 150 years of early Christianity in China. "Daqin" formerly referred to the Roman Empire. Many ministers and soldiers of the Yuan Dynasty were Nestorians.

Sorghaghtani Beki, the wife of Genghis Khan's fourth son Tolui, was the niece of the leader of the Khereid Mongol confederation, and a Nestorian Christian. She was dubbed "Mother of Four Emperors" due to the lofty positions eventually held by her four sons: Möngke succeeded Ögedei as the Mongol's Great Khan; Kublai succeeded Möngke and established the Yuan Dynasty, and was posthumously designated Emperor Shizu of Yuan; Hulagu founded the Ilkhanate in the southwestern portion of the Mongol Empire; and Ariq Böke was elected as the Khan of Khans in Mongolia after a struggle with Kublai.

Over the last 100 years, dozens of tombstones and crucifix-shaped ornaments inscribed with Syriac script have been unearthed, from western Xinjiang to eastern Inner Mongolia and southward to Quanzhou in Fujian Province, illustrating how widespread Nestorianism was in China.

A relative latecomer to the Silk Road, Islam, was founded in Mecca in 622. By 700, the Arabs were traversing the Silk Road and controlled Khorasan, then the easternmost province of Persia, and located in what are now parts of northeastern Iran, southern Turkmenistan and northern Afghanistan.

In 751, Gao Xianzhi, Military Commissioner of the Western Regions for the Tang, led an army from Qiuci to Samarkand to quell turmoil there. They fatefully encountered the Arabian army at Talas (now a Kyrgyz city bordering Kazakhstan), where the Chinese were defeated and retreated. This marked the start of the decline of the Tang Empire in Central Asia, and the beginning of Islam becoming the dominant religion on the Silk Road.

Initially, Persian-speaking Sufis roamed the steppes of Central Asia, persuading many nomadic Turkic tribes to abandon animistic Shamanism in favor of monotheistic Islam. Many Turks were sold as slaves or soldiers serving the Persian nobility, and eventually Turkic converts to Islam undertook Jihad, attacking infidel regimes, and Buddhists and Manichaeans in the Tarim Basin and Hindus in the Indus Valley were gradually Islamized.

In China's case, the first Muslims to enter the country would have been Arab traders who arrived in Tang-era Guangzhou via the Maritime Silk Road in 651.

When the Lu Anshi Rebellion broke out in 755, the Tang court invited the Uyghurs, Tibetans and Arabs to Chang'an to help crush the uprising. Some Arab soldiers preferred to remain in China after the war, and this was likely what kickstarted Muslim settlement along the Silk Road and into the Central Plain.

Each of the three Mongol Westward Expeditions undertaken in the first third of the thirteenth century brought back many captured soldiers and craftsmen, most of whom were Muslim. Throughout the Yuan, the Muslim population increased significantly, and they spread throughout the country, but settled mainly in the northwest and Yunnan in the southwest.

Meanwhile, Muslim merchants of Arab and Persian descent had settled along the Southeast coast since the Tang Dynasty, and some became local leaders and gained appointment by the imperial court. For example, Pu Shougeng, a Muslim from West Asia, was a Muslim merchant and administrator under the Song and Yuan.

In short, most of the Chinese-speaking Muslims in China today belong to the Hui ethnic group, which tends to concentrate in certain communities dispersed throughout China.

The Turkic-speaking peoples of Central Asia and Xinjiang have all been Islamized (with the exception of the Yugurs, a group of less than 20,000 people living near Gansu's Zhangye, who practice Tibetan Buddhism), and form a predominantly Islamic minority in northwestern China.

Among them, the most distinctive are the Uyghurs and the Salars. The Uyghurs originated in the Mongolian Plateau and originally called themselves Huihe, but later changed their name to Huihu (now Weiwuer in Chinese, Uyghur in Turkic and European languages) during the Tang, and penetrated Xinjiang via the Hexi Corridor in the ninth century. Their culture is long-established and their numbers much greater than those of other Turkophone peoples, making them the single most populous ethnicity in Xinjiang.

The ancestors of the Salar people migrated eastward from present-day Turkmenistan in the thirteenth century as a result of political conflict while under Mongolian rule.

The Turkic-speaking peoples migrated from the Mongolian Plateau to the west, with the Oghuz Turks gradually moving westward to present-day Uzbekistan and Turkmenistan in the seventh century, and entering the Persian cultural sphere.

The Salars, on the other hand, migrated back eastward many centuries later. Their migratory journey was arduous and their numbers dwindled, finally settling on the border between China's Qinghai and Gansu Provinces, not far from the source of the Yellow River. The Salars now boast a population of about 130,000 and live in mixed communities along with the Han, Hui and Tibetans, but the majority of the population still maintains the beliefs and core practices of Islam.

CHAPTER 9

The New Silk Road: Strategic Thinking

SEA POWER, TERRESTRIAL POWER AND GEOPOLITICS

For thousands of years before Europe's Age of Exploration, the middle swath of the Eurasian continent was the principal passage for human commercial and cultural contacts. The "Oasis Silk Road" pioneered by the diplomat-explorer Zhang Qian to the Western Regions in the late second century BCE, was located in this region.

The land and sea travels of the Polos family between Italy and China during the thirteenth century were not only remarkable examples of East–West interaction, but also the harbinger of geographical explorations by the Europeans. The launch of the maritime-driven Age of Exploration in the sixteenth century saw the traditional land-based Silk Road gradually lose its former brilliance, although its geographical dominance of Central Eurasia did not end. From the seventeenth century onward, the mighty Tsarist Russians nibbled at and then swallowed up this land that had once witnessed such glory. Compared to the rest of Eurasia, it became even more isolated and backward due to the growing prosperity of maritime transport in the eighteenth century. Henceforth, the ancient trade corridor that passed through Central and West Asia on its way to Europe recalled the forlorn ambience of Tang Dynasty poet Du Fu's verse:

> War-steed neighs, cold wind moans
> Sun sets on the once glorious banner.

The middle of the nineteenth century was an era when the European powers competed for world hegemony. On the Eurasian continent, Russia occupied its middle portion, Central Asia, while Britain controlled the South Asian subcontinent. Russia sought to push south to Afghanistan and thereby compete with Britain in the South Asian arena. But the British aimed to control Afghanistan and encircle Iran to prevent the Russians from moving southward.

Thus, central Eurasia became the setting for "The Great Game," an iconic geopolitical conflict played out in the nineteenth century by Great Britain and Tsarist Russia.

In the end, both foes failed to vanquish Afghanistan—"the graveyard of empires"—and reluctantly agreed to slightly alter the chessboard by adding a narrow "finger," the Wakhan Corridor, to the eastern part of Afghanistan's territory, so that it bordered directly on China and functioned to separate British-controlled South Asia from Russian-controlled Central Asia. With Afghanistan now serving as a buffer zone between Britain and Russia, both colonial empires then turned their attention to Xinjiang, China. Each stationed diplomatic staff at their enormous consulates in Kashgar, in part, to seek new benefits in Xinjiang but also to monitor one another's movements.

In the nineteenth century, there commenced the rise of a new power outside of Eurasia—the United States. In 1877, a professor of history at the US Naval Academy, Alfred Thayer Mahan, wrote a book entitled *The Influence of Sea Power upon History*. It advanced the "sea power doctrine," which posited that whichever country possessed naval superiority would dominate the course of world history.

Regardless of whether naval power can really change the course of history, this book did indeed influence the strategic thinking of the United States, Britain, Japan and other naval powers. Japan's subsequent Pacific War was guided by Mahan's "theory of naval power," which is still the basic creed of the US Navy.

In 1904, Sir Halford John Mackinder, an early geopolitical scholar and director of the London School of Economics, presented his paper, *The Geographical Pivot of History*, at the annual meeting of the Royal Geographical Society. A naval power strategist, Mackinder proposed the "Heartland Theory" of terrestrial power: Whoever controls the Eastern European Plain controls the "Heartland" of the "World Island," and whoever controls the "World Island" possesses mastery over the entire world.

This theory had considerable influence on later strategists in Russia, Germany and the United States. One of the motives for the Nazis to kickstart World War II was to gain control of the "Heartland." Some American strategists also often emphasized the importance of "Central Eurasia," and the aggressive policies of the United States and the European Union toward Ukraine in recent years have more or less reflected this geopolitical ideology.

The "Pivot to Asia" policy proposed by the United States some years ago incorporates Mahan's "Sea Power Doctrine" and Mackinder's geopolitical theory. In recent years, the United States has proposed the Indo-Pacific Strategy, which envisages the Indian Ocean and the Pacific Ocean as a single entity and seeks to bring India, which has never allied with Pacific countries, into the US–Australia–Japan military alliance.

At the same time, the Americans see themselves as dominant at sea, but are poised to accelerate the integration of its Navy as a ship-to-shore connector with the Coast Guard, which has special functions, and the Marine Corps, which can deliver weapons of sustained lethality in the Western Pacific.

McKinder's theory is typical of nineteenth-century Eurocentrism and can no longer encompass today's strategic space. While modern geostrategy cannot discount two-dimensional geography, the role of the third dimension (air), the fourth dimension (outer space) and even the fifth dimension (telecom network) absolutely cannot be ignored.

It is worth mentioning here that in Mackinder's two-dimensional geographic thinking, the "Heartland" he refers to is intimately related to the "Silk Road." To illustrate his theory, Mackinder also cites the formation of the Mongolian and Russian empires as case studies. From this, it can be seen that the strategic location of the Silk Road is indeed very important. The Belt & Road Initiative proposed by China in recent years certainly holds such a strategic significance.

New Era, New Power, New Reasoning

The invention of the airplane by the Wright brothers in 1903 added an important new dimension to human activity. In World War I, both the British and the Germans established an air force—exploiting an invention that was but a decade old—and dispatched their pilots to engage in fighting.

Manfred von Richthofen, better known as the "Red Baron," was Germany's ace fighter pilot of the era, and he notched up 80 victories in air combat. Baron von *Richthofen,* the geographer who proposed the term "Seidenstraße" back in the nineteenth century—"silk road" in English—for the network of trade routes that extended from China to India and to Central Asia, also happened to be the Red Baron's uncle.

In 1971, the prototype of the lightning-fast and now far-reaching Internet emerged in the United States, formally ushering the world into the era of "globalization." Since then, the five dimensions of land, sea, air, space and network have been interacting with each other; land power, sea power, air power, outer space power and network power have become factors that every strategist needs to consider comprehensively.

After the Soviet Union's dissolution in 1991, the "remote regions" of Central Eurasia, which had been almost forgotten, received renewed attention. Here, the five newly independent countries—Kazakhstan, Kyrgyzstan, Tajikistan, Turkmenistan and Uzbekistan—were at first unstable, with ethnic tensions rising, religious extremists fomenting trouble and, in some cases, civil war breaking out.

Russia later sought to bring these five former Soviet republics back into its sphere of influence. Exploiting their economic and cultural power, the United States, Western Europe, Japan, South Korea, India, Pakistan and Turkey have all in turn essayed to fill this "vacuum." China, as a major power neighboring these countries, naturally played its part too.

In the aftermath of the devastating 9/11 attack, the United States dispatched a large military force to Afghanistan and increased its influence in the nearby region. This seemed to be the resurrection of the nineteenth-century terrestrial-power theory in the twenty-first century, but more than a decade of war—reportedly at a cost of more than $2 trillion—forced the United States to revise its strategic thinking. In 2021, the Americans officially withdrew completely from Afghanistan.

Just before and after 9/11, the implementation of China's "Great Western Development Strategy," and the emergence of security issues in Xinjiang also prompted the Chinese government to link the development of its western region with the question of national security, and furthermore, to associate these factors with the future development of Central Eurasia.

In 2006, the United States launched its "Greater Central Asia Partnership," which envisaged the formation of a north–south economic cooperation zone. Centered on Afghanistan, with the five Central Asian countries to the north and Pakistan and India to the south, the five Central Asian countries (i.e., the five "Stans") would supply Afghanistan, Pakistan and India with oil, natural gas and electricity. To borrow a term from the end of China's Warring States period (second century BCE), this plan could be referred to as a "Vertical Alliance" strategy. However, since the situation in Afghanistan was never promising and goodwill between India and Pakistan has been difficult to establish, the chances of success for a "vertical alliance" are not good. It has become even less viable since the Taliban takeover of Afghanistan.

After several years of observation, I published an article entitled *Greater Central Asia and the New Silk Road* in Beijing-based *Caijing* magazine (2013.9.2 issue), in which I mentioned that "China has to deal with the maritime powers regarding sea routes, especially in strategically located straits, in order to ensure the right to free navigation. In the land area of 'Greater Central Asia' (Central Eurasia), there is also a need for cooperation and mutual assistance with the countries concerned to ensure that the 'New Silk Road' is stable and peaceful."

Meanwhile, in the autumn of 2013, the Chinese government proposed the twin concepts of the "Silk Road Economic Belt" and the "21st Century Maritime Silk Road," now better known simply as the Belt & Road Initiative. This initiative advocated utilizing international cooperation to drive East–West development among the countries of the Eurasian continent, and thereby revitalize what was historically its longest and most extensive trade network. This notion is similar to the "Horizontal Alliance" strategy employed during China's Warring States period, and its realization would spur economic and cultural development in the Central Eurasian region, which is currently lagging.

This represents a fresh model of international cooperation and development. It is a rejection of the nineteenth-century, zero-sum "Great Game" and twentieth-century binary Cold War ideology, in which enemies "faced off against one another." It embodies an inclusive mindset, i.e., "There's food enough for everyone, and if there's an issue, let's talk it over."

However, given the historical inertia of international politics and the current balance of power contrasts among the major players, the degree of difficulty in implementing this grand strategy should not be underestimated. China's diplomatic, military, and economic decision-makers need to thoroughly grasp the actual needs and social conditions of the region, and let the results and satisfaction among participating countries confirm the value and significance of this initiative.

Silk Road Rules of Conduct

China is both an inland and a maritime country. It is also a country with a shortage of fossil energy sources, other than coal, and needs to import large amounts of fuel. China's energy strategy therefore requires taking into account the security and reliability of both sea and land transport.

In recent years, China's maritime power has been on the increase. However, as Australia, Japan and the United States are concerned about the rise of China, and as the Philippines, Vietnam, Indonesia and India take the opportunity to participate in this entanglement, it will be very difficult for China to exploit marine resources in the East China Sea and South China Sea on a large scale, nor will it be easy to maintain sovereignty and rights over the territorial waters and its Exclusive Economic Zone in the South China Sea.

The Diaoyu Islands issue—Japan claims them as its Senkaku Islands—is one of the most difficult international strategic equations and its resolution is somewhat linked to the resolution of the South China Sea issue.

Present in the United States during 1971–1975, I actively participated in the "Baodiao Movement" (lit., "the campaign to protect the Diaoyu Islands") that was undertaken by overseas Chinese in North America. At the time, I believed in the principle that Chinese territory could not be gifted to or acquired by a third party. I believe that reasoning still stands today.

But I have come to realize that China is no longer the sick man of East Asia who can be dismembered at will, and that although she was bullied in the past, she need not allow emotional grievances to become a burden when considering international strategic issues, for this would reduce her flexibility.

The important starting point for consideration is that China is not, and should not be, the new hegemon of Asia that makes its neighbors tremble. As the world's most populous country and the second largest economy, China must take into account the common destiny of all mankind and take action, or not, as appropriate.

The United States currently controls the Hormuz Strait at the entrance to the Persian Gulf, the Bab-el-Mandeb Strait at the southern end of the Red Sea, and the Malacca Strait north of Singapore, and is the de facto master of the Indian Ocean. India does not wish to and could not change this status quo, and Russia, Japan and China must all acknowledge this fact.

As regards the terrestrial Eurasian heartland, Russia, India, the United States and China each have different requisites and considerations.

Russia, which once ruled this region, is still very strong and will not be willing to cede its advantages to others. In this regard, the majority of the Russian people will support the government's actions. The question is whether in the future Russia's overall economic capacity will be able to support its ventures there. It's recent actions in Ukraine, Kazakhstan and Georgia show that it still harbors territorial and other geopolitical ambitions in this region, but its capability of execution is another matter.

The United States still possesses significant influence in Afghanistan, Kyrgyzstan, Uzbekistan and Pakistan. But it does not share a border with any of the countries in this relatively underdeveloped region, nor does it have historical roots there, and the American public does not recognize the strategic importance of this region. Among the many global hotspots, it is probably not a region for which any US government would expend endless amounts of human and material resources, especially given recent costly failures in Afghanistan.

China is the key source of commodities for the Five Central Asian countries, and a big-time purchaser of their oil and natural gas. There is already an oil pipeline between China and Kazakhstan that doesn't pass through Russia, and several natural gas pipelines are being laid from Turkmenistan to Xinjiang of China via Uzbekistan. Russia has also concluded a long-term agreement to supply oil and natural gas to China and has built a new pipeline completed in 2023. These new facilities represent a marvelous achievement!

Most Chinese have only a vague understanding of "Central Eurasia," being limited to emotive concepts such as "terrorism," "religious extremism" and "East Turkistan" (a separatist movement in Xinjiang).

When it comes to Xinjiang, I cannot disagree that it may cause the Chinese government to perceive it as a thorny issue. The combination of religious extremists and terrorists in Xinjiang has seriously damaged social stability in the past few years, and some of the government's responses in the past 10 years, either at the Autonomous Region or the municipal/county levels, have been portrayed as suppression of human rights and religious freedom.

Despite numerous allegations in the international media the basic fact is that Xinjiang is becoming a more peaceful and prosperous society.

China's current development strategy is to make Kashgar the twenty-first-century "Pearl of the Silk Road," restoring its former glory, so that the oasis city of yesteryear can contribute positively to the economic and cultural development of the entire Central Asian region. The soundness of this policy is irrefutable.

Additionally, the China–Pakistan Economic Corridor, which China will construct with Pakistan between Gwadar Port and Kashgar, will connect the inland city of Kashgar to the Indian Ocean via some 700 kilometers of road and high-speed rail. This corridor will benefit far more than just Pakistan and China's Xinjiang Uygur Autonomous Region; it will also reduce transport costs for a significant portion of China's energy imports, and lessen the risk of depending on energy that currently must pass through the Malacca Strait.

Development of renewable energy sources and the success of fracking technology—extracting oil from shale rock formations—will render the United States much less dependent on the Middle East and Central Asia for energy supply. Which is to say, the Central Eurasia energy and trade network is becoming increasingly essential to China but gradually less important to the Americans.

However, the terrestrial and marine "big chessboard" of the twenty-first century will not be a replay of the "zero-sum" game of the nineteenth and twentieth centuries. China and Russia should cooperate on many fronts in Central Eurasia, but without the need to join forces against the United States; China and Europe should also strive to create a win–win situation for everyone, including coordinating their policies toward Iran, and not hindering Russia's development.

The economic potential of the region badly needs development, and as in China 40 years ago, the bottleneck lies in infrastructure. Roads, railroads, airports, port facilities and telecom network construction all require an injection of funds and technology. The region is so vast, and there is so much infrastructure to be built, that no one has the financial resources to do it alone, and no one has the manpower to do it all.

Compared to several maritime powers today, China's maritime might is still weak, and its ability to project power in the Indian Ocean, which is crucial to the maritime Silk Road, is even less impressive. Therefore, the swagger and bombast flooding the media at present increasingly makes one feel that the Belt & Road Initiative, a profound concept that constitutes a long-term vision, has not yet percolated into the minds of certain China-based "rhetorical patriots."

Those who are concerned about the development of China and world peace best not forget: "Building together, owning together, utilizing together" and "mutual trust, mutual benefit, and mutual respect" should be the guideline for attitudes and behavior along the "New Silk Road."

CHAPTER 10

Frankincense, Oil and Geopolitics

THE 2015 DOHA FORUM

Founded in just 1971, the diminutive nation of Qatar located on the western coast of the Persian Gulf—covering over 11,000 square kilometers and numbering about two million residents—is quite active in the international arena. It established the Al Jazeera TV stations whose English and Arabic channels have both proven influential, hosted the WTO's current Doha Round negotiations, held the 2006 Asian Games, and commissioned I. M. Pei to design the novel and elegant Museum of Islamic Art whose collection comprises a large number of treasures. And that's not to mention Qatar won the right to host the FIFA World Cup in 2022.

The average person is less likely to know that for more than twenty years, the Foreign Ministry of Qatar has hosted the annual Doha Forum, where government dignitaries and academics are invited to discuss the prospects for economic development in the Middle East. In May 2015, this forum was co-organized by the Center for Middle East Development of the University of California at Los Angeles (UCLA), and counted more than two hundred participants. In addition to the opening and closing ceremonies, the forum was divided into six streams carried out simultaneously in four venues for a total of twenty-four sessions, each with its own topic. Based on my observations, each event sparked lively debates on and off the stage.

Due to several events that captured the world's attention just before the forum opening, regardless of the scheduled topic of any given session, there were always speakers who touched on issues associated with these events. By my count, issues of concern to all are listed here in the order of the level of interest they generated in 2015: (1) Negotiations on limiting Iran's nuclear program; (2) The unstable political situation in Arab countries, including the "Islamic State (Daesh)" phenomenon; (3) China's rise, and the establishment of the Asia Infrastructure Investment Bank; and (4) Low oil prices and economic development in the Middle East.

The participants can be divided into: (1) Residents of various countries in the Middle East; (2) Middle Eastern emigrants to Europe, America and Australia; (3) Europeans and Americans without Middle Eastern roots; and (4) Asians from outside the Middle East. The perspective and emphasis of people in these four categories differ. If I must summarize, I'd say that the great majority of attendees currently based in the Middle East—one Israeli excepted—attribute the instability of today's Arab societies to the manner in which the British and French carved up Arab territory after World War I and acted as temporary "trustees" thereof; the favoritism Israel enjoyed at the hands of the West once it was founded; and the unprovoked war against Saddam Hussein's Iraq waged by the United States.

Some of the Middle Eastern émigrés to the West, however, pointed out that there are divergent views and contradictions within Middle Eastern societies themselves. Among the Europeans and Americans, some participants were concerned with progress in human rights and the establishment of civil society, while others focused on the impact of China's rise on the Middle East. Two speakers in particular somewhat overstated their concerns on this account, and were taken to task for this on the spot by Chinese scholars. Scholars from countries such as China, Japan and India unanimously agreed that the relationship between the rest of Asia and the Middle East will be closer in the future, and that China will play an increasingly significant role there.

To summarize the viewpoints expressed by speakers at the forum, I realize that "war and peace" will have connotations for the Middle East that Tolstoy never imagined when he penned his masterpiece: War, long or short, with or without American "boots on the ground," will not easily engender a clear outcome; and peace, be it due to a balance of forces or an extreme imbalance, will not easily endure.

Frankincense and Oil

On the morning of May 12, I delivered my scheduled speech entitled, "Frankincense and Oil."

The climate of the Arabian Peninsula (south of the Euphrates) is extremely hot and arid, and the terrain comprises mainly mountains and desert, but few rivers. Unlike neighboring Mesopotamia, Persia and Egypt, the peninsula did not develop an agricultural civilization. Instead, given its locations at the intersection point of three continents—Asia, Africa and Europe—trade emerged as the primary economic activity.

Frankincense, myrrh and pearls produced in the Arabian Peninsula spread across these continents in very early times. Since the seasonal winds of the Indian Ocean, known as "trade winds," facilitated ocean navigation, two thousand years ago the southern portion of the Arabian Peninsula (modern-day Oman and Yemen) was already in frequent contact with the coasts of western India and eastern Africa. India's spices, precious stones and sophisticated cotton textiles, along with Africa's ivory, rhinoceros horns and gold and other goods were shipped first to Yemen and Oman, and then re-exported to destinations throughout the three continents. But these items were not daily necessities, so trade volume was limited and very sensitive to war and changeable weather conditions.

Actions of the Colonialists

In the nineteenth century, Britain and France became industrialized colonial empires, and large volumes of their manufactured products were distributed throughout Africa and Asia. Demand for raw materials increased among advanced European countries, and therefore trade via the Indian Ocean rose sharply, far exceeding levels of international commerce during the Yuan period (thirteenth–fourteenth centuries) when Eurasian contacts were already unimpeded, as well as the period when the Portuguese and Dutch dominated Indian Ocean trade (sixteenth–eighteenth centuries).

Since the twentieth century, the use of petroleum worldwide has increased considerably and it has gradually become a necessity and a key strategic resource.

Since the period prior to the outbreak of World War I and after World War II, vast reserves of oil and natural gas have been discovered around the Caspian Sea and inside the Strait of Hormuz in what is known as the Persian Gulf, depending on one's preference.

By the way, the Chinese are hardly strangers to the gulf region. Beginning with the envoy Gan Ying (circa 97 CE) in the Han dynasty, and followed by Du Huan during the Tang, Wang Dayuan during the Yuan, and the great Ming dynasty naval explorer Zheng He (c.1418), there have been many official contacts between the Chinese empire and the gulf region.

There are those who judge that God has been especially generous to Muslims, since the vast majority of the inhabitants of the Caspian Sea and Persian Gulf regions are devotees of Islam. But prior to World War II, these areas were largely in the hands of the British and the Russians. The Soviet Union directly ruled the territory around the Caspian Sea—Azerbaijan, Kazakhstan and Turkmenistan—and could thus exploit underground resources there without much ado. In the Persian Gulf area, Britain implemented a calculated two-pronged strategy of provocation and mediation that stimulated constant warring between the various Arab tribes and gulf emirates, all once part of the Ottoman Empire. This culminated in the formation of several regimes that were reliant upon the British.

With the discovery of oil in the gulf in 1930, oil companies based in countries such as Britain, the United States, France and The Netherlands inked many different agreements with gulf countries. Generally speaking, these companies obtained the right to exploit an oil field and market its oil, in exchange for a small percentage of the revenues generated by oil sales. Today, these agreements appear very unequal, because once the host country signed, matters such as whether or not to exploit its own underground resources, how much to exploit, how to determine the selling price, and where the oil should be shipped were entirely determined by the multinationals. Only Iran succeeded early on in winning concessions and "repatriating" exploitation rights.

But the Arab emirs were no fools. They recognized that they simply did not possess the necessary human resources and know-how to exploit these resources, and rather than hoard their underground wealth and live in poverty, they chose to use it to generate money that could be used to recruit or train talent, purchase equipment and lay the groundwork for future exploitation by the Gulf States themselves.

Relations Between Middle Eastern Oil-Producing Countries

After World War II, the establishment of Israel in Palestine, America's strong support for it, and the reality of Israel's repeated battlefield victories over its Arab neighbors constituted a massive blow to Arabs, regardless of their class background. A sense of powerlessness and of being persecuted took root in the Arab psyche.

In 1959, the Organization of Petroleum Exporting Countries (OPEC) was established. This signified the initial attempt of oil-producing/exporting countries to seize the initiative by coordinating with one another. In the 1960s, European national economies took off and their demand for oil increased markedly. The price of oil soared, and producers recorded skyrocketing increases in wealth. In 1973 when Syria and Egypt launched their surprise attack on Israel, oil-producing Arab countries exploited their oil as a weapon, a strategic move that had considerable impact. As a result, the price of crude oil shot up from US$3.5 to US$15 per barrel. Having accumulated piles of "petrodollars," the producers took the opportunity to adjust their relations with oil multinationals in their own favor, seizing the initiative and reclaiming oil field exploration and production rights.

Iran, Iraq and Saudi Arabia are the leading oil exporters in the Middle East. They are also regional powers, but their relations are quite complex. Iran's 1979 revolution led by Shiite clerics initiated an Islamic revival movement that continues to this day. This has pushed the Gulf states to actively promote their Sunni Wahhabi doctrine of faith, but the specter of spreading Shiite influence worries the Sunni rulers of the gulf too. Therefore, while the ruling class on the Arabian Peninsula have mostly been hostile to Israel, they are even more opposed to an Iran that is, ironically, more strongly anti-Israel.

During 1980–1988, Iraq and Iran fought a war that inflicted heavy damage on both parties, but one in which victor and vanquished were not perfectly evident. Having survived the war, Iran's cleric-dominated regime consolidated its rule. Meanwhile, Iraq's Saddam Hussein exercised an even more arbitrary dictatorship. Although Iraq's oil revenues were greatly reduced due to the ravages of war, Saddam continued to maintain armed forces numbering almost one million. On the one hand, he suppressed the Kurds whom he suspected of separatism, and on the other, he mobilized his troops to "recover" sovereignty over Kuwait—hived off from Iraq and designated a British protectorate in 1932—because Kuwait refused to recognize Iraq's right of access to the Persian Gulf. In fact, Kuwait had achieved independence in 1961.

After the collapse of the Soviet Union in 1990, the United States became the unrivaled global superpower. Its first big move was to use high-tech driven, overwhelming force to annihilate the same Iraqi military that America had so heavily armed during Iran–Iraq war of the 1980s. In order to win recognition and financial support from other countries for Operation Desert Storm, the United States recruited allies into a coalition force that numbered thirty-nine countries. Waging the 1990–1991 Persian Gulf War cost more than US$60 billion—more than half the burden shouldered by Kuwait itself—while the remainder was shared among coalition members.

THE WAR IN IRAQ AND OIL PRICES

After years of embargo, sanctions and cat-and-mouse on-site weapons inspections, in 2003 the Americans led several coalition allies in an attack on Iraq, the objective being to "locate and destroy weapons of mass destruction." Saddam was executed and many of his followers were sentenced to prison. Meanwhile, Iraq's armed forces, consisting of hundreds of thousands of soldiers, were disbanded—and many then became high-potential candidates for recruitment, first by a very active Al-Qaeda, and eventually by ISIS.

In coordination with a handful of Iraqi politicians newly returned from exile overseas, the United States took the initiative to introduce a new constitution that effectively handed political power over to the Shiites, who constitute the majority of the Iraqi population, and who had suffered repression under Saddam. Conveniently, this new, pro-American government handled tenders for oil field exploitation and oil production. At the time, the Kurdistan Regional Government enshrined in the new constitution undertook to invite—without the consent of the central government in Baghdad—international tenders for exploration of oil fields within Kurdistan. This move triggered a major northward flow of capital. In fact, the once considerable momentum of ISIS was fueled by the steady income from its control of certain oil fields in northern Iraq not under control of the Kurdish authorities.

Just as the US military prepared to withdraw from Iraq, America's subprime mortgage crisis set off a global financial tsunami. Oil prices soared, at one point reaching US$145 per barrel of crude oil, compared to just US$30–40 prior to the invasion of Iraq. Yet a few years later when the Ukraine crisis erupted, the price plummeted again to the "low price" of US$50 or so. However, since the Russian–Ukraine war began in early 2022, the oil price went into another round of up-and-down while the supply and pricing of natural gas became the major concern.

During the years of high oil prices, breakthroughs in fracking technology—the use of hydraulic fracturing to retrieve vast amounts of natural gas and oil from shale formations—took place, permitting increased production of both on American soil. The United States is self-sufficient in these energy sources, but the low price of oil is a body blow to countries for which it is the primary source of income. They include some the Americans hardly classify as friendly, such as Russia, Iran and Venezuela, but also include allies such as the Gulf States that are blessed with large sovereign funds. Their ability to buy US Treasury Bonds in support of the United States has weakened, and they are increasingly anxious about the outlook for their own futures.

Pax Americana and New Geopolitics

The Roman Empire attained its acme during the rule of Augustus, when he ruled vast swaths of Western Europe, North Africa and West Asia. Troops were stationed throughout the empire and Roman law was implemented, freeing this huge territory of the blight of war for two centuries. Historians termed this "Pax Romana." During the thirteenth–fourteenth centuries, the Mongols ruled a large portion of the Eurasian continent, and many historians employ the Latin phrase "Pax Mongolica" to describe the reign of the Mongol khans despite repeated internecine war among themselves. Naturally enough, many have dubbed America's contemporary global hegemony, "Pax Americana."

By the middle of the twentieth century, the United States accounted for about half of global GDP. In the 1950s, Europe's economy also began to revive, so during the latter half of the twentieth century the volume of cross-Atlantic trade far exceeded that of the Indian Ocean. In the closing years of the twentieth century, however, one Asian country after another underwent rapid development. As predicted by British historian Arnold Toynbee, the twenty-first century will be the Asian century.

By the middle of the twenty-first century, estimates are that in GDP terms the top six national economies will be: China (2nd since 2014),

United States (1st in the past 100 years), India (6th in 2021), Japan (3rd in 2021), Russia (11th in 2021) and Indonesia (15th in 2021). Given that four-and-a-half of these countries are located in Asia, Indian Ocean trade is set to thrive once again, and by then the South China Sea will be the world's most important trade thoroughfare.

Even if China's national GDP ranks first in the world, however, the per capita GDP of the United States, Japan and several European countries will all continue to exceed China's by far; China itself estimates that by the mid-twenty-first century it will rank as a "moderately developed country," which seems to be an appropriate description.

The United States is truly blessed. To the east lies the Atlantic Ocean, to the west the Pacific Ocean, to the south is Mexico, a much weaker country, and to the north is its brotherly neighbor Canada. Thus America's territory is quite safe. Its capacity for innovation and economic dynamism has led the world for more than a century and shows no sign of receding, and its military might invincible.

America's current concerns are the threat of terrorism, whether due to religious extremism or ethnic hatred, and the loss of global dominance to China once it has completed its rise.

The threat of terrorism targeting the United States is grounded in reality. The events of 9/11 aside, for two centuries the American mainland has never experienced attack by an external force. The vast majority of terrorists driven by misguided religious fervor are truly keen to pierce that protective bubble, however.

Given the twin threats facing the world now—climate change and pandemic—American concerns about China are superfluous. These worries are mainly due to the fact that—compared to twenty-five years ago when US dominance was at its height—its advantage has indeed diminished in relative terms. This engenders a sense of unease among many Americans.

In fact, the situation in which the economic development of China and India, both countries with huge populations and ancient civilizations, fell so far behind the West is a historical anomaly. Prior to the mid-eighteenth century, the two countries together accounted for about seventy percent of global GDP. Barring the unforeseen, their return to the ranks of great and powerful nations is to be expected. Nevertheless, this does not signify that either one of the two is capable of assuming the role played by the United States, on account of the latter's geographical advantages, cultural attractiveness and technological innovativeness.

As for China, it does not harbor intentions for global hegemony, nor does it possess the means to achieve it. China has fourteen land neighbors, including four that are nuclear-armed, and it has unresolved border disputes with India. Among its nine maritime neighbors are a strong Japan, and several South China Sea countries with which it has ongoing territorial disputes. To cope with such a complex and difficult geopolitical situation, China must closely observe the overall situation, act calmly and be a good neighbor.

Clearly, only within a peaceful environment can China develop and progress. Any thought to ending "Pax Americana" is a delusion and would harm China itself. Conversely, any concrete military action taken by the United States to contain China's rise would be short-sighted, and a miscalculation of China's depth and resilience.

In my article *The New Silk Road* published in the September 2, 2013 edition of the Chinese-language *Caijing* (Issue 367), I stated that "China is both a landlocked and a maritime country." "Regarding sea routes, especially those involving strategically placed straits, China must deal with other maritime powers in order to ensure the right of safe navigation." "On the ground in Central Asia, China must also cooperate with the relevant countries to achieve a win–win outcome, ensuring a stable and peaceful New Silk Road." Safe maritime navigation, and stability and peace on land, are China's genuine needs. This is consistent with statements by the United States, and does not in any way signify a conflict with America's fundamental interests.

Future Energy Demands

From the perspective of energy demand, China and India will lead the world in the twenty-first century. Over the next twenty years, these two countries will account for sixty percent of new electricity generated globally. Southeast and South Asian countries will also enter a stage of rapid development and require more energy. The state of energy conservation methodology and alternative carbon–neutral energy source development throughout Asia lags behind Europe and the United States, so Asia's dependence on Middle Eastern oil and gas will rise rather than fall. By 2025 or so, China will overtake the European Union as the world's largest importer of oil.

Many African countries possess abundant energy reserves, but Africa is about to enter a period in which per capita energy consumption will rise rapidly. Whether the African continent can become energy self-sufficient is a question no one can answer at the moment. What is certain, however, is that Africa's demand for energy will lag behind Asia's, and Africa will not become an important market for Middle Eastern oil.

By 2035, just three countries—the United States, Russia and Saudi Arabia—will account for thirty-five percent of global supply of liquid energy. OPEC's share will be about forty percent, unaltered from 2013.

However, the future of fossil fuels, liquid or gas, is itself in question. Global warming due to carbon emission is threatening the well-being and even continued existence of human societies. With advanced technology, alternative sources of energy, such as solar, wind and tidal, are gradually maturing. Thus, the patterns of worldwide energy consumption are difficult to estimate.

WHITHER THE MIDDLE EAST?

Seen in this light, and putting aside the issue of how each country will deal with carbon emissions, the Middle East's oil will still have thirsty buyers, mostly Asian countries, for quite some time. But how long this demand will last is far from certain.

More than two millennia ago, the Arabian Peninsula's frankincense was sold mainly to Asia's India and Iran. Eight hundred years ago, the Crusades brought West Europe into close contact with the Middle East. Several Latin Kingdoms established by West European crusaders in Syria and Palestine ruled for more than a century; in 1270, King Louis IX of France died in the midst of a crusade, and the Catholic Church, which considered him a martyr, canonized him as "Saint Louis." During the sixteenth–seventeenth centuries, the Ottoman Empire was the most powerful country in Europe. It twice laid siege to Vienna and almost captured it.

Beginning in the eighteenth century, conflicts between Europe and the Middle East saw the advantage frequently seesaw between the two. At the end of the eighteenth century, however, Napoleon led his troops to invade Egypt, ushering in a period of constant bad blood between Europe and the Middle East. With the onset of the nineteenth century, European scholars began to research Middle Eastern languages, cultures and societies. They founded "oriental studies" in order to help mankind better understand the region's ancient civilization. During the same period, Ottoman Turkey, Egypt and Persia began to study Western Europe's science, technology and laws and institutions, as they undertook their trek toward modernization.

Ever since oil became the principal product of many Middle Eastern countries, the United States and EU member countries have become exploiters and purchasers of that oil, as well as investors in, and management consultants and arms suppliers to the Middle East. And yet, the citizens of each Middle Eastern country—as displayed at the Doha Forum mentioned above—suffer from a love–hate complex with these same Americans and Europeans. They don't deny that they are well acquainted with these Westerners, but when it comes to Asian buyers, particularly those in East Asia, they are plainly unfamiliar.

Based on the estimates cited above, the Middle East oil-producing countries needn't worry about sufficient purchasers for their goods in the near future, but they may not be knowledgeable about the histories, cultures or societies of their new customers.

For Asian countries, the Middle East is the region where it is most convenient to source the energy they need. But given the region's volatility and unstable output, Asian buyers cannot be sure that supply can be guaranteed. And more importantly, will transport of the oil be safe?

Unquestionably, problem-free navigation in the Indian Ocean, especially in the Strait of Hormuz and the Strait of Malacca, and safe navigation in the South China Sea, are extremely important as the volume of oil transported in these waterways is set to increase substantially in the near future.

During the Iran—Iraq War, for example, oil transport was affected by military operations: A 500,000-ton supertanker owned by Chinese Hong Kong's Orient Overseas Container Line (OOCL) was bombed and sunk by the Iraqi Air Force. In the future when the Indian Ocean becomes the world's most important site for maritime trade, the importance of safety at sea will increase greatly; given the conflicting interests of the major global powers, it's predictable that the moves they make will exacerbate the drama that is to be played out in the Middle East and Indian Ocean.

For the peoples of both oil importing and exporting countries, peace in the Indian Ocean would be the greatest blessing they can pray for from their respective divinity, be it Allah, God, Brahma, Buddha, the Jade Emperor or the Heavens!

CHAPTER 11

China and Pakistan: A Historical View

China and Pakistan have been and will forever be close neighbors.

The two countries have been "Friends in Deed" for the past 65 years and will continue to be for many more.

As China–Pakistan celebrate their 65 years of neighborly relations, I shall attempt to recall some historical "characters" who have been trendsetters and guiding lights for the modern-day populations of China and Pakistan.

To look back at what these figures did is to light the chandeliers in our memory palace and the lighting will be a source of inspiration for us all.

Let me start with two anecdotes. Some twenty years ago, when I was Dean of Engineering at China's Hong Kong University of Science and Technology, I recruited from the United States a young scholar in Computer Science. He is of Pakistani origin and introduced me to the music of Nusrat Fateh Ali Khan whose amazing voice was at once stimulating and mesmerizing to me. I also enjoyed listening to Pakistani popular songs some of which seemed to have been derived from Sufi music.

Some 15 years ago, my computer scientist friend brought back from Pakistan a hard-bound copy of the Holy Quran. It is an Arabic-Chinese bilingual version, translated by Professor Ma Jian of Peking University and published in Rawalpindi. It now sits in my own library.

The Indus Valley Figurines: Who Are We?

As if they wanted to play games with us, the early residents of the Indus River Valley who created a brilliant civilization 5,000 years ago and were sophisticated in many respects have left no clues as to who they were, where they came from and with whom they had the most contact. Also, as if to underscore the point that the human race is from but one origin, the early clay figurines discovered in the Indus River Valley show a remarkable similarity to those found at other Neolithic sites on the Eurasian continent.

A reasonable guess is that these early residents of the Indus River Valley were at least in contact with the Sumerians and Akkadians in Mesopotamia. I was pleasantly surprised when I first noticed that similar cylindrical seals were used in both civilizations about 4,500 years ago.

While the descendants of Mesopotamians in the early bronze-age are well documented, the identity of the residents in Mohenjo Daro, Harappa and other sites remains unknown. In Mohenjo Daro, the well laid-out "city" of brick-houses along with community baths typified an advanced agricultural society; indeed, they gave the world cotton and probably the technique of weaving. The makers of such articles as a 5,000-year-old pottery piece with a mystic bird painted on it remain unidentified. A well-proportioned male torso cast in bronze is also an enigma for scholars. Indeed, a great deal more needs to be learned about this vanished ancient civilization.

Whereas the legitimate proprietors of these sites and artifacts live in Pakistan today, we are all indebted to the creators of the marvelous civilization of the Indus River Valley. That we belong to the community of shared destiny for all mankind is given proof by these mysterious "characters."

The Gandhara Statues: We Belong to Everyone

Following the expeditions of Alexander the Great, the Greco-Bactrians in Taxila made a town in the Hellenistic style which was marveled by the Scythians and Parthians who ruled this area subsequently.

Kushan Empire was later founded by Yuezhi people who migrated to this area from present-day China about 200 BCE; it later expanded to the Ganges Plain to the east and Tianshan Mountains to the north during the reign of King Kanishka. Later, Buddhists in Gandhara (near Peshawar today) made statues of Buddha and Bodhisattvas in the Greek tradition using images of Apollo and Athena as the basic design, but always with a tint of local color added. The Gandhara Buddhist art gained admiration from believers in Mahayana Buddhism and spread in China, then to South Korea, Japan and Vietnam.

The Chinese monk Fa Xian saw in the early fifth century hundreds of stupas and monasteries near Peshawar. However, Xuan Zang (玄 奘) in the seventh century lamented the destruction of Buddhist temples when he passed through this area. It was probably the Hephthalites (also known as White Huns) who reduced the Buddhist structures to rubbles.

Nevertheless, in the annals of religious art, Gandhara ranks very high to this day. The name Gandhara art reflects the place of its origin, but its sphere of intellectual influence has encompassed Central Asia, East Asia, Southeast Asia and beyond. Who can say that this is not an excellent example of shared heritage and destiny of different peoples?

CHENG HE AND CHEN CHENG: WE ARE FRIENDS FROM AFAR

Most people know that Admiral Zheng He was an outstanding navigator, effective military commander and accomplished diplomat. But few are aware that he was a Muslim with family lines directly traceable to Central Asia. Moreover, among his lieutenants, several were Chinese Muslims of Perso-Arabic descent, therefore conversant in the Persian and Arabic languages. He died on his 7th and last voyage and was given an Islamic burial in the sea.

Cheng He's seven voyages ranged in time from 1405 to 1433; covering south India, the Persian Gulf, Yemen, Somalia and Kenya.

While these voyages were well recorded, the real purpose of his missions was not spelled out in any of the documents in the palace archive of Ming Dynasty. I have posited that he was probably instructed by Emperor Yongle to establish a dependable communication route to the Timurids who were then in a dominant position in Central and West Asia, also able to influence the Mongol forces still struggling with the newly established Ming Dynasty. Due to intermittent military actions by the Ming and the Mongols, the land routes from the interior of China to Central Asia were often blocked and unreliable at best. So Cheng He came by sea to the Timurid territories to seek friendship.

In the same era, two Ming Chinese emissaries, Guo Ji and Chen Cheng, made their way overland from Beijing to Central Asia on a number of occasions.

Guo Ji and his colleagues went to Samarkand first in 1387 during Timur's ascendency, but were detained for nearly 20 years until Timur's death. Soon after his return to China, Guo Ji was sent to Central Asia again in 1407, both to assert Ming's interest in Central Asia and to make certain that the internecine war of succession among Timur's offspring would not cause the Silk Road to be closed.

The more accomplished diplomat was Chen Cheng, who had learned Mongolian and Tibetan languages and worked for many years near the Oirat Mongols and the East Chagatai Khanate. He led Ming delegations to Central Asia three times, in 1413, 1416 and 1418. Chen Cheng's mission was probably meant to convince Timur's successors that the Great Ming of China was so affluent and powerful that it would be futile to invade China as Timur tried to do just before his death. On the contrary, the new Timurid leadership should be shown that it would be beneficial for them to be friends with Ming. Chen Cheng visited Herat, capital of the Timurids in 1414. He was well received by Timur's son Shah Rukh who was impressed by Chen Cheng's knowledge and arguments and decided to send a large delegation to Beijing, presenting to Emperor Yongle his father's favorite war horse, as a symbolic recognition of China's suzerainty.

At the beginning of the sixteenth century, the Timurids fortune waned and were driven out of Central Asia by the Uzbeks, nomadic Mongols from the Kazakh steppes and descendants of Batu, grandson of Genghis Khan. The last Timurid ruler, Zahir-ud-Din Babur, had to go into exile in Fergana and Afghanistan. This, of course, had a great deal to do with the history of Moghul India, hence the modern-day Pakistan.

Babur and Akbar: We Bestow Order and Harmony

One of the most talented and captivating personalities in Central Asia in the fifteenth–sixteenth century was Babur, founder of the Moghul Empire. I visited Lahore some years ago and marveled at his good fortune in settling in Lahore after a series of political and military setbacks. While I cannot read his autobiography *Baburnama* written in his Turki (or Chagatai) language, I bought an English copy of Tabaqat-i-Baburi, his biography written by Zain Khan. I learned much wisdom in this book.

Babur, the "Renaissance Prince" in the European parlance, was not aware that the Europeans had rounded the Cape of Good Hope and reached India just before he set out from Lahore to defeat the various armies in India. One reason for Babur's military victories was the use of guns. Here history shows a number of ironies: First, the Turki- and Persian-speaking Babur was culturally not Mongol even though his mother had direct lineage to Genghis Khan; second, he suffered at the hands of his distant cousins from the steppes who were Mongols and called themselves Uzbeks; third, Babur benefited from the gunpowder that the Mongols had earlier introduced to Central Asia; fourthly, the empire that Babur founded on the Indian subcontinent was named Moghul, meaning Mongol in Persian.

Akbar, grandson of Babur and the greatest of the Moghul emperors, created a huge empire probably unforeseen by his grandfather. He took seriously his responsibility of ruling a large and diverse population in India, so he often had Muslim ulema as well as Sufis in his court to discuss religion and philosophy along with Hindu, Christian and Zoroastrian scholars. While his attempts to harmonize Islam, Hinduism, Christianity and Zoroastrianism were not put into full practice, his open-mindedness and desire for social harmony should be a source of inspiration for any country with a diverse population. Indeed, Akbar would have been happy with the phrase "community of shared destiny of all mankind."

Karakoram Mountains: We Are Not Your Barriers

The mountains that lie west of the Himalayas are forbidding and seemingly insurmountable. It is said that the Karakoram is India's natural "Great Wall." But anyone who has cast an eye on the breath-taking Karakoram Highway will know that nature never intended to separate determined peoples on both sides of these glacier-dotted mountains.

The determination of the Pakistani and Chinese governments was a primary reason for the completion of this highway. The heroism and sacrifices of the engineers and construction workers over a 20-year period will forever be remembered. More than 500 of them gave their lives to this 1,200 km highway, the highest cross-border road in the world. These heroes, may their souls rest in eternal peace, serve to remind us that the bonds between China and Pakistan are indeed strong.

THE CHINA–PAKISTAN ECONOMIC CORRIDOR: WE BRING PROSPERITY

When I first visited Kashgar in the summer of 1987, I met in the hotel dining room a group of Pakistani businessmen who had just come over to China, in several stages, along the yet to be inaugurated Karakoram Highway. When I asked how long the trip took, a middle-aged man from Karachi replied: "Too long!"

With China's One-Belt-One-Road initiative and the China–Pakistan Economic Corridor, the group of businessmen I met in Kashgar would have been pleased with the idea of high-speed trains crossing the Chinese–Pakistan border. So will be tens of thousands of businesspeople, scholars and tourists in the future.

The China–Pakistan Economic Corridor, in addition to attracting various industries to the new towns to be built along it, will also have a humanistic dimension to it. The small children who live along the Corridor will have their eyes opened to the outside world, their education opportunities enhanced and their career choices broadened. It is these future citizens, both Chinese and Pakistani, who will build a community of common destiny and usher in a new era of China–Pakistan relationship.

CHAPTER 12

Tempest in Eurasia: Russia, Ukraine and Georgia

Prelude to the Russo-Ukrainian War

In recent years, Ukraine's political scene and the ongoing test of strength between foreign heavyweights have ranked as top news items in terms of their implications for global strategy. Since 2019, even US domestic politics have been impacted, and after Russia's invasion of Ukraine in 2022, war and peace in the Dnieper River basin have become the focus of international attention.

In February 2014, Ukraine's president Yanukovych suddenly fled to Russia after a series of political moves by his opponents and what he claimed to be gunshots at him. He was then voted out of office by the national parliament, and a pro-Western acting president and interim government took power. In March, the Russian Federation annexed Crimea after a hastily arranged and disputed referendum showed that 98 percent of Crimean voters wished to leave Ukraine and join Russia. In early April, pro-Russian groups in Ukraine's two easternmost oblasts, Donetsk and Luhansk, established militias and demanded independence or the right to join Russia.

Ukraine then elected Petro Poroshenko, a pro-Western businessman and politician, as President in late May 2014 and a partial civil war ensued. In mid-June, Russia ceased national gas exports to Ukraine.

At the end of June, the EU signed a partnership agreement with three former Soviet republics—Ukraine, Georgia and Moldova—extending "zero import tariff" treatment to them. In July, Ukraine's pro-Western government decided to dispatch troops against armed strongholds in eastern Ukraine. Efforts by France, Germany and Russia to negotiate a cease-fire proved fruitless. The West demanded that Russia immediately rein in the armed Ukrainian rebels, or else they would strengthen sanctions against Russia.

When Russia struck back in March 2014 during the Ukraine crisis, its policy decision was clear and its execution resolute. As part of his "rapid reaction force" deployment, Putin delivered a televised speech during which he spoke passionately, citing historical details and portraying the nation's current standing in a way capable of galvanizing Russian nationalist sentiments. The basis for these feelings is the hegemony of northern Eurasia achieved by the Russians, little by little, over several centuries. But this nationalism and its interpretation of recent history are not convincing either to the mainstream population in Ukraine or to the non-Russian peoples within the borders of the present-day Russian Federation.

Subsequently, a full civil war between pro-Russia militias and Ukrainian government forces broke out in Donbas (abbreviation for Donetsk Coal Basin in easternmost Ukraine) and has continued for over 8 years.

Surrounded by the Black Sea and the Sea of Azov, the Crimean Peninsula, with its warm-water harbor Sevastopol, holds a commanding position in the Black Sea region. During the sixth–tenth centuries, Kipchak Turkic tribes continued to settle there and became Crimea's most populous indigenous people. After Mongol's mid-thirteenth-century conquest of much of Eastern Europe, Crimea was ruled by Mongol-Turkic clans, known as Crimean Tatars—similar to but different from the more numerous Volga Tatars—for over 400 years.

In the late eighteenth century, the Russian Empire defeated the Crimean Khanate, at the time a dependency of the Ottoman Empire, and annexed Crimea. Ethnic Russians, Ukrainians and others quickly poured in. After the October Revolution in 1917, Crimea became a part of the Russian Socialist Republic.

During WWII, Stalin ordered the massive deportation of Crimean Tatars to Central Asia. In 1954, Khrushchev, perhaps attempting to redress what Stalin did to the Crimean Tatars, ordered that Crimea be transferred from Russia to Ukraine. Since then, ethnic Russians have constituted roughly 70 percent of the Crimean population, with Ukrainians, Crimean Tatars and other ethnicities comprising the remainder.

12 TEMPEST IN EURASIA: RUSSIA, UKRAINE AND GEORGIA

Developments in the state of affairs of Ukraine and Georgia are part and parcel of the major powers' strategic global configuration, a configuration that is inseparable from Eurasian history and reality on the ground. The United States seeks to use its naval power to restrict and dominate land-based forces; the EU seeks to extend its influence eastward to a region that the earlier British geopolitical scholar, Halford Mackinder, termed the "heartland of the World Island," which coincides with areas the ancient Silk Road passed through, i.e., the Ukrainian-Russian Steppe and Southern Caucasus. Meanwhile, China is promoting the emergence of a "Silk Road Economic Belt" and constructing a high-speed railway to replace the camel caravans of yore.

Throughout the eventful situation in recent years, the West staunchly supported the Ukrainian government while condemning Russia and slapping it with numerous sanctions. For its part, Russia declared that it was obligated to protect ethnic Russians in Ukraine and elsewhere, and Putin repeatedly trumpeted what can be called Tsarist Russian nationalism.

Meanwhile, as a side show, a near farce took place in the interlude.

Mikheil Saakashvili, who ascended to the presidency after he successfully led the "Rose Revolution" in Georgia, lost popular support shortly afterward and was prosecuted for corruption and abuse of power. He chose exile in Ukraine, obtained Ukrainian citizenship, and was appointed by his old friend President Poroshenko to be governor of Odesa Oblast which administers the most important Ukrainian seaport. Within two years, Saakashvili had a falling out with his old buddy Poroshenko. This time the Georgian left to take up residency in... Poland. Then in 2019, just before the Ukrainian presidential election, Saakashvili led a small contingent of his followers to sneak into Ukraine, and positioned himself as a potential candidate for the presidency, thereby setting the stage for yet another round of drama.

In the end, after many roadshows and media headlines, Volodymyr Zelenskyy, a lawyer-actor who once played the role of Ukrainian president on TV, was elected President in May 2019.

SHARED ROOTS

Actually, Ukrainians and Russians share the same origins. During Russia's period of expansion (1650–1900), many Ukrainians participated and acquitted themselves gloriously. One could compare this to the role many Scots played in the expansion of the British Empire. However, ethnic, linguistic and historical differences between the Russians and Ukrainians are less marked than those that distinguish the Scottish from the English.

The northern shore of the Black Sea—home to the steppes that traverse the northwest part of the Eurasian continent, i.e., modern-day Ukraine—is the birthplace of the world's Indo-European languages.

About 6,000 years ago, tribes speaking a "proto-Indo-European" tongue resided there, though their traces have since disappeared. Some 5,000–3,000 years before our era, they migrated outward in three waves, eventually spreading throughout what are today Europe, Iran, Afghanistan, Pakistan and well over half of India.

The earliest settlers in the Tarim Basin in today's Xinjiang and those who lived a nomadic existence in the Hexi Corridor in Gansu, the Yuezhi, migrated there from Ukraine via the Eurasian Steppe some 4,000 years ago. Their "Tocharian language," as it is labeled by some linguists, shares a similar grammar and some vocabulary with the language of the Hittites who ruled Asia Minor 4,000–3,500 years ago, as well as the Celtic languages of what are now Ireland, Wales and Scotland.

It was also about 6,000 years ago that the Indo-Aryans on the Ukrainian Steppe first tamed the horse, making cavalry the fiercest mobile fighting force prior to the tank. Mastery of horses stimulated communications on the Eurasian continent, and also endowed steppe nomads with a military advantage. In the first half of the thirteenth century, the Mongols exploited this superiority to conquer the Slavs who lived on the northern shores of the Black Sea, ruling them for the next 250 years.

While the Slavs do speak an Indo-European tongue, it is not a direct descendent of those spoken by "proto-Indo-European" tribes. In fact, during the era of the Greek city-states, the northern shores of the Black Sea served as Athens' granary; the geographically prominent Crimea was long ruled by the Greeks.

Beginning with the sixth century, the forests and plains of East Europe were inhabited by Eastern Slavs who occasionally came into contact with the Norman Vikings of the Baltic Sea region. In the ninth century, a group of Vikings followed the Dnieper River southward, first ruling the Eastern Slavs there and then gradually integrating with them. In what is today Kyiv, the capital of Ukraine, they established a feudal principality known as "Kievan Rus."

In the late tenth century, the rulers of Kievan Rus commanded their subjects to convert to the Greek Orthodox faith. This meant they also adopted the Cyrillic Alphabet that Greek missionaries had created for

Slavic languages. The establishment of the principality, conversion to Greek Orthodoxy, and use of the new script all marked the commencement of the recorded history of the Slavs. This is the foundation of a shared civilization and national origins of today's Russians, Ukrainians and Belarusians.

Turkic, Norman, Slavic and Mongolian Peoples

From the late sixth century onwards, Turkic tribes migrated westward from the Mongolian Plateau in large numbers. In the eighth century, some of these tribes scattered among the Ural Mountains, the Volga River and along the northern shore of the Caspian Sea. Among them, an alliance of Khazar tribes grew quite strong in the ninth–tenth centuries. Its turf extended to the entire northern shore of the Black Sea—modern-day Ukraine. Unlike other Turkic speakers, the Khazar did not become followers of Islam or Christianity. They instead chose Judaism, and functioned as a buffer between the Arab and Byzantine Empires.

During this period, the Norman Vikings proceeded south from the Baltic Sea and entered the region north of the Black Sea. In order to counter the power of the Khazar, they joined with the Slavs to establish the Kievan Rus principality, and eventually merged with them.

The Khazar went into decline in the twelfth century, but another horde of Mongols on horses came from the east in the thirteenth century. They quickly conquered Kievan Rus and other Slavic alliances. The commander of this great army was Batu Khan, grandson of Genghis Khan. He proceeded west along the Eurasian Steppe, conquering and incorporating the Turkic-speaking Kipchak.

In the years before and after 1240, his troops plundered Kyiv, Moscow, Vladimir and other Slavic cities, and destroyed Kievan Rus. This marked the start of separate paths of development for the Ukrainians, Russians and Belarusians.

The Grand Principality of Moscow and the Kipchak, Crimean and Kazan Khanates

In 1241, Batu had led his conquering troops as far West as the Danube River Basin, and was closing in on the Adriatic Sea. Just then the Great Khan Ögedei passed away, and Batu decided to lead his troops back east in order to compete for the position of the Great Khan. But on his way he learned that his cousin Güyük had already succeeded Ögedei, so Batu built his capital at Saray on the lower Volga, and established the Kipchak Khanate, commonly known in Europe as the "Golden Horde" that ruled much of Eastern Europe and what is now Kazakhstan.

In the subsequent three centuries, the Kipchak Khanate and other Mongol Khanates that split from the Kipchak Khanate all promoted east–west interaction across the Eurasian Steppe. This fostered north–south communications between the northern steppe and Asia Minor, the Caucasus, Persia and agricultural regions in Central Asia, stimulating more frequent trade and cultural interaction throughout Eurasia. During this period, the Mongols gradually merged with the Islamized Turkic tribes located north of the Black Sea and the Caspian Sea, evolving into what the Slavs collectively label "Tatars."

In the middle of the fifteenth century, a Tatar clan founded the Crimean Khanate, elevating an 11th-generation grandson of Genghis Khan as its khan. Another group of Tatars led by a 10th-generation grandson of Genghis Khan, founded the Kazan Khanate in the middle reaches of the Volga River. At that time, the Grand Principality of Moscow founded by Russians after the destruction of Kievan Rus was still a vassal of the Kipchak Khanate. During the fifteenth–sixteenth centuries, the Crimean and Kazan Khanates and the Grand Duchy of Moscow were all granted titles of nobility by the Kipchak Khanate. They paid tribute to it, and regularly intermarried with it. Later, the Grand Principality/Duchy of Moscow grew stronger and named itself the "Tsardom of Russia." In its turn, it also conferred titles upon Tatar princes and other high nobles, and often invited Tatar nobles to serve in the Moscow palace.

During the fifteenth–eighteenth centuries, the Crimean Khanate was an important force in Eastern Europe. It often invaded and looted regions inhabited by Slavs, particularly to take slaves for sale to the great power of the era, the Ottoman Empire. At the time Crimea was the slave trade center of Europe; because the Qur'an prohibits enslaving Muslims, there was strong demand for Christian slaves among Muslims across the Middle East.

The Ottoman dominion extended over the Crimean Khanate, the Caucasus, and most of the territory around the Black Sea during the seventeenth–nineteenth centuries. Russia also grew strong during this same period. It vanquished many regions, and continually expanded to the east and west. During its expansion, Russia established Cossack

Corps—comprised mainly of Ukrainians and Poles—and permitted them to establish autonomous local governments in newly conquered territory.

The coat of arms of the Tsardom of Russia (later changed to Imperial Russia) was a double-headed eagle; one looking eastward, the other westward, symbolizing that Russia faces the entire Eurasian continent. Significantly, the term "tsar" comes from the Roman Empire's title, "Caesar," for after the Ottomans destroyed the Byzantine Empire in 1453, Russia claimed for itself the role of the latter's successor. It is evident that even before it became truly powerful, Russia already possessed great ambition and exploited it to inspire its subjects.

Proud but Isolated Georgia

Like Ukraine, Georgia has also been designated as a newfound "partner" by the EU. This country covers 70,000 square meters and numbers just five million inhabitants. Georgian does not belong to the Indo-European family of languages. The Georgians are indigenous to the Caucasus, unrelated to any of the peoples mentioned previously, and they adopted Christianity and created their own script at least five hundred years before the Slavs. These facts have combined to endow these people with a strong sense of pride.

The bulk of Georgia's territory lies to the south of the Greater Caucasus Mountains. To the north are autonomous republics in the Russian Federation, including those which have seen frequent terrorist incidents in recent years: Ingushetia, Chechnya and Dagestan.

I have traveled in Georgia, entering southern Georgia via a land route from Armenia and exiting from the east for Azerbaijan. The Georgian border guards were neatly groomed, courteous and did things by the book. Border guards in Eastern Europe and Western Asia are no match when it comes to the latter; perhaps Georgia's level of civility is one reason why the EU selected it for partnership.

Tbilisi, Georgia's capital, is located on both sides of the Mtkvari River valley. The river still flows through the city founded 1,500 years ago, and the mountains still tower over it on either side, but Tbilisi has been ravaged by war 29 times! Arabs, Turks, Mongols, Persians and Russians have all taken turns pillaging and burning it. Yet each time the city was rebuilt.

The Tbilisi I encountered is a European-style city, and almost all the buildings were newly constructed or rebuilt over the last two centuries.

The presidential palace, the new bridge spanning the Mtkvari, and the Sheraton Hotel radiate a dynamic, twenty-first-century ambience. Strolling through the Old City reconstructed after the eighteenth century, I found displayed in antique stores historical reminders that do not require a written explanation: Persian pen cases, Ottoman jewelry, and Russian dolls. These common items evoked for me the unique history of the city, a history for the most part engendered by the city's location rather than actions taken by the Georgians themselves.

But there have been exceptions. At the end of the eighteenth century, in order to contend with pressure from both the Persians and Ottomans, the Georgian king sought protection from the Russians. That was the equivalent of opening the door to a wolf, and henceforth Georgia figured upon Imperial Russia's map. Even the Georgian church—with a history five hundred years longer—ended up in the embrace of the Russian Orthodox Church.

In 2003, thirteen years after independence from the Soviet Union, US-educated Mikheil Saakashvili led a crowd of citizens, roses in their hands, to storm government buildings and seize power. Then-president and former Soviet Minister of Foreign Affairs Eduard Shevardnadze was forced to vacate his post, and Saakashvili—who took a totally pro-Western line—became president. This was Georgia's famous "Rose Revolution."

On the opening day of the 2008 Beijing Olympics, Saakashvili ordered the army to attack South Ossetia, which had until then enjoyed de facto autonomy, and this incurred the wrath of the Russians; the Russian army easily defeated the Georgians as the West looked on. Today, only Russia and a handful of other countries recognize the sovereignty of South Ossetia and another Georgian autonomous region, Abkhazia.

Without question, Georgia's most famous personality is Joseph Stalin. I once visited the Stalin Museum located in Gori where he grew up. The museum is a stately three-story building right next to the little house where Stalin came into the world. Many historical photos and items are on display. Among them, the most famous is one that captures Lenin flanked by Stalin on the left and Trotsky on the right. Lenin was a Russian reportedly of part Tatar descent; Stalin was Georgian, while Trotsky was Jewish. This photo bears witness to the fact that the Soviet Revolution was erected on the foundations of multi-ethnic Imperial Russia.

Outside the museum stood a statue of Stalin on a high pedestal. I took two photos in front of the statue at 17:00 on June 22, 2010. Just three days later at 03:00, the statue was quietly removed, according to a Reuters' report.

The son of a cobbler, Stalin was a former seminary student and professional revolutionary who once ruled the Soviet Union and headed the international communist movement for almost thirty years. During World War II, Stalin led the Soviet Union's "Great Patriotic War." Because of his leadership during the war, his memory is still cherished by many Russians. His rejection of Hitler's proposal to hand over a German marshal captured by the Soviets, in exchange for a Soviet captain, Stalin's own son, remains one of the legends that made him famous. He employed extremely brutal methods to purge dissidents, however, and for this he has been spurned by history.

Indeed, many of Stalin's lesser-known decisions continue to impact the lives of tens of millions of people even in our day.

For example, Stalin was the Soviet Union's first Commissar for Nationality Affairs. Born and raised in the Caucasus with its complex relations between different peoples, he was naturally familiar with ethnic issues in the Soviet Union. Although he agreed with Lenin's basic policy that ethnic minorities should enjoy autonomy in regions where they were concentrated, in order to "divide and rule," he intentionally drew boundaries that grouped several different ethnicities. Today, the root of ethnic conflicts in several Central Asian countries can be traced back to Stalin's approach, even clashes in twenty-first-century Georgia and Ukraine.

UKRAINE'S DESTINY

Now let's return to Ukraine. Due to its location and other factors, in the late fifteenth century while Moscow was gaining in strength, Ukraine was ruled by Roman Catholic countries such as Lithuania and Poland. As a result many Ukrainians converted to Roman Catholicism. This is the origin of the division of Ukraine into eastern and western regions, a split with a history of some five centuries.

After 1650, the Ukrainians allied with Russia in order to resist the Polish. Soon thereafter, Ukraine was divided between Russia and Poland, with the eastern portion incorporated into Tsarist Russia, commencing its Russification. As Russia continued to expand, virtually all of Ukraine eventually came under Russian control, except a small area ruled by Austria. Long-term Russification gradually assimilated eastern Ukraine, but since most of Ukraine's population in the west was influenced by Poland,

Austria and also by the Roman Catholic Church, it remained dissatisfied with Russian rule.

After the October Revolution in Russia, once again Ukraine was carved up: western Ukraine went to Poland while the east reverted to Russia. When the Soviet Union was inaugurated, Ukraine, again with adjustments in territory and population, was among the first republics to join, although many Ukrainians were not pleased with the new arrangement. During World War II when the Nazis invaded Ukraine, many western Ukrainians treated the Germans as liberators and welcomed the invaders with open arms.

Following World War II, the two camps led by the United States and the Soviet Union maintained the Cold War for 45 years. The Americans implemented a policy of encirclement and containment against the Soviet Union, and supported opponents living within its borders. This approach has been used throughout human history, and is the easiest way for domestic opponents to gain support from abroad. Throughout the Cold War, many anticommunist Ukrainians in the West publicized their opposition to the Soviet Union, and the United States continuously financed a Ukrainian government-in-exile.

After the dissolution of the Soviet Union, Russia descended into difficulties that could not easily be remedied. The Warsaw Pact disbanded, and several original members—including East Germany, Czechoslovakia and Poland—immediately made plans to join NATO, so NATO loomed at Russia's door. Of the 15 former Soviet republics, the three Baltic countries were originally considered part of the West. But now, even Ukraine, the second biggest, desired EU membership and wished to join NATO. Although there were no public statements by either the United States or Russia just before or after the demise of the Soviet Union, the Russians have claimed, with confirmation by some participants at the time, that the United States had promised not to increase the number of member states of NATO.

During the Yeltsin years, the president was totally unable to cope with these issues as he drowned his troubles in liquor. This gave Ukraine some time in which it could maneuver freely. After Putin came to power, however, Russian power was somewhat restored, and he excelled at managing and even exploiting international political developments. But even so, Russia came up with the short end of the stick on two occasions: Georgia's "Rose Revolution" in 2003 and Ukraine's "Orange Revolution" in 2004.

The internal strife in Ukraine that commenced in autumn 2014 is reflection of a very significant strategic game on the global stage. Regarding the "Ukraine question" this time around, Russia appears determined not to come out as the loser. Ukraine is thus destined to become the venue for a tug-of-war between the EU and Russia, and may well become the board for a global chess-game involving the strategies of several heavyweights.

Pawns in a Strategic Game: Ukraine and Georgia

The United States is the world's most powerful country. Its emblem is an American bald eagle with one claw clutching an olive branch and the other claw, a bundle of arrows. Accordingly, the United States has historically pursued a foreign policy that combines soft and hard power, and seeks solutions that are both just and beneficial to its national interest.

It is in the ancient homeland of the Indo-European languages—Ukraine, and the home of Caucasians, Georgia—that Russia's double-headed eagle and the American bald eagle have rather different strategic thinking and master plans.

Russia's current strategic goal is to integrate its Soviet-era Asian hinterland with the European frontier, attract European capital and talent with the level of modernization it has already achieved, and exploit its overall national power to meet the challenges posed by the United States, EU or other countries. Russia definitely does not want to see Ukraine and Georgia become outposts of NATO and the EU at its frontier, and is even less keen to see control of its network of Ukraine-based, EU-bound oil and natural gas pipelines under threat.

Russia cannot afford failure at its front door. One fortuitous solution for Russia would be a Ukraine where its eastern and western regions take their own paths. Meanwhile, Russia's Georgian strategy is to continue to suppress the latter, ensuring it cannot effect a real connection with EU.

The US global strategy is rather different. It seeks to use its geographical advantage of facing both the Pacific and the Atlantic, in conjunction with its current overall national strength, to dominate future trade and economic development on both sides of the Atlantic as well as the Pacific, and thereby prevent any Eurasian player from emerging to challenge its sea-based hegemony over the Eurasian landmass. If problems frequently erupt in Russia's neighborhood, this is in line with America's strategic interests.

The "Silk Road Economic Belt" concept advocated by China, however, is not in sync with America's global strategy. Does this mean that China and Russia will join forces to deal with the United States (and the EU)? I don't foresee such a turn of events, because the pair lack mutual trust and overlapping interests.

Freedom, democracy and human rights are values long espoused by the United States. Since a majority of the residents of western Ukraine are willing to damage Ukraine–Russia relations in their pursuit, the Americans will no doubt wholeheartedly support them.

As long as a considerable number of Ukrainians are keen to join the EU, the United States and EU will naturally welcome their entry. If long-term domestic friction causes Ukraine's factories to shut down, farmland to lay barren and energy supplies to fall short, all of this may give Germany a headache—but it won't unduly bother the Americans and the British who are not even members of EU.

If Ukraine's leaders cannot stabilize society and eliminate the barriers between the country's east and west, then Ukrainians—regardless of their location—cannot emerge as winners. As for the Caucasus to the east of the Black Sea, if the Georgian leaders prove incapable of overcoming the destiny assigned to them by their geography, then the Georgians may remain proud, but inevitably isolated too.

Tough but Vulnerable

The Soviet Union had many weak points, the key one being its inability to fully integrate the territories and many peoples that came with their conquest; and secondly, the inefficiency of the *nomenklatura* and its monopolization of power. In 1985, just as Mikhail Gorbachev initiated *perestroika*—the radical restructuring of the Soviet economic and political systems—I visited the Soviet Union and experienced first-hand the mediocrity and ineptness of the bureaucracy.

Not long after, I came across an article by an American scholar predicting that the Soviet Union would break up because of discontent of the peoples of the Baltic Sea, Caucasus and Central Asia. At the time it struck me as wishful thinking, but a few years later history provided its own answer.

After the Soviet Union's implosion, ethnic conflicts markedly diminished. But Russia, now a federation, still suffers from ethnic problems. The states of Dagestan, Chechnya and Ingushetia in North Caucasus are obvious cases in point. Since Putin took power, ethnic conflicts have not been handled well. No real progress has been made in reducing the bureaucracy's inefficiency or loosening its stranglehold on power.

In addition, as an open society with free flow of information now, a considerable number of Russian citizens aspire to the Western lifestyle and social system, and welcome Russia's "Europeanization." In fact, this mindset began to insinuate itself in society back during Peter the Great's reign at the outset of the eighteenth century, so it's hardly a new phenomenon.

At a time when Russia opposes a West that is drawing ever closer, Russia finds itself short on stamina. Although Putin's government seems to have obtained positive domestic support for its stand on the "Ukraine question" since 2014, that doesn't guarantee majority approval for the war efforts in the future or even now. Yes, I've visited Russia six times over the last two decades and I've seen the huge social changes with my own eyes. But, in the grand scheme of things, I consider Putin's success in Crimea only a moderate victory, not a major turning point for the nation. And his recent decision to start a war with Ukraine was a gamble that is not likely to pay off in the long run whatever the outcome of the battlefields.

Russia currently relies mainly on energy exports to prop up its economy, but the United States has entered the top ranks of the oil-exporting countries. Meanwhile, energy-saving know-how is maturing in Western Europe, and provision of energy via the Mediterranean has increased significantly. Therefore, Russia's use of oil and gas supply as an effective weapon will gradually diminish. The fact that EU has imposed embargo on Russian oil and petroleum products in mid-2022 shows that EU is already not critically dependent on Russia's energy supply.

On the other hand, even Western countries that support Ukraine and Georgia in breaking with Russia find it difficult to forecast accurately the actual outcome of their own actions.

The EU does possess the means to formulate strategy regarding how to make Ukraine and Georgia its would-be partners. However, willingness to implement it suffers from a lack of unanimity. Brexit represents an incredible fracture of Europe. The EU's own problems will make its leadership think twice about making Russia a permanent enemy.

During the 1961 Cuban Missile Crisis, President John F. Kennedy loudly warned off the Soviet Union's Khrushchev, and attained total victory as a result. Kennedy even flew to Berlin to make himself heard; less than 30 years later, the Berlin Wall fell.

Indeed, one-third of the world's GDP was produced by the United States back then, but today that figure has dropped to one-fourth, while the US debt burden has multiplied many times over. After decades of huge fiscal deficits, coupled with continuous wars in Afghanistan, Iraq and indirectly in Libya and Syria, US financial strength has markedly deteriorated. The unfair distribution of economic resources exposed by the financial tsunami in 2008–2010, and a substantial increase in election campaign costs, has generated severe doubts—a new-fangled phenomenon—among many Americans concerning the country's social justice and election system.

When I went to lecture in Ukraine in 2011, former prime minister Yulia Tymoshenko was in prison, a situation that was a source of much argument in society. I spoke with some young Ukrainians about this. Whether they lived in the eastern or western part of Ukraine, and spoke Ukrainian or Russian at home, they all hoped for an independent and peaceful country with corruption-free officials. If the United States, EU and Russia do not agree on divvying up Ukraine again, then it is the young Ukrainians who are most entitled to say what they want for their country.

Eurasia was the first to domesticate the horse, and traditionally offered good access to myriad destinations. Why can't it once again serve as a key artery facilitating east–west trade between Europe and Asia?

PART IV

Survey of Greater Central Asia

CHAPTER 13

Greater Central Asia and the New Silk Road

My interest in "Greater Central Asia" began with two texts in my elementary school textbook, "Ban Chao Discards his Pen to Join the Army," and "Be a Settler on the Frontier." Ban Chao was a Chinese diplomat, explorer, and general who re-established control over the Tarim Basin on behalf of the Eastern Han dynasty in the first century.

My father told me that shortly after the Xinhai Revolution in 1911, my paternal grandfather, who was an elementary school teacher, was drafted into the Liaoning army for an expedition to enforce the Republic of China's claim to "Outer" Mongolia (now an independent republic), where Czarist Russia was instigating an independence movement. However, the troops were disbanded before they could move out due to a lack of funds and supplies.

In the 1960s, when I was a doctoral student in the United States, I bought a copy of Owen Lattimore's 1940 edition of *Inner Asian Frontiers of China* at a used bookstore. This tome opened my eyes to China's northern and western frontiers. Over the years, I have traveled to various parts of the Asian interior and have accumulated much direct understanding of the region. In this chapter, I combine my personal experience with the trajectory of history to briefly analyze Greater Central Asia, the heartland of the Eurasian continent.

I will also offer some thoughts on the "New Silk Road" since President Xi Jinping's Belt and Road Initiative was launched.

For thousands of years before Europe's Age of Discovery beginning in the 1400s, the central zone of the Eurasian continent served as the principal route for human commercial and cultural contacts. The "Silk Road," which was pioneered by Zhang Qian's passage to the West in late second century BCE, is a very descriptive name. But the beginning of the maritime era—the Age of Sail—in the sixteenth century caused both Great Central Asia and its portion of the Silk Road to lose their luster. From the seventeenth century onward, mighty Imperial Russia gradually eroded and swallowed up this formerly glorious territory. The prosperity of maritime transport made it a closed and backward region, and other than archeologists, historians and exiled Russians, few Europeans would have a long sojourn in this once prosperous and much traveled heartland of Eurasia.

After the Soviet Union's dissolution in 1991, this "remote region," almost forgotten by the world, was once again a focal point. I am writing this chapter because of my affection for it over the years, but also because of the current context of the twenty-first century.

What Constitutes "Greater Central Asia"?

"Central Asia," "Greater Central Asia" and "Inner Asia" are all geographical concepts that refer to the central region of Asia, but also have historical and cultural meanings that are difficult to define in terms of latitude and longitude or mountain ranges and rivers. Even expert references such as *Encyclopedia Britannica* and the *Soviet Encyclopedic Dictionary* have delineated them rather differently.

In recent years, some European and American scholars have coined the term "Central Eurasia," i.e., "the middle part of the Eurasian continent" or "Middle Eurasia" to describe Greater Central Asia, thereby highlighting the region's location and historic origins.

According to the outline prepared by UNESCO for publication of its *History of Civilizations of Central Asia*, in its broadest sense "Central Asia" comprises: "The Mongolian Plateau, the Hexi Corridor, Qinghai, Xinjiang, the Amu Darya and Syr Darya basins, the southern Kazakhstan steppe, northeastern Iran, northern Afghanistan, and northwestern Pakistan." This outline was developed prior to the Soviet invasion of Afghanistan in 1979, was agreed upon by multinational experts and is fairly free of political influence.

As per this outline, I divide Greater Central Asia into two parts, a "Central Region" and a "Peripheral Region." The Central Region refers to Kazakhstan, Uzbekistan, Turkmenistan, Kyrgyzstan and Tajikistan. They all declared independence from the Soviet Union in 1991 in accordance with Soviet-era borders and are internationally recognized as the five Central Asian states, colloquially referred to as "the Stans." Their territories cover roughly the Amu Darya and Syr Darya river basins plus the Kazakhstan steppe.

The Peripheral Region groups territories administered by seven countries: the Republic of Mongolia; Russian Federation (Republics of Buryatia, Tuva and Altai); China (Inner Mongolia, Ningxia, Gansu, Qinghai and Xinjiang); India (northwestern India and part of Kashmir); Pakistan (northwestern Pakistan and part of Kashmir); and northern Afghanistan and northeastern Iran.

Three Environments, Three Cultures

In terms of geographical characteristics, Greater Central Asia can be divided into three environments and three corresponding modes of livelihood:

The first is the Asian steppe in the north. This region is generally flat, stretching from the Mongolian Plateau in the east to the north of the Caspian Sea in the west, and bordering Siberia's evergreen coniferous forests to the north. The vast grasslands there are suitable for nomadic herding, and most of their pre-modern inhabitants were free-ranging nomads; their societies were composed mainly of groups with horizontal links rather than vertically linked units ruled from the top, and tribal alliances were erratic.

Secondly, there are the deserts and oases in the south. This region has a very arid climate, but there are many underground rivers that irrigate the oases. Traditionally, the oases have been densely populated, mainly for agriculture, but also for commerce.

This region extends from the Hexi Corridor in the east to the Caspian Sea in the west. It is bounded to the south by the Qilian Mountains and several mountain ranges to the west, and to the far west by the Iranian Plateau. Because of the complex irrigation systems required by oasis inhabitants and the need to centralize human and material resources, there was a tendency toward a vertical hierarchical society. For centuries, interaction between nomadic and agrarian societies—both conflictual and mutually beneficial—has been a constant theme throughout the history of Greater Central Asia.

The third is the alpine region. It includes the western Tien Shan and the Pamir Plateau, the Kashmir and Karakoram Mountains south of the desert, the border provinces and tribal areas of northwestern Pakistan, and northern Afghanistan. These high-altitude mountains constitute a difficult environment, and as a result, the inhabitants are rugged and fiercely independent, but ally to resist intruders.

Closely related to Greater Central Asia is the fascinating Silk Road.

Turbulent Times Along the Silk Road

The German geographer Baron von Richthofen introduced the concept of the Silk Road at the end of the nineteenth century to describe the commercial routes in the central part of the Eurasian continent. The Silk Road is not a road per se, but a *network* of roads between East Asia and Eastern Europe; the central part of this network roughly coincides with Greater Central Asia.

I first set foot on the Silk Road in 1978 when I traveled from Xi'an to Baoji in Shaanxi Province, the easternmost section of the Silk Road. But it was not until the summer of 1987 that I actually penetrated the once uncharted "Western Regions" and experienced the charms of the Silk Road, as my wife and I journeyed from Lanzhou through the Hexi Corridor to Dunhuang, home to the Buddhist temple-caves of Mogao, and then through Turpan and Urumqi to reach Kashgar, "Pearl of the Silk Road," located near the border with Afghanistan, Kyrgyzstan, Tajikistan and Pakistan.

Soon after our journey, the Soviet Union collapsed, and the heart of Greater Central Asia transformed dramatically. The five newly independent countries were initially unstable, with ethnic tensions, religious extremism, and even civil war emerging in some. Later, Russia tried to bring the five "Stans" back into its sphere of influence; meanwhile, the United States, Western Europe, Turkey, India and Pakistan, and Japan and South Korea essayed to exploit their economic and cultural power to fill this vacuum.

As a neighboring country, China, of course, did not merely look on from the sidelines.

In June 2001, six countries—China, Russia, Kazakhstan, Kyrgyzstan, Tajikistan and Uzbekistan—announced the establishment of the Shanghai

Cooperation Organization (SCO). This was an attempt to form a non-aligned, non-confrontational organization that does not target any other country. Since India, Pakistan and Iran joined, there are now nine full members and three observer states, Afghanistan, Belarus and Mongolia.

Immediately after the terrorist attacks of September 11, 2001, the United States dispatched troops to Afghanistan, determined to eliminate the Taliban regime—some of whose predecessors, the Mujahadeen, had ironically received considerable US support when they fought to expel the Soviets—and established military bases in many parts of Greater Central Asia.

During 2002–2006, on four occasions I traveled widely in Xinjiang Uygur Autonomous Region and also visited India and Pakistan five times. In 2007, my wife and I traveled by car around Uzbekistan, penetrating deep into the heart of Central Asia.

In November of 2007, I delivered a keynote speech on the Buddhist monk Xuanzang and the Silk Road at a conference in Xi'an on the theme of "The New Silk Road and Harmonious Society" (Chapter 6).

In Xuanzang's era—the first half of the seventh century—the network of trade routes that formed the Silk Road connected the Byzantine Empire, the Arabian Peninsula, the Sassanid Persian Empire, India, Tibetan territory in modern-day Qinghai province, and the Tang Empire. In the twenty-first century, this Greater Central Asia that was already integrated and well connected 1400 years ago, can and should now be better integrated into the global economy through railroads, roads, airlines, oil and gas pipelines, telecommunications, and the Internet.

During my seven in-depth tours of Greater Central Asia between 2008 and 2017, I sensed that the region would become a vast and attractive setting for another round of cooperation—and competition—among powerful players and that its economic, cultural and political development would receive widespread attention. This is the "New Silk Road" to which we are all looking forward.

CHAPTER 14

Migration of Populations Within Greater Central Asia

Greater Central Asia includes all of Kazakhstan, Uzbekistan, Turkmenistan, Kyrgyzstan, Tajikistan—commonly referred to as "the Stans"—and the Republic of Mongolia, as well as parts of Russia, China, Afghanistan, Iran, Pakistan and India. To understand this complex region in the twenty-first century, it's important to have a basic grasp of its convoluted history.

CLUES TO UNDERSTANDING GREATER CENTRAL ASIA

I read many a tome on the subject and took a pile of notes, and one day I had an epiphany that gifted me with a clue. This clue can be described as an outline of the history of Greater Central Asia. Once I had this framework in hand, details were secondary, and the "warp" and "weft" of the region's past became evident.

The history of Greater Central Asia is inseparable from the Silk Road, and the relationship between the Chinese and neighboring peoples is also intertwined with silk. China enjoyed sole ownership of this "intellectual property" of sorts for more than three millennia. But according to Xuanzang's account in his *Great Tang Records on the Western Regions*, a Chinese princess on her way to marry the Prince of Khotan smuggled silk cocoons out of the empire, and they were subsequently secreted to present-day Uzbekistan by a Sogdian trader. Otherwise, China's monopoly on sericulture and hugely profitable exports to Central Asia, Western Asia and Europe would have continued for many more centuries.

In the Chinese script, several of the terms mentioned above—"warp and weft," "clue," "intertwined" and "relationship"—all contain the radical that denotes "silk," which should give you an idea of the influence this fiber has had on Chinese culture.

Today, China envisions a "New Silk Road" to develop its western territories and secure energy supplies. But in my opinion, in addition to accelerating the construction of the twenty-first-century "road," we must also come up with a twenty-first-century equivalent to the prized silk of yore.

But to get back to my main point: My fundamental take on human history is that "geography determines historical development."

In the northern part of Greater Central Asia, at about 45–50° north—Xinjiang's Urumqi is located at 44°—lies the Eurasian Steppe that extends from the Danube River in the west to the Greater *Khingan* Mountain Range in the east. It includes the steppes of Ukraine, southern Russia, Kazakhstan, Dzungaria (northern Xinjiang, China), and Mongolia. This vast expanse of space has been home to nomadic and semi-nomadic peoples since 5,000 years ago and is a gateway between the eastern and western parts of the Eurasian continent. It is also dubbed the "Grassland Silk Road" because nomads spread Chinese silk to West Asia via this temperate route.

In second-century BCE, the Han dynasty diplomat-explorer Zhang Qian pioneered the Silk Road through the desert and a string of oases, with its main artery located at 35–40° north (Kashgar is located at 39.5°). The peoples of the oases were mainly sedentary agriculturalists, with a few engaged in long-distance trade.

These two roughly parallel east–west corridors made Greater Central Asia an axis and hub for interaction between Eurasian civilizations. European, Middle Eastern, Indian and Chinese civilizations converged and developed in Central Asia, and then branched out. The clues to understanding the formation of ethnic groups, language change, religious thought, political systems, and economic activities in Greater Central Asia are the population movements that took place over time.

The Warp and Weft of History

Tens of thousands of years ago, modern Homo sapiens roamed in large groups. The waves of migration described in this chapter are the more numerous and distant population movements that commended about 5,000 years ago. Horses were already being used for transportation, and animal-drawn vehicles were available in the Middle East. There were nomadic tribes speaking Indo-European languages in the steppes of Ukraine and southern Russia, and speakers of Altaic tongues in the steppes of northern Mongolia. Beginning 4,500 years ago, these steppe tribes migrated one after another, either from west to east or from east to west, which we can describe as the "weft" of population movement.

Nomadic herders from the northern steppe and settled agricultural populations in the south have always interacted with each other. But purposeful and large-scale population movements began 4,000 years ago, mostly by northern tribes moving south, and sometimes by southerners moving north. These movements constitute the "warp" of population movement.

The historical tapestry of the Greater Central Asia region thus comprises the warp and weft woven during various periods. East–west and north–south population movements in this broad region can be divided into three eras:

4,500–2,300 Years Ago: Indo-European Tribes Migrate Eastward in Four Waves

The first wave was the Tocharians. A group of Proto-Indo-European speakers moved eastward to the northern foothills of the Altai Mountains about 4,500 years ago. At about the same time, another group of Proto-Indo-European speakers entered the northern foothills of the Tianshan Mountains (south of the Altai) and later entered the Hexi Corridor from there. Known to modern European scholars as Tocharians, Chinese historical texts refer to them as Yuezhi.

These Indo-European-speaking groups brought with them domesticated horses and bronzeware. Some Tocharians reached Turpan and Loulan in eastern Xinjiang about 4,000 years ago and then moved into the Tarim Basin—which may not previously have been inhabited by humans—establishing oasis states such as Kucha and Agni (Yanqi in Chinese) and evolved into settled farmers. It was the Tocharians who brought wheat from West Asia to East Asia. The fact that domesticated horses, bronzeware and wheat were introduced by the Tocharians suffices to highlight the fact that the Chinese civilization had multiple origins.

In addition, the easternmost part of the Indo-European-speaking, white-skinned population (including the Tocharians) was located between Loulan and Dunhuang, and further east was the area inhabited by the Altaic-speaking population of North Asia. Since ancient times, Loulan had a reputation for producing great beauties, and those women were most likely the result of melding genes from these two distinct peoples.

The second wave was the Aryans. Tribes speaking an eastern branch of a Proto-Indo-European language, which evolved into Indo-Iranian, entered the steppes of Central Asia, the Iranian plateau, and Afghanistan about 3,800 years ago using oxen- and horse-drawn carts. They were known as Aryans, a term that originally meant "a noble."

About 3,200 years ago, a group of Aryans crossed into Afghanistan via a pass in the Hindu Kush, and moved south to the Indus and Ganges valleys, vanquishing the indigenous, dark-skinned Dravidians and gradually integrating with them to form what we know today as Hindu civilization. The early Aryans had long oral epics that were sourced from the classical scriptures of Zoroastrianism and Brahmanism (predecessor of Hinduism), so there is a high degree of homogeneity between classical Persian and Indian civilizations.

The third wave was the Scythians. This is a term used by ancient Greek historians to refer to a very widespread group of people who spoke an Eastern Iranian language. They moved eastward and southward from the Black Sea and the Caspian Sea beginning 2,700–2,100 years ago. Some formerly controlled trade on the steppes, and as a result gathered a great deal of wealth and established humankind's first steppe empire. Archaeological discoveries prove that the Scythians built royal tombs in many parts of the steppe and collected a large number of elaborate gold ornaments. The Scythian tribesmen wore tall, pointed helmets that were easily recognizable.

About 2,500 years ago, after the establishment of the Achaemenid dynasty in which a Western Iranian tongue was spoken, the Scythians submitted to Persia. Persian inscriptions refer to the Scythians as Sakas, while China's *History of the Former Han* refers to them as the "Sai."

After Zhang Qian's opening of the Western Regions in the late second century BC, the Han Empire had dealings with several Scythian-ruled kingdoms, including Wusun (present-day Ili River valley) and Kangju (Syr

Darya River valley, now southeastern Kazakhstan). The oasis kingdoms of Shule (present-day Kashgar) and Khotan were also established by the Scythians during the Eastern Han (25–220). The Scythians and Sogdians who were active during the Sui and Tang dynasties were closely related by language and genealogy—both were Indo-European-speaking people from the northern coast of the Black Sea—but their lifestyles were distinct because of where they lived. The Sogdians were mainly agriculturalists, while the Scythians were on the whole nomadic or semi-nomadic herders.

The fourth wave was the Greeks. When Alexander the Great arrived in present-day Tajikistan, he took a 16-year-old Sogdian princess, Roxana, as his first wife (327 BCE). As Alexander returned westward, in addition to leading most of his troops back to Babylon and marrying a Persian princess, he also left behind many of his men and founded many cities in his name along the way.

Some of them founded the Kingdom of Bactria (Daxia in Chinese) in what is now eastern Afghanistan and northwestern Pakistan. Later, when King Ashoka of India (269–232 BCE) was promoting Buddhism by force, the Greco-Bactrian people in Central Asia also converted to Buddhism.

But their view of the deity differed from that of early Buddhists who did not create concrete images of the Buddha. They sculpted a statue of the Buddha based on the form and sculptural techniques of the Greek pantheon and thus created what is known as Gandharan Buddhist art. This style spread to China, South Korea, Japan and Vietnam, and had a profound impact. This Greek population was soon lost, however, immersed in many subsequent waves of migration from Greater Central Asia.

Second Century BCE to Eighth Century CE: Altaic Tribes Migrate from East to West in Three Waves

The First Wave Was the Xiongnu. A nomadic people, they originated in the Khangai Mountains on the Mongolian Plateau, and their speech was probably a Mongolic tongue which, along with Tungusic and Turkic, are considered Altaic languages.

To the east of the Xiongnu were the Donghu and to the west were Indo-European-speaking Tocharians and Scythians, also nomads. To the south of the Mongolian Plateau was a farming population composed of Han Chinese. Complementarity between farming and nomadic civilizations was quite high, so the Han region was very attractive to the Xiongnu.

During the Warring States period (fifth to third centuries BCE), the Xiongnu took advantage of warfare among the Chinese and gradually pushed southward, crossing the Yin Mountains and forcing their way to the Hetao region. After the fall of the Qin Dynasty in 206 BCE, the Xiongnu extended their power to the Hexi Corridor and the northern foot of the Tianshan Mountains.

Under Emperor Wu of Han (r. 141 to 87 BCE), however, at great cost to his military, the Xiongnu were eventually defeated and then divided: The Southern Xiongnu surrendered to the Han, while the Northern Xiongnu retreated to the north.

In the Eastern Han dynasty (202 BCE to 220 CE), the Northern Xiongnu were driven out again and gradually moved westward. Their westward movement triggered a wave of migrations of many tribes, so much so that Europe was invaded by "barbarians" from the Ural Mountains. In what are now the five countries of Central Asia, the emergence of the Xiongnu forced some of the original inhabitants to relocate southward, impacting present-day Afghanistan, Pakistan, and northwestern India, and constituting what can be described as the "warp" of Greater Central Asian history.

The Second Wave Were the Hephthalites. According to Chinese chronicles, they belonged to a Mongolic-speaking people who later migrated to Central Asia. They were very active in Greater Central Asia during the second-to-fifth centuries CE, defeating the Kushan empire founded by the Tocharians (Yuezhi), occupying much of present-day Afghanistan and Uzbekistan, and penetrating deep into western India where they established a kingdom.

By the fifth century, the area ruled by the Hephthalites stretched from the Pamir Mountains in the east to the Caspian Sea in the west. After the rise of the Turkic peoples, their western branch entered Hephthalite territory, initiating a series of unceasing clashes. It was only later when the Western Turkic forces joined with the Persians further west to attack the Hephthalites that the latter were vanquished. This marked the moment when the Hephthalites relinquished their dominant role on the Greater Central Asian stage to the Turkophones.

There is still controversy among scholars worldwide about the ethnicity and language of the Hephthalites. Some believe that they were a branch of Indo-European-speaking Persians, while most Chinese scholars believe that they spoke an Altaic language. The fact is that the Hephthalites operated for centuries in Central Eurasia, a region with a very complex demographic composition, and they inevitably allied and intermarried with many different people and tribes. Thus, while there may have been some Indo-European-speaking tribes among the Hephthalites, the leaders of the confederation would likely have been speakers of an Altaic tongue, for otherwise there would have been records of this in Chinese historical sources.

The Third Wave Was the Tujüe or Turkic Peoples. They originated in the upper Yenisei River in the northern part of the Mongolian Plateau, and initially constituted a part of the tribal alliance/confederation founded by the Rouran, who dubbed the Turkic tribes "blacksmith slaves" due to their superior ironwork.

The Tujüe established their own khanate during the sixth–seventh centuries and then separated into two branches. The Eastern Turkic people were initially strong in their dealings with Sui and Tang, but they eventually became vassals. Meanwhile, the Western Turkic people, after defeating the Hephthalites, continued migrating and became a major force that greatly influenced the history of Greater Central Asia. Some entered the Urals and the Volga River region, while others crossed the Syr Darya River to the south and set foot into the Persian world.

The westernmost of the Turkic tribes entered Asia Minor at the end of the eleventh century and gradually conquered and assimilated the Greeks and Armenians there, eventually establishing the Ottoman Empire that dominated Eastern Europe, North Africa and West Asia during the fifteenth–nineteenth centuries.

From the tenth century onward, the Turkic peoples, now scattered throughout the region, gradually abandoning their Shamanism for Islam. The population of Greater Central Asia gradually underwent Turkification and Islamization. Today, four of the five Central Asian countries are basically Turkophone, and only Tajikistan has a predominantly Iranian-speaking population.

In China's Xinjiang, the original Tujüe, Scythians, Han Chinese and Qiang were gradually conquered after the tenth century by the Huihu who migrated from the Mongolian highlands to the northern and southern foothills of the Tianshan Mountains, where they intermarried with the locals to form a new ethnic group, the Uyghurs.

This new ethnicity spoke the Turkic language of the Huihe, was genetically quite mixed, and successively practiced Shamanism, Buddhism, and Manichaeism. During the eleventh–fifteenth centuries, the Uyghurs underwent a rather long process before they were fully Islamized.

In terms of the experiences of Turkification and Islamization, Xinjiang and Asia Minor (Turkey's Anatolia), which are very far apart, had fairly similar processes and roughly the same timing. However, the two new ethnic groups in these regions—the Uyghurs and the Turkish—are actually rather different in terms of their genealogical origins.

Their languages have common historical origins but exhibit distinct regional differences. The physical differences within the Uyghur population (excluding nearby Turkic peoples such as the Kazakhs) and within the Turkish population (excluding non-Turkic peoples such as the Kurds) are each so great that each could serve as a museum of ethnic folklore.

In general, there is no mistaking the traces of geography and history. Among the Uyghurs, a higher percentage of their faces, nostrils, eyes, and hair resemble the Mongolian people than do the Turks, and this percentage is highest in the Hami region of eastern Xinjiang. Turks as a whole are closer in appearance to Iranians and Greeks.

Located northwest of China's Xinjiang and northeast of Turkey are the Volga Tatars who are also Turkophone. I have twice visited the Republic of Tatarstan in Russia. It is difficult to distinguish between ethnic Russians and Tatars by appearance or language because of the 800 years of Turkic-Mongolian-Slavic admixture and 450 years of Russian rule. This further shows that the continual and sustained migration of Turkic groups has over the past 1400 years spread their languages over the entire Central Eurasia.

Eighth–Twentieth Centuries: Successive Invasions by Arabs, Mongols, and Russians

After vanquishing Persia, the Arabs entered Greater Central Asia in the early eighth century. Their population was concentrated in the military and religious upper classes, so they were a minority within the total population. However, because of their Islamic faith, the Arabs have had long-lasting, profound cultural impact.

After the Arab troops entered Central Asia, they inevitably came into direct contact with the power of the Tang Dynasty. In 751, a local incident in the Central Asian Kingdom of Shi (modern Tashkent), led Go

Seonji, the Tang dynasty's military governor in Qiuci (modern Kuche, Xinjiang) to lead a large contingent of Tang troops to quell this minor uprising. Unforeseen by Go, his forces encountered the Arab army and were badly defeated at the Battle of Talus. Among the captured Tang soldiers were skilled paper makers who were later settled in Samarkand by their captors. Thus, the first papermaking atelier west of China came into being in the mid-eighth century and was one of the material reasons for the later blossoming of Arab-Islamic civilization.

On the other hand, during the An Lushan Rebellion just four years later, the Tang court invited the Arab army to hasten east and help quell an uprising led by the eponymous general reputedly of Sogdian and Turkic extraction descent. This represents the first time that the Arabs crossed the Hexi Corridor into the Chinese heartland, i.e., the Central Plains. Almost all of the Arabs who entered China stayed and entered Chinese society. They and their offspring thus formed the earliest sizable Muslim community in China.

The Mongols advanced westward three times in the thirteenth century and established the most extensive empire in world history. Two centuries later, Genghis Khan's legal system for the Mongol nation still existed, but the Mongols themselves had gradually become Turkicized and Islamized.

Timur, who dominated Central Asia and Western Asia in the fourteenth–fifteenth centuries with Samarkand in Uzbekistan as the capital of his Timurid dynasty, claimed to be a Mongol nobleman. In fact, he was from a Turkicized Mongolian tribe and not a descendant of Genghis Khan, so he modestly designated himself "Emir" throughout his life—not daring to claim the sacred Mongolian title of "Khan."

His sixth-generation grandson, Babur, was indeed descended from Genghis Khan on his maternal side. In the early sixteenth century, Babur was expelled from his country. He first went south to Afghanistan and eventually made his way to North India, where he founded the Mughal Empire (1526–1857).

This was a period of population movement in Greater Central Asia. After the fall of the Timurid Empire, three khanates emerged in its core region (present-day Uzbekistan), founded by descendants of Batu (the grandson of Genghis Khan), who had come south from the Kipchak steppes.

This is another example of the east–west "warp," which constitutes the tapestry of the history of Greater Central Asia. Xinjiang of China, Kyrgyzstan, and southeastern Kazakhstan continued to be ruled by descendants of Chagatai, Genghis Khan's second son, for several centuries.

From the thirteenth to the twentieth centuries, the political power of the descendants of Genghis Khan—known as the Golden Clan—was strong in Greater Central Asia. The last two Mongol khans were the Emir of Bukhara, who was forced to abdicate by the Soviet regime in 1920, and the ninth Khan of Kumul (Maqsud Shah), whose khanate in northeastern Xinjiang was abolished by the Xinjiang governor Jin Shuren in 1930.

The Russians embraced Christianity and acquired the Cyrillic script in the tenth century and were conquered by the Mongols in the thirteenth century. The first czar of all of Russia, Ivan the Terrible (1547–1584), freed his people from the Mongol yoke and began to expand eastward. In the sixteenth century, the Russians conquered the Tatar Khanate in the middle reaches of the Volga River, formerly part of the Kipchak Khanate (the Golden Horde). They moved eastward to the Outer Khingan Range during the seventeenth century. In the eighteenth century, they conquered most of Kazakhstan, and in the nineteenth century, the Russian czar ruled all of Greater Central Asia west of Xinjiang region and north of Afghanistan.

After the incorporation of the five Central Asian states into the Soviet Union, a national delineation project under Stalin's influence began to define the ethnicities and redraw the boundaries of the region. Even today, those boundaries remain unchanged. After the Soviet Union collapsed, all five became independent and have lost some of their ethnic Russians, but the working language in each country is still predominantly Russian.

After 1991, Russia lost the Soviet Union's territory on the west, hence lacking maneuverability versus Europe; it lost its traditional buffer zone between Iran and Turkey in the South Caucasus, highlighting the unrest in Russia's North Caucasus; and it lost energy- and mineral-rich five Central Asian states at its south-central borders.

One of the manifestations of Putin's drive for Russian strength in recent years has been to take advantage of the US involvement in Afghanistan to try to reduce this superpower's influence in Greater Central Asia, and thus to resurrect Russia's dominance over the five Central Asian countries. However, the people of these lands have not been amicable with Russia and show no signs of "welcoming the king's troops with a hearty meal."

The influence of the Russians on the modern history of Greater Central Asia can be considered profound. The future of Greater Central Asia will also be impacted depending upon the nature of Russia's interaction with the "five-Stans" as well as its actions vis-à-vis the United States, China and India.

CHAPTER 15

Greater Central Asia: A Cultural Mosaic

It is difficult to obtain a well-rounded picture of Greater Central Asia due to its vast territory, lengthy history, multiple ethnicities, and diverse languages and faiths. However, without appreciating its cultural context, it would be impossible to truly understand its social, economic, and political status quo. This chapter separately examines Greater Central Asia's five regions—northeast (Lake Baikal), southeast (Hexi Corridor), west (Aral Sea), southwest (Lahore) and central (Tajikistan)—in order to piece together a mosaic that captures the cultural contours of Greater Central Asia.

Herding Sheep by Lake Baikal

As a child, I used to sing this ditty about Su Wu, the Han envoy taken captive by the Xiongnu:

> Su Wu herded sheep by the North Sea
> Naught but snow and ice twixt Earth and Sky.
> Nineteen long years detained was he
> With snow for water, and felt to stave off hunger.

In the summer of 2012, I flew from Mongolia's Ulaanbaatar to Ulan-Ude, the capital of the Republic of Buryatia, a republic of the Russia Federation. It is a fascinating city hosting both Russian Orthodox churches and Tibetan Buddhist temples, with about 400,000 inhabitants,

65% of whom are Russians. The Buryats number about 500,000, and most inhabit small towns and villages east of Ulan-Ude.

Naturally, I had to check out Su Wu's "North Sea"—Lake Baikal, of course—the world's deepest and most capacious freshwater lake. My amateur tour guide from a local museum brought along his pharmacist wife and their two young boys. They spoke to one another in Russian and qualified as Russified Buryats, but also knew Buryat, a Mongolic tongue. Both come from secular families but maintain some shamanic customs. At the urging of an American missionary, a decade ago the couple were baptized as Southern Baptist Christians.

History of Lake Baikal

East of Lake Baikal is where the Xiongnu, Xianbei, Rouran (or Avar in some European accounts), Tujüe (Turkic tribes), Khitan and Mongolian peoples roamed before their rise to power. This great lake played a nurturing role for them and thus an important role in world history. Since these and several other ethnicities or states that emerged later played an important role in the development of Greater Central Asia, it's important to give a brief account of the major historical events that involved them.

In third century BCE, the Xiongnu rose to power but were contained by the Han Empire after second century BCE. During first century CE, the Han dynasty entered the Tarim Basin, and the Silk Road began to flourish.

In the fourth century, the proto-Mongolic Xianbei appeared on the scene and ruled northern China. They promoted Buddhism and initiated Sinification.

In the sixth century, the Tujüe broke away from the Rouran and rose on the Mongolian Plateau. They subsequently split in two: The Eastern Tujüe migrated south to the Yin Mountains where they were subdued by the Tang, while the Western branch crossed the Pamir Mountains (mainly located in modern Tajikistan) and continued westward.

At the beginning of the eighth century, Arab-Islamic forces entered the Persian world and reached as far east as the Syr Darya and the Pamir Plateau. However, by the middle of the century, the Tang dynasty withdrew from the Western Regions, and the Tibetans took advantage of the situation to enter the Hexi Corridor and Tarim Basin.

In the tenth century, the Tujüe underwent Islamization and established several regimes that implemented Turkification and Islamic policies in their dominions.

At the beginning of the thirteenth century, the Mongols rose to power and over a period of 40 years, Genghis Khan and his descendants undertook three Westward Expeditions and proved themselves invincible warriors.

During the fourteenth century, the Mongols ruling the Islamic areas converted to Islam, and those Mongols who ruled regions with Turkic populations willingly Turkified. Nonetheless, the Mongol ruling class maintained political power for more than 500 years.

At the beginning of the sixteenth century, Europeans reached Asia by sea and the land-based Silk Road declined. During the seventeenth–eighteenth centuries, Russia conquered the Tartars in the Volga region and the Kazakhs in the Siberian steppe. Meanwhile, the Manchu-ruled Qing dynasty controlled the Mongolian Plateau, Inner Mongolia and the North–South route through the Tianshan Mountains.

In the nineteenth–twentieth centuries, Russia ruled most of Greater Central Asia, but with the collapse of the Soviet Union in 1991, Greater Central Asia entered a new, uncharted era.

Greater Central Asia as Seen from Southern Gansu and the Hexi Corridor

In the summer of 1987, to attend a conference I traveled from the United States to Lanzhou, capital of Gansu Province. Afterward, the organizers arranged tours of the Bingling Temple Grottoes, Liujiaxia Reservoir, Dongxiang County (where half of the population are Mongolian-speaking Muslims), and Labrang Monastery in Gannan Tibetan Autonomous Prefecture. It is no coincidence that this land, where the Tibetan and Loess Plateaux meet, is also a border area between Han Chinese and Tibetan cultures.

Then we proceeded to Dunhuang. Dunhuang is located at the far western portion of the Hexi Corridor (aka Gansu Corridor), between the Gobi Desert and towering mountains. Before the Han dynasty, it was an outlying area of Chinese culture and a dividing line between the Caucasian and Mongolian populations. After the Tibetans flourished during the Tang, Dunhuang became the point of intersection of Han, Tibetan and Central Asian civilizations.

In 2009, I traveled by car across the entire Hexi Corridor in five days, with a three-day stop in Dunhuang. This trip gave me a true understanding of the meaning of "Greater Central Asia." It is not just a geographical concept, nor is it limited to international politics, but is more of a concept of overall cultural development. Modern-day Republic of Mongolia—and China's Inner Mongolia, Hexi Corridor, Ningxia, southern Gansu Province and eastern Qinghai Province—are indeed culturally and economically part and parcel of Greater Central Asia.

In the thirteenth century, a group of Turkic tribes, Muslims who spoke the Oghuz branch of the Turkic languages, migrated eastward from what is now Turkmenistan. After a long journey, they settled in eastern Qinghai, not far from the source of the Yellow River, supposedly because the water there was sweet and refreshing, similar to the water they left behind further west.

Since the tenth century, this area has been inhabited by a mixture of Han Chinese and Tibetans, as well as many Muslim soldiers resettled there during the Mongol-ruled Yuan dynasty (1271–1368). Today, the most numerous of the Muslim ethnic groups who live near Gansu's Linxia are the Dongxiang who speak a Mongolic tongue; the Salars still speak a Turkic dialect and number about 120,000; and the smallest of the three are the Bonan, who speak a distinctive Mongolian dialect of the same name.

Scientists and "Father of Algebra"

My wife and I traveled to Uzbekistan in 2007 and visited one of the first UNESCO World Heritage Sites, the ancient city of Khiva and the nearby city of Urgench. In addition to the well-preserved buildings of sixteenth-century Khiva, there is a monument that is not part of the tangible cultural heritage: The statue of the most famous local, Muḥammad ibn Mūsā al-Khwārizmī (783–840). He is known as the "Father of Algebra," and the modern term—algorithm—is a corruption of the latter part of his name that identified him as a native of Khwarazm. He attained notoriety and moved to Baghdad, where he published monographs on mathematics and astronomy in Arabic and introduced Indian decimal mathematics to the Arab world. His works were translated into Latin in the twelfth century, thanks to which Europeans learned the most advanced mathematics and astronomy of the time.

Sixteenth-century architecture of the ancient city of Khiva in western Uzbekistan

The region of Khwarazm, located between the Turkic nomads of the lower Syr Darya and the Persian farmers of the lower Amu Darya, rose to prominence in the middle of the eleventh century when the king was a Turkic soldier of slave origin. In the early twelfth century, it became Khwarazmia, the empire that ruled the Persian world.

In 1218, Genghis Khan was so enraged by the insult visited upon his envoy to Khwarazm that he suspended his attack on the Western Xia in order to launch an expedition to punish the Khwarazmians. Within three years Khwarazm was razed, and while the eldest son of the dead Shah fought on in various parts of Khwarazmia in an attempt to rebuild his homeland, his forces were eventually annihilated in 1231.

Khwarazm, now known as Karakalpakstan, is today an autonomous republic within Uzbekistan. Most inhabitants speak Karakalpak, a Turkic tongue that differs from Uzbek, and is closer to Kazakh and Kyrgyz.

While traveling around Uzbekistan in the fall of 2007, I hired a driver—a Karakalpak native—who taught English at a local high school, and he served as my tour guide for all of eight days. His language skills were impressive, speaking English with us, Uzbek with strangers, Russian with the tour manager, and a hodgepodge of Karakalpak and Uzbek with his family on the phone.

In addition to Khwarazm, two other world-class scientists have emerged from Greater Central Asia. One was Ibn Sina (Avicenna), an eleventh-century medical scientist and philosopher. A Persian born near today's Bukhara in Uzbekistan, he relocated to Baghdad and wrote the *Canon of Medicine*, the basic textbook of Arabic medicine. It was translated into Latin in the twelfth century and served as the textbook of medical schools throughout Europe until the seventeenth century.

Another scientist was Timur's grandson, Ulugh Beg, who ruled Samarkand. He built the world's most advanced astronomical observatory there and led a team of astronomers who mapped the positions of more than 1,000 planets, making him one of the world's most prolific astronomers before Copernicus. Ibn Sina and Ulugh Beg were also scholars and philosophers of Islamic doctrine and works by both of these men in this domain have come down to us.

LAHORE: SIGHTS AND THOUGHTS

In the fall of 2006, I accepted an invitation to visit Punjab University, one of Pakistan's most prestigious academic institutions. At the time, Pakistan was under military rule and the university president was a lieutenant general in the army. When he learned of my interest in culture and religion, he immediately instructed his subordinates to change my itinerary by combining several tours on campus into one symposium, adding more time for off-campus visits, and sending a young faculty member and a car to accompany me.

Lahore is the capital of the Punjab, Pakistan's most populous province, and the cultural nerve center of the country. Since the eleventh century, Lahore has been the frontier base of various Turkic Muslim regimes in India, so there are many magnificent mosques and squares in the city.

After losing both his homeland of Ferghana and his beloved Samarkand, Babur, the sixth-generation grandson of Timur, wandered for many years in eastern Uzbekistan and northern Afghanistan. In 1526, he established himself in Lahore. Skilled in both literary and martial arts, Babur was not only the founder of the Mughal Empire but also established a tradition of writing in Chagatai, a Central Asian Turkic literary language written with a script that is a slight variation of the Perso-Arabic alphabet. Today's Uighur script is based on Chagatai's.

My Lahore sojourn yielded two things. First, I saw a number of Gandhara art treasures in the museum, and second, I took a private taxi ride to the Pakistan-India border to observe the "patriotic spectacle" that is the flag-lowering ceremony that begins two hours before sunset every day. I was lucky enough to be helped to squeeze into the stands and see the Pakistani army put on a good show. Whenever the specially trained Pakistani soldiers goosestepped until their boot-tips were higher than their heads, the Pakistani audience shouted and cheered, interspersed with chants of *Allahu Akbar* as they endeavored to outdo the Indian honor guard performing just across the border.

The traumatic partition of India in 1947 divided British India into two independent dominions: India and Pakistan. While the Islamic Republic of Pakistan is officially Muslim, India itself is home to some 11% of Muslims worldwide, slightly more numerous than the total population of Pakistan. The official language of Pakistan is Urdu, but only seven percent of the population speaks Urdu as their mother tongue; India has many times more native Urdu speakers than its Muslim neighbor. Spoken Urdu was developed in and near the military bases of the Delhi Sultanate and the Mughal Empire. It is essentially the same as Hindi (the official language of India), provided you discount Urdu's Arabic and Persian loanwords. Besides, Urdu is written in Arabic alphabet while Hindi is written in the Devanagari script derived from Brahmi.

In fact, nearly one-half of Pakistanis speak Punjabi, and the other side of the India-Pakistan border is the Indian province of Punjab, where the language is almost identical. The actors in the "patriotic spectacle" at the border to which I was privy are ironically two families of the same race who speak the same language but embrace different faiths.

CENTRAL AND SOUTHERN ASIA: LIKE "LIPS AND TEETH"

Prior to the European occupation of India, invaders had historically come south from the Hindu Kush Mountains in Afghanistan. In the second century, the Yuezhi established the Kushan Empire that included the Tarim Basin, Pamir Mountains, Amu Darya Basin, Hindu Kush Mountains and the Ganges Valley, thereby uniting South and Central Asia.

In the sixteenth century, Babur moved south from the Hindu Kush to establish the Mughal Empire, and from then on relations between Central and South Asia became closer, with frequent exchanges of people, goods and information. In the eighteenth century, the Mughal Empire began to decline when the Persian king Nadir invaded India, sacked Delhi, and whisked away the Mughal emperor's jeweled peacock throne as a trophy.

In the nineteenth century, British India, which dominated South Asia, was keen to extend its realm north into Central Asia, while Russia, which ruled Central Asia, tried to block its expansion. Afghanistan famously became the chessboard upon which the "Great Game," an iconic political and diplomatic confrontation between the two empires, was played out until the early twentieth century.

Immediately after the infamous coordinated suicide terrorist attacks of September 11, 2001, the United States believed that Osama bin Laden, the leader of the Islamist terrorist organization Al-Qaeda, was hiding in Afghanistan, and dispatched troops to Afghanistan to uproot the Taliban regime that hosted him. It should be noted that while Pakistan was a quickly recruited ally in Bush's "War on Terror," there were Taliban elements in Pakistan and many Taliban sympathizers there too.

During the Soviet-Afghan War (1979–1989), the Pakistanis felt threatened by a common enemy, so they helped the Mujahadeen resist the Soviets, with considerable support, material-wise, from the United States. Perhaps not surprisingly, when US troops arrived in Afghanistan, there were also Pakistanis who clandestinely supported Afghan Taliban activities in the border areas.

In view of India's long-term rivalry with Pakistan and its desire to exert influence in a region historically vital to its own security, India also gave a special hand to the post-Taliban Afghan government and hoped to establish a north–south axis of the economic and military alliance between Central Asia and South Asia. Such a geopolitical consideration still exists today, even though the current government of India is led by the BJP, a party with a strong pro-Hindu and anti-Muslim stance.

The Sogdian Homeland

In the summer of 2011, my wife and I visited Tajikistan. The most memorable trip was by off-road vehicle from Panjakent on the western border of Tajikistan to Khujand on the Syr Darya River. Panjakent was once a major town on the Silk Road and the easternmost outpost of the ancient

Sogdians in Transoxiana, and remnants of an early Sogdian castle still remain there.

After King Cyrus founded the Persian empire, both the agricultural Sogdians and the nomadic Scythians submitted to him. Bukhara, Samarkand and Panjakent in Zeravshan valley became important towns on the Silk Road and strongholds of Sogdian merchants.

In fourth century, the Sogdians became active on the Silk Road. A letter written in 313 by a Sogdian merchant who came from this area to do business in Wuwei, Gansu was never delivered to his family but was left at the base of a Great Wall beacon west of the Yumen Pass. It was not until the early twentieth century that it was discovered by British-Hungarian archaeologist Aurel Stein and dispatched to the British Museum. After decades of work, this letter and several others that suffered the same fate were finally deciphered, giving the world a better understanding of the situation of merchants on the Silk Road in that era.

We drove through lofty mountains and high peaks, mostly uninhabited, encountering the occasional dwelling. We passed a tunnel built with the help of the Iranian government, but just a few years after it was completed, the road surface was already uneven and water dripped constantly from the tunnel ceiling.

We passed two other tunnels built with Chinese aid, both in good condition, so the people in the environs were very friendly to us and even the women were willing to take pictures with me.

As we lingered amidst this desolate high-altitude scenery, we encountered a team of road construction workers from Sichuan. After exchanging just a few words, I felt warm and fuzzy. There they were, laboring hard in the deserted mountains of a foreign land, and their relatives—likely living off their repatriated earnings—probably couldn't imagine their loneliness. I hope they're at least appreciated by the locals.

Tradition and Modern: Kazakhstan's Old and New Capital

Territory-wise, Kazakhstan is the largest country in the Greater Central Asia region and possesses the world's largest reserves of oil, natural gas, uranium, chromium and titanium. It is also the youngest of these countries.

The Kazakh nation was formed only after the fifteenth century. Although the Kazakhs are a Turkic-speaking people, it originated in the division of the Kipchak Khanate, which was established by the Mongols on the steppes of South Russia and Central Asia.

In the middle of the fifteenth century, the Kazakhs were only part of the newly formed "Uzbek" tribal alliance led by the descendants of Jochi, the eldest son of Genghis Khan. During a subsequent struggle on the steppe, a Mongolian nobleman, Burunduk, broke away from the original tribal alliance and declared himself khan. From this time on, the term "Kazakh" referred to those who abandoned the alliance.

View of Tianshan Mountains from southern Almaty in Kazakhstan

The Khazakh Khanate was attacked for a long time by both the Russians and the Dzungars, a confederation of Mongol Oirat tribes. The Kazakhs successfully resisted the latter but lost to the former. At the beginning of the nineteenth century, the khanate was deposed and entirely occupied by Czarist Russia. Among the countries of Greater Central Asia, Kazakhstan was under Russian rule for the longest time and was most influenced by Russia.

Its former capital, Almaty, was established by Russia in the mid-nineteenth century as a new city on the site of the old Silk Road and served as the administrative center of Russia in the Ili and Chu River basins.

With the dissolution of the Soviet Union in 1991 Kazakhstan became independent, and three years later it was announced that the capital would be relocated to an ordinary provincial town in the center of the country. The purpose of the move was self-evident: First, they did not want their capital to be too close to China, and secondly, they wanted to use the new capital to boost their economy and the people's enthusiasm for their newly independent country.

In 1997, Kazakhstan moved its capital and named its provincial capital "Astana," the Kazakh version of *Astane*, the ancient Persian word for "capital." It is the coldest capital in the world, save Mongolia's Ulaanbaatar, but the enthusiasm for national construction I sensed there was much greater than that of the Mongolians, who were positively disgusted with the congested state of traffic in their capital.

Astana was renamed Nur-Sultan in 2019 in honor of its first president, Nursultan Nazarbayev, who moved the capital there and resigned on his own accord. However, demands are growing in Kazakhstan for the capital city to be returned to its original name of Astana following widespread civil unrest in early January 2022.

I first visited Astana alone in 2011, and then in 2012 with my wife to witness President Nazarbayev's masterpiece, and I definitely felt the new capital is an experiment worth observing. The old part of the capital is the cultural district, while the new part is the administrative and commercial district. The culture in the old district is nothing to write home about, but the new district inspires great hope.

A large six-story shopping mall in the form of a yurt symbolizes that the Kazakhs have not completely abandoned their nomadic traditions. Nazarbayev University, named after the now truly retired president, is an English-medium institution and has a well-developed biotechnology institute headed by my alumnus, a PhD from Northwestern University.

I went to the old parliament building in Almaty to meet the new head of the building, the British Dean of the International Business Academy. He told me that during more than four years in Kazakhstan, not a day passed when he was not surprised by the new atmosphere of the country. He also hinted that the longer he lives in the country, the more he realizes that combining tradition and modernity is not an easy task.

Out of courtesy and out of my good wishes for Kazakhstan, I did not tell the Englishman that the key to melding tradition with modernity has been debated in China for four or five generations now. I can only hope that the 500-year-old Kazakh nation will not spend the next 100 years obsessing over the relationship between tradition and modernity, between heritage and innovation.

CHAPTER 16

My Journeys to Xinjiang: From Dream to Reality

The seeds of my dream journey to Xinjiang in China's remote far west were planted early. While a pupil at primary school, in my textbook I read *Zhang Qian's Diplomatic Mission to the Western Regions* and *Ban Chao Swaps His Writing Brush for the Sword*; on the radio, I learned to sing *Girl from Daban City*, Wang Luobin's adaptation of a Uyghur folk song; and at home, I heard my elders discuss Sheng Shicai, the warlord who ruled Xinjiang during the 30s and 40s, and Burhan Shahidi, a Uyghur scholar-politician prominent in both pre- and post-1949 China.

In the summer of 1987, I returned to China for a series of lectures, and as was customary at the time, the work unit that invited me to speak offered me two weeks of free travel in the country in lieu of remuneration in foreign currency which it lacked. Twice previously my requests to go to Xinjiang had been politely refused, but this time it was quickly agreed. In mid-August, my wife and I flew to Urumqi for three days and then onto Kashgar for a four-day stay. My childhood dream had become a reality!

One cannot compare the Xinjiang of thirty-five years ago with today's, and our experience at Kashgar airport back then illustrates this.

Before our Kashgar-Urumqi flight departed, it was discovered that one of our aircraft's wheels had a problem. Several mechanics spent more than two hours repairing it but to no avail. By then it was dark. Since the airport was not equipped with runway lighting, nighttime departure was not feasible. We passengers were bundled off in a large bus to a hotel for the night, but our luggage remained on the plane, so we couldn't switch out of our sweat-soaked garb.

Early the next morning, a civilian flight carrying passengers detoured to Kashgar, dropped off a replacement wheel and immediately took off again. The new wheel was smoothly installed, and—without testing the new hardware—we were promptly boarded and on our way to Urumqi.

Motivated by an obsession of a sort, in the following three decades I've visited Xinjiang several times. Thanks to this infatuation, I've gradually gained an understanding of Xinjiang and can bear witness to its evolution.

Hami Wheat and "Hami Melon"

More than four millennia ago, tribes speaking an Indo-European tongue, whose members featured deep-set eyes and noses with a prominent bridge, took advantage of the horses they had domesticated to migrate eastward along the Eurasian grasslands from the northern shore of the Black Sea to the northern foothills of the Altai Mountains. One of their branches, dubbed "Tocharian" by archaeologists, crossed the Altai and proceeded south to the grasslands of northern Xinjiang of China. Some of the Tocharians continued onwards, relocating southeast to the Hexi Corridor. These are the "Yuezhi" referred to in ancient Chinese-language historical texts.

Amidst the Balikun Grasslands near Hami stands a stone structure dating from 3200 years ago. Pottery and carbonized wheat grains have been unearthed there, and scholars believe this may have been the site of the Yuezhi royal court. It was the Yuezhi (i.e., Tocharians) who introduced wheat from West Asia via the Hexi Corridor, and this is how the Central Plains of China came to cultivate this grain—a key phenomenon in the history of human civilization!

Hami was traditionally a strategic location along the Silk Road. Even today, Hami remains the key entry and exit point between Xinjiang Uygur Autonomous Region and China's interior.

During the fourteenth–fifteenth centuries, Hami belonged to the Eastern Chagatai Khanate governed by Genghis Khan's descendants. After Emperor Yongle of Ming relocated the capital from Nanjing to Beijing, he had to deal concurrently with the Western (Oirat) Mongols and the Northern Yuan that had retreated to the Mongolian Plateau. In 1402 he invested Hami's Mongol ruler, Engke Temur, as Prince Zhongshun.

In the middle of the Ming Dynasty, Hami's rulers converted to Islam. During the early Qing, the Dzungar tribe in Western Mongolia came to prominence, first laying waste to the Yarkand Khanate established in southern Xinjiang by East Chagatai Khanate's nobility, and then challenging the authority of the Qing in Mongolia. Finding himself squeezed between two great forces, the Hami ruler chose to seek protection by becoming a vassal of the Qing. He dispatched a special envoy to seek an audience with Emperor Kangxi and presented him with a sweet type of muskmelon in tribute. Kangxi named this Xinjiang specialty "Hami melon," and conferred its giver with the title "Hereditary Prince."

Although Xinjiang's politics have always been complex, the rule of this Hami princely domain continued unbroken for another 233 years. It was only in 1930 that the warlord Feng Yuxiang chased the ninth in the line of hereditary rulers from his palace. Today, the restored Hami Palace is an important tourist attraction.

More widely known than the Hami Palace is the fruit itself, the Hami melon whose taste resembles that of a cantaloupe. But among growers in Shanshan, some two hundred kilometers west of Hami, the association of "Hami melon" (*hami gua*) with that city leaves a less sweet taste in their mouths—one farmer complained to me that the primary cultivation site for the sweet and crisp melon is Shanshan, not Hami!

Turpan: Ancient Documents, Origins of Its People

After the Tocharians arrived in the grasslands of northeastern Xinjiang, some continued onwards to places such as Turpan (Turfan), Shanshan (Piqan), Yanqi (Karashar) and Kuqa (Kucha), becoming the earliest people to be located on the edge of southern Xinjiang's deserts.

The Turpan region is an intermountain basin in the eastern portion of the Tianshan Mountains. While the climate is torrid, it is a fertile territory rich in resources that attracted a large population for thousands of years that engaged in both agriculture and commerce. During the Western Han, it was here that the Tocharians established Jiaohe, the capital of Jushi Kingdom, about ten kilometers from modern-day Turpan.

I visited the Jiaohe Ruins twice. Even two millennia later, you can make out the contours of the city, and its estimated population once approached ten thousand. During the Six Dynasties period (220–589), a large number of Han Chinese fled to the Turpan area to escape war, and many northern nomadic peoples also based themselves there. In 450 CE, the Jushi Kingdom was destroyed by the nomadic Rouran, and thereafter Turpan was governed by a succession of four Han Chinese clans, known collectively as the Gaochang Kingdom. In 640, the Tang sacked Gaochang and established the Anxi Garrison in Turpan. Later, Turpan was ruled for a period by the Tibetan (Tubo) people from the south.

In ancient times, the Silk Road between Dunhuang and Persia comprised three routes: Northern, middle and southern. Turpan served as a hub for the former two. During the fourth–ninth centuries, one of the most active peoples on the Silk Road were the Sogdians, and they were concentrated in Turpan. They introduced Zoroastrianism, Manichaeism and Nestorianism (i.e., Christian Church of the East) to Turpan, from where it spread to the Mongolian Plateau and Hexi Corridor.

During the eighth century, due to contact with the Sogdians, the nomadic Huihe (renamed Huihu at the end of the eighth century, and ancestors of the modern-day Uyghurs) abandoned Shamanism, converted to Manichaeism and created their own script based upon the Sogdian alphabet. Since the Huihe were already on good terms with the Tang and familiar with Han culture, they disregarded the Sogdian practice of writing from right to left and elected instead to write top to bottom in imitation of *hanzi*.

In the middle of the ninth century, the Huihu fled the Mongolian Plateau when attacked by the Kirghiz who came from the northern Mongolian Plateau. A portion of the Huihu relocated south to the Hexi Corridor; others proceeded westward to the Turpan region where they supplanted the Gaochang Kingdom, a Buddhist state strongly influenced by Han culture, and founded the Kingdom of Qocho that practiced Manichaeism. However, influenced by the region's deep-rooted Buddhist faith, Gaochang's Huihu rulers gradually became Buddhists themselves. Meanwhile, during the same period, a group of Huihu migrated to a distant location west of Congling (Pamir Plateau). They joined forces with an earlier arrival, the Turkic Karluks and also began to interact with the Persian-speaking, Muslim Samanids.

During the latter half of the tenth century, the great majority of the Huihu abandoned their nomadic lifestyle in favor of sedentary farming and established the Kara-khanate that followed Islamic law. Henceforth, they were based in Kashgar and gradually expanded eastward. At around the same time, the Kingdom of Qocho—Buddhist by then—slowly expanded westward, extending its dominance over Urumqi, Yanqi, Kuqa and Aksu, and at one time, occupied Khotan and Kashgar too.

16 MY JOURNEYS TO XINJIANG: FROM DREAM TO REALITY

Early in the eleventh century, the Muslim Karakhanids first launched jihad against Buddhist regions Yarkand (Shache) and Yutian (Kingdom of Khotan), and finding itself victorious, moved against the Kingdom of Qocho too. By the beginning of the twelfth century, all of the peoples in Xinjiang, whether speaking a form of Eastern Iranian, Han or Tubo, were governed by the Huihu, and they gradually adopted the language of their rulers. The terms denominating this language varied over the centuries, but it has been known as "Uyghur" since the last years of the Qing.

During the twelfth–fourteenth centuries, Xinjiang was ruled first by the Western Liao (Kara-Khitai founded by the Khitai's Yelü Dashi), and then by the Mongols headed by Genghis Khan. The Gaochang Khanate was a vassal state of both. After centuries of war and integration, the population of Xinjiang was fully Islamized in the sixteenth century.

Today, the Turpan region is home to handwritten manuscripts employing various ancient Silk Road scripts, including Tocharian, Han, Sogdian, Manichaean, Tubo and Huihu. Various peoples, languages, religions and lifestyles once met and flourished here, and Turpan's contemporary population and culture reflect this historical process.

URUMQI'S ERDAOQIAO AND AN ELDERLY TURKIC LANGUAGE SCHOLAR

Urumqi is Mongolian for "beautiful pasture," but during the Tang it was known as "Luntai," and then as "Dihua" during the last years of the Qing and the Republican Era. The soil to the north is suitable for nomadic use rather than farming, so its residents frequently changed. Urumqi served as the headquarters of the "Northern Garrison Command" that governed northern Xinjiang during the Tang.

Over the last three decades, I've visited Urumqi nine times. Since 1987, each time I've noted visible changes in the city. Its progress is not only reflected in the new airport, high-rises and five-star hotels. An important indicator of its development is the area near Erdaoqiao where the Uyghur population is concentrated. When I first went, there were many street vendors hawking lamb kebabs near Erdaoqiao, and the Grand Bazaar featured daily-use items such as nylon shirts and rubber sandals. Later, dance halls and the Grand Theater were built in the vicinity, and the Grand Bazaar became the Xinjiang International Grand Bazaar. In the summer of 2011, I had a hearty dinner at a restaurant next to the Grand Theatre. On Jiefang South Road, the area's main thoroughfare, I also noted a rather modern-looking store specializing in Turkish goods, and a shop selling Qinnuri-Sultan brand name clothing.

From these changes, I fully comprehend that economic openness and social tolerance are the best policies for Xinjiang's construction. Nonetheless, I also know that since its establishment as a province in 1884, in the course of its overall development, Xinjiang has also experienced some very stormy weather.

Amidst these tempests, one scholar who remained in his post and devoted most of his life to the study of Turkic languages was a close friend, Professor Chen Zongzhen, who passed away in early 2018. In the 1950s, he studied Uyghur in Beijing and later transferred to Urumqi to research Uyghur and other Turkic tongues. Along with fellow scholars, he spent many years of hard work creating and launching a Romanized alphabet for modern Uyghur that had similarities with scripts used for Turkish, Azerbaijani, Turkmen and Uzbek over the last century. In fact, the "New Uyghur Script" was officially recognized by the Autonomous Region authorities and taught for several years in elementary schools during and after the Cultural Revolution, but this approach was abandoned in the early 80s in favor of re-instituting the traditional Arabic-based script.

Due to the vagaries wrought by the Cultural Revolution, Professor Chen served for several years as a Han-Uyghur translator in a rural county in southern Xinjiang, and Uyghur intellectuals universally praise his grasp of the spoken language as smooth, precise and native. His academic achievements were not in the field of translation studies, however; they focused on the historical evolution of and comparison between the various languages that comprise the Turkic language group. He authored many works, and even in his eighties published a 600-plus-page tome, entitled *History of the Uyghur Language*, containing more than 700,000 words. His entire family resided in Xinjiang for many years and contributed much to it. May the memory of the venerable professor's fine character and scholarship be passed on for generations!

Korla's Hong Konger

Modern-day Korla, home to the Yanqi Kingdom during the Han, was once a point of intersection for nomadic and agricultural lifestyles.

Proceeding south along the mountainous China National Highway, Korla is just a few hours ride away from Urumqi. But today's Korla is not primarily nomadic or agricultural. It is home to many oil companies and banks, a city where the modern real economy's petrochemical industry and virtual economy's financial industry converge. It has arguably inherited the historical role of playing host to two distinct clientele.

I have a memorable impression of contemporary Korla: It is home to a four-star hotel that is not luxurious but leaves the traveler feeling warm and cozy. During my stay, I chatted with the general manager. A native of Hong Kong, he has lived in Xinjiang for more than a decade and his children were born and raised there. From what he said, I gather he is still nostalgic about Hong Kong, but he confided that he had decided to settle in Xinjiang; his children's reaction aside, even he found Hong Kong too muggy for comfort. As a Hong Konger myself, I like to think that the hotel guests enjoy their stay thanks to the experience and vision that this general manager has transported with him to his new hometown.

KUCHA'S MURALS AND *PIPA* TUNES

Kucha (Qiu'ci) is located on the northern edge of the Tarim Basin. It was the site of the Anxi Garrison Command during the days of the Tang Dynasty and served as its headquarters during the period when the Tang, Tubo and Arabs competed for dominance in much of Central Asia.

In third century BCE, the Xiongnu made their entrance into the Hexi Corridor. Most of the Yuezhi were forced to migrate westward, crossing Congling until they reached the Ili River Basin. Later, pressured by the nomadic Wusun—also displaced by the Xiongnu—the Yuezhi moved southward, crossing the Amu Darya and settling in what is now Afghanistan. The Yuezhi supplanted the Kingdom of Bactria, founded by troops that had accompanied Alexander the Great in his eastward conquests, with the Kushan Dynasty. The Kushan established relations with the Han, Parthian and Roman Empires, and thus became one of the four great Eurasian empires. Kushan Empire's territories covered modern-day Afghanistan, Pakistan, northwestern India, and parts of Central Asia. Its sphere of influence reached northeast to what is now Kucha.

The Kushan Dynasty adopted the Buddhism of India's Mauryan Dynasty and facilitated the faith's spread eastward. At its height, the Subashi Temple, founded in Kucha during the third century, lodged ten thousand monks. Kumarajiva entered the monkhood there, and Xuan Zang lingered there for two months during his years-long overland journey to India. Although abandoned for almost a millennium, the temple's majestic contours are still visible.

Kucha is also a world-famous site for Buddhist art, and a large number of exquisite murals are intact at the Kizil Caves.

Two things about my visit to Kucha are particularly memorable. The first is that we reached the Kizil Caves near closing time, so staff suggested we return the following morning. We explained that we had other sites on our agenda the next day, and for this trip we had especially invited Lin Meicun, professor of archaeology at Peking University. Fortunately, two of the staff were graduates of Lanzhou University's Department of Archaeology, and when they learned Professor Lin was in our group, they immediately consented to take us up to the rock-cut grottos. Assuming the gray-haired man among us must be the renowned scholar, they made their way straight to me. "I *am* a professor, but my surname is not Lin," I said bashfully.

Being in Kucha, of course, I had to go see the statue of Kumarajiva. His father was an Indian aristocrat whose political mishaps landed him in Central Asia where he took the younger sister of the King of Qiu'ci as his wife. Under the influence of his mother, Kumarajiva entered a temple, took his vows as a monk, and went to study in India. Proficient in Sanskrit and Qiu'ci script (a variety of Tocharian), and knowledgeable in both Mahayana and Hinayana (Theravada) Buddhism, Kumarajiva's reputation spread far and wide. After Fu Jian, Emperor of Former Qin, united northern China, he intended to make Buddhism the state religion. He dispatched General Lü Guang to attack Qiu'ci, and bring Kumarajiva to the capital Chang'an. But while Kumarajiva was passing through Liangzhou, Fu Jian was killed and the Former Qin fell. Kumarajiva therefore spent the next sixteen years in Liangzhou (modern-day Wuwei, Gansu), and mastered the Han Chinese language. It was not until the Later Qin Emperor Yao Xing retook Liangzhou that Kumarajiva could proceed to Chang'an where he preached the Buddhist canon to the elite, and headed up its translation, becoming the most accomplished translator in the history of Chinese Buddhism. The *Heart Sutra*, *Diamond Sutra*, *Lotus Sutra* and three hundred other texts were all translated under his leadership. "Form is no different to emptiness, emptiness is no different to form" from the *Heart Sutra* were rendered by his calligraphy brush in Chinese.

In Chang'an, the Tang capital, the most popular music in the court came from Qiu'ci. Although the *pipa*, a pear-shaped, four-stringed musical instrument (sometimes referred to as the Chinese lute) is widely believed to be native to China, it actually originated in Central Asia; there are *pipa* painted on the walls of the Kizil Caves.

There was a *pipa* virtuoso in our group, the Central Conservatory of Music's Professor Zhang Hongyan. This was the second of my most memorable moments in Kucha—when she played three tunes on her *pipa* right at the foot of Kumarajiva's statue! Granted, there was no amphitheater, no entrance ticket, but it was by far the most meaningful *pipa* performance I've ever attended, not to mention a fine example of unscripted "cultural interaction" on the Silk Road.

Khotan: *Gangzi Rou* and Donkey-Powered Cart

Located in southwestern part of Tarim Basin on the desert edge, Khotan (now Hetian) was long known as Yutian, and renowned for the lovely jade (*yu*) mined there. The earliest residents of Yutian were Scythians who spoke an Eastern Iranian tongue, Saka, but there were also Indians and Qiang. Yutian became a Buddhist state quite early, and possessed its own scripts: Kharosthi at first, and after the fifth century, Saka employed the Brahmi abugida. Of all the states located in the "Western Regions" (the Han Chinese term for Xinjiang and areas further west), Yutian had the closest relations with the Central Plains, the heartland of Chinese civilization, and was the first in the Western Regions to have hosted sericulture and silk manufacture.

We visited many cultural relics and historic sites and came into contact with many locals. At a dance hall one night we encountered numerous fashionably attired couples engaged in social dancing. To see such a dance floor scene in a town that is said to have a heavily "Islamic ambience" made me cognizant of Hetian's diversity: Here one finds trendy types who yearn for modernity, but there are also those who dress conservatively and are nostalgic for a distant, more chaste past. The sentiments of the majority, however, lay somewhere in between.

During those few days we spent in Hetian, there were two additional things that impressed me. The first was a place of worship for my "five viscera" (key internal organs according to traditional Chinese medicine), located near the iconic statue of Uncle Kurban and Chairman Mao shaking hands. A stall there offers a traditional dish, *gangzi rou*. Fat mutton is first simmered at length in a *gangzi*, an enamel cup, muttering *gulu-gulu* as the broth bubbles. It is customarily eaten by dipping *nang* (a flatbread similar to Indian *naan*) into the broth. Most of the dozen or so travelers in our group were not keen to partake of this delicacy, but I am naturally curious and had the nerve to try a cup. I was duly encouraged by the praise of the stall owner and a few fellow gourmands nearby.

The other is the tale of a rustic farmer. My wife and I asked the locals to help hire a donkey cart to take us into the depths of the desert to visit the ruins of Ruwake Buddhist Temple. Although it is a county-level protected site, anyone unfamiliar with the path might not be able to get there or find his way out again. We came and went, toured the site and took pictures without a hitch. When we arrived back in town, the cart came to a halt. We spotted friends who had gone to a different site and we all began chatting about what we'd seen. A few moments later we turned around only to realize the farmer whose donkey-cart had transported us was nowhere to be seen. What about his three hours of unpaid labor? We asked around at length before we found someone who knew where he lived. So we went, located his place and knocked at the door. Yes, it was him, our donkey-cart chauffeur. It turned out that he had been too bashful to interrupt our enthusiastic chat, so he just slipped away quietly. I handed him the money, shook hands and we bade each other farewell. Two strangers—one good-willed and the other sincerely thankful. Although we did not speak one another's language and are unlikely to meet again in this life, I believe that both of us will cherish that handshake.

Kashgar: Cultural and Religious Status

During the Han (206 BCE–220 CE), Kashgar was known as the Shule Kingdom, and both the diplomatic envoy Zhang Qian and General Ban Chao passed through this oasis state. Under the Han, it was one of the four towns housing a garrison under the Anxi Garrison Command, and also the site where the northern, middle and southern Silk Roads converged, and thus a veritable "Silk Road Pearl."

The early inhabitants of Kashgar were Scythians, whose culture was a fusion of Persian, Indian and Chinese elements. Beginning with the Kara-Khanid Khanate founded sometime in the ninth century, Kashgar was the center of Islamic culture in Xinjiang for a millennium.

The eleventh century saw two renowned authors emerge in Kashgar: Yusuf Khass Hajib, author of *Qutadğu Bilig* (*Kutadgu Bilig*), or *Wisdom Which Brings Good Fortune*, and Mahmud Kashgari, who compiled

Dīwān Luğāt al-Turk, or *Compendium of the Language of the Turks*, in Arabic.

In the fourteenth century, the Chagatai Khanate split into two: Xinjiang was claimed by the East Chagatai Khanate, while territory west of the Tianshan Mountains was governed by the West Chagatai Khanate. Eventually, the reins of power in the West Chagatai Khanate were grabbed by Timur, a member of the Turkified Mongolian Barlas tribe. Conferring himself with the title "Amir Timur," he led several successful military campaigns and founded an empire that occupied the lion's share of Central and West Asia. His son, Shah Rukh, declared himself Khan, the first in a line of nine. The Timurid Empire engendered a host of talented men and featured a vibrant and prosperous culture.

At the turn of the fifteenth–sixteenth centuries, Persian served as the court's written language alongside a script known as "Chagatai." A Central Asian Turkic language, it employs the Arabic script but contains certain grammatical elements and loan words from both Arabic and Persian. During the seventeenth–nineteenth centuries, the Uzbeks adopted Chagatai as their script.

Kashgar is just one mountain away from the Ferghana region of the Timurid Empire (and the Uzbek Shaybanid Dynasty that supplanted it), so it was influenced by the latter's language and faith. Naturally, Chagatai became the text of the Yarkand Khanate and the source of the Uyghur script.

It was during the period of the Yarkand Khanate (fifteenth–seventeenth centuries) that the Uyghur—Huihu-speaking devotees of Islam, an amalgamation of the Tocharians, Scythians, Qiang, Han, Sogdians, Huihu and Mongols—coalesced into a distinct people. On the cultural level, it was in Kashgar that original writing in Uyghur emerged, along with performances of that quintessentially Uyghur music form, the Twelve Muqam. In terms of religion, various Sufi sects have become the focus of belief among the Uyghur. Naqshbandi, which originated in the Timur era, evolved into the most important order of Sufism in Xinjiang. Until the twentieth century, Sufi masters (Khawāja, Khoja) and groups of local nobility (Beys, Begs) formed the upper-level network of Uyghur society.

Differences in the interests of local factions led to the division of the Khoja into the "Black Mountain" sect (*Qarataghlik*) which was based in Yarkand, and the "White Mountain" sect (*Aqtaghlik*) based in Kashgar. Both sects possessed considerable human and material resources, and their influence extended from nobility to the common people. As with many societies throughout human history, the interests of competing factions among the upper class were often expressed—or concealed—via religious differences.

During the eighteenth–twentieth centuries, Kashgar was China's most important city in southern Xinjiang, but it was also one of the objects of the heated competition—the "Great Game" as it is known—for Central Asian territory between Imperial Russia and the British Empire.

In the mid-nineteenth century, the Khanate of Kokand in Fergana Valley exercised great influence over Kashgar and the rest of southern Xinjiang. Born in Fergana, soldier of fortune and Muslim leader Muhammad Yaqub Beg (Agubo) invaded Xinjiang and declared himself its ruler. He ruled southern Xinjiang according to Sharia for more than a decade, and also occupied areas such as Turpan. Yaqub Beg was pro-British and anti-Russian and expressed his fealty to the Ottoman Sultan, who conferred the title of "Amir" upon him. Eventually, Qing loyalist General Zuo Zongtang led troops to Xinjiang and defeated Yaqub Beg's forces at Turpan, and Yaqub Beg died suddenly in Yanqi. This appreciably altered the political situation in Xinjiang.

After Xinjiang was established as a province under the Qing in 1884, the political center was relocated to Urumqi. Thereafter, a relatively pacific, almost isolated, and thus underdeveloped Kashgar continued to exist until my encounter with it on my first trip in 1987.

Sixteen years on, and Kashgar had become a new city with modern streets, modern architecture and many fashionably dressed citizens. Kashgar's Old Town, Id Kah Mosque and the Apak Hoga Mausoleum—said to house the tomb of the "Fragrant Concubine" who once resided in the Qianlong Emperor's Beijing harem—had all become tourist destinations, adding a bit of shine to this Silk Road pearl with a medieval flavor.

At a stall hawking musical instruments, with my modest haggling skills I managed to purchase a *dutar*, a traditional long-necked two-stringed lute. Later, a Uyghur musician told me that the asking price and the instrument's tone were both very good, so the money I shelled out was worthwhile.

In Yengisar near Kashgar, we spotted a pair of veiled women in full-length black robes. They were also wearing a *niqab*, a facial covering that reveals only the eyes via a slit. To eat, they had to lift their veils in order to put their spoons to their lips. While this may be an expression of religious piety, it struck me as rather inconvenient.

Over the past three decades, the city of Kashgar has modernized, but the number of women donning *hijab* (fully concealing the hair) and veils has increased. Of course, this is true overseas as well.

In my opinion, on the one hand, the conservative and "retro" tendencies among Muslims, and anti-Muslim discrimination among people of other faiths on the other, are mutually reinforcing. I sincerely hope that Kashgar, long the religious and cultural heartland of southern Xinjiang, can overcome these two tendencies.

Yining: Nomads and Border Town

Yining, formerly Ili, is the capital of the Ili Kazak Autonomous Prefecture. During the Qing, the general responsible for maintaining order on the two main routes connecting southern and northern Xinjiang was stationed there.

The Dzungar Khanate, which once ruled all of Xinjiang, also took Ili as its capital. Ili belonged to the Wusun Kingdom during the Han, and Princess Xijun, who was given in marriage to the Wusun leader—famous for her poem lamenting her "exile" to a foreign land—probably resided in what is modern-day Yining.

Historically, the Tianshan Mountains have generally marked the division of Xinjiang into two, with northern Xinjiang home to nomadic peoples, while southern Xinjiang is largely devoted to farming. Today, herders in the grasslands of northern Xinjiang are mainly Kazakhs.

According to what appears to be a credible story of the origins of the Kazakhs, in the fifteenth century the White Horde in the eastern part of the Golden Horde split, and some tribes with mutual blood ties, known as the Kazakhs (meaning "those who leave"), departed together. Like Uyghur, Kazakh is a Turkic language, but the Kazakh way of life is closer to that of Mongolians.

During the eighteenth–nineteenth centuries, Russia gradually occupied all of Central Asia. In 1864, Russia wrested large areas of the Ili River Basin from the hands of the Qing. Many Kazakh herders did not want to live under Russian rule, so they came to Ili, Tacheng and Altay where they were accepted by the Qing.

The climate in southern Xinjiang is fairly warm, and the oases and the outer margins of the desert can be cultivated. Although there is little rainfall, underground rivers and qanat can be used for irrigation.

Northern Xinjiang has always been dominated by grazing, while agriculture and forestry remain undeveloped. The Chinese official Lin Zexu was demoted and dispatched to Ili after the First Opium War, where he focused his attention on water conservancy. Soon after irrigation canals were completed, a new wave of Uyghur famers (an earlier wave came in the eighteenth century when Qianlong Emperor unified Xinjiang) arrived in Ili from southern Xinjiang. Today, many of the Yining's Uyghur residents are their descendants.

Located to the west of Yining is the Qapqal (Chabuchar) Xibe Autonomous County, populated by a few tens of thousands of Xibe or Xibo. The Xibe and Manchu languages are similar. Their ancestors were dispatched by the Qianlong Emperor and trudged thousands of miles to Ili. Today, China's Manchu—still based largely in the northeast, their traditional homeland—can rarely speak, read or write Manchu, but many Xibe in this corner of Xinjiang still maintain their language, spoken and written. Most of the staff who manage the Manchu archives in Beijing's Forbidden City are reportedly Xibe.

I had the opportunity to go to Yining twice in 2005. The first time, I went southwest to Chabuchar and the Zhaosu Grasslands, and the next time to the northwest, home to Huocheng County and the territory on the edge of Sayram Lake, and the dry port at Khorgos just then under construction. Khorgos has been a major traffic artery since ancient times.

When I snapped a souvenir photo standing at the sign marking the end point of China National Highway 312, I thought traffic would one day be very busy. I hadn't imagined that in less than a decade, the Belt and Road Initiative would launch, and Khoros Port would be elevated to a full-fledged city. I assume the throughput of this, the most northwestern inland port in the country, will inevitably exceed that of several inland ports in China's Northeast!

Altay: Tuva and an Eight-Year-Old Girl

Altay is the most important city in northern Xinjiang and can be reached directly by plane. Kazakhs account for a high proportion of the population, and they are generally fluent Mandarin speakers.

It was in order to visit Kanas Lake that we went to Altay. But the sight of the lovely multi-colored waters of the lake aside, my chat with the young daughter of the guide as we drove there turned out to be an unexpected benefit. The guide was the son of members of the

Xinjiang Production and Construction Corps—known as *bingtuan*—who chauffeured individual travelers in his own SUV.

The moment before we set off, he asked if we'd mind if his daughter joined us. She was well-behaved and wouldn't bother us, he assured. Since there was a vacant seat anyway, we agreed. When I got in the SUV, we found a clever and pretty young lady already on board. Along the way, we discovered this little miss was knowledgeable indeed. We talked and talked, and eventually, we two oldsters and this eight-year-old began repeating Tang-era poems from memory. We each took our turn reciting a line—in rotation—and by golly, for the most part she was up to the challenge.

From our experience in remote Altay, I must say that people who are worried that Chinese traditional culture will be eroded and diluted by foreign influences are overly pessimistic!

During our short time at Kanas Lake, I reaped another harvest: I had contact with Tuva within China's borders. The lake is located at the junction of China, Kazakhstan, Russia and Mongolia. The lifestyle of the Tuva people in that area has been deeply influenced by the Mongols, but they still speak a Turkic tongue. Most Tuva live in the Tuvan Republic of the Russian Federation, and some live in the western Mongolia. I had never before set eyes on a Tuva, and I did not even know there were any in China's Xinjiang.

We visited a few of their tents and witnessed a magical musical performance. A Tuva musician put a tiny reed-like instrument in his mouth, blew on it and emitted two distinct yet harmonious melodies—like a Bach fugue. Mind you, a Bach fugue requires ten fingers playing piano keys, but a Tuva need only hold a small reed in his mouth, and by manipulating it with his tongue and lips, the musician can generate a melodious tune that is neither urgent nor languid.

My *Journey to Xinjiang* is not yet over. If given the chance, I will continue to dream the dream of my youth, and once again set out to experience the newest reality of Xinjiang.

PART V

Portrait of India

CHAPTER 17

Experiencing Emerging India

At the end of March in 2014, I went to Vienna to participate in a small-scale conference, "Interfaith Dialogue: Global Ethnics in Decision-making." A total of thirty persons attended, one-half of whom were retired heads of government and one-half "high-level experts" from various religious and cultural backgrounds. Only one Chinese and one Indian were in attendance. The latter is not just a person of great prestige in his homeland; I later learned that many Chinese know of him and refer to him as "Guruji," a transliteration of his Indian title signifying "great spiritual teacher." His statements generated animated discussion.

I am neither a spokesperson for a given religion nor a specialist in Confucianism, but during my speech I recited in Chinese, and distributed in the original and in English translation, the section on "Utopia" in the "Book of Rites" (Li Ji, Liyun Datong Pian). I did so in order to offer a simple explanation of Chinese political philosophy from Confucius' time onwards, and this also attracted a lot of attention.

The banquet marking the opening of the conference was held at City Hall by the Mayor of Vienna and doubled as a celebration for Germany's former Chancellor Helmut Schmidt, who had just turned ninety-five. Speaking in English, France's former President Valéry d'Estaing delivered the complimentary address in which he spoke highly of Schmidt's vision and character. He closed by citing Confucius: "Benevolence is initially difficult but ultimately triumphs."

Indian Affinities

In September, I received a letter of invitation from the India Foundation to attend the "India Ideas Conclave" in Goa during December 19–21, 2014. The Reception Committee Chairperson, Sri Sri Shankar, was the same spiritual teacher I had first met in Vienna six months previously. In India, when "Sri" precedes the surname it functions as an honorific; "Sri Sri" naturally indicates a greater honorific, signifying "Revered Master." Additionally, he invited me to join another dozen or so conclave attendees for a three-day sojourn at "The Art of Living Ashram," which he founded in southern India's Bangalore.

Upon receipt of the invitation, I immediately changed my earlier plans, and decided to visit India for the seventh time. Several reasons were responsible for my rapid decision:

Firstly, China and India are countries with ancient civilizations. Everyone in the world today who wears cotton clothing, uses cane sugar, eats chicken meat, plays chess, throws dice, or uses decimal-based numbers should be grateful to the ancient Indians; and whoever wears silk, eats pork, employs coal for fire, uses paper, or ploughs his fields with a water buffalo, should be grateful to the Chinese of old. Beginning with the sixteenth century, China and India both suffered invasion and plunder at the hands of European colonial powers, but in the middle of the twentieth century each took a separate path to autonomy and revival. Looking ahead to the middle of the twenty-first century, the retired politicians and academics who met in Goa at the year-end of 2014 all judge that China and India will undergo vigorous development, and the map of global power relationships will inevitably be altered as a result.

Secondly, in recent years China and India have experimented with reform and innovation. Both face many difficulties, among which is how to deal with indigenous cultural traditions. On the one hand, they need to overcome some old customs and practices that impede social progress, but they also cannot break entirely with tradition.

Thirdly, both are populous countries, which, while still underdeveloped, nonetheless constitute major economic powers in their own right. Many predict that in less than two decades, the three largest economies worldwide will be China, the US and India, in that order. President Obama's recent flurry of overseas meetings with the leaders of China and India illustrate how heavily they weigh in the minds of US policymakers.

Fourth, China and India are destined to be neighbors, yet the Chinese people's understanding of India is quite vague. The typical Indian also has a very limited understanding of his Chinese counterpart, and impressions tend to be negative. These factors are unfavorable to the development of bilateral relations and the generation of benefits for both peoples.

This paper and my plan for the subsequent publication of several essays are motivated by the reasons noted above. Unlike my knowledge of Europe, Central Asia and the Middle East, the process of familiarizing myself with India has not included long-term and systematic reading, and therefore my writing about India may capture only a partial image of the "Big Elephant."

Bangalore and Soft Power

With a population of 8.5 million, Bangalore, the capital of southern India's Karnataka State, ranks as the nation's third-largest city. I first went to Bangalore in 2003 because it was India's industrial and technology center. I visited the Indian Institute of Science (established in early twentieth century), the Tata Institute of Fundamental Research (founded in 1954 by Tata Group, India's largest Industrial conglomerate), and several biotechnology and IT firms. Over the years, much global talent and capital have flowed into newly developed districts of Bangalore where industrial parks like "Electronic City" have transformed the city into a world-class center for software development. Bangalore styles itself as Asia's "Silicon Valley."

Economically speaking, over the last decade Bangalore has recorded considerable progress. If you compare the neighborhoods and environment surrounding the science parks with those of a typical inner-city residential district, the contrast illustrates that while India's technology elite is now handsomely remunerated, the gap between rich and poor is still serious. Even so, Bangalore's level of illiteracy is quite low, and slum areas are much reduced there compared to cities such as Mumbai (formerly Bombay), Kolkata (Calcutta) and Chennai (Madras).

If we posit that today's "Bollywood"—the center of Hindi-based film production named after Bombay + Hollywood—is an expression of India's soft power rooted in financial and technical advantages afforded Mumbai under the British, then Bangalore, thanks to its pleasant climate and social ambience, has become a good place for nourishing mind and body that represents different aspects of India's soft power: Yoga, meditation and spiritual cultivation.

"The Art of Living Ashram" where I checked in on the morning of December 16, 2014, is such a venue.

Its founder Sri Sri Ravi Shankar was born into an upper-class family in southern India, and by the age of four he could recite many Sanskrit Vedic scriptures. He was tutored by a teacher who helped organize the non-violent movement along with Mahatma Gandhi and graduated with a dual degree in physics and Vedic literature. In 1981, at 25 years of age, Sri Sri Ravi Shankar founded the Art of Living Foundation, a non-profit NGO that, while rooted in Hinduism, is not a religious body. More than three decades on, it is now India's largest NGO.

During my three days with him, I could sense his easygoing style and personal charisma. In addition to being a spiritual leader, he is also an ambitious corporate planner and manager. During the daytime, he must meet a steady stream of visitors, and at night in the square, he converses with thousands of people using English and a hodgepodge of Indian dialects. News of these activities spread rapidly via Twitter and the Internet. Many public spaces in cities throughout India display his portrait in advertisements for his Art of Living Foundation. It's no exaggeration to say that he is a household name in India.

Based on his practice of yoga, Sri Sri Ravi Shankar has created his own unique rhythmic breathing and meditation techniques, and they serve as the core of training undertaken at his foundation's ashrams. Ideologically speaking, he preaches a humane, religiously tolerant world free of stress and violence. In terms of action, he frequently moves among violent zones of conflict such as Iraqi Kurdistan. Thanks to his tens of millions of followers in India, and close relations with the leadership of the Bharatiya Janata Party (BJP) that is currently in power, he possesses great influence and is considered India's "Ambassador of Peace." Similarly, because his foundation has branches in more than 150 countries and regions, he also enjoys great renown on the global stage. Some Westerners even use the same title as for the Pope—"His Holiness"—when referring to or addressing him.

On December 18, the ashram organized a novel Christmas party. Those of us who were guests from outside Bangalore, and several Muslim leaders in the region as well as the Auxiliary Bishop of the Catholic Diocese of Bangalore, were invited to take a seat on a spacious, meticulously decorated stage. Two savvy Masters of Ceremony hosted the event attended by at least five thousand persons. A choir, consisting of students from the tuition-free elementary school established by Art of Living, performed English Christmas carols that sounded exceedingly familiar to Western ears.

Guests on stage such as the former prime ministers of the Netherlands, Slovenia, Jordan and Lithuania, a senior German Member of the EU Parliament, and the former Deputy Speaker of the Belgian Parliament, were invited to take turns telling how they felt. The former Lutheran Bishop of Oslo, currently a member of the Nobel Peace Prize Selection Committee, also gave a short and very fitting speech. Just when I was congratulating myself that since I do not belong to any religion and therefore needn't speak, the Master of Ceremony read out my name, and politely invited me to take my place at the microphone, center stage!

Bangalore's population breakdown is about 79% Hindu, 13% Muslim, 6% Christian and 1% Agni. The latter refers to Jainism, a religion that evolved from Brahmanism prior to Buddhism, and advocates *ahimsa* (non-injury to all life) and vegetarianism. The proportion of Hindus and Muslims in Bangalore is roughly the same as nationwide, but the number of Christians in the city is disproportionately higher. That night, Muslim and Christian representatives—without exception—deeply praised the morality integrity and wisdom of our host and expounded upon the adage that "all men are brothers." For his part, Sri Sri Ravi Shankar mentioned the death of more than two hundred young students due to the terrorist attacks of the previous day in Pakistan and expressed his deep condolences to their surviving family members.

India and Pakistan have seen many military conflicts, and rifts between religions have generated many violent conflicts within India proper. But on the whole, the fact that a populous country comprising various languages, religions, regions and castes has been able to maintain overall social stability and economic progress some sixty-eight years after independence is undeniably a miracle of sorts. Many people believe that India will eventually emerge as leader of the subcontinent, precisely because it possesses unmatched religious and social traditions. Therein lies its soft power!

Closed-Door Brainstorming Session in Goa

Prior to being forcibly retaken by India in 1961, for over 450 years Goa was a colony of Portugal.

The Portuguese occupied Goa at virtually the same time as the troops of Babur, Genghis Khan's descendant, migrated south into India from Central Asia. Babur founded the Mughal Empire—"Mughal" is a variant of Mongol—that would rule India for some 350 years.

During the sixteenth century in both Spain and Portugal, the Catholic Church instituted the Inquisition to persecute Muslims and Jews who had already resided there for eight centuries. Goa followed suit and established a religious court to try believers deemed unfaithful to Catholicism.

In the autumn of 2006, I did a one-month stint as a visiting scholar at the University of Delhi. One Friday I took the opportunity to fly to Goa. As soon as we hit the ground I could see that its level of development far surpassed that of its neighboring states. My three days there were very comfortable and pleasant.

This time my impressions weren't particularly strong, however, since the starting point of our flight was the relatively new-look and scenic Bangalore. Nonetheless, Goa had progressed over the last eight years. The hotel where we lodged and held our meeting was recently built. It comprised several small buildings, amidst which were a lawn, pond and trees. A nice place for a vacation indeed.

Our meeting schedule was very tight, however, and did not afford any opportunity to enjoy a vacation. There were about 250 attendees, mostly Indian, and not a few foreigners too. The goal of the conference was to contribute strategies and advice for India's future development. To encourage a spirit of criticism and uninhibited speech, the media was barred. Since the event was held just a few months after the BJP had taken power thanks to its overwhelming victory at the polls, participants were primarily BJP supporters, or even core party members.

The Opening Ceremony was hosted by Sri Sri Ravi Shankar, and he delivered the keynote address too. The Indian Defence Minister and the Chief Minister of Goa were Guests of Honor, but they were not joined by a third invitee, Prime Minister Modi, who was unexpectedly otherwise engaged. "Development Mantra for India," the closing speech, was given by India's Minister of Foreign Affairs. Clearly, this conference was closely associated with the party in power.

Many speakers voiced pointed criticism of India's current situation. Some considered that rapid urbanization would only result in greater impoverishment of the countryside. Instead, agricultural technology should be modernized in order to increase output and benefit farmers. Some found all of India, urban and rural, excessively dirty; everyone has to use toilets, but no one is willing to clean them. Some brought up gender inequality and lamented the gratuitous wastage of female productivity. Yet others recommended that "every last person" should enjoy the benefits of social welfare.

During the full two-day conference, I especially noted three points, and sought opportunities to discuss them:

1. Should India develop its manufacturing sector? One author recently wrote a book entitled, "Make in India," which has won strong support from the new government. Of course, this title is a clever response to the well-known slogan, "Made in China." The latter expresses a finished action, while the former is a *call to action*, i.e., "India, make it!" This proposal has implications for India's import policies, human resources, energy supply and ecosystem. Given the existing technical level of India's manufacturing, and its relatively complete range of industries—coupled with low wages—there is no reason that India cannot energetically develop its manufacturing sector to meet domestic demand. It can undertake OEM business for multinationals, or even replace China as the "world's factory." If India has not done so to date, it is probably because its economic policymakers have chosen an alternative path of development.
2. India is a "secular" nation populated by a large majority of Hindu devotees. When the National Congress Party (Congress) was in power, however, it did its utmost to treat the various religions equally. The BJP, on the other hand, has a distinctly pro-Hindu color to it. In this regard, Prime Minister Narendra Modi has a controversial record, and he was harshly criticized for failing to prevent the 2002 anti-Muslim Gujarat riots when he was the Chief Minister of Gujarat. He was refused a visa for entry to the US in 2005 over related concerns, but in a remarkable diplomatic turn-about, in late 2014 he was welcomed in New York City and Washington D.C. on a whirlwind, five-day official visit as India's prime minister. In the future, besides growing the economy and fighting corruption, will the BJP choose to emphasize the traditions of Hinduism, and undermine peaceful coexistence between Hindus and Muslims? At the Goa conference, one European speaker denigrated the Islamic faith and even impugned the character of the

Prophet Muhammad himself. Although others spoke out to criticize him, in the audience many were busy applauding this speaker. This is a minor episode, but one that suffices to cause alarm.
3. Bilateral relations between India and three countries—Pakistan, China and the US. In my formal speech to the conference, I emphasized the historical origins of China and India and the benefits of Sino-Indian friendship. I mentioned that historically speaking, China has been an importer of Indian culture: Buddhism, which originated in India, altered the Chinese people's views of the world and life and death, and Indian art influenced China's architecture, sculpture, painting and dance. Many attendees posed questions and made comments after my speech. One, in particular, was a bit biting: Since you Chinese are so talented at imitation, quipped the questioner, and formerly imitated us in a big way, haven't you now turned your attention to imitating American culture?

I told him that China has its own traditions and has functioned as a major culture exporter; paper, printing technology, gunpowder and the compass are examples. What I didn't say was, the only way to make up for the questioner's ignorance and envy would be to enrich his knowledge of China post-haste. After the conference, a columnist told me that China and India should indeed collaborate amicably, but only on condition that China ceased supporting Pakistan. It appears that be it China or India, when considering diplomacy, one must learn to see things from the other's perspective and recognize one another as big countries and permanent neighbors.

CALCUTTA AND VESTIGES OF THE BRITISH RAJ

From the seventeenth century to the early twentieth century—over more than two hundred years—the headquarters of British rule in India were located in Calcutta, now known as Kolkata.

In 1690 the British obtained permission to conduct trade from the hands of the Mughal Dynasty's Bengal-based military governor, and henceforth Calcutta served as the base of operations of the British East India Company, in whose guise Britain gradually swallowed India. In 1858, the British exiled to Myanmar the aging Mughal emperor who still harbored illusions of rallying his people to expulse the colonialists. The British officially undertook to rule India and declared Queen

Victoria "Empress of India." Thereafter, Britain dispatched a Viceroy (lit., deputy king) to govern India who was stationed in Calcutta. In the early twentieth century, Britain decided to relocate its headquarters outside Delhi, the former capital under the Mughals, and built a new city on the southern outskirts to serve as its capital—dubbed New Delhi—in 1934.

On my way back from Goa to Hong Kong, I made a point of sojourning for two days in Kolkata. I was keen to witness for myself this metropolis that was once the center of British colonial rule and experience the lingering ambience of British culture there.

Judging solely from the landscape, the majority of important structures in today's Kolkata are leftovers of the British Raj. Among them, the most imposing is the Victoria Memorial constructed from white marble. In 1858, after their troops had crushed the first large-scale anti-colonial uprising, some British soldiers damaged the façade of the Taj Mahal by extracting inlaid precious stones to serve as "war trophies." Some Indians said that since the British had damaged the Mughal Dynasty's most elegant and refined architectural gem, they should compensate with a structure of comparable beauty. Three hundred years after their occupation of the city, the British did indeed build the Victoria Memorial. Strolling in the surrounding gardens and streets, I could definitely sense the intersection of times ancient and modern.

The large hotels and restaurants in the city center remain impressive. I had dinner at the most upmarket among them, the Oberoi Grand Hotel. As I eyed the tastefully decorated interior and enjoyed service by well-trained waiting staff, I was reminded of the legacy of British colonial rule, but I could also see India's future.

Ironically, the greatest legacy of the British is their language. About four hundred million people in India can use English with varying degrees of fluency, to read, write and converse, making it the most populous country in the world to widely employ English. There are hundreds of dialects and thirty or so official languages, but English is the only universally accepted one; English and Hindi are the two legally enshrined national languages, but many Indians do not accept the supremacy of Hindi. And of course, English remains a useful tool permitting (fairly) smooth communication with foreigners.

The second legacy is parliamentary politics, although endemic vote buying and corruption among politicians dilute its salutary role in Indian society. For a huge and complex nation such as India, centralized power would be almost impossible to implement, and the parliamentary system is arguably the only option for violent conflict.

The third legacy of colonial rule is the independence of the justice system vis-à-vis the legislative and executive branches of the government. In spite of its inefficiency and relative corruption, the judiciary remains a source of protection for vulnerable members of society.

The fourth is the civil service system, even though it is both bloated and inefficient. Civil servants at the national, state and district levels provide continuity and policy advice as power rotates erratically between competing political parties. Otherwise, India's governance would be an even more daunting task.

The fifth legacy of the British is the system of education, especially at the tertiary level. If a region's educational infrastructure is incomplete, society as a whole will be incapable of meeting the challenges of modernization; its elites will not possess the requisite knowledge, skills and creativity to solve problems and plan for the future.

These key aspects inherited from the colonial ruler have not only helped this sixty-eight-year-old nation to avoid becoming a "failed state." They have also enabled India to implement considerable development and innovation leading to achievements that are evident today.

In the coming decades, India may well undergo even more vigorous development. This is predicted by many experts, and I also have a premonition that this is the case. Here's why:

> Firstly, India is a genuinely pluralistic society. The Hindu tradition is colorful and variegated. Obedience and unanimity are not absolute requirements, so Indian culture does not contain factors that hinder creative thinking—and innovation is precisely the most important element in international competition today.
>
> Secondly, while no society has achieved total equality, India's caste system actually functions to deepen inequality. Social inequality has led India to neglect education opportunities and health care for about one-half of its population. This is a huge shortcoming of Indian society and is the very inverse of the concepts enshrined in the previously cited section on "Utopia" in the Confucian "Book of Rites." If this situation is not ameliorated, India will never be a truly great and powerful nation. But this is not a fatal weakness either; India's progress over the last sixty-eight years is a persuasive illustration of this. India has long had a very populous stratum

of elite talent, and thanks to their energetic efforts they have been able to move society in the direction of progress. Independent development of nuclear power, outer space-bound satellite launches and exploitation of modern biotechnology to produce traditional Vedic medicines are all outstanding achievements of India's elites.

Thirdly, India currently has strong industrial, R&D and financial systems in place. They all possess the potential to transition from a focus on output quantity to quality output, and thus become powerful engines for India's development.

In recent years, India's overall trend has been progressive. The upper-class elites are optimistic about the future. I browsed finance magazines in Kolkata, and there were not a few financial commentators who held positive attitudes about the outlook for economic development in the next few years. This optimism may be based on their personal experience, or perhaps their religious beliefs.

I possess neither their experience nor their religious beliefs. I can only say that I am cautiously optimistic regarding India's future development.

CHAPTER 18

Getting Acquainted with the Indian Elephant

Birthplace of Hinduism and Buddhism, India is an ancient country with five thousand years of civilization. China's architecture, sculpture, music, dance and martial arts have all been deeply influenced by those of India. The largest nation in the Indian Ocean region, India is also strategically located, bordered by the sea on three sides and the Himalayas to the north. The current population exceeds 1.3 billion, and India's GDP ranked number 5 worldwide in 2021.

Despite their country's close relations with India—China is its biggest trading partner—the great majority of Chinese perceive India as alien, even mysterious. While regrettable, this is hardly surprising given India's huge size and complexity.

ETHNICITIES AND TONGUES

India is a very colorful land, worthy of the label "multicultural museum of humanity."

If we first look at the peoples of India in terms of pigmentation, we find that dark-skinned, flat-nosed Dravidians reside mainly in the south. They were the earliest inhabitants of the Indian subcontinent, and their ancestors were likely the creators of the Indus Valley civilization who lived more than 5000 years ago. Fair-skinned, high-nosed Aryans are mainly located in the north and west of India. Their ancestors are principally nomadic tribes that invaded the northwest some 3000–3500 years ago, but some are descendants of Muslims who entered India from Persia or Central Asia over the last millennium. Along the borderlands to the east and north are peoples with light-brown skin with nose bridges of middling height, who belong to Tibeto-Burman ethnic groups, and have thrived in those regions for several thousands of years.

In fact, through a melding process lasting more than 3000 years, today the great majority of Indians represent a mixture of Dravidian and Aryan ancestry in varying proportions. Within the same district, town or even village, you can find individuals with very distinctive facial characteristics and skin color.

India possesses 120-plus languages, each of which has more than one million speakers, and more than 1500 dialects. Including the federal and state levels, there are 22 official languages, of which 15 are Indo-Iranian tongues that belong to the Indo-European family of languages, four categorize as members of the Dravidian language family, two are Tibeto-Burman tongues in the Sino-Tibetan family, and there is even one Austroasiatic language that belongs to the Munda family. According to statistics, the mother tongue of three out of four Indians is a member of the Indo-Iranian family of languages, and these speakers live mainly in northern, central and western India. Another twenty percent who speak a Dravidian tongue reside mainly in the southeast. Due to India's linguistic hodgepodge, many people can speak several languages.

The constitution designates the language spoken by inhabitants of northern and central India—Hindi—as the national language, and the Devanagari script, written from left to right with symmetrical rounded shapes within squared outlines, as its official written form. Approximately 350 million Indians are native speakers of Hindi, and almost all educated Indians can speak and write the language. But in many places, especially the south, Hindi is still not recognized as India's "national language."

As a result, English remains the nation's most widely used working language, making it the "unofficial" national language. In fact, only about twenty percent of the population can speak and write English fluently; the other eighty percent have no need or opportunity to use it. The population that is fluent in English reflects the proportion of contemporary Indian society that has received a decent education. Some families among the elite have employed English for generations, and their speech is natural and elegant. No matter how intelligent they are, those persons who are the first generation in their family to receive an education cannot possibly catch up to the former and inevitably feel somewhat inferior.

Of course, as the number of well-educated Indians increases substantially in the future, a simultaneous increase in the number of fluent English speakers will occur.

Alongside the gradual popularization of English, a brand of "localism" has sprung up over the last three decades. This phenomenon is related to the growth of locally based mass media, as well as to politicians who deliberately speak in dialect to cater to voters in the middle and lower classes. Some members of parliament (MPs) insist upon speaking the dialect of their constituency when in parliament, which places the federal officials they are interrogating in an awkward position. For this reason, when federal ministers prepare for a Q & A session they often bring along several assistants fluent in various languages. Besides revealing India's multi-ethnic reality, this also reflects some people's anxiety about losing their self-identity.

"As countries grow increasingly 'globalized', they grow increasingly 'localized' on the domestic front." This phenomenon that first emerged in Europe is even more evident in the Indian context. India's constitution proposed that by 1965, Hindi should replace English as the official national language, but to date this has remained unachievable. At the time, who would have imagined that English would actually become India's competitive advantage in the twenty-first century?

Rebellion, Independence, Constitution

Prior to independence in 1947, the subjects of British India, including today's Pakistan and Bangladesh, engaged in a resistance movement lasting nearly a century. In its early period, it was led mainly by the Indian National Congress, and later the Muslim League also participated. After World War II, the British were powerless to prevent independence and therefore decided to withdraw. At this point, a fundamental contradiction occurred between these two large organizations that had joined hands for more than fifty years in the struggle for independence: the Indian National Congress energetically advocated for the establishment of a single united, multi-religious but secular state comprising all territory in British India, while the Muslim League firmly insisted that areas with an absolute Muslim majority should form a separate Islamic country. During 1946–1947, bloody conflicts occurred between various religious groups throughout India, and therefore Britain decided to grant India independence earlier than previously envisioned.

Mediation was undertaken by Lord Mountbatten, Queen Elizabeth who has recently passed away, and the Indian National Congress and the Muslim League reached a partition agreement for the establishment of two countries, India and Pakistan. Crucially, Britain was empowered to delineate their borders. British India comprised more than 550 autonomous states, and according to the agreement, the Maharajah of each of these states was free to decide which country to join. The northernmost state of Kashmir was overwhelmingly Muslim, but its Maharajah was a Hindu. He hesitated at length, but after the sudden outbreak of violent conflicts between religious groups, he opted for India. This triggered the pre-independence war between Pakistan and India. For nearly seventy years, India and Pakistan have each occupied its half of Kashmir, and this has become the principal source of hostility between the two.

During the early period of independence, more than one million persons lost their lives due to religious conflicts, and more than ten million fled their homes in India or Pakistan. It was only in 1971 after repeated wars that India, Pakistan and Bangladesh took shape as we know them today, and experienced relative stability.

Given its starting point of violent conflict and unrest, it has truly been no easy feat for India to insist upon religious equality and maintain social stability. One important factor was the policy of religious neutrality maintained by India's founding Prime Minister Jawaharlal Nehru. Perhaps a more deep-seated reason, however, is Hinduism's strong, intrinsic vein of tolerance.

Unlike in China, virtually everyone in India is a believer. The overwhelming number are Hindus (roughly 81%), followed by Muslims (roughly 14%), Christians (about 2%) and Sikhs (about 2%). Those professing faith in Buddhism, Jainism, Zoroastrianism, Judaism and other religions altogether constitute less than one percent of the total population.

In formulating the constitution, the upper-class Hindu elite demonstrated tolerance and vision. Implemented in 1950, the constitution emphasized the protection of human rights. It abolished the "untouchable" caste that Hindus traditionally reserved for *dalit*, historically disadvantaged communities who were segregated from mainstream society. Henceforth they belonged to the new category of "Scheduled Castes" and were granted guaranteed quotas for places at school and in the civil service.

I was formally invited to visit India in 2002 and met the Acting Minister of Culture, a woman with Tibeto-Burman facial features. She presented me with a large volume, a replica of the constitution, and pointed out that—in 1950 or 2002 for that matter—this was an enlightened constitution.

Religious Society, Secular Nation

Religious faith is a top priority for the people of India. After repeated debate, the Constituent Assembly decided to refer to "deity" in the preamble to the constitution but did not cite any term for this concept commonly used by a specific religious community. The constitution expressly guarantees that all citizens possess freedom of religious belief, practice and propagation. Otherwise, the government was to maintain religious neutrality.

Regarding the right to religious practice, however, the framers of the constitution faced a very thorny problem. Ancient Hindu Vedic scriptures stressed the sanctity of cattle, especially cows. After the middle ages, Hindus ceased slaughtering cattle and eating beef. For centuries since, unowned cattle have wandered unhindered through the main thoroughfares and alleyways of Indian towns. Meanwhile, Muslims ruled India during much of the twelfth to nineteenth centuries, a period that saw the Muslim population double. Muslims not only eat beef, but at the end of the Hajj they celebrate Eid al-Adha (lit., "feast of the sacrifice") when the wealthy should slaughter cows or sheep and distribute the meat among the poor.

Thus the dilemma: How could the religious practices of *both* Hindus and Muslims receive equal protection before the law?

After repeated debate, a result was arrived at: The constitution itself does not mention the question of the slaughter of cattle for food, but in an appendix, "The Directive Principles of State Policy," it takes the moderate stand that each state may legislate regarding matters such as the protection of the livestock industry, and limitations on the slaughter of milk cows, cattle used for farming and other animals. Based on this directive, many individual states later prohibited or restricted slaughter.

Killing cattle for food has long been a big issue in India. It is not just the modern-day Republic of India that has used legal means such as appendices to the constitution to empower state governments to limit cattle slaughter; even during Mughal rule, for the sake of social harmony several Muslim monarchs issued edicts prohibiting their slaughter. However the British were dominant colonial masters who loved their beef, so during the British Raj wherever colonists resided there were busy slaughterhouses. This practice at odds with Hindu custom sparked several riots, and to some extent fueled the independence movement.

Muslims consider pork *haram* and do not eat it. While pork is openly sold and bought in today's India, most Hindu devotees are also accustomed to doing without it. During my seven trips to India, I have seen restaurant menus featuring mutton, chicken, fish, shrimp and vegetarian cuisine, but never beef or pork dishes. I assume this reflects wisdom borne of the long-term social practices of India's multi-religious society.

Based on this wisdom, India's founders struck a balance: To construct a secular state within a devoutly religious society, government and religion must be separated. This is why a Sikh once served as prime minister for a long period, and several Muslims have held the title of president, including one who was a leader in nuclear research. All of these are sterling examples for all of mankind. Nonetheless, in a society where Hindus constitute an absolute majority, long-term maintenance of a secular nation is not an easy task.

The Bharatiya Janata Party (BJP), which emphasizes Hindu traditions, won a huge victory at the polls in 2014. Since then, several states have strengthened controls against cross-border cattle sales and slaughter. In fact, there is a history of businesspeople who open and operate slaughterhouses and traffic the animals and their flesh across state lines, and many farmers raise cows expressly to sell their meat. If we examine history, however, we find that in early Brahmanism it was not forbidden to slaughter cattle. Back then, not only was beef eaten, but it was even used in sacrificial offerings to the deities. But in a society where most people eat neither pork nor beef, to insist in 2015 upon strictly implementing laws forbidding cattle slaughter is undoubtedly not aimed at ending illegal slaughter of the animal per se; rather, it is to highlight the BJP's positioning as protector of Hindu traditions.

I have the impression that the precarious balance between India's religion-based society and secular state is being sorely tested.

Democracy, Rule of Law, Corruption and Electoral Bribery

Prior to British rule, India never had a united, centralized government. After independence, under the shadow of constant threats of renewed religious riots, India adopted federalism and parliamentary democracy.

Since India had never experienced a unified regime, given the great differences between the states in terms of language, religion and geography, the choice of federalism was quite natural.

As regards parliamentary democracy, India had no such tradition either. The percentage of illiterates in the population upon independence exceeded 85 percent—it's still well over 20 percent—and this was at odds with the educated electorate necessitated by American- and European-style parliamentary democracy. Nonetheless, it was India's best option. Military dictatorship was not on the cards, because at the time there were no well-trained troops under a unified command, and no military strongman who could have controlled the overall situation. So if democratic elections had not been implemented, it would have been impossible to avoid the chaos of constant riots.

In the seventy-five years since independence, the achievements of India's democracy are very commendable. Actual progress on the ground, however, has fallen short when compared with initial expectations. This is not difficult to understand.

The successful implementation of a parliamentary democratic system requires two basic pre-conditions: A visible one—an independent and credible judicial system and a clean, efficient and politically neutral civil service; and an invisible one that is even more crucial—an electorate with civic awareness and a grasp of the concept of rule by law. Fortunately, in 1947 the British handed over to the Indians a judicial system and experienced civil servants. Given that there was no better option, and aware that conditions were not ideal, there was little to do but forge ahead.

Mahatma Gandhi's designated heir, Jawaharlal Nehru, drew on his tenacious personal beliefs and the prestige he accumulated during years of pre-independence struggle to lead the Indian National Congress and serve continuously as the first prime minister of India until he died in office in 1964. This period laid the foundation for India's democratic constitutionalism and established a framework for the development of Indian society.

Two years after Nehru's death, his only child Indira Gandhi (unrelated to "Father of the Nation" Mahatma Gandhi) commenced her seventeen years as the head of government, enjoying a hold on power that was twice interrupted by election defeats. With her authoritarian style, she monopolized power. In 1984, she ordered the army to mount an assault on the Golden Temple, a holy Sikh shrine that had been occupied by Sikh separatists. This inflicted serious damage on the temple and infuriated many devout Sikhs. Just a few months later, a pair of her Sikh bodyguards shot and killed her in her residence. News of her assassination caused anti-Sikh riots to break out in New Delhi and many other places, culminating in some 3000 casualties.

Rajiv Gandhi, Mrs. Gandhi's elder son, took over from his mother as prime minister for five years. Even after an election defeat in 1989, he continued to serve as Congress Party Chairman. In 1991, a female Tamil extremist detonated a bomb hidden under her clothing, killing Rajiv and about twenty-five others on the spot.

The successive assassinations of mother and son highlighted that India's democratic electoral system had not resolved the problems posed by intense religious and separatist passions.

Another of India's nagging problems—albeit in common with countries worldwide—is the trafficking of political favors in exchange for hard cash.

During the forty years when three generations of the Nehru "dynasty" held power, despite occasional corruption and vote-buying scandals, the Indian electorate was essentially satisfied with the performance of Congress under the Gandhi's. In a dozen or so elections, in six of them Congress took more than half the seats in parliament. Ironically, the fact that Congress also *lost* several elections during this period served to increase the electorate's trust in India's electoral system.

Once the Nehru family found itself in the opposition, however, India's money politics were gradually exposed. In order to facilitate raising funds for Congress, Indira Gandhi altered the government's fiscal policy and thereby opened the door wide to collusion between officials and businesspeople. Sanjay Gandhi, her youngest son, participated in politics at an early age, and his penchant for corruption and bribe taking was common knowledge. When Rajiv took over the prime minister slot from his mother, along with his defense minister he allegedly pocketed bribes from Swiss arms dealers. He was prosecuted for this. To clear Rajiv's name, his family members and supporters energetically followed the legal proceedings to their termination thirteen years later. He was ultimately acquitted, though long dead by then.

Prime Minister P. V. Narasimha Rao served from 1991 to 1996, but when he left his post he was jailed for accepting bribes. When he was prime minister, virtually all of his cabinet ministers presented themselves to a financial tycoon for his "blessing." Money politics and bribery of MPs have long plagued India's political circles, damaging the people's confidence in the electoral system.

In fact, the concept of the rule of law and sense of civic consciousness among the common people are still weak. For a small amount of money, or because they have been instructed to do so by a relative, a poor person often votes for candidates about whom they are ignorant. And MPs are quite willing to break the law in the rush to obtain campaign funds or increase revenues.

India's judicial system, while independent, is seriously short of manpower and funds, so it is unable to cope with the large number of corruption cases and related litigation. Predictably, officials and MPs who engage in corrupt behavior are unwilling to increase the budget or staffing for the judiciary and anti-corruption bodies.

As in other underdeveloped countries, democracy and the rule of law have failed to curb corruption in India.

Great Wealth, Extreme Poverty and Tardy Justice

According to global per capita GDP ranking in 2021, India figured 146th down on the list, compared to China at 72nd. The two countries each have populations totaling around 1.3 billion, but over 400 million Indians live below the poverty line with a daily income of less than US$2.15, a standard to measure poverty according to the World Bank in 2021.

Despite such widespread poverty, India is home to many mega rich, and some tycoons enjoy flaunting their wealth ostentatiously. When their daughter gets married, for instance, they insist on hosting a non-stop, ten-day banquet to which they invite a host of international dignitaries, and star actors, singers and footballers with whom they had no previous ties whatsoever.

I've visited slums in Mumbai located not too far from the mansions of the super-rich, and I've been to slums in Chennai, Kolkata and Lucknow too. Their facades differ, but in common is the space where several members of a family are crammed into a "home" that is so shabby it can't be called a room. Without running water or sewers—there aren't even latrines. Cost-free electricity is "sourced" on the spot by tapping into an electricity cable.

Big city slum residents do not, in fact, lead the most miserable lives in India—that status is reserved for poor peasants in the countryside who depend on the vagaries of the weather for survival. But many of these poor residents in the cities are actually peasants who have been deprived of their land.

When I was in the United States, I was advisor to an Indian postdoctoral researcher born into a family of farmers who tilled their own land. He was a graduate of the Indian Institute of Technology Madras. He earned his PhD at the State University of New York, had a solid educational foundation, and was both smart and studious. During his second year of work with me, out of the blue, he requested a month's leave during the Easter break to deal with a family matter. Although the timing struck me as odd, and he hadn't explained his reasons clearly, I acquiesced.

Two months later he finally returned, his head shaven and a very depressed look on his face. After several chats, I finally learned that his father had borrowed money at a high rate of interest that he couldn't pay back, and his creditor threatened him. The previous year his father had used his own land as collateral to borrow some money from a relative in order to pay off this debt.

One year later, their relative had come with a few people in tow, unceremoniously occupied his father's land, and tried to force him to vacate his house. The anxious old man was on the verge of suicide—the reason why his son with the PhD had left America in such a rush. He found someone to intervene and negotiate the matter, but both land and livestock ended up in the hands of the aggressive relative. To ensure that his father was shielded from further harassment, his son the PhD signed the agreement. Then he shaved his head and went to a Vishnu temple. There he made a solemn vow to the deity that he would return to the United States and earn money in order to support his father and uneducated siblings back in India.

I've since recounted this story to a few Indian friends. They all said that in the countryside, it's commonplace for a farmer who cultivates his own plot to lose his land and become destitute. I also queried my postdoctoral student: Since your father owned land, why not borrow money from a bank in order to repay the debt, instead of pawning his land to a relative at a cheap price? My student explained that one needs an acquaintance to gain access to a bank loan, and after his father had paid this middleman a sizeable "gratitude fee" for his service, the money left over wouldn't have sufficed to pay off his creditor.

So I asked him: Since the land your father mortgaged was worth far more than the loan he obtained, later on why didn't he go to court to prevent his relatives from forcibly seizing his land, and then sell the land to pay off the debt? He replied that the relative in question was very influential, and it was questionable if the court would even accept to adjudicate the matter. And even if it did, who knew when it would actually hear the case? The courts are useless—you must rely on the gods!

The banks and courts of today's India have progressed greatly since then. But as far as I know, poor farmers still find it difficult to borrow money for the seeds they sow, and the objectionable practice of charging an "introduction fee" and "handling fee" remains. Instances where the court refuses to adjudicate an injustice or the hearing is delayed interminably, still exist.

In any society, that there are laws on the books is better than the law of the jungle; that there are courts is better than no courts at all. But this reminds me of an adage in English: *Justice delayed is justice denied*.

Tradition vs. Westernization: The Sole Option?

Upper-class Indians generally speak very literate English and understand Western culture and social etiquette. For this reason, Indians deal with Europeans and Americans with greater ease than do the Chinese. Today, Indians serving as senior managers in large companies in the West—such as the Fortune 500—vastly outnumber the Chinese who hold such positions. This reflects the high level of adaptation Indians have achieved in European and North American societies, but it is also just one aspect of their "Westernization."

On the other hand, even very Westernized Indians also retain many aspects of traditional Indian culture. For instance, most Indian women prefer traditional clothing. Men dressed in modern gear are also numerous, but a large proportion still dress traditionally.

Then there is one's personal name. Many Chinese like to take a foreign name, explaining that it's easier for foreigners to say and remember. This is true, of course, but many Indian names are both hard to pronounce and recall. Yet for decades, I have not encountered any Indian who has opted to drop his own first name in favor of a Westernized one.

Less easily noted is the fact that young people in India commonly accept an "arranged marriage" as per the wishes of their parents.

While teaching at Montreal's McGill University in the eighties, I had an excellent Indian doctoral student. As a young student, he worked hard on his homework and earned the opportunity to study at the Indian Institute of Technology Mumbai for his BA and MS, and then came to Canada for his PhD. His interests were broad, and he was familiar with both Western literature and music. At McGill, he met a female student of Indian ancestry and the two soon had feelings for one another. But before they could socialize much, they broke up; her parents didn't approve of the match. During summer vacation the following year he returned to India, ostensibly to visit his mother. Back in Canada in time for the new school year, he sported a ring on his finger and said he had married; his bride was also an engineering student. Apparently, his mother had her eye on this girl as a match for her son, so she summoned him home over the summer to tie the knot promptly. I can't even count the number of similar stories that I've heard.

I've attended Indian-style weddings in both North America and India. Almost without exception, the bride, groom and their families don gorgeous, colorful traditional Indian garb. There are no pristine white wedding gowns or bevies of bridesmaids and best men and other details of Western etiquette that the Chinese have appropriated—Lu Xün famously dubbed it "grabism"—for whatever reason. As per Indian custom, Hindu scriptures are typically recited, the parents offer their blessings, ash is smeared on the heads of the bride and groom, and rings are exchanged. Then it's onto the feasting and dancing, normally to the tune of Indian—not Western—music.

There are two very popular forms of athletics in India: One thanks to the British, cricket, and the other is one that originated in India several thousands of years ago—yoga. Cricket is still cherished in the lands formerly ruled by the British Empire, and the Indian team often takes the annual world title. Meanwhile, yoga is recognized worldwide as a healthy activity for mind and body. If we describe India as a country where things Western and traditional coexist in harmony, then cricket and yoga are excellent examples.

Indians have never negated their own culture, and their borrowing from foreign customs is quite selective. It seems almost none of India's "fashionable" personalities are keen to transplant Valentine's Day, Halloween or Thanksgiving Day—holidays that are unrelated to India's history or culture—and promote their celebration by the average Indian who hasn't a clue as to their real significance.

In the closing years of the nineteenth century, it suddenly became the vogue for the Indian elite to engage in religious reform and literary rejuvenation. Tellingly, this trend actually acted to strengthen Indian nationalism. Most Chinese intellectuals are familiar with the Bengali poet Rabindranath Tagore and his energetic advocacy for absorbing the culture of others to serve as "nutrients" for Indian culture. He believed that Indian culture possessed its own unique tenacity and vitality, and it could withstand the shock of contact with other cultures. This confidence was the result of his judgment: Indian culture possesses an innate resistance to rupture.

Tagore was dead right. One hundred years on, despite its embrace of things Western, India has absolutely not lost its sense of self.

CHAPTER 19

India's "Special Administrative Region"—Pondicherry

When *Life of Pi* captured a second Oscar for Taiwan-born Chinese director Ang Lee, the film received big-time coverage in Chinese media worldwide. Barely mentioned, however, was the starting point for Pi's journey adrift on the open sea with a Bengal tiger—his hometown Pondicherry, India's own "Special Administrative Region."

TAMIL NADU'S ANCIENT TONGUE

Over the past decade, I've gone to India five times for a total stay of more than two months and traveled to many locales. But after viewing *Life of Pi* in mid-December 2012, I felt a strong impulse to go and see young Pi's hometown for myself. By the end of December, that impulse had metamorphosed into a plane ticket, and I found myself boarding a plane for my sixth trip to India.

The first stop after my flight from China's Hong Kong SAR via Singapore was Chennai, the capital of the southern Indian state of Tamil Nadu. Dubbed Madras by the British, with a population numbering five million Chennai ranks as India's fifth largest metropolis. Tamil Nadu is located in the country's southeastern-most region and faces Sri Lanka from which it is separated by the Indian Ocean. Residents of both Tamil Nadu and northern Sri Lanka are dark-skinned Tamils who speak the ancient Tamil tongue.

Typically quite long, Tamil surnames are difficult to remember. Forty years previously, the first postdoctoral student I advised was a Tamil who had graduated from the Indian Institute of Technology Madras. I recall the first time we chatted about the prestigious technology institutes in New Delhi, Mumbai and Madras. He explained that residents of these cities don't speak regional "dialects"; they speak three distinct *languages*.

If you wish to speak of India's various tongues, you should begin with the ancient civilization of the Indus Valley. Archaeologists have ascertained that 4500 years ago the valley already possessed a fairly well-developed agricultural civilization, and it is reasonably supposed that residents of that era were black-skinned Dravidians. Approximately 3500 years ago, white-skinned Aryans—whose origins lay in the southern Russian Steppes—migrated continuously through passes in the Hindu Kush Mountains of northwest India, down into the Indus and Ganges basins, and then expanded towards the south of India. They possessed the Vedas, ancient canons of early Brahmanism that were formerly passed down orally in Sanskrit, and which continue even today to constitute the primordial source of the diverse Hindu faith.

Thanks to more than three thousand years of intermarriage and melding between Aryans and India's indigenous peoples, plus nearly two millennia of large-scale intermarriage with waves of India-bound Central Asian peoples such as the Scythians ("Sakas"), Yue-Chi, Hepthalites ("White Huns"), Persians and Turkic-speaking tribes who migrated south at various periods of time, it's no exaggeration to say that India is a virtual anthropology museum featuring more than one billion specimens.

In general, inhabitants of northwest India tend to have paler complexions, taller physiques and speak a language fairly closely related to Sanskrit; southerners tend to be darker and shorter and speak a language belonging to the Dravidian family that includes Tamil and official languages of three other southern states.

Prior to independence in 1947, India had never experienced a unified national government. The Chola Dynasty that ruled southern India for almost one millennium was put in place by the Tamils. During the Middle Ages, they excluded once-flourishing Buddhism while energetically reviving Brahmanism. They built a large number of temples in the south—30,000 are extant today—thereby leaving behind a precious cultural legacy.

Snapshot of Chennai

Over the last three decades, the governance of Tamil Nadu has alternated between two opposing parties, but both have stressed Tamil culture. They have redesignated all names dating from the British Raj (1858–1947), so Madras is now known as Chennai.

My wife and I visited Chennai for two days. This seaside city was Britain's earliest base in India, and today it is commercially developed and hosts many sites of historical interest. Buildings constructed during British rule such as the University of Madras and Fort St George, and George Town, the governmental and commercial center, are all architecturally quite unique. The layout of these structures clearly conveys Britain's basic policy of safeguarding commercial interests through the combined use of military, governmental and cultural power.

The still-extant St Andrew's Kirk, St George's Cathedral and the Madras Club embody the British practice of not mixing with the locals, which necessitated separate churches and clubs for the colonial ruling class. Great Britain was jointly created overseas by the "merger" of the peoples of England and Scotland. That there remained a distinction between the English and the Scots, however, is evidenced by the appellations given these churches, which are named after the patron saints of Scotland and England, respectively.

Another highlight among Chennai's tourist destinations is a visit to the Pantheon Complex, which represents traditional Indian culture. The National Art Gallery, featuring a bronze statue of Shiva the Cosmic Dancer, possesses many fine works of south Indian art. But in terms of artistic excellence and sheer volume, it is outranked by the collections of London's British Museum, Musée Guimet in Paris and the New York Metropolitan Museum.

The National Art Gallery was built in a gorgeous and majestic Mughal style (*see text below*) that showcases India's cultural diversity. Hinduism is based on a strict caste system, while the principle of Islamic social organization is equality among all Muslims, so during the Mughal reign, many Hindus converted to Islam. In India's big cities today, many Muslims inhabit main streets, and what greets the eye is a polarized Muslim community: one that targets tourists and hosts elegant mosques, palaces and mansions; and another poor and dirty Muslim residential quarter with cramped, shabby shops.

We hired a chauffeured sedan to take us to Pondicherry. Along the way we came across several finely decorated, glorious Chola period temples as well as crude, dilapidated houses of the common people. Small town residents sauntered down the road with their cows, and on the highways, gas-powered car and bull-driven carts shouldered one another magnanimously.

Britain and France Battle for India

Proceeding from Tamil Nadu to Pondicherry requires passing through a frontier outpost where a vehicle fee is collected, but travel documents are not inspected. Upon entry one immediately discovers many bilingual signs in Tamil and French, because before Pondicherry was designated a "Special Administrative Region" in 1954, it had been under French rule for more than three centuries.

In 1498, the Portuguese Vasco da Gama and his crew rounded the Cape of Good Hope at the tip of southern Africa and arrived at Calicut—where China's great Muslim admiral and explorer Zheng He may have died earlier that century—in southwestern India. This pioneered the first direct trade route between Europe and Asia and broke the centuries-long Arab monopoly on Indian Ocean navigation.

During the sixteenth and seventeenth centuries, one after another the Dutch, British and French established a string of footholds along the Indian coastline. At the time, the Mughals, who had migrated south from Central Asia in the sixteenth century, ruled the lion's portion of northern India. The term "Mughal" refers to Mongols, descendants of Timur who once sacked Delhi. Although they were also distant relatives of Genghis Khan a, they had long since been Turkified and Islamized.

In South India, there were also a number of local governments that were beyond Mughal control, including one entrenched in the southwest, the Kingdom of Maratha that was founded by a warrior caste, or "Maravar." While they willingly joined forces with the Europeans to combat Mughal power, they also frequently attacked European strongholds.

Britain and France each operated an East India Company incorporated by Royal Charter. The British commenced business earlier and had a larger trading scope, and as France's power was initially no match for Britain's, the companies coexisted peacefully. Later, the British discovered a rapid rise in France's trading volume and military forces, signaling the "rise of a great nation," and they began to focus on containing the French. This generated a lot of friction.

The most intense conflicts occurred on India's east coast. With the consent of the local authorities, in 1654 the British constructed a fortress on the coastal banana tree plantation of a farmer named Madras. They designated it "Madras," and appointed a governor there. In 1664, the French set up headquarters in Pondicherry, a natural port 130 kilometers south of Madras.

Two themes dominated eighteenth-century Indian history: The gradual disintegration of the Mughal Empire due to internal divisions, and the rivalry between Britain and France on the fringes of that splintering empire.

Despite the existence of various forces within India engaged in mutual slaughter in pursuit of a portion of territory within the Mughal Empire, from today's perspective, only Britain and France genuinely possessed the capability to replace the Mughal dynasty. In 1746 France fought a brilliantly successful battle and seized Madras, Britain's main stronghold in southeast India.

The French did not honor their agreement to hand over Madras to the Mughals in return for their neutrality during the Anglo-French hostilities, however, and became the target of a military offensive led by the *Nawab*, an Urdu title bestowed by the Mughal Emperor on a semi-autonomous provincial ruler. In the resulting battle, two hundred French troops and seven hundred French-trained indigenous soldiers routed the *Nawab's* ten thousand strong force.

This military campaign was a portent of things to come; India would eventually fall into European hands.

By mid-eighteenth century, the military might of the British and French were evenly matched. For which country India would become a jewel in its crown was indeed difficult to predict. But it appears that, in this case, fate had indeed ordained that "God Save the Queen!" Robert Clive (1725–1774), a young British officer with a fiery temper—he once attempted suicide during a quarrel—exhibited exceptional valor in a 1751 battle against the French. This lifted the morale of his fellow soldiers and forced the relatively superior French troops to surrender.

Clive also performed outstandingly in battles against Indian forces and was appointed Governor of Madras. He appropriated the plan of the French whom he had defeated, and thereby laid a solid foundation for further development of the British Empire in India. After his return to his homeland, he became one of the three richest men in Britain. He was put on trial for corruption, however, and this time successfully committed suicide at the age of forty-nine. Today, a large statue of this compulsive adventurist and colonialist stands in the heart of London, both In memory of Clive and also of Great Britain's colonialist past.

The French Governor of Pondicherry, the Marquis Joseph-François Dupleix (1697–1763), was a highly talented man of great intelligence and courage, but the times were not in his favor. Motivated by envy of the governor, after the sea battle with the British in 1746 the French admiral Mahé, renowned for his military strategy, refused to sail into the port at Pondicherry, lest his fleet should come under the control of Dupleix. Instead, he purposely led his fleet to far-away Mauritius in the southern hemisphere.

After this defeat, Dupleix attempted to turn the tide by pouring capital into constructing fortifications and expanding French influence via bribery and negotiations. Investors in the French East India Company, however, vigorously criticized these measures because profits were meager. Summoned back to France in 1754, Dupleix became destitute, and his later years were lonely and desolate.

During this period, the great European powers engaged in the Seven Years' War. As a result, the possession of several colonies of the belligerents—mainly Britain and France—switched hands. In 1761, British troops captured Pondicherry. French military facilities were largely destroyed, greatly weakening French power in India. By the beginning of the nineteenth century, French India comprised just a few small pieces of territory along the eastern and western coastlines.

INDIA'S UNION TERRITORY

In 1857, a great nationwide rebellion gripped India, and many Britons met their end. The uprising lasted nearly one year and was dubbed the "Indian Mutiny" by the British; contemporary Indians referred to it as "India's First War of Independence." After the rebellion subsided, the British King appointed a Viceroy to directly rule India, which included the future Pakistan and Bangladesh. Beyond Britain's direct jurisdiction, there were also more than five hundred Princely States of various types and sizes, as well as Portuguese and French colonies.

When India gained independence from Britain in 1947, Portugal and France initially retained their colonies. Located in southwestern India,

Portugal's Goa was forcibly retaken by the Indian Army in 1956 and is now an Indian state. French India comprised four small plots of land whose total land area was smaller than one-half of today's Hong Kong Special Administrative Region. With defeat in Vietnam in 1954, France was forced to withdraw from Indochina, and India took advantage of this opportunity to negotiate with the retreating colonial power. India took over administration of the four plots of French-occupied land and formed the Union Territory of Pondicherry. The capital was established in the city of Pondicherry proper. Dubbed "Puducherry" in Tamil, it means "new town."

The other three parts of the Union Territory are located along the eastern and western coastlines: Mahé, which is named after the eighteenth-century French Admiral, faces the Arabian Sea and is surrounded by Kerala; Yanam, which faces the Bay of Bengal and is surrounded by Andhra Pradesh; and Kārikāl, which is south of Pondicherry and surrounded by Tamil Nadu. While English and Hindi are the Union Territory's lingua franca, there are four official languages: Tamil, Andhra Pradesh Telugu, Kerala Malayalam and French.

The Cabinet directly administers the Union Territory of Pondicherry, which is not represented in India's Federal Parliament. It has its own parliament that can pass laws for the Special Administrative Region, but they take effect subject to New Delhi's approval. The territory was established almost sixty years ago, and its current population numbers about 1.3 million. Education level and per capita income still rank among the highest in the country.

Culture and Customs of Pondicherry

Pondicherry is a small town. In the past, it was divided into the "Ville Blanche" ("White City") inhabited by Europeans, and the "Ville Noire" ("Black City") inhabited by Indians. The White City is one of contemporary India's tourist destinations. The streets are laid out on a grid pattern like a checkerboard, with tree-lined boulevards dotted by grand European-style mansions; the seaside features many white villas, just like France's small provincial towns on the Mediterranean coast.

When the French withdrew, they promised to grant local residents French nationality, and many Indian residents chose to take up the offer at the time. Six decades later, however, the number of French passport holders has greatly diminished, and few locals now speak fluent French.

But still on the ground are a rather large Consulat Général de France and several French cultural institutions, including the École Française d'Extrême-Orient (French School of Asian Studies), famous for its archaeological and historical research, and the Lycée Française that is recognized by France's Ministry of Education.

We stayed in a small inn, Hôtel de L'Orient, located on Rue Romain Rolland, named after the French novelist. It's located just three blocks from the Bay of Bengal. In the evening, strollers on the seaside promenade are a veritable potpourri: women in their eye-catching *sari* and headscarves, and many men in their drab clothing and full-face beards. Under the setting sun, the contrast appears a tad incongruent.

A new administrative headquarters, the Chief Secretariat, has been constructed on the seaside boulevard. The city also possesses a nineteenth-century Catholic Church, inside of which hangs "Assumption of the Virgin," an oil painting bequeathed by Napoleon III. Most of the devotees we encountered were middle-aged Tamil-speaking women.

We also visited a colorful Hindu temple. Sri Aurobindo, a scholar who was among the first to advocate India's independence, took up residence in the French colony in order to avoid persecution by the British authorities, and it was in this temple that he grasped the truth about yoga, and expounded upon its essence. Aurobindo Ashram, the spiritual center named in his honor, regularly hosts people of diverse backgrounds who go there to study and interact, and it has become one of southern India's noteworthy cultural venues.

On a pitch in front of a residential area, we found a group of Indian men engaged in lobbing metal balls toward a small wooden ball placed some distance away. This is pétanque, a pastime native to France's Provence. Just which country's passport they were holding I can't say, but my guess is that, after all these years, they should be Indian citizens!

At the end of the seaside promenade stood a sign in English: "Pondicherry isn't the same when you litter!" Ironically, there was a pile of debris right in front of the sign. It was a short walk from the garbage mound to a noisy, bustling little market. Next to it stood a finely decorated Hindu temple, and by its entrance was a live elephant for souvenir photos. Attached to the sacred animal's right hind leg was a thick metal chain.

Some liken India to an elephant. For more than a decade, I have witnessed the elephant's wisdom and strength, but I have not yet gauged its speed when it really begins to gallop. This Pondicherry elephant was shackled and thus moved with difficulty. Those fond of analogies might wonder: Is that shackle locked in place by the traditions of Indian society, the influence of the former colonial master or the corruption and incompetence of contemporary Indian bureaucrats and politicians?

CHAPTER 20

India's Take on "Belt and Road"

Since autumn 2013 when China formally proposed its strategic vision of a "Silk Road Economic Belt" and "21st Century Maritime Silk Road" (jointly dubbed "Belt and Road"), China has moved to establish even closer relations with countries along these land and sea routes. Fast-developing India, however, has yet to clearly express its attitude regarding the Belt and Road Initiative. This essay intends to explore—from the point of view of Indian history—the considerations that may inform India's academic elite and government decision-makers as they assess China's initiative.

Ancient Civilization, Massive Population, Advantageous Geography

Most Chinese know that India is heir to an ancient civilization. Five thousand years ago in the Indus Valley urban construction was already well developed, and even included sewers. This culture, which later suddenly vanished, has been termed "Indic Civilization." Beginning 3,500 years ago, successive waves of Aryans entered India bringing the Vedas and laying the foundations of a caste system and a host of separate kingdoms now known as "Hindu Civilization." One thousand years ago, waves of Islamized Turkic peoples came separately from Central Asia and established sultanates of various sizes, with Delhi being the political center. About five hundred years ago, a different group of Muslims with

Turkic origins—descendants of Timur and Genghis Khan—came south from Central Asia and founded the Mughal Dynasty that ruled India for 330 years. Over the last millennium, India has formed a "dual" society in which Islam and Hinduism coexist. It expresses itself via a modern "Indian Civilization" that accommodates diverse elements.

Each with a population of 1.4 billion in 2021, India and China are at par as the most populous nations on earth, but within this decade, India will probably overtake China. Ranking 6 in GDP in 2021, India's economy has developed rapidly in recent years and annual growth should exceed eight percent throughout the next decade. By 2030, predictions are that in GDP terms China will rank Number 1, followed by the United States and then India.

Chinese generally fail to note that India benefits from an extremely advantageous location. India finds itself at the center point between three continents—Europe, Asia and Africa. To India's north lay the Himalayas, its northwest affords access to Central Asia and China's Xinjiang and Tibet, and Bangladesh, Myanmar and southeastern Tibet are linked to northeastern India. Such contacts have enabled India to maintain smooth commercial and cultural exchanges with the rest of Asia since ancient times. These land-based links happen to be located on the "Oasis Silk Route" that cuts across swaths of temperate climes in Eurasia, as well as connecting to the "Southern Silk Road" that crosses both temperate and tropical regions.

India's west coast faces the Arabian Sea and thus directly accesses the Persian Gulf and the Arabian Peninsula. Just 1,200 kilometers lie between Mumbai and the Strait of Hormuz, while the Gulf of Aden is 1,700 km from the Indian metropolis. (By comparison, the distance between Guangzhou and the Strait of Hormuz is approximately 5,000 km.) The Bay of Bengal on India's east coast faces Myanmar, Thailand and Malaysia; at its most narrow the distance is just 200 km. All of southern India is surrounded by the Indian Ocean, with Indonesia's Sumatra to the east, various African countries to India's west, South Africa's Cape Town to the southwest, Australia's Perth to the southeast, and Antarctica due d south.

It is worth noting that among the countries that border the Indian Ocean, only one is on hostile terms with India, and ironically it is one with shared "roots": Pakistan. It aside, among all of India's nearby and distant land-based neighbors, the sole country to make the Indians uneasy is China.

India's Early Maritime Navigation

As early as 5,000 years ago, there were frequent exchanges between India and Mesopotamia, located north of the Persian Gulf. One piece of evidence of this is the cylinder seals that both employed. About 3,000 years ago, the Egyptians and Phoenicians (and later the Greeks) discovered the maritime route that led from the Mediterranean to the Red Sea, then into the Indian Ocean from the southern end of the Red Sea, and finally arrived at India. In the fourth century BCE, the construction of the Port of Alexandria transformed this into the principal route for contact between Europe and Asia. Henceforth, Indian spices, ivory, pearls and hardwood furniture were constantly transported via this sea lane—known as the "Spice Route"—to North Africa and Europe.

Just when made-in-China silk became fashionable in the Roman Empire—prompting fears that Rome was squandering its wealth on this expensive imported material—large amounts of Indian spices began to appear in the food eaten by the residents of Rome. Of 468 recipes noted in *Apicius* (a collection of Roman recipes, possibly named after its gourmet author), some 349 required pepper. Of course, the Roman Empire exported fine glass (as evidenced by its presence in the Nanyue King's Mausoleum in Guangzhou) and liquor to India and China, as well as copper and tin that served as ballast cargo.

Starting in the first century, India exported large quantities of cotton, firstly to the Arabian Peninsula and Southeast Asia, and then to areas on the western edges of the Indian Ocean, such as East Africa.

Around 150 BC, Greek sailors discovered monsoon winds in the Indian Ocean that blew from south to north in the summer and the opposite direction in the winter. The winds occurred on both the eastern and western coasts of India. Henceforth navigating the Indian Ocean no longer required following the coastline, and the length of time required for each voyage could be estimated. Thanks to these seasonal winds—better known as "trade winds"—the Indian Ocean progressively evolved into a maritime trade region for Asia, Europe and Africa, and southern India emerged as an entrepôt for trade between Europe, West Asia, East Africa and China.

Several of China's most famous monks were able to go to India to fetch the Buddhist scriptures thanks to the convenience offered by land and maritime silk routes. In 399, Faxian set out by land for northern

India, traversing Xinjiang's Tarim Basin in China and Central Asia's Gandhara. After living along the middle reaches of the Ganges for seven or eight years, he continued eastward and at a port not far from where the Ganges reaches the ocean, he caught a large boat capable of transporting more than two hundred passengers. After several brushes with danger, he reached Sri Lanka. Two years later, he took a commercial vessel to eastern Sumatra, and after a rest, prepared to continue northward to Guangzhou. But his vessel encountered strong winds and drifted at sea for more than three months. Eventually, he switched boats and returned to China at Jiaozhou Bay in Shandong.

Two centuries after Faxian's stay in India, in 645 Tang Xuanzang completed his entire 18-year round trip over the land-based Silk Road. Later, Tang Dynasty's Yijing also went to India, going and returning on the ocean, while Hyecho, a native of Silla (modern-day South Korea) who studied Buddhism in China under the Tang, voyaged to India by boat but returned overland via China.

When Buddhism entered China, it not only benefited from the Indian scriptures and art. Chinese monks and scholars also mastered Sanskrit and Indian phonology. As a mnemonic device, the monks annotated the Sanskrit texts with Chinese characters. This inspired the use of the *fanqie* method in ancient dictionaries to specify the pronunciation of a Chinese character. It consisted of using two characters—one with the same initial (sound), and a second to indicate the final (sound)—in combination to represent the full, accurate pronunciation of a given character (*hanzi*). The thirty-six "key-letters" used in the ancient Chinese study of phonetics and rhyme also owe their origins to the Sanskrit "alphabet."

In 751, the Tang Dynasty army suffered a disastrous defeat at the hands of the Arab army in what is known as the Battle of Talas (a site near the borders of modern-day Kyrgyzstan and Kazakhstan), and the Tang had no choice but to withdraw from Central Asia. Coming on the heels of that defeat, the An Lushan Rebellion also acted to reduce Silk Road traffic. Meanwhile, the emerging Arab Abbasid Dynasty constructed a new capital at Baghdad, near the old one at Babylon. It worked to ensure that Baghdad maintained its position as a key city in the land transport network, and also opened a host of sea routes linking it with many other countries.

During this period, the numbers invented in India (from 0 to 9) spread to the Arab world—eventually dubbed "Arabic numerals" by

Europeans—and became the standard arithmetic symbols used up to our day. Indian and Persian legends were compiled in the classic *Arabian Nights* (aka *One Thousand and One Nights*).

THE INDIAN OCEAN: AN INLAND ARAB SEA

Beginning in the ninth century, the Chinese empire in East Asia declined while the Arab empire in West Asia expanded. In China, economic growth in the south overtook the north, and Guangzhou, Quanzhou and other southeastern cities gradually replaced Chang'an and Luoyang as international trade centers. Accordingly, the importance of maritime communications gradually exceeded those carried out via the Eurasian land mass.

The adventures of Sinbad the Sailor in *Arabian Nights* were of course fictional and even fantastical, but the tales accurately captured the contemporary Arab yearning to sail the high seas.

Although India was still at the center of trade in the Indian Ocean region, after the tenth century it was not the Indians who dominated Indian Ocean trade; this role was played by Arabs and Persians. They lived in clusters on the edges of the Indian Ocean, including Sumatra, various places along the east African coast, and Guangzhou. During the late Tang, the Huang Chao Agrarian Rebellion (874–884) spread to Guangzhou. Arab and Persian merchants killed in the *fan fang* (neighborhoods inhabited principally by foreigners) numbered in the tens of thousands, a statistic that illustrates the importance of maritime trade then, as well as the nationalities of the key players.

During this period, the Indian Ocean was effectively the "inland sea" of the Arabs.

MARITIME AND LAND-BASED TRADE UNDER THE MONGOLS

After three successful military campaigns conducted to the west, the Mongols gradually established the largest empire in human history. The Mongolian empire comprised four entities with complex political relations: the Kipchak Khanate, based in east European and north Asian territories whose populations were mainly Slavs and Kipchak Turks; the Il Khanate, comprising areas belonging to the Persians but also including various maritime and land-based trade routes; the Chagatai Khanate, mainly in Central Asia, and including part of modern-day Xinjiang Uygur Autonomous Region inhabited by Turkic peoples; and Da-Yuan, territory inherited from the Southern Song of imperial China, also known as the Yuan Dynasty (1271–1368). Like the second century Roman Empire, the Persian Parthian Empire, India's Kushan Empire and China's Han Dynasty, the four *ulus* established by the Mongols were linked with one another and cut across the Eurasian continent.

In order to stimulate commerce and increase tax revenues, the Mongols built roads and bridges, dredged the Beijing-Hangzhou Grand Canal and established official courier stations and inns (*caravanserai*) along trade routes.

During the thirteenth and fourteenth centuries, political and commercial decisions reached by the four Khanates, and the relations between them, rendered maritime and land-based communications equally important. This was no historical accident; it was a key strategy applied by Kublai Khan that was intended to maintain relations between his China-based Yuan Dynasty and the other three essentially independent Khanates, thereby influencing them and keeping them in check.

Thanks to two or three decades of effort, Kublai Khan completed a network of maritime and land routes. As a result, during this period many travelers from distant foreign lands to the west arrived in China and bore witness to the prosperity and affluence of Mongol-ruled Cathay. Some were missionaries, some merchants, some simply adventurers. Among them were the Italian Marco Polo and Ibn Battuta, a Muslim explorer of Berber descent. In the late thirteenth century, traveling on land Marco Polo reached Dadu, the capital of China under the Mongols, located in what is now Beijing; a few years later he left Hangzhou on a ship bound for Persia, from where he returned to Italy. In mid-fourteenth century, Ibn Battuta arrived in China by sea and departed on a ship too, bound for his native Morocco (Map 20.1).

The Yuan Dynasty's Eurasian trade and cultural exchanges can be considered a prototype for "globalization" of that era. In today's vernacular, the Mongol's network was simply "Globalization 1.0."

The Indian Ocean After the Sixteenth Century

After Portugal's captain Vasco da Gama rounded the Cape of Good Hope to reach Calicut on the southwestern shore of India, over the next two decades Portuguese vessels established bases at several sites on the eastern

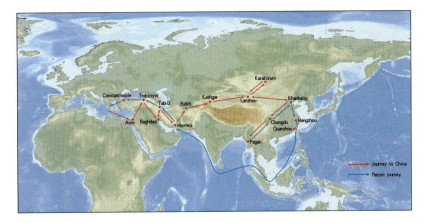

Map 20.1 Travel route of Marco Polo (thirteenth century)

and western coasts of India, including Goa and Cochin, and grabbed Malacca in the southern Malay Peninsula in Portugal's name of too. By the middle of the sixteenth century, the Portuguese had largely destroyed the commercial network established in the Indian Ocean by the Arabs during the ninth–fifteenth centuries, and Portugal had passed its own laws designating this occupied territory as Portuguese. Henceforth, India's southern coastline became even more crucial as a transportation hub and transit point for trade between Asia, Europe and Africa, and also as a Catholic missionary base. Thereafter, the ones to dominate Indian Ocean trade and to obtain huge benefits therefrom were all Europeans—first, it was the Portuguese, then the Dutch and the French, and finally, the British.

Belt and Road: But How Do the Indians See It?

No matter what era, location, physical environment, availability of raw materials, human talent, internal cohesion and strategic thinking are determining factors in achieving a nation's long-term goals. Naturally, the success—or failure—of China's recently launched "Belt and Road" strategy will also depend on these factors.

From the geographical point of view, India occupies a very important position. To a great extent, India's perceptions and decision-making regarding the "Belt and Road Initiative" will impact its implementation.

So how does India perceive the Belt and Road?

Based on my personal understanding of India and information gleaned from the media, I believe many of India's elite do not greatly accept or appreciate the Belt and Road; in fact, many even dislike it. If China's academic elite and decision-makers can put themselves in the shoes of their Indian counterparts, or at least attempt to comprehend their reactions, then China may make a more appropriate response to potential challenges.

The Indian Ocean region has long been an important region for economic and cultural interaction between Europe, Africa and Asia. The achievement of India's independence in 1947, most of India's elite believe, was the result of nearly a century of anti-colonial struggle. Therefore, they argue that India is the natural inheritor of the benefits abandoned by the colonialists. Based on this reasoning, it follows that India should be the master of the Indian Ocean—indeed, it owes its very name to the country. During the Cold War India did not join any camp, insisting on a policy of non-alignment. Nehru and his fellow comrades possessed the ambition and mindset of a large country, and naturally believed an independent India would inevitably become a powerful nation.

Starting in the twelfth century, and especially since the sixteenth, the landlocked countries of Central Asia have enjoyed close links with India, and people and ideas have frequently trafficked between them, so the Indian people have an emotional attachment to those lands. Clearly, India has made many contributions to the Silk Road, and feels as if it should have a say in related matters.

Seen in terms of practical benefits, India's demand for energy is becoming more and more acute, and it hopes that Central Asian countries will supply a portion of those needs. In recent years, the United States has put forward proposals such as "Great Central Asia" and the "New Silk Road," advocating that oil and natural gas produced in Central Asia should be transported south to Afghanistan and then onto Pakistan and India, thereby establishing a north-to-south energy corridor. But under agreements reached between China, Central Asian countries and Russia, Central Asian and Russian energy resources would be transported to China. This east–west solution and the north–south one advocated by the Americans are a modern-day version of the two opposing strategies for dealing with the increasingly powerful state of Qin during the latter years (334–249 BC) of China's Warring States period. (*One school advocated a north–south alliance in which they would ally to repel Qin; the east–west alliance called for each of the states on the east to join forces with Qin which is on the west.*) Undeniably, China's construction of oil and gas pipelines in several Central Asian countries does represent a potential challenge to India's national interests.

To India's north, east and south are Nepal, Bangladesh, Myanmar, Sri Lanka and the Maldives, all countries with which India undeniably shares historical origins. It is unimaginable that India would remain indifferent to their agreements with third countries.

China has its determination to "rejuvenate the Chinese nation," and its "China dream." For its part, India has its "vision of a powerful India" and its own "Indian dream."

These two dreams are not inherently a reason for conflict, and accommodations could be made so as to realize both. But as international relations have evolved over the last half a century—particularly after the two countries engaged in armed conflict in 1962—media, academia and political circles in the West have continued to compare the pair, and this has engendered a widespread sense of estrangement among the Indian elite vis-à-vis China.

Three Sorts of Reactions

India does not lack for talented, broad-minded officials. Even if they are dissatisfied with the as-yet-unclear Belt and Road blueprint put forth by China, they do not easily reveal their discontent on the diplomatic stage.

Based on media coverage, it appears that to date there have been three reactions within India to China's Belt and Road Initiative:

> The first is of the opinion that India should participate in the construction of Belt and Road projects. For example, India has already begun exploring with China the construction of a high-speed railway from New Delhi in the northwest to Chennai in the southeast. This is a positive reaction. Those who advocate this believe that by actually taking part in certain projects in the Belt and Road plan, India will gain a voice for itself as well as potential influence.

The second reaction is that China simply intends to invade the Indian Ocean in order to seek harbors in the Maldives, Sri Lanka, Myanmar and especially Pakistan, and to construct railways linking some of those harbors with China. China is also engaged in deflecting Indian and Russian interests in Central Asia. This group of people judges that Belt and Road is not in India's best interests, and therefore India should boycott it and resist its realization. At times India exhibits exceptional friendliness to Japan and the United States. The goal: To use these two countries to contain China and ensure it cannot fully exercise its naval power in the Indian Ocean. In its relations with Russia, Iran and even Turkey, India has a similar motivation—it hopes to curb China's influence in Central Asia. None of this signifies that India wants the Japanese or the Americans to have a greater say in the Indian Ocean, or that Russia, Iran and Turkey should be more powerful in Central Asia; India is simply applying the strategic principle of befriending distant nations while taking the offensive against those nearby.

The third reaction is that as a big country, India should not rush to make its position known. China's initial moves on the chessboard should be observed, and if they are unwise, India needn't bother opposing them; but if those moves are adroit or compatible with India's interests and ideals, then India can consider a more positive response. Now is not the moment to take a stand.

Tenor of Sino-Indian Relations

In the end, which of these attitudes will be accepted or translated into action by India's government? At present, this is not clear. But we can find some answers by examining basic tendencies in the history of Sino-Indian relations over the most recent five decades.

Firstly, there has not been substantive progress regarding boundary disputes for several decades. Currently, both countries are led by assertive governments, and neither is willing to make concessions that would satisfy the other party. Therefore, no major breakthrough regarding the territorial disputes can occur in the short term. Both parties are willing, however, to shelve this dispute for now, and seek cultural and economic exchanges and cooperation, and this is proving to be a feasible direction.

Secondly, the strongest hostile force facing India is Pakistan. China's support for Pakistan is one reason why Sino-Indian relations cannot be upgraded. India is also very concerned about the situation in Afghanistan and desires to exert its influence there. India's level of concern regarding Afghanistan is not necessarily less intense than that it feels about Pakistan, but since Pakistan lies between India and Afghanistan, the former finds it difficult to fully bring its power to bear. In any case, both India and Pakistan are already members of the Shanghai Cooperation Organization. Any improvement in the relationship between Pakistan and India will simultaneously benefit Sino-Indian relations.

May Each Party's Beauty Shine Forth

In March 2015, India launched an initiative of its own, entitled "Cotton Route," that includes areas on the fringes of the Indian Ocean region. Cotton has long been a major Indian export, similar in importance to silk for China. Although silk was sold widely, it was nonetheless a luxury item, while cotton—a necessity—was distributed to many more destinations. So India's proposed "Cotton Route" can be compared to China's "Silk Road," and the two might even be competitors.

Silk, however, was hardly China's sole export. From the Tang to the Qing dynasties, porcelain ("China") was a major part of its exports, and tea as well. As far as China is concerned, the appellation "Silk Road" is merely an easily comprehended symbol.

Since the Chinese have their silk, tea and porcelain, and India its cotton and spices, then why don't the two countries find a way to "appreciate the beauty of others," as per the Chinese adage, and politely use the appellation familiar to the other party in future communications? If for the moment that's not feasible, then they can at least agree to "let each party's beauty shine forth," with each country employing the slogan most pleasing to its own ear.

Intriguingly, the English phrase "Belt and Road" is a "fuzzy" slogan of sorts. It refers to one belt and one road, but it does not specify *which* belt or road. If China and India can reach some sort of consensus regarding these etiquettes, it might lower the tension, psychologically speaking. Putting the Belt and Road Initiative into action could then possibly bring great benefits to both parties.

In fact, as China and India undergo modernization, there are many aspects of the process that are suitable for cooperation and mutual borrowing. Limiting carbon emissions and air pollution management are two obvious examples.

In my own experience a few years ago, the air in both Beijing and New Delhi made people uncomfortable and often badly inhibited visibility.

Hopefully, the elite of both nations can put aside the annoying ambience caused by the smog, and brainstorm to generate refreshing new topics for consideration. I am even more hopeful that the leaders of both nations will not allow the haze to blind them to the reality that—over there on the opposite side of the Himalayas—stands a potential partner.

PART VI

Persian Cultural Sphere

CHAPTER 21

Early Civilizations on the Iranian Plateau

Geography and Human Environment

Persian civilization is one of the oldest in the world and was deeply influential in both West and South Asia. The core area of Persian civilization was the Iranian Plateau, but the Persian cultural sphere extends far beyond the plateau. Roughly speaking, it stretches from the Pamir Plateau and the Indus River in the east to the Syrian Desert in the west, from the Aral Sea and Syr Darya River in the northeast to the Caucasus Mountains in the northwest, and in the south, it reaches the Persian Gulf, the Gulf of Oman and the Arabian Sea.

The Iranian Plateau is northeast of Mesopotamia and the Persian Gulf, and its western limit is the 2,000-kilometer-long Zagros Mountains, with the northwestern end close to the Caucasus Mountains and the southeastern part extending east of the Persian Gulf. Its furthest eastern and southern reaches are within the Baluchistan region, which today falls within Iran and Pakistan, respectively.

Although designated a "plateau," there are actually some lowlands within this geographical unit. The entire plateau is characterized by a distinct water system, and the rivers are relatively short and carry low volumes of water flow. Therefore, from an agricultural point of view, the plateau is not considered a fertile region.

Archaeological evidence indicates that the Iranian Plateau was one of the first regions in the world to develop agriculture, nearly 10,000 years ago. This basically means that the plateau was the birthplace of humankind's agricultural revolution during the Neolithic Age. Interestingly, agricultural cultivation in the Mesopotamian Plain, the plateau's neighbor to the west, arose later yet the region entered the civilized era—complete with a script and institutions in place—earlier than the Iranian Plateau.

In terms of transportation, the Iranian Plateau was home to major arteries linking Europe and Asia. As early as the Neolithic era, humans had already pioneered trade routes. Obsidian mined in Asia Minor, for example, reached present-day Afghanistan and India via an Iran-Mesopotamia trade route, and Iran imported Afghanistan's lapis lazuli using the same corridor. Thus, before agriculture was widely practiced, the Iranian Plateau already functioned as an important trade artery between West Asia, Mesopotamia's Euphrates and Tigris rivers and modern-day Turkey, and was known for its "Obsidian Route" and "Lapis Lazuli Passage." Some trading post sites along these routes have been excavated by archaeologists.

Three Early Civilizations

Like all early societies, civilization in the Iranian Plateau commenced with the era of city-states and kingdoms. The first city-states were located in the Elam region in the southwest. Other early states formed in the Zagros Mountains, while the latest to take shape were the Median and Persian empires, which were both founded by Aryans in western Iran.

Cultures in the Elam region that predate the arrival of the Aryans are described below.

Elam was located in the western part of the Iranian Plateau and eastern Mesopotamia where natural conditions were relatively favorable, such as pastures suitable for developing pastoralism, fertile plains amenable to irrigation, and rich timber and mineral resources for various handicrafts. Therefore, it is not surprising that the region was where civilization first emerged in Iran.

Through research, we now know that although they had male leaders, the early city-states in the Elam region maintained a matrilineal form of society, with the general order of succession passing from brother to brother and only later father to son. In order to maintain the characteristics of matrilineal society, there were often cases where siblings married to maintain power within a common matrilineal lineage.

The Elam region both traded with and waged war against neighboring countries. The Sumerians in Mesopotamia (lit., the land between two rivers) invaded the region, and the Akkadian Kingdom, which unified the southern part of the two river basins, also conquered Elam.

Thus, the early civilizations of Elam were heavily influenced by Mesopotamia, with Akkadian and Kassite civilizations being the most influential. Elamite civilization began to master Mesopotamian pictographs, which later evolved into linear script, around 6,000 years ago. Cuneiform and modified linear writing have been found in Susa, the capital of the Elamites, and in Anshan, another notable trading city.

Later, the Elamites borrowed Mesopotamian cuneiform script and further transformed their linear writing into the Elamites' own cuneiform script. At this time, Akkadian was the common language in their capital Susa, and many legal and religious documents were written in Akkadian.

The center of Elam culture was at Susa, and remains unearthed there show that, in addition to possessing native Elam characteristics, Susa's culture was significantly influenced by the temple cities of the two river basins.

But in general, early Elam culture was an offshoot of Kassite culture in the two river basins. For a long time, the Kassites were the dominant player in Mesopotamia. The Kassite Kingdom was connected to Egypt in the west on the one hand and influenced Iran in the east on the other. The Kassites also maintained a network of trade routes from Central Asia through Iran to Mesopotamia and westward to Egypt.

These trade routes can arguably be described as precursors of the Silk Road. Initially, the Silk Road linked East Asia with Central Asia, and only later did it extend to the Mediterranean Sea. The ancient trade route of the Kassite era was mainly from Central Asia to Egypt, with Elam on the Iranian Plateau playing the role of a transit point during this period.

Aryans: Masters of Iran

About 6,000 years ago, a group of Indo-European-speaking tribes resided in the vast steppe north of the Black Sea, from the Danube in the west to Central Asia. Most lived as nomads, while a few engaged in settled farming. Probably due to climate change, as the Bronze Age commenced they began to migrate in various directions about 5,000 years ago. Some entered the vast areas of Central Asia, West Asia and South Asia, and are called Aryans by scholars. Aryan meant "noble," the derivation of the name for the country we know today as Iran.

About 1,000 years later, the Aryans set out from their second homeland in Central Asia and once again migrated with their oxcarts and horse herds. Some went south and east to India, and these were Indo-Aryans who spoke Vedic and Sanskrit. Another wing traveled west and south and became the Aryan- (or Iranian-) speaking West Iranians. A third group, the Scythians who can be labeled East Iranians, relocated to the steppes in the east. The Aryans who migrated to Transoxiana in Central Asia and practiced agriculture were the later Sogdians and Khorezmians, also known as Southern Iranians.

In short, by 3,000 years ago, the Aryans had largely occupied the "Persian cultural sphere" mentioned above and formed the mainstream population that would eventually create Persian civilization.

THE MEDIAN AND PERSIAN KINGDOMS

The Aryans had already entered the Bronze Age and practiced a clear social division of labor before penetrating the Iranian Plateau and India. They had a traditional history passed on by word of mouth, the renowned *Avesta*. According to this oral epic, society consisted of three castes: Priests, warriors, and farmers (or herdsmen), which were also the origin of the Hindu caste system.

In the western and northwestern parts of the Iranian Plateau, a federation of mainly nomadic tribes took shape that distinguished three strata: Priests, warriors and nomads. It was later unified under the Medes Kingdom.

In the Persian (Pars or Fars) region of the southwestern Iranian Plateau, tribal groups or city-states gradually emerged where the sedentary population practiced agriculture. These were the people who later established the earliest Persian Empire, a unified kingdom that granted autonomy to certain city-states and distant regions.

Here it is necessary to mention a phenomenon that has occurred at various stages of history all over the globe, i.e., when a given region's self-governing tribes or city-states are faced with external pressure—provided they share similar cultures—they tend to merge and establish a unified kingdom. Once this kingdom has concentrated a sizeable population and resources, it is also likely to expand outward again and construct an empire.

This recurring phenomenon may have first occurred on the Iranian Plateau. After the Persians, who spoke the Indo-European West Iranian language, had established their power and city-states on the Iranian Plateau, they had to face several countries in the west that were more developed and powerful.

The Medians faced several Semitic-speaking countries in the western Iranian Plateau and eastern Mesopotamia, the closest being their neighbor Elam, and the Neo-Babylonian Empire in southern Mesopotamia and Assyria in the north. On the one hand, these states were role models to the emerging Medians and Persians, but they also exerted strong external pressure against their development. Medes first replaced Elam, and later implemented a foreign policy that joined hands with the Neo-Babylonians to defeat Assyria.

Persia, on the other hand, started from two places, Susa and Esan, and absorbed Elam. The Medians arose earlier, were more powerful and maintained a largely nomadic lifestyle, while Persians led a predominantly agrarian lifestyle.

Around the end of the eighth and start of the seventh centuries BCE, the Medians and Persians had amassed more power in West Asia than the previous Mesopotamian states and became the newly dominant powers among the hegemonic states of West Asia.

After centuries of integration, struggle and competition, the descendants of the Indo-European-speaking Aryans—Medians and Persians—were finally united by Achaemenes, a Median nobleman, who consolidated the kingdoms ruled by the Persians and Medians. The Achaemenid Empire (555–330 BCE), also known as the First Persian Empire, encompassed more territory than any previous empire in history.

THE ACHAEMENID EMPIRE

The details of how the descendants of Achaemenes inherited the Persian throne are not known to us. But they did use Persia as a base to overturn the Medes Dynasty, whose military had been more powerful. So, although it was Persia that incorporated Medes, the Persian kings who achieved unification were actually Median nobles who had migrated southward and inherited the Persian throne. Thus, unlike Egypt in North Africa and China in East Asia, which were founded on agriculture, the Persian Empire featured both agrarian and nomadic lifestyles from the beginning.

The Persian king, a noble of Median descent who integrated Medes to form the Achaemenid Empire, was Cyrus the Great. In 555 BCE, it was Cyrus who founded what was then the earliest and largest empire in history. His martial achievements were brilliant: To the west, he defeated several important Mesopotamian states, and to the east, he extended Persian power into Afghanistan and Pakistan. By this time the Persians had fully entered the Iron Age, which provided the material conditions for their forceful expansion by furnishing them with state-of-the-art weaponry.

Cyrus moved westward to consolidate Median forces that were already present in Mesopotamia and retook Babylon. He forbade his soldiers to engage in looting, preserved the city's buildings, and freed tens of thousands of Jews taken captive by the Babylonians in Palestine. He allowed them to return to their homeland and rebuild the Temple of Jerusalem that had been destroyed by order of Nebuchadnezzar II, king of the Babylonians.

Successor to Cyrus was Darius, a distant nephew. There are no clear historical records of the origin of either ruler, but in view of the Persian Empire's later development, Darius was unquestionably the most suitable monarch to consolidate and expand the empire at that time.

Darius the Great (reigned 522–486) first quelled some still-rebellious Elam, Median and Babylonian forces, including religious leaders. He then divided the vast lands occupied under Cyrus and those during his own reign into twenty provinces. After his total victory, Darius inscribed the saga of his acquisition of the throne and crushing of the rebellions in three cuneiform scripts (Elamite and Babylonian, and the Old Persian whose usage began during his reign) on a cliff in western Iran, which is known as the Behistun Inscription.

Darius first instituted the concept of checks and balances in the Persian Empire he founded. He assigned a governor to each *satrap* or province to manage taxation, finance and civil affairs. At the same time, he divided the country into five large military districts, each with a number of sub-districts. In order to supervise and restrain one another, governors and sub-district heads were not mutually subordinate. This was one reason why the emperor of the Persian Empire was able to remain seated on his throne in Susa while retaining remote control of such a large territory.

There were also several other policies that led to the effective rule of the Persian Empire. First of all, it was governed in a conciliatory manner, and although the empire had a strong military force and dispatched administrative heads to the provinces, the center relied mainly on local powerful people to handle local affairs, including tax collection, and did not attempt to micromanage affairs from the capital.

Secondly, the early empire devoted itself to constructing roadside inns and roads, among which the best built and maintained, which led straight to Susa for the emperor's exclusive use, was dubbed the "Royal Way." It took only a few days to proceed from Susa to the Aegean Sea, a distance of some 2,400 kilometers.

Thirdly, Darius stationed intelligence officers in various places who were imaginatively called the "Eyes of the Emperor." The intelligence obtained by these agents from spying and surreptitious visits were collected in the capital and used by the emperor and his ministers as a basis for their policy decisions.

The military achievements of the Achaemenid Persian Empire were very great, and its administrative achievements were also remarkable. But the empire's most significant contribution to human civilization was in the religious domain.

It designated the religion of Zoroaster, a prophet born about 100 years before the founding of the Persian Empire, as the state religion, and relied on the power of the state to preach this relatively primitive, but very creative, view of the universe, society and life and death.

Zoroaster's creed spread widely in the Iranian-speaking world and had a profound influence on later generations. This was a great contribution of the Persians to world civilization. Unlike adherents to the Bahai faith—which originated in nineteenth-century Iran—Zoroastrians are a legally recognized and tolerated community in today's Islamic Republic of Iran.

This book's collection of essays on the Persian cultural sphere could also be entitled *Iran: An Empire of the Mind*. The earliest manifestation of this power in Persian civilization was Zoroastrianism. Later on, we will also talk about the Persian influence and contribution to the development of Islamic civilization, as well as later Persian contributions to world civilization in terms of history, literature, philosophy, painting, mathematics, medicine and architecture.

Grecian Influence

After the establishment of the Persian Empire, which ruled over a vast area of West Asia, Northeast Africa and a corner of Europe, only the Greek city-states had the power to rival Persia. Had they been united, as were Persia and Medes, the Achaemenids might not have been able to handily rule such a vast territory with many different faiths for long.

However, divisions among the Greeks allowed the Persians to cross the Bosporus and capture Macedonia and part of Thrace in fifth century BCE. Later, the disunity of the Greek city-states allowed Macedonia, north of them, to unify Greece, and Macedonia's Prince Alexander led his army to successfully lay siege to the Persian capital and occupy most of the empire's territory.

The history of Alexander the Great's eastern conquests has long been known. In 336 BCE—at the tender age of twenty—he commanded his army and exploited his innovative form of warfare, the Phalanx that featured soldiers with lances arrayed in a matrix, to destroy the Levant, travel south and destroy Persian rule in Egypt, return to attack Babylon and Persia, and then move east into present-day Afghanistan, reaching as far as Pakistan and crossing the Indus River.

After their decade-long campaign, his restless Greek-Macedonian soldiers became homesick and restive. This convinced Alexander that the time had come to return to the west. As he passed through the Persian capital Susa he married a Persian princess, donned royal Persian robes and welcomed the prostrations of his subjects, demonstrating that he was indeed the Emperor of Persia, and willing to integrate with peoples of the East.

At his wedding banquet, he even encouraged his ten thousand subordinates to marry local Persian maidens and wear Persian garb.

But shortly after the celebration, Alexander the Great expired at the age of just 32.

After Alexander's death, the huge territory he had conquered were divided up among four of his generals. Ptolemy occupied Egypt and established the Ptolemaic Dynasty. Seleucus, who was at Alexander's side during his conquest of Persia and Central Asia, took over West and Central Asia and established the Seleucid Dynasty, with its capital first in Babylon in the east, but later moved to Antioch (modern Syria's main seaport Latakia) on the eastern coast of the Mediterranean, in order to solidify his rule of Greece to the west.

After 322 BCE, the Seleucid Kingdom governed the Levant, Mesopotamia, Persia, Afghanistan, and parts of Central Asia. Henceforth, the Balkans, Asia Minor, Egypt (Ptolemaic Kingdom), West Asia and parts of Central Asia (Seleucid Kingdom) were greatly influenced by

Greek civilization, marking the commencement of what historians label the "Hellenistic Age."

The Greek influence in Asia and Africa was not only what Alexander hoped to see, but it also caused some degree of fusion of the Egyptian—Greek and Persian—Greek civilizations, which contributed to the revival of Persia as we shall see in the chapters that follow.

CHAPTER 22

Renascence of Persian Culture

HELLENIZATION AND PERSIANIZATION

Alexander died soon after he vanquished the entire Persian Empire. His general Seleucus founded the Seleucid Empire largely within the boundaries of Alexander's conquests, and ruled territory roughly equivalent to the size of the former Persian Empire. It extended as far west as modern Syria and Lebanon, and east to Pakistan.

During the Alexandrian conquest and Seleucid reign, the Greeks founded a number of city-states in various parts of the country, accounting for a significant percentage of the population of the Seleucid Empire.

Throughout almost 300 years of Hellenization, Persians in the East were influenced by Greek culture and vice-versa. In fact, Alexander foresaw the inevitable interaction between and integration of Eastern and Western civilizations. He recruited many Persian soldiers in the course of his eastern conquests, so the forces in Alexander's decade-long "Eastern Campaign" was also partly manned by Persians.

The cities of the Seleucid Empire featured two systems, ranging from the democracy of the Hellenistic city-states in the west to the imperial autocracy of the Persian region to the east. Although the Seleucids main territories lay in the east, the ruling elite originated in the west, so early on the capital was moved from Babylon to Antioch in the far west.

This westward relocation was not just due to the Seleucid's psychological emphasis on the west, as there were also certain interests to be considered. Antioch was the western terminus of a key trade route between Europe and Asia—the Silk Road—and another important hub of the trade route was Petra, in modern Jordan's southwest. Petra was located between the territories of Egypt, ruled by the Greek Ptolemies, and the Seleucid Empire. Since the Seleucids had psychological and strategic reasons for devoting their strength to these two major western towns, they handed over the administration of the eastern portion of their empire mainly to the Persians.

Nonetheless, the Greeks left an important legacy throughout ancient Persia, especially in what are now Afghanistan and Pakistan. For example, Gandhara culture, born of interaction between Hellenistic and Indian cultures, became a source of Asian Buddhist art.

The Hellenistic Period endured nearly three centuries, but not the rule of the Seleucids. While they focused their efforts on fighting Egypt's Ptolemaic Dynasty, a nomadic power emerged in their eastern provinces—the Parthians.

Before describing the establishment of the Parthian Empire and its culture, it makes sense to talk about Zoroastrians and their religion.

Al Sig Canyon: Entrance to the Silk Road city of Petra in southwestern Jordan

The Prophet Born Smiling

Around 630 BCE, Zoroaster, who was born into a priestly family in what is now Afghanistan, presented his views on the universe and life and they have been passed down orally for generations. There is no definitive proof of his life, although some people believe he was born around 700 BCE in modern Azerbaijan. In any case, centuries after his death, his followers compiled his thoughts in the *Avesta*. Because the Avesta does not mention any Persian or Median characters or events, Zoroaster must have lived earlier than the period of Persia and Media, but certainly not later than the establishment of the Achaemenid Dynasty (550 BCE), since the Achaemenids regarded Zoroastrianism as their primary faith.

Legend has it that the prophet came into the world with a smile on his face. Zoroaster's ideas would have reflected the more complex living conditions of the nomadic Aryans during migration since some Aryans turned to sedentary farming as they interacted with different groups of people. His religious thought was a response to the new situation and represented the first relatively complete religious system to emerge anywhere.

A tenth-century Islamic mausoleum in Bukhara, central Uzbekistan, is decorated with a representation of the sun's rays on the dome, suggesting that Zoroastrianism, which had a unique place in cultural circles before Islamic culture entered the Persian world, was still influential

The basic concept of the *Avesta* is cosmic dualism. Good and evil are represented by two separate divinities. One is called Ahura Mazda, the source of light and life, the symbol of wisdom, goodness, truthfulness and creation. The other is called Ahriman (considered by one sect to be Mazda's twin brother), the primeval root of darkness and death, and a symbol of ignorance, evil, hypocrisy and destruction. In the entire universe and throughout one's life, good and evil coexist; but after a long struggle, good will eventually triumph over evil. Sometime in the future, Saoshyant, a savior born of a virgin will miraculously descend and judge the world, ending the Mazda era.

The religion created by Zoroaster emphasized ethics and morality. He explained the relationship between human behavior and the future like this: If one strictly abides by the principles of good thinking, good speech, and good deeds, they shall be put to the test in the future "Last Judgment" and enjoy eternal bliss in Heaven at the behest of the savior Saoshyant. But the power to determine whether a person does good or evil comes not from Mazda's compassion nor is it tempted by Ahriman but is determined by one's own free will.

In its subsequent development, Zoroastrianism emphasized the use of fire, a symbol of light, as an altar for religious veneration, and was thus sometimes considered the religion of "fire worship."

Subsequent developments added a number of deities and rituals, dividing the religion into two different wings. One school of thought particularly emphasized the identity and power of Ahura Mazda and is therefore dubbed "Mazdaism." The other advocated the coexistence of two principal deities and dualism—black vs. white, good vs. evil. This was an internal division in the history of Zoroastrianism, but for world civilization, Zoroastrian ideas about the opposition of good and evil, messianism, apocalyptic judgment, and free will were important inspirations for later Judaism, Christianity and Islam. Persia is said to be an "empire of the mind," and the teachings of Zoroastrianism exemplify this.

Parthian Empire: Founded on Horseback

After the Seleucid Empire governed for several generations, the ruling elite saw many feuds and was divided by internal struggles, which led to the expansion of local power in the Persian territories. On the eastern shore of the Caspian Sea dwelled the Parthians, a largely nomadic tribe of fierce horsemen who spoke a language similar to Persian. They unified

Persia under the leadership of the Arsaces clan, and expanded into western Mesopotamia and eastern Afghanistan, founding the Parthian Empire that lasted nearly four centuries (247 BCE to 224 CE).

The mounted Parthians took their world by storm, but could not rule it astride their horses, so they employed many Greek-inspired methods to govern it and were avid students of Hellenistic culture.

Their territory was vast and comprised three distinct regions and economies: Farming in the plains of Mesopotamia to the west and fertile oases of southwestern Central Asia; artisanal and commercial activities in established Hellenistic cities and others that predated them in the east; and nomadic way of life in the steppe areas.

Fortified by its tripartite economy and powerful army, the Parthian Empire played a key role in the period from 200 BCE to 200 CE when trade on the Eurasian continent flourished thanks to the Silk Road. This empire's role in Eurasian trade is also confirmed by archaeological discoveries of Parthian currency in Central Asia and western China, all of which were labeled in Greek, suggesting that the Parthian Empire was still in its Hellenistic period.

In ancient Persia's Mazdaism, there was a mystical association centering on Mithra, the Sun God. Although worship of Mithra was not a mainstream belief in the Parthian Empire, many Roman soldiers, who often battled Parthian troops, gradually embraced Mithra worship.

Rome's Emperor Aurelian (r. 270–275) declared the Sun God as head divinity in the Roman pantheon, yet another example of the East's Persian influence on civilization in the West.

PERSIA PUSHES BACK AGAINST THE ROMANS

After the Parthian Empire had been established for about 100 years, Grecian power on the Balkan Peninsula was eclipsed by the Italic Peninsula's Romans, so that Rome became the West's representative and the Parthian Dynasty of Persia emblematic of the East. There were direct conflicts between the two empires, as well as much trade.

One of the two focal points of conflict was Armenia, located to the northwest of Persia in what are now the South Caucasus and northeastern Turkey. Armenia had always been within the Persian sphere of influence, and for a time was even a Persian province. However with the expansion of the Roman Empire, its borders were pushed to the Euphrates River, and Armenia near Parthia effectively became a Roman protectorate.

Another area of conflict was present-day Palmyra in Syria, a major town on the Silk Road that could be reached only after crossing the Euphrates and part of the Syrian Desert.

A high point in the rivalry between the Parthian and Roman empires occurred a few years prior to 50 BCE. Marcus Licinius Crassus, one of the three most famous Roman generals, led an attack on Parthia with tens of thousands of troops in order to show that he could compete with Pompey and Caesar in military achievements on behalf of the empire. But the Parthian cavalry were fine archers, while the Roman soldiers excelled at fighting on flat ground in close quarters. Crassus was not only defeated but also killed.

History has it that at the very moment, Crassus was slain by the Persians, the Persian king was watching a Greek play in his court. In other words, the Hellenized Parthian Empire was still entertaining itself with Greek drama more than a century after expelling the Greeks. Ironically, the general of the Roman Empire—who succeeded the Greeks as representatives of Western civilization—was rudely dispatched by the Parthian Empire's Persian army.

Like all dynasties, the Parthian Empire may have been able to resist this particular attack, but its long rivalry with another empire inevitably sapped its strength.

A more fatal blow came from internecine struggles: Power passed from one emperor to another fifteen times over a century, with each monarch averaging less than seven years on the throne. This was obviously very disadvantageous for a dynasty's unity. The decline of the Parthian dynasty created the conditions for the establishment of another famous one in Persia's history, the Sassanid Dynasty.

Zoroastrianism and Manichaeism Under the Sassanids

During the latter part of the Parthian Empire, Persian culture integrated a sizeable amount of Greek culture, but basic Persian beliefs in Zoroastrianism and Mazda worship were restored, bringing the curtain down on the Hellenistic Period. The Parthian Empire gradually declined and, in the face of strong external enemies and internal struggles, gave way to another dynasty.

In third century, a nobleman in southwestern modern Iran's Fars Province defeated the Parthian army and founded the Sassanid Dynasty. Ardashir I named it in honor of his grandfather, Sassan.

From the outset, Zoroastrianism was designated as the state religion. Although Zoroastrianism was already the dominant faith among Persians at this time, there was a distinction between eastern and western sects, and the Sassanids did their utmost to render them mutually compatible.

Among the dynasties of Persia, the Sassanids (224–651) had the most frequent contacts with China. Their rule coincided with the period between the Wei and Jin Dynasties and the beginning of the Tang dynasty when the Silk Road gradually opened to Persia and then westward to the Mediterranean.

History is replete with examples of how an empire virtually requires one or more external enemies in order to remain strong. For the Sassanids, that meant the Roman Empire based in the Italic Peninsula, and then its successor, the Eastern Roman Empire, i.e., Greek-speaking Byzantium, based in Constantinople.

In addition to the enemies of the Sassanids in the west, there was also a rising rival in the east, the Hephthalites. Speakers of an Altaic language, they were a nomadic people similar to the Huns and arrived in Central Asia around the fifth century. The Hephthalites were also known as White Huns, possibly because the ruling elite later intermarried with Altaic-speaking North Asians and Persian-speaking Central Asians.

Although the Hephthalites shared a border with the Persian Sassanids and often had conflicts with them, the Hephthalites encouraged the latter to fight with the Byzantines and even helped them do so. With strong foes to the east and west, and inadequate tax revenues, although the Sassanid Dynasty was one of the most illustrious dynasties in Persian history—and endured almost four centuries—it proved unable to provide its inhabitants with genuine peace or prosperity.

From the perspective of the Persian cultural world, the Sassanid Empire was the purest representation of Persian civilization and the acme of Persian culture renascence in the post-Hellenistic era. It is therefore not hard to understand why the Sassanid Empire and several of its monarchs have enjoyed a very positive and prominent position in post-empire chronicles, and even in contemporary Iran's history books.

The early Persian empire was governed mainly by locally autonomous administrations. The local authorities had a great deal of autonomy with the approval of the central government, but centralization greatly increased during the Sassanid Empire. The empire's territory extended as far east as the Indus River, and almost all of Central Asia belonged to it, while its rule over its subjects was more meticulous than in previous generations. For example, the faith and behavior of the East Iranian-speaking Sogdians living between the Oxus (Amu Darya) and the Jaxartes (Syr Darya) were regulated by the Sassanid Empire.

Since the Sassanid Empire placed special emphasis on religious beliefs and highlighted native Persian culture, Zoroastrian clergy possessed superior political influence and power, and acquired economic power too. As a result, the construction of fire altars became popular and the clergy enjoyed high social status. Against a background of widespread discontent among Persians with the corruption and domination of the religious elite, a different faith thrived: Manichaeism.

Any chaotic period in history is likely to see the emergence of new religions. In 216 CE, a descendant of the Parthian royal family born in Mesopotamia, Mani, founded a new religion influenced by Christian mysticism and based on the basic concept of Zoroastrian dualism. The prophet himself was lame, possibly a Christian in his early years, and influenced by Neo-platonism.

In the religion he founded, there was an aversion to the human body and the belief that purity of spirit was noble and something for which to strive. Manichaeism is also dualistic but differs from Zoroastrianism's dualism in that it professes good and evil both exist, but these two forces are manifested differently during three eras. The opposing forces are Ahura Mazda, the God of Good, and Ahriman, the God of Evil, and the three eras refer to the struggle between Light and Darkness over time.

In the beginning, Light and Darkness are separate and independent of one another; during the middle era, Darkness invades Light, they become entangled and engage in repeated struggle, and initially Darkness dominates but then Light appears to somewhat recover; and during the final phase, the pair return to their primordial separate state. (Zoroastrianism, on the other hand, professes that after a struggle, Light is eventually victorious and destroys Darkness).

The two forces are manifested in humankind via a struggle between the spiritual and the corporeal: The soul is holy, but is bound to the flesh, which is unclean. To restore purity and light, the holy soul should abandon material pleasure, not possess property, or marry, raise children or eat meat, and so forth, so that after death one can enter the underworld and ascend into the Light, and separate from the Darkness to which the physical body is forever bound.

This was in fact an other-worldly, even pessimistic religion. But in those days, this faith spread rapidly not only within Persia but also to Central Asia, Sogdiana, and then via itinerant Sogdians to the Turkophone peoples of the northern steppes, and even to China's Central Plains.

Manichaeism was one of the "Three Alien Religions" purportedly exterminated by Emperor Wu Zong of Tang (reigned 840–846), so it did not exist openly in China for long. Manichaeism later went underground, and this secret brotherhood was known as the Religion of Light (*ming jiao*), which existed until the early years of the Ming Dynasty.

Anushirvan and the Sassanian Renascence

According to the *Avesta*, there were three castes, and another was added later, making four castes in Sassanian society. At the top was the priestly caste; then came nobility and warriors, then the newly added caste of scribes, and at the bottom were those subject to tax, i.e., farmers, herdsmen, craftsmen, merchants, and other commoners. This division of labor and method of operating a society was not unfeasible, but in this hierarchy, priests and warriors/nobles often possessed the lion's share of society's assets, fostering a form of "wealth gap."

After the Manichaeans came out against the official state religion, an extreme faction emerged among them. This faction believed that since all sins in the world derived mainly from wealth and lust, these should be totally banned or all inhabitants should be equal; there should not be a situation where the rich had land and a bevy of wives and concubines, while a poor man had no wife or plot of land to call his own.

Under the initiative of a leading figure named Mazdak, a movement began throughout the Sassanid Empire to confiscate the wealthy's property and divide it equally among all. Some places even had special venues where men freely "shared" women. This movement caused great social chaos, but King Kavad chose to support it at first in order to contain the power of the priests and nobles so that they would not threaten him. He later attempted to violently suppress the Mazdak rebellion but died suddenly.

Almost simultaneously with the Mazdaq unrest, Sassanian rule was threatened by the Hephthalites. Upon King Kavad's sudden passing,

Prince Khosrow succeeded to the throne in 531 CE. After quelling the Mazdak uprising, Khosrow I proceeded to restore social order by gifting heirless wealth and land to charitable organizations. He then ordered his administration to reform the tax system; undertake a new census; conduct land surveys and assess the output of various types of land, and compile two sets of national tax registers. In addition, the king greatly enhanced irrigation works rehabilitated farmland, and increased agricultural productivity.

Khosrow's reign was the most prosperous and dynamic period of Persian culture. The monarch studied Greek philosophy as well as Indian knowledge of various kinds, including chess, an Indian invention. He ordered the translation of important Greek, Syriac, and Indian scholarly and religious works (including some Neo-Platonic works) into Persian Pahlavi (Middle Persian) and introduced chess to his people. The monarch led scholars to compile a complete history of their own country, a specialty of the Greeks and Chinese but a practice heretofore neglected by the Persians and Indians.

Khosrow was not only able to defeat external foes and pacify domestic turmoil, but he also grew the economy and promoted culture. Knowledgeable, a strategic thinker, rich in leadership ability, he was also a master of on-the-ground implementation.

Because of his great achievements, he was designated *Anushirvan*— "Immortal Soul"—by his descendants. Others dubbed him "Dispenser of Justice" or the "Philosopher-Emperor." His reign (531–579) marked the end of the Sassanian renascence. Although the Sassanids defeated the Hephthalites and later defeated Byzantium, occupied Jerusalem, and even entered Asia Minor, they were never able to thoroughly resolve the problems of envy and rivalry between the royal family and the clergy.

At the beginning of the Sassanid Dynasty, King Ardashir ("Ardashir the Unifier") told his son that the church and the throne were interdependent. Without the church's support, a king could not reign, and without his support, neither could the church flourish; both must be considered such that a balance was maintained.

In fact, during the Sassanian era, Zoroastrianism was the state religion, and the founding monarchs of the empire were themselves of priestly lineage, but they were unable to heed this sagely advice. By mid-seventh century, the empire's treasury was empty, the people impoverished, and national unity had been dealt a heavy blow by the struggle between the religious and royal powers.

This offered an excellent opportunity for a new force to emerge from the Arabian Peninsula and penetrate the Persian cultural sphere that had radiated such a powerful influence for over a millennium.

CHAPTER 23

Islam and the Invaders

The two most influential events over thousands of years of Persian history were the mid-sixth-century BCE establishment of the Achaemenid Empire with its practice of Zoroastrianism, and the conquest of the Sassanid Dynasty by the Arabs in mid-seventh century CE, when Islamization began. Henceforth for almost a millennium, much of the Persian cultural sphere was ruled by Arabs, Turkic peoples and the Mongols.

In the seventh century, when the Byzantine and Sassanid empires were exhausted from battling one another, many tribes in the Arabian Peninsula, which had been exceptionally scattered and had their own idols and rituals, converted one by one to Islam under the guidance of the Prophet Muhammad. Now united, the Arabs expanded outwards with unprecedented speed and scope. Expression of this unity was naturally conquest by the sword and the extension of their dominion, but the internal impetus for this manifestation was rooted in the religious zeal of the newly converted Arabs.

At the beginning of the Arab expansion, the leadership made a decision that seemed out of line with the rules of war, but one it had to be extremely confident and courageous to make. After they had vanquished the Eastern Roman Empire's territory in the northern Arabian Peninsula (today's Iraq, Jordan, Israel including Palestine, Lebanon and Syria), the Arabs promptly attacked Byzantium's Egypt and Tunisia to the west while simultaneously opening a front to the east, targeting the Persian Sassanids.

These two majestic empires—the Eastern Roman Empire (Byzantium based in Constantinople) and Persia—that represented the grand civilizations of the West and East respectively, had struggled against each other for centuries, yet were crushed by an emerging Arab entity with no such glorious history, a civilization that paled by comparison, and whose population was markedly smaller. The chief reason for this is that these empires had long been at war, debilitating both sides; the common folk were so impoverished, and taxes so burdensome, that they were unwilling to prop up their emperors when under threat.

The Arab expeditions had three objectives: First, to act as invaders and rule over the majority of the conquered; second, to propagate Islam; and third, to Arabize the ruled. This triple objective was the same be it in Egypt, the Levant or Iran.

History demonstrates that Arabization and Islamization were almost completely successful in Egypt and Tunisia. Within two centuries of the Arab conquest of Egypt, spoken and written Arabic had become the working and living languages of the entire Egyptian population, but because Islamic doctrine respects the beliefs of Jews and Christians, some Egyptians—one in ten is a Coptic Christian—have resisted Islamization to our day, and the same is true of the Jews.

Arabization and Islamization were also quite successful in the Levant, the original territory of the Eastern Roman Empire. The language and script in these areas were completely Arabized, and the vast majority of the population practiced Islam. Of course, for the same reasons as in Egypt, a small number of Christians did not convert, and the Jews had long been driven out of Palestine by the Romans.

Persia: Islamization and Arabization

Through economic and administrative means, the imposition of a head tax on the Zoroastrians, and a number of pro-Muslim administrative measures, the Arabs, previously inexperienced in governance and with a level of civilization incomparable to that of Persia, accomplished two of their three goals—successfully ruling the Persians and making Islam the dominant religion within the Persian sphere.

There were many Arabs who believed that Islam was a revelation from God to the Prophet Muhammad made in the Arabic language, a religion bestowed upon the Arabs, and that other peoples need not be Muslim, or indeed even qualify as such. During Muhammad's life, his attitudes toward the Jews around Medina shifted from initially respecting them and calling for coexistence, while later rebuking them and placing restrictions on the Jewish tribes. But in any case, Islam recognizes Jews and Christians, who are also monotheistic "People of the Book" who can maintain their religious beliefs and community autonomy, provided they pay a head tax (*Jiziya*) to their Muslim rulers.

The biggest question facing the Arabs after they ruled Persia was determining whether Zoroastrianism was a monotheistic or polytheistic faith. Were its devotees a people possessing a sacred canon? There were two considerations related to this question. On the theoretical level: Should Zoroastrians be forced to practice Islam? The second was a practical one. If everyone became a Muslim and was exempt from the head tax, how to compensate for the loss of government revenue? Ultimately, the Arabs concluded that *Avesta* was a holy scripture and worship centered mainly upon Mazda, and therefore Zoroastrianism qualified as a monotheistic religion. But in their hearts and their actions, Arab Muslims discriminated against Zoroastrians.

Perhaps to the surprise of the Arabs, within less than a hundred years the vast majority of the residents in the Persian cultural sphere had converted to Islam. Many did so to avoid paying the poll tax and to improve their social status, but the Islamic concept of equality also appealed to lower-caste Persians.

Once converted, believers needed to learn Arabic and employ it in religious activities, so Arabic vocabulary appeared widely in Persian. Soon the Persians abandoned the Pahlavi script in favor of a slightly altered form of written Arabic, i.e., the Perso-Arabic script. In essence, the Persian language and grammar did not really change, just the alphabet. For Persians, this inevitably led to intermingling of Pahlavi, Arabic and Persian terminology.

Interestingly, Persian—already rich in administrative, financial, philosophical, physical and medical terms—also quietly seeped into Arabic thanks in part to their similar scripts.

To summarize, it is a fact that the Arabs easily conquered the Iranian Plateau. Although they did not do their utmost to promote the Islamization of the Persians, the vast majority converted to Islam, and the Arabic script and language were widely accepted even while the man-in-the-street continued to speak Persian.

Persianization of Islam

Given Persia's large population, vast territory, and long history of its civilization, it was unlikely that Islam would remain unchanged once many Persians converted to Islam.

In the eighth century, the freshly converted Persian Muslims were dubbed *Mawali* by the Arabs, a somewhat contemptuous term for non-Arab Muslims, and they responded by launching the Shu'ubiyah protest movement based on Persian nationalism. In some places, Arab military and government officials demanded that Persians who had converted to Islam continue to pay the head tax, and many discriminatory laws were imposed on the Mawali in their daily lives and work.

Animosity between the new converts and the ruling Arab dynasty was particularly evident in Khorasan of eastern Persia. Far from the two river valleys where the Arabs were concentrated, Khorasan was even farther from Damascus, seat of the Umayyad Caliphate. In cooperation with the Abbasids (descendants of Muhammad's uncle Abbas), who had opposed the Umayyad Dynasty for many years, a Mawali named Abu Muslim formed an army in his hometown Khorasan in 746; brandishing its iconic Black Banner, it defeated the Umayyad army stationed there in 749. He then led his troops westward and joined forces with the Abbasids to storm Damascus.

The Umayyad Dynasty, whose successive caliphs were overly fond of liquor and things carnal and ignorant of world affairs, quickly collapsed, although a young prince whose mother was Moroccan fled across the Strait of Gibraltar with the help of a loyal servant, and later established a post-Umayyad regime in Iberia.

After the Abbasids took control of the caliphate, they initially relocated the capital eastward to an area with a large Persian population, near the former Sassanid capital of Ctesiphon. In the early Abbasid period, Abu Muslim figured prominently. But the ever-suspicious Caliph Mansur, fearful that the Persian would grow too powerful, plotted his assassination that was carried out in 755. Abu Muslim's violent elimination was driven by a personal feud with the caliph, and it did not deter large numbers of senior officials of Persian origin from later holding high positions in the Abbasid court or receiving honorary titles.

The Abbasid capital, Baghdad, was established in 762 as the new center of Islamic rule. Located on the Tigris at the edges of the Persian cultural sphere, it was mainly inhabited by Arabs. But mosques built by the new dynasty were in the Persian style, and in fact, the Arabs did not have mosques with a distinctly Arab air about them; the Prophet himself had resided in a modest dwelling in Medina that doubled as a *masjid* or mosque, namely a place for praying.

The Umayyads had built large Byzantine-style mosques in Damascus, while the Abbasids chose to erect magnificent, Persian-inspired mosques in Baghdad. As time went on, the Abbasid caliphs ceased dealing specifically with affairs of state except in their role as religious leaders, because the later caliphs adopted the long-established Persian system in which a vizier (i.e., prime minister) headed the government.

After the ninth century, although the caliphs themselves were Arab and traced their descent from Muhammad's paternal uncle Al-Abbas, many had Persian mothers, and their viziers were often Persian as well. The use of Arabic in the court and on important occasions meant most Persian intellectuals were fluent in both Persian and spoken Arabic and many Persians wrote in Arabic as well.

Before the Arab invasion, the Persians had a long history of governance and a tradition of cultural excellence. Drawing on the strengths of the Persians, the Abbasid Caliphate (750–1258) was able to develop one of the most glorious civilizations in the world during the Middle Ages, giving birth to the Islamic Golden Age that many Muslims still recall with nostalgia today.

ISLAMIC CIVILIZATION: THE PERSO-ARABIC VERSION

Islam's "Golden Age" generally refers to the Arabo-Islamic civilization of the ninth–twelfth centuries. Although this is a common expression, it ignores the Persian contribution.

Soon after the Abbasid Caliphate founded Baghdad, the Palace of Wisdom (Grand Library of Baghdad) was founded, and a translation campaign was launched that lasted more than one hundred years. There was certainly a lot of Persian involvement, and the translations were mainly from classical Greek philosophical, literary and scientific texts, as well as Persian and Indian ones. From this foundation, Islam developed its own Islamic doctrine, theology and jurisprudence, as well as its own philosophy, mathematics, astronomy and medicine.

Even in popular literature such as the classic *Arabian Nights* (*One Thousand and One Nights*), most of the tales were Persian in origin, with a few being Indian.

As regards serious religious questions, there are four major schools of jurisprudence in Sunni Islam, two of which were founded by Persians. Doctrine-wise, Islamic scholars have raised two questions that have not been definitively answered to our day.

Firstly, since the Qur'an was a revelation from Allah to humankind, and every word within it is sacred, is the Qur'an Allah Himself or His Creation? Later mainstream theologians believed that the Qur'an was not Allah's Creation but Himself speaking. As a matter of fact, however, the Qur'an was compiled and transcribed by believers after the death of Muhammad by order of several of the first caliphs. Logically, if the Qur'an is the very word of Allah, then the language must have come into existence later than Allah and therefore have been created by Him.

Secondly, if God is omniscient—all-knowing as regards the past, present and future—and each human being's destiny has been preordained, then why does man sin? How could God have predestined His creatures to sin and be punished for their misdeeds? The orthodox Islamic explanation is that God gifted humankind with free will at the same time that He created all things, so each person chooses of their own volition whether to follow the Qur'an or draw near to Satan. Such is the result of the free will bequeathed to humankind by God.

Some Islamic scholars have wondered that if man does possess free will, should he use his God-given free will and inferential powers to interpret the universe created by God? Medical, chemical, physical, astronomical, geographic, and mathematical sciences were all important subjects in this regard, and the study of these domains by Muslim scholars during the Golden Age provided later European scholars with important insights and potential lines of inquiry. The contribution of the Persian-speaking peoples in these areas was quite significant.

Nowadays, it is widely held that higher algebra was an Arab invention. It is true that such a book was first written in Arabic, but its author was a Persian named Muhammad ibn Musa al-Khwarizmi, who was born at the end of the eighth century in Khwarazm (modern-day Uzbekistan), near the Aral Sea.

There was also a very gifted philosopher and physician, a Persian born in Bukhara (modern-day Uzbekistan) at the end of the tenth century, named Avicenna (Ibn Sina). He was able to recite the entire Qur'an by the age of 10, studied medicine with an Indian physician at 16, and began practicing it when just 18. When the ruler of the Samanid Dynasty became seriously ill and royal physicians were unable to help, Avicenna was summoned to the palace and cured the sultan.

He wrote extensively, including the encyclopedic *Canon of Medicine* which encompassed disease, diagnosis, treatment, and pharmacology. This medical classic, penned in Arabic and later translated into Latin, was used as a textbook by many European medical schools from the 12th to the seventeenth centuries.

Well versed in Aristotelian philosophy, Avicenna was later punished for renouncing the Islamic dogma.

During the Yuan Dynasty, the main contents of the *Canon* were also introduced to China's medical community and have had a significant impact on Chinese medicine down to our day.

During the 400 years between the Arab conquest of Persia in the mid-seventh century and the Golden Age of Islamic civilization in the eleventh, although the Arabs governed the Persians in political, military and religious terms, it was the Persians who transformed the Arabs culturally, ideologically and lifestyle-wise. Therefore, the so-called Arabo-Islamic civilization we speak of today might more appropriately be referred to as "Perso-Arabic" Islamic civilization.

THE PERSIANS ESTABLISH REGIONAL REGIMES

Since Baghdad, the Abbasid's capital, was not far from traditional Persian territory, and there were frequent internal struggles within the caliphate, the Persians with their robust cultural power and cohesion had opportunities to establish local regimes on their own. From the ninth century onward, several local rulers in the Persian cultural sphere established virtually independent regimes. "Virtually," because most still recognized the Caliph of Baghdad as their sovereign and cited him in the sermon at the *Jummah* (Friday prayers)—although as time passed some local heads were mentioned instead—and the currency they minted was still issued in the name of the caliph. But in essence, these were Persian regimes over which the Arabs could not enforce de facto jurisdiction.

The earliest such local regime may well have been the Tahirid Dynasty in 820 (present-day southeastern Turkmenistan), with its capital located in the Silk Road oasis town of Merv. Shortly afterward, the Saffarid Dynasty (867–1003) was founded by a coppersmith—*saffar* means coppersmith—from the Sistan region (modern-day western Pakistan and eastern Iran). These Persian-established local authorities often did not claim the title of "Shah," but used the Arabic "Emir" meaning general or military governor, and sometimes called themselves "Malik" (meaning duke or prince), indicating that they dared not "share the high ground" occupied by a caliph.

Two regimes were dominant in the eastern part of the Persian sphere. One was the Samanid Dynasty, which defeated the Saffarids. For more than 100 years, from 892 to 999, the Samanids established a fairly strong and stable regime with Bukhara as its capital. Large numbers of Turkic slaves were sold to various parts of Persia in Transoxiana south of the Syr Darya and north of the Amu Darya, so Bukhara became the principal slave market in the Persian realm during that period.

The Amu Darya region in the ninth–tenth centuries was a place where Turkic-speaking nomadic populations migrated southward from the northern grasslands, East Iranian-speaking Sogdians engaged in sedentary agriculture and trade and frequently intermingled with speakers of other types of Iranian from southern Amu Darya (today's Afghanistan), and western Persian populations.

Since the Samanids had their capital there, they had to interact with various populations. In an era when Arabic was prevalent, motivated both by appreciation for ancient Persian civilization and a practical need for communication between assorted Central Asian peoples, the Samanids consciously undertook to unify various Iranian languages into the standard lingua franca of the Sassanid era—Persian—and based it upon the dialect spoken in Fars.

Nowadays the Persian-speaking population of Uzbekistan, the main population of Tajikistan, and the second largest ethnic group in Afghanistan, the Tajiks, all speak the standard Farsi of today's Iran. For political reasons, Farsi or the standard Persian language, has been known as Dari in Afghanistan and has been its official language since the twentieth century. The largest ethnicity in Afghanistan, the Pashtuns, speak a language that is very similar to the official language Dari.

This linguistic unification, which occurred in the tenth century, led to the conversion of various Turkophone peoples to "standard" Persian at the time of Persification. Modern-day Iran aside, during the twelfth–eighteenth centuries the Persian sphere also included Turkmenistan, Afghanistan, most of Pakistan, western India and southeastern Turkey. Because of the use of a common language, Sufi orders were widely established, and Persian poetry easily circulated in these areas.

Another local Persian regime was the Buyid (Buwayhid) Dynasty (945–1055) in western Persia, founded by the son of a Persian family, Ali ibn Buya. The Buyids were Shiites, but they claimed to be descendants of the Sassanids and formerly occupied senior posts in the armed forces during Samanid rule (819–999), so they possessed military power.

Later, when the caliphate in Baghdad was in decline and reduced to recruiting Turkic soldiers to serve in the royal guardian brigade, the Buyids brought their troops into Baghdad to rescue the caliph who was being manipulated by his guards. Thereafter several caliphs effectively became puppets of the Buyid Dynasty. This was indeed a rare occurrence in Islamic history—a Sunni caliph taking orders from a Shiite warlord.

Both the Samanid and Buyid Dynasties claimed to be the descendants of important Sassanid figures, and the Samanids even declared themselves to be the progeniture of a Zoroastrian noble. They lived during an era when various ethnic groups of Turkic origin were entering the Persian world in Central Asia in large numbers and gradually undergoing Persianization. This added a new dimension to the history of these local Persian regimes.

Invasion by Turkic Peoples and Mongols

The Turkophone tribes first appeared in the upper reaches of the Yenisei River in the northwestern part of the Mongolian Plateau. During China's Sui Dynasty (581–618), they conquered various peoples and tribes of the steppe and established the Turkic Khanate. As a result of intermittent attacks by the Sui (581–618) and Tang (618–907), the Khanate split into the Eastern and Western Turkic Khanates. The latter covered today's western Xinjiang Uygur Autonomous Region, and Uzbekistan and Kyrgyzstan. Some of the western Turkic tribes, known in history books as the Oghuz Turks, continued to move westward.

The Oghuz reached the Aral Sea and crossed the Syr Darya River to the south into the Persian world. Since they had already encountered many Persian Sufis on the steppes, some of the Turkophone tribes had converted to Islam, but most still practiced their original Shamanism or maintained their Buddhist faith. Since they were not Muslims, many of them sold their services as slave soldiers or domestic slaves of the Persian upper class and thus entered cities such as Bukhara and Samarkand, both now located in Uzbekistan. Among these soldiers from the Turkic-speaking tribesmen, there were later those who took control of the military and thereby gained political power.

Persianized Turkic soldiers also began to establish their local regimes on Persian territory. For example, Persians governed what is now Ghazni in Afghanistan, but their rule was usurped in the early eleventh century by the military power of the Oghuz Turks, who established the Ghaznavid Dynasty (977–1186) that repeatedly threatened northwestern territories of the Indian subcontinent.

The Oghuz continued to migrate westward, establishing the vast and populous Seljuk Khanate in Persia and Iraq during the eleventh–thirteenth centuries. They still labeled the land they ruled "Khanate" according to the custom of nomadic steppe herders. The two brothers who ruled the Seljuk Khanate were both very capable, and one led his troops into Asia Minor, into what are today Turkey and Armenia. The other besieged Baghdad and was crowned by the caliph as a sultan. He later expelled the Shiite Buyids and became the de facto ruler of Sunni Islam.

By this time, although members of the various Turkic tribal confederations had mastered Persian, they practiced a trilingual system of sorts: Arabic for religious rituals, Persian as the administrative language, and Turkic dialects in their daily lives.

The period when the Seljuks controlled the Abbasid Caliphate and ruled the Persian region was a period of considerable economic and cultural development. They essentially adopted the Abbasid's efficient Persian-style administration for their Seljuk Khanate, and even appointed the brilliant Persian scholar, Nizam al-Mulk, as their vizier. This famous minister authored the *Siyasatnameh* (The Book of Governance) which became renowned throughout the Islamic world.

The Seljuks who entered Asia Minor soon established a state based in what is now Konya in south-central Turkey, and proudly accepted the title of "Sultan" bestowed upon them by the Caliph of Baghdad. They called their state the Rum Seljuk Sultanate, a reference to the Christian dwellers of the former Eastern Roman Empire.

During the reign of one of the earliest Turkic regimes established in Iran, the Ghaznavid Dynasty (977–1186), there emerged a poet of Persian origin named Ferdowsi. He continued the unfinished work of a poet from the Sassanid era and wrote a collection of tales of Persian monarchs who pioneered "the Persian empire on horseback," entitled

Shahnameh (Book of Kings). Born in the present-day Iranian province of Khorasan, Ferdowsi devoted more than 30 years to creating this epic poem—consisting of some 50,000 couplets—that is virtually pure Persian, as he sought to avoid the Arabic vocabulary that had long been embedded in Persian.

From its genesis in 1000 to the present day, the *Book of Kings* has been treated as a literary treasure by the Persians, studied by every schoolchild, and there is hardly an Iranian alive who does not know the history recounted therein; it is virtually a national history of Persian culture and its folk. Completion of this massive work coincided with the fall of the Samanid Dynasty, so Ferdowsi dedicated it to the king of the Ghaznavid Dynasty in the southeast. But the latter being of Turkic stock who had just gained power, their regime not only did not value this epic that consciously glorified Persian culture, but they didn't even want to hear of it, so Ferdowsi received no reward for his life's work. Fortunately, the manuscript was not destroyed and has survived to become an Iranian national treasure.

At the time when the Seljuks were gradually moving their focus to Asia Minor (modern Turkey's Anatolian heartland), Khwarazm was the dominant regime in the Persian cultural sphere. The conflict between the Khwarezmians, based in a large oasis region on the Amu Darya river delta in western Central Asia, and the emerging Mongols, caused the latter to initiate three expeditions to the west.

The Mongols invaded Persia three times, and each time they brutally massacred the dwellers of many cities and destroyed their mosques.

After the third expedition, Genghis Khan's grandson, Hulagu Khan, established the Ilkhanate in 1256 with Persia as his center and his capital at Tabriz, in northwest Iran. The rulers of the Ilkhanate were initially very unfriendly to Muslims. They considered themselves Shamanists, while the wives of the Great Khan (Kublai Khan) and Hulagu both came from a Mongolian clan that was Nestorian Christians. Therefore, they often carried out violent activities to destroy the Islamic culture at the very heart of the Islamic way of life.

Of course, these activities were not sustainable in the long run, for Persians and Arabs greatly outnumbered the Mongols. After more than 30 years and the reign of several khans, the ruler of the Ilkhanate, Ghazan, decided to convert to Islam in 1295 and became a defender and rebuilder of Islamic culture. Thereafter, Islam held sway in the Mongol Ilkhanate. Of course, there were very few Mongols in the Ilkhanate and after a few generations, they were assimilated into the local population and there was effectively no Mongolian regime or separate Mongolian ethnicity to speak of.

It should be noted that in the early years of the Ilkhanate, even though the rulers adhered to Mongolian traditions and did not believe in Islam, they appointed some locals as viziers or key advisors, including Ata-Malek Juvayni. He traveled to the Mongolian capital Karakorum, and his book, *Tarikh-i Jahangushay* (History of the World Conqueror), is considered by later scholars to be an extremely important record of the conquests by Genghis Khan and his descendants.

In addition, there was Rashid al-Din Tabib, a scholar of Jewish origin who converted to Islam. He served as vizier to Ghazan Khan and was later tasked to lead scholars from different countries and religions in compiling the renowned *Jamiʿal-tawarikh* (Compendium of Chronicles), arguably "the first book of world history."

Ghazan himself instituted many reforms, but also went to the extreme in one regard—he ordered the destruction of many Christian churches and Zoroastrian temples because he had converted to Islam.

We can summarize the experience of foreign invaders in the Persian domain as follows: The Persians were a highly civilized people who mastered the art of governance early on. The Arabs conquered the Persian Empire, and the vanquished converted to Islam, but they did not abandon their language or methods of administration. The Turkic interlopers enjoyed great power for a period but were gradually Persianized. Practitioners of brutal massacres who proudly placed the skulls of their victims in pyramid-shaped piles, the Mongol rulers, who also initially destroyed mosques and forbade Muslims from slaughtering livestock by letting them bleed to death—in the halal fashion—eventually were Persianized as well, adopting the language, lifestyle and Islamic faith of the people they conquered.

The Timurid Empire and Islamic Renaissance

Timur (1336–1405) was born near the historic city of Samarkand in present-day Uzbekistan and belonged to a branch of Mongols that became Turkified once it settled near Samarkand in the early thirteenth century. During his childhood, the Mongolian Ilkhanate was already in decline. Timur married a princess of the Eastern Chagatai Khanate and was proud to be a royal son-in-law of Genghis Khan's "Golden Family."

But since he was not a member by blood, he never dared take the title of "Khan," opting for "Emir" instead.

After raising troops in his native Samarkand and taking control of the Western Chagatai Khanate, Timur conquered much of the world under the banner of the Islamic Jihad and *yassa*—a secretive legal code decreed by Genghis Khan—and never lost a battle. He invaded India, captured all of present-day Iran, occupied the Caucasus, and at one point battled all the way to present-day Turkey. His war record far surpassed that of the founder of the Ilkhanate, Hulagu Khan, and Timur eventually founded his own Timurid Empire.

During his reign and that of his son Shah Rukh (1405–47) and grandson Ulugh Beg (1447–49), politics were a combination of Mongolian and Arabic practices, the legal system drew on Turkic customs and Genghis Khan's reign, and culture was a fusion of Persian and Turkic influences.

With such a hybrid ideology and system of governance, Timur established a new-fangled empire that not only compensated for the damage and unpleasant memories of more than 100 years of Mongol rule on Islamic civilization but also succeeded in birthing a Perso-Islamic cultural renaissance. This renaissance coincided with the European Renaissance and was expressed mainly in the domains of literature, painting, and architecture.

Successive rulers of the Timurid Khanate were all dedicated to the development of Persian culture, rewarding poets, encouraging Persian-style miniature painting and promoting mathematics and astronomy.

Timur was born in Central Asia, and although he belonged to the Persian cultural circle, Central Asia was already dominated by Turkic languages. His son Shah Rukh moved the khanate capital from Samarkand to Herat (present-day Afghanistan), where the court languages—a Central Asian Turkic language (today's Uzbek) and Dari Persian (Afghan's dominant tongue that is essentially Farsi)—were equally esteemed.

Timur's tomb in Samarkand

Timur's grandson Ulugh Beg built many important Islamic buildings in Bukhara, including mosques and madrasas. He was also an astronomer who constructed the Ulugh Bey Observatory in Samarkand—the most advanced in the world at the time—and recorded the positions of more than 1,000 stars and trajectories of some planets. He personally delivered lectures at madrasas.

It was at the height of the Timurid Empire that the master miniaturist, Behzad, painted his most important works in Herat, where he headed the Royal Workshop, and for some time headed such a workshop in Tabriz as well. It was also in Herat that Jami, the great master of Persian Sufi poetry who authored the *Seven Thrones*, became famous. Many important and innovative Islamic structures were built during the Timurid Khanate. The mosque and madrasa embracing the famous Registan in central Samarkand were outstanding examples of Islamic architecture during this period, both characterized by an innovative use of blue tiles for decoration.

The history of Persia demonstrates that this imaginative, creative, and infectious ancient civilization did indeed undergo thousands of years of fluctuations. That's the fascinating thing about the history of civilization—its never-ending cycle of nadirs and zeniths.

Bukhara: Phoenixes and sun on portal of Nadir Divan-Begi Madrasah

CHAPTER 24

Persian Poetry and Painting

PERSIAN CULTURAL AWARENESS: INSPIRED BY INVADERS

Beginning in the mid-seventh century, the birthplace of the powerful and far-reaching Persian civilization, the Iranian Plateau, was first occupied by Arabs, and thereafter Hephthalites, Seljuk Turks, Khwarizmis, Mongols and Turkmens, respectively, took turns as the region's rulers. As a conveyor of culture, Persian civilization continued to exist, but the Persian Empire and monarchy were interrupted for almost a full millennium.

During those 1,000 years, the great majority of the invaders converted to Islam, and almost all became speakers of Persian. Thus, while Persia was conquered many times over, its new rulers were consistently assimilated in terms of language and religion.

Gradually, a desire was born among those who perceived themselves as Persians to protect and develop indigenous culture. In the ninth century, the Sunni Samanid Dynasty emerged in Central Asia. Although it governed in the name of the Baghdad-based Caliph, this was a Persianate dynasty that consciously promoted Persian literature.

The Persians had long been successful in architecture, painting, music and literature, all of which reached notable heights under the Sasanids (224–651 CE). As a form of literary expression, however, poetry was not paramount in early Persian culture. In the seventh century, after the Arabs pacified Persia the vast majority of Persians embraced the faith of their conquerors, and many became fluent in Arabic as well. Given Arabic's rhythmic nature and ease of rhyme, poetry has traditionally been highly esteemed among Arabophones.

As a result of the integration of the two peoples, the Persians also began to value poetry. During the ninth–tenth centuries, the Persophone rulers of states forged in the Khorasan region (modern-day Uzbekistan and Afghanistan), such as the Samanid Dynasty (819–999) and Ghaznavid Dynasty (977–1186), also revered their bards. Persian verse was often recited in the court where poets enjoyed high status, and this substantially impacted oral and written language.

The Samanid Dynasty was founded by descendants of Sasanid royalty who migrated eastward to the Khorasan region after the fall of their dynasty. More than a century later, they situated their capital in Bukhara (modern-day Uzbekistan) and established a Persian-dominated kingdom where poets were encouraged to create poetry in Dari, the court language of the erstwhile Sasanids. Under the impetus of the royal family, Dari poetry spread widely, to the extent that during the ninth–tenth century members of the cultural elite in Eastern Persia became speakers of "Dari-style Farsi," the West Iranian language whose origins lay in southwestern Persia's Fars region. This court language became known simply as "Farsi."

The time when the Persian language prevailed also happened to occur when Sufi mysticism was rapidly evolving among the Persian cultural elite. Therefore, Sufi philosophy and the sentiments of Sufists often found expression in concise lines of Persian verse. The Sufis regarded the relationship between man and God as the most important religious experience and theological proposition, and the search for oneness with God as the greatest yearning and consolation. Thanks to the passion for Sufism and its subsequent spread, during the ninth–tenth centuries poetry became the dominant form of literary expression among the Persian cultural elite.

Hallmarks and Evolution of Persian Four-line Verse

Although Persian verse existed during the Sasanian era, it was not until the ninth–tenth centuries that several of its practitioners attained renown. At that time, a poem comprised four-line stanzas, often two couplets, and a rhyming scheme emphasizing the last syllable of each line, which is quite similar to the quatrains that prevailed in China under the Tang (618–907).

Professor Mu Hongyan of Beijing Foreign Studies University has analyzed the similarities and differences between Persian four-line poems—known as *ruba'i*—and Tang era quatrains. Citing the research of the Italian scholar Alessandro Bausani, as well as studies of a Chinese expert of Persian literature, Yang Xianyi, Mu asserts that *ruba'i*, along with the poetic form of Turkic-speaking peoples in Central Asia quite possibly both originated in the Chinese quatrain. It is indeed interesting to note the similarities in time, geographical contiguity and similar format of the poetic styles in these distinctly different languages.

The Persian *ruba'i* and Chinese quatrain do share similar characteristics. Both are short and pithy, and well suited to expressing a fleeting sentiment or intuitive idea. In four brief lines, the poet is constrained to employ metaphors that compellingly convey the desired message.

Among the early Persian poets, the most famous was Rudaki (858–941), born in Rudak, Khorasan in what is now Tajikistan. A traditional Muslim who was not a Sufist, he was respected by the Samanid court, and is considered the pioneer of the Persian four-line poem.

A few centuries later saw the appearance of Omar Khayyam (1048–1131), a famous poet native to Nishapur, now in northeastern Iran. He was also an astronomer and a mathematician who deeply respected rationalism, which distinguished him neatly from other poets who were devotees of Sufi mysticism. Although he penned only quatrains, his verse was incisive and topics wide-ranging. He is considered the quintessential *ruba'i* poet.

Perhaps due to his broad base of knowledge and devotion to rationalist thought, Khayyam had much in common with European scholars of the Renaissance and Enlightenment periods, so he is very popular in the West. His poems on love, suffering, social injustice, and the mysteries of the universe have been widely translated into European languages, the most renowned interpretation unquestionably being Edward FitzGerald's *Rubáiyát of Omar Khayyám*, a selection of quatrains—controversially attributed to Khayyam—published in 1859.

After the twelfth century, other genres of Persian verse did appear, but the four-line *ruba'i* remained the favorite.

To facilitate a comparison of Chinese and Persian love quatrains, here are two examples that Professor Mu cited in her work: The first is one of the known *Zhuzhi Ci (Bamboo Branch Song)*, a short poem inspired by a Sichuan folk ballad and composed by Tang poet Liu Yuxi (772–842); the second is by Rumi (1207–1273, also known as Mawlawi or

Mevlana), who resided in the Seljuk Sultanate of Rum, located in what is now south-central Turkey.

Liu Yuxi's poem:

> **Red Blossoms**
> (to the tune of "Bamboo Branch Song")
> Red blossoms of mountain peach crowd the uplands,
> Spring waters of Shu rivers buffet the mountains as they flow.
> Crimson blossoms so quickly fading, like my lover's ardor;
> flowing waters so endless, like the sorrow I feel.
>
> (by Liu Yuxi, tr. by Burton Watson)

And Rumi's quatrain:

> Entangling, entangling like a net was her lustrous mane
> How doubly honey-sweet her ruby lips.
> Our vow to rendezvous
> Empty, empty yet teeming with separation's pain.

Although the first is an English rendition direct from the original Chinese, and the second is based upon a Chinese translation from Persian, it is evident both poems are concise and spare, and deal with romance. Liu Yuxi was writing about mortal love between man and woman, and is free of metaphor, while Rumi's poem is also infused with the religious air of a Sufi love poem.

SUFI POETRY: INTOXICATED BY ROMANCE

In the centuries that followed Rudaki and Omar Khayyam, many famous poets also composed verse in Persian, and not just native speakers; they included Seljuk Turks, Khwarizmis, Azeris, as well as Ottomans and even Indians under Mughal rule. We can say that the dissemination of medieval and pre-modern Persian literature more or less coincided with the territories governed during the ancient Persian Empire, i.e., from the Aegean Sea in the west to the Indus River in the east.

Born a decade after Khayyam in Ganjah (now Azerbaijan) was Nizami Ganjavi (1141–1209), who is renowned for his *Panj Ganj* (*Five Treasures*). One of the quintet, *Leyla and Majnun*, is his recognized masterpiece. Derived from Arab legends, it recounts a tragic romance between a young man and woman from different tribes that ends in death for the couple. Here's a brief excerpt from the epic:

> If not for the passionate fire burning in my heart for you,
> The tears I have shed would have drowned me long ago.
> If not for the teardrops welling in my eyes for you,
> Sorrowful flames would have reduced me to cinders long ago.

In fact, three of the most famous Persian-language Sufi poets lived in a territory governed by the Mongols. During the rule of the Ilkhanate (1256–1335), whose core territory lay in parts of today's Iran, Azerbaijan and Turkey, there were frequent exchanges of literature and art between Persia and China.

When the Mongols invaded, southwestern Iran's Shiraz was spared the horde's customary ransacking and massacres, because the local ruler wisely paid a hefty sum instead. Society remained relatively tranquil, and perhaps this is how the city survived to eventually nurture a pair of world-renowned poets: Saadi of Shiraz (1210–1291), and Hafez (1315–1390). The former's *Bustan* (*The Orchard*) and *Gulistan* (*The Rose Garden*), and the latter's *Collection of Lyrical Poetry*, are well known throughout the Persian world, and most any Persian speaker can recite from them at will. In the entirety of Persian literary history, aside from Ferdowsi's 50,000-line epic poem *Shahnameh* (*The Book of Kings*), several hundred of Hafez's lyrical poems are possibly the most widely cited.

Saadi was born into a family of modest means and lost his father at an early age. As an adult, he studied Arabic literature and Islamic law in Baghdad, and traveled throughout the Middle East as a Sufi beggar. His works included poetry and short stories, and his writing was imbued with profound philosophical thought and social significance. One of his famous phrases:

> Almighty Allah cherishes
> Both those who are wealthy yet humble like the poor
> And those who are poor yet generous like the wealthy.

Hafez was a writer who belonged to no religious order and held no government post. He put to memory Islam's holiest text—in Arabic, "hafez" signifies one who has memorized the *Qur'an*—during childhood. From his prolific poems, we can see that it is not "fine wine" that flows from his liquor goblet; it is the pursuit of spiritual freedom, wild and uninhibited, a genuine, sensual spontaneity. Because of this, literature lovers worldwide, especially in Europe, revere Hafez's verse.

Another extremely important Sufi poet was Rumi, leader of the Sufi Order. When he wrote about drinking, he distinguished between "God's wine" and "Satan's wine." He wrote of the love between human beings and God as "romance," and also used the love between a man and a woman as a metaphor for human beings' love for God. He believed that the source of all pain was estrangement from God, so the search for oneness with God and maintenance of that unity was surely humankind's most noble pursuit.

Since there exist other hidden metaphors for beautiful women and fine wine in the verse of Sufi poets, to comprehend Sufi mystical poetry one must recognize that authors are subtly employing them to express their sentiments for God, and attempting to put into words the indescribable joy of that instant when unity with God is achieved.

Via their literary expression, these Sufis were actually modifying fundamental Islamic doctrine that asserts "there is no deity but God ('lā ʾilāha ʾillā -llāh')." According to the *Shahada*, one of the Five Pillars of Islam, all things on earth were created by and belong to God. Sufi mysticism considers that everything in existence is part of God's divinity, so poets often described in their verse the ecstasy born of their love for God and His omnipresence. They altered their focus from "returning to God after death" to "oneness with God in this world," and described the relationship between God and humankind—formerly that of Creator and his creation—as a relationship between lovers. For this reason, I entitled this section "Intoxicated by Romance."

By the fifteenth century, the center of Persian poetry creation had shifted to the east (modern-day Afghanistan). The focus of the Persian Renaissance was then firmly on Central Asia, due to the fact that the Turko-Mongol Timurid Dynasty (1370–1507), although Turkophone, was deeply influenced by Persian literary and high culture. The thirteenth-century Mongol invasion had weakened Persian culture, and so, ironically, it was descendants of the Turkified Mongols who spearheaded this Persianate revival.

The Timurid era saw the emergence of several important Persian poets, the most famous being Jami (1414–1492), whose collected verse epitomized Persian poetry and pushed it to its greatest heights. He was born into a family of Sufists, mainly resided in Herat (now in Afghanistan), then capital of the Timur Khanate, and was a key member of the *Naqshbandi Order of Sufism*. In addition to being a principal exponent of Sufi mysticism, Jami also delved into Islamic Sunni doctrine and philosophy and advocated the cultivation of self within this life and for eternity. His poems and essays were numerous, his language elegant and fresh in style, and his writing was appreciated both by court scholars and the common folk. *Haft Awrang* (*Seven Thrones*), a collection of seven poems, is his most renowned work.

Taking a broader and longer view, one can see that Persian civilization, in addition to developing distinctive military bodies, and political and legal systems, also created Zoroastrianism. After their conversion to Islam, however, in literature, the Persians began to emphasize poetry, and since this more or less coincided with the spread of Sufism, the literary genre of Sufi love poetry was born.

From Bas-Reliefs to Persian Miniatures

Sophisticated artistic expression manifested itself very early in Persian civilization. There are vivid reliefs in the Persepolis Palace ("Apadana") built 2,300 years ago. Mani (c. 216–274), Manichaeism's founder, was an artist and painter. Manichaeism greatly esteemed painting and employed materials such as gold foil to create art with particularly vivid colors.

During the Ilkhanate (1236–1335) established by the Mongols after their conquest of West Asia, Persia and China enjoyed frequent contact. Persian art in several domains underwent considerable evolution thanks to the two-way flow of people and historical chronicles and was especially evident in the arts of porcelain and painting.

By this period, Persianate societies had long been Islamized, and consistent with Islamic tradition, painting was not encouraged. In particular, portraits of people and even representations of animals were frowned upon, so as not to violate the taboo against idolatry; therefore flora, geometric shapes and artistic calligraphy became the mainstay.

In the era when the Mongols ruled Central and West Asia, the Chinese art of painting spread to Persia. Many professional painters were influenced by it, and a certain "Chinese style" manifested itself in their works. As noted earlier, this is when Persian literature flourished. Poetic output was prolific, and it coincided with the period when Sufi mysticism came to dominate mainstream Persian culture.

Many epics and poetry collections appeared, such as *The Book of Kings*, *Five Treasures* and *Rose Garden*, and most were tales with historical significance and dramatic storylines. Accordingly, a new artistic genre appeared: Illustrations that graphically expressed a story's plot. Very fine brushwork and variegated colors were required to create pleasing images, and this came to be known as "miniature painting."

Persian miniatures featured people, objects and scenery. Because these illustrations required very fine brush strokes and minute detail, they drew upon and eventually surpassed *gongbi* painting—a form of realism achieved via meticulous brushwork—that had originated in China. It was generally practiced by professional painters for utilitarian purposes, as opposed to the category of *literati* painting that was the product of leisurely scholars with a creative impetus. *Gongbi* could take the form of a portrait, flora, *nature morte* or even a landscape, but was never intended to express a philosophical mindset or a spiritual yearning.

Miniature painting in the Persian world represented a newly developed genre that emerged after earlier Persian traditions were jettisoned. It differed from both classical Chinese painting and European painting during the Renaissance, both in terms of theory and painting techniques, and it fused Persian and Islamic characteristics.

Miniatures later spread to Mughal India and Ottoman Turkey, and the Arab region too. Because religious beliefs in the latter are more conservative, the art of miniature illustration—due to its association with Sufism, which was and is considered heretical by some Muslims—was also practiced among Arabs, but never prevailed. By contrast, Persian-style miniatures became the favored form of painting in Turkey, India and the entire Persianate world, and its works are considered the acme of illustrative art.

As a form of artistic expression, the concepts represented by Persian miniature painting, and the techniques employed, may be contrasted with those of the Italian Renaissance, and China from the Tang and Song Dynasties onward.

Miniature Painting Guide: *My Name Is Red*

In the summer of 2003, I accidentally came into possession of an English translation of *My Name is Red*, a novel by the Turkish novelist Orhan Pamuk. Right from the start I could hardly let go of it. But the plot twists and turns, and a book-length tale revolving around a group of court-appointed miniature painters, like a miniature itself, requires a close read for fuller comprehension.

After reading the novel, I deeply admired the author. Six months later, thanks to a friend's introduction, I went to Istanbul to meet Orhan Pamuk. Our chat went very well, so I invited him to give a lecture at the City University of Hong Kong, and to be the special guest at a "City Cultural Salon" held monthly at my home.

Orhan Pamuk studied architecture, but as fate would have it he became a novelist, not an architect. In order to write *My Name is Red*, he spent years in libraries researching background materials for this murder mystery set in late sixteenth-century-Istanbul. I was very pleased that two years after his Hong Kong visit, he won the Nobel Prize for Literature in 2006, the first-ever Turkophone writer to be so honored. When the award was announced, I just happened to be in Istanbul and even met his sister-in-law!

My Name is Red is indeed an intriguing novel. But for me personally, its value also lies in the multi-dimensional, in-depth introduction the author provides to the painting of miniatures; the novel itself resembles a *muraqqa*, an album of Islamic miniatures and calligraphy. While weaving his tale, the author subtly reveals his profound views on several questions. The clash between Persian miniatures and Italian Renaissance paintings triggers a bizarre murder, which drives the main axis of the novel.

Let's start with European painting and its genesis in the Renaissance jump-started by the Italians. First of all, the artist selects his own location before painting the scene that he observes. Distance vis-à-vis the painter is defined by relative size, demonstrating the concept of three-dimensional perspective. People or objects are distinguished by nuances of color and light, and day and night are completely distinct, which conveys light and shadow perspectives. During the Renaissance, Europeans began to pursue humanism, and drawing the world as seen by the human eye is itself a manifestation of humanism.

The principles and methods of classical Chinese *literati* painting since the Tang and Song Dynasties (seventh–thirteenth centuries), however, are distinct from those in Europe inspired by the Renaissance. Within the same tableau, the painter could observe from various locations the persons and scenes he wished to paint. This multi-point perspective, as opposed to fixed-point, means that artistic conception trumps realistic portraiture. Within the same painting, the artist can switch suddenly from looking up at a mountain to gazing down from its summit. The person or object to be highlighted can be portrayed quite large, and objects that serve as a foil need not be conveyed proportionally.

But the Chinese painter nonetheless had certain rules to follow: Nighttime must be dark and daytime bright, flora gaily colored, mountains and trees portrayed with peculiarity, and so on.

Miniatures were all illustrations for a book and placed adjacent to the related text. The topic of the miniature could be found in those words, so the illustration was simply the graphic expression of a given scene in the tale. This format represented a challenge to the miniaturist in that his depiction was juxtaposed with the text it sought to interpret, and also provided a limited space for its creative expression.

Since many of the classics destined for illustration expressed Sufi-inspired illusory experience, the artists accordingly depicted them from a Sufist "combined human and divine" angle. The fundamental argument of the miniaturist was that the human eye cannot detect reality; what it "sees" is an illusion. Therefore, they did not use what the human eye perceived as their benchmark for illustration. All the matter that populates our universe, animate and inanimate, is Allah's creation and is constantly visible to Him. The view of the human eye might be blocked, but this did not alter the fact that beyond those mountains and walls lay other people or objects.

The miniaturist believed that since Allah created the world thusly, it was entirely permissible to depict the world behind those walls. Additionally, the key personages in the text were naturally depicted larger, similarly to Chinese-style painting. Illustration was not limited to reality as perceived by the human eye, and this is the first characteristic of the Persian miniature.

The miniaturist's use of light, however, was distinct from that of Chinese or European painters. The Persians preferred strong primary colors, avoiding intermediate tints, resulting in very bright illustrations. To this end, a steed could be blue or red. Of course, daylight action required a bright background, and to indicate nighttime, the moon would be visible in the sky. This was the second characteristic of the Persian miniature.

The main characteristic of miniature illustrations is detail, a painting technique that is hard on the eyes, leading to a loss of vision for some in old age. This is portrayed in Pamuk's novel, in which an elderly illustrator can continue to work even after he goes blind, because he distinctly recalls how each detail is conveyed via his brushstrokes. In other words, miniature painting is a stylized, conceptual art, a bit like the face masks employed in Peking Opera. When it came to people, each had a certain look; there were stereotypes for painting a horse too.

The reason is that, for one, in Islamic culture there was little traditional emphasis on the depiction of people or animals; a horse is a horse, a *conceptualized* horse, not a specific horse. As intriguingly argued in China by Master Gongsun Long three centuries before Jesus, specifically defining a given horse as "white" implied that a yellow or black one was *not* a horse, so strictly speaking, there was no such thing as a "white horse"! It didn't matter what the characters in the story looked like—since no one had actually seen them—so stylized faces did not pose a problem.

Orthodox Islamic scholars were not in favor of drawing the human figure, so for artists, it was not only easier to avoid doing so in their miniatures, but it had the advantage of lessening critical voices and increasing legitimacy in terms of Islamic doctrine. So, stylization was the third characteristic of miniature painting.

From the development of Persian poetry and painting, we can see that the evolution of culture was closely related to Persian society's interaction with the outside world. Both poetry and painting were externally influenced, but the Persians nonetheless created unique modes of verse and illustration originating primarily in their own cultural roots.

Although miniatures were dominated by Sufists, in the Persian cultural circles of the fourteenth–sixteenth centuries, the overall style remained roughly similar regardless of the painter's personal faith; there were no "anti-Sufi" or "non-Sufi" schools of painting as such.

During the period of Mongol rule, the Buddhist art of Dunhuang frescoes entered the Persian conscience, and Chinese-style twisted tree roots, wispy clouds, mythical unicorns, dragons and phoenixes began popping up in fourteenth–fifteenth-century miniatures. The master miniaturist Kamaleddin Behzad (1450–1531) is believed to have executed a famous illustration, Prophet Muhammad's Ascension, included in *Seven Thrones*, the famous poetry anthology. He introduced the concept of Buddhism into this miniature, and even the figurative representations therein were drawn upon Chinese Buddhist paintings.

Persian culture possesses its own profound heritage but has also been capable of continuously integrating foreign elements. Therefore, it has repeatedly rejuvenated itself and created a dynamic culture that is at once "refreshingly new yet ancient."

CHAPTER 25

Shia Islam and the Safavid Dynasty

During Iraq's civil war (2006–2008), Sunni terrorists twice bombed the tomb of Hasan ibn Ali al-Askari, the 11th Imam in Twelver Shia Islam, in eastern Iraq's Samarra, highlighting the schism and even hatred between the Sunnis and Shiites.

In fact, both sects hold sacred and read the identical Qur'an, and the basic doctrine is the same. The difference between the two branches is even more subtle than those that distinguish Catholicism, Orthodox Christianity and Protestantism.

Of the approximately 1.7 billion Muslims in the world today, about 85% are Sunnis and 15% Shiites. Because almost all Iranians are Shiites, and Iran has been in the news so often since Iran's Islamic Revolution triumphed in 1979, the largely interchangeable terms "Shia" and "Shiite" have become commonplace.

In 680 CE, Husayn, the grandson of the Prophet Muhammad, crossed the desert from Mecca in the Arabian Peninsula to Kufa in eastern Iraq with a few hundred men. An Umayyad army intercepted them at Karbala, a short distance from Kufa.

Husayn offered to remain behind, provided his men could continue their march. But having entirely encircled them, the Umayyad troops would not even permit Husayn's followers to fetch water at the river.

After consulting the capital at Damascus, the Umayyad army demanded that Husayn swear allegiance to Khalifa Yezid of Damascus, the son of Muawiyah, founder and first Caliph of the Umayyad Caliphate.

Husayn refused this condition, and the Umayyads began to slaughter the interlopers.

Badly outnumbered, almost all Husayn's men and relatives were slain. Hussein was the last survivor, his arms still cradling his dead two-year-old son pierced by an arrow. But soon Husayn too was knocked to the ground, and an Umayyad officer speared his body. His decapitated skull was sent back to Damascus in a honey jar.

This tragedy is an oft-repeated saga passed down among Shiites. During the days when Husayn was besieged, some people in Kufa learned of it and considered going to his rescue at Karbala but did not do so because of their small number and lack of determination. Afterward, those Kufa residents regretted their inaction and cowardice, and so, each year on the tenth day of Muharram, the first month in the Islamic lunar calendar, they mourn the *Ashura* (Arabic for 10), and re-enact the tragedy of Karbala. On this day many devotees wail and flagellate themselves.

This custom highlights the fact that while Sunnis and Shiites share the same Qur'anic beliefs and rites, the latter are endowed with a deep sense of grief, remorse and humiliation.

Strictly speaking, "Shia" is not a self-referential name for believers. In Arabic, Shia means follower, partisan, party or faction. Since the passing of Muhammad, there has always been a group of people faithful to the memory of Ali ibn Abi Talib, and they are known as Shia, i.e., a shortened term denoting "faction (of Ali)."

Ali was Muhammad's cousin and son-in-law too, since he married Muhammad's daughter Fatima. They had two sons, Hassan, the eldest, and Husayn, who was slain by the Umayyads. Shiites believe that only the descendants of Muhammad, i.e., the descendants of Ali, can justly serve as heirs of the Prophet—"Kalifa" or "Caliph" in Arabic—and thus as the religious and political leader of all Muslims.

But Sunnis believe that any Muslim can become the Caliph and lead the *ummah* (worldwide community of Muslims). The four successors in the early years of Islam are known collectively as the Rashidun ("Rightly Guided") Caliphs: Abu Bakr, Umar, Uthman, and Ali. Most Shiites believe that Ali should have been Muhammad's successor long before, and therefore have little respect for or even recognize the three who preceded him.

Christianity split into several branches three hundred years after the death of Jesus, while Islam underwent a serious and bloody split less than fifty years after Muhammad passed away. Three of the four Rashidun Caliphs, including Ali, died by assassination.

Ali was the fourth and last of the Rashiduns, but his reign (656–661) was short. A loyal and humble man who spent much time in prayer and meditation, and who rarely quarreled with others, it took more than twenty years before he was elected Caliph after the third was dispatched. His selection led to a direct challenge on the part of Muawiyah, Governor of Syria. The two sides fought to a standstill, but after "divine arbitration," Ali's side was defeated.

Muawiyah, a Meccan nobleman and nephew of the third Caliph Uthman, had opposed Muhammad at one point in the past. Immediately after his successful challenge to Ali, he established the Umayyad dynasty centered on his family, with its capital in Damascus, a city he had conquered and administered. Ali's followers rejected Muawiyah, and Muawiyah's descendants despised and suppressed them. As a result, Ali's disciples felt a sense of loss and humiliation even before the tragedy at Karbala.

After the Karbala massacre, the Shiites began to form their own administrative system and elect their own leader, whom they dubbed "Imam." This title originally referred to the leader of daily prayers in a mosque, but later it also referred to the supreme leader of the Shiites. Sunni Muslims today still call the presiding cleric at any mosque imam, but in the Persian-speaking world Muslims refer to this cleric as *Akhund*—*Ahong* in Chinese—which suggests that historically, Chinese Islam was heavily influenced by Persia.

During the seventh and eighth centuries, the Sunni heirs in Damascus gradually formed a family dynasty, and established a patrilineal system of succession, i.e., from father to son or brother to brother. Descendants of Abbas, Muhammads uncle, took advantage of the victory of the Persian Muslim revolt in the east and joined forces with other opponents of the Umayyads to overthrow their caliphate in the Abbasid Revolution of 750 CE. The Abbasids then established their dynasty in eastern Iraq and soon built a new capital in Baghdad. Their dynasty lasted until its destruction by the Mongols in 1258.

In contrast to the Sunnis, Shiite Muslims have never embraced the concept of a capital city, but have remained scattered throughout the world, with diverse sub-sects and doctrines of their own. Northern Iran, Egypt, Tunisia, Morocco, and Yemen have all experienced Shiite rule, but none comprised a capital for the entire Shiite community.

Schisms occurred several times in the course of Shia Islam's development. The first major schism occurred during the reign of Zayd ibn Ali, the Fifth Imam and grandson of Husayn. He raised an army in Kufa in an attempt to overthrow the Umayyads but died in battle in 740. Those who recognize only Zayd but not the Sixth Imam are known as the Zaydis or the Fiver Shias. This school was closer to the Sunnis in its religious views, recognizing the three Rushidun Caliphs before Ali and permitting several caliphs to coexist, each exercising power independently in his own territory.

In fact, religion does not necessarily need to be protected by a regime, because faith is after all a spiritual domain, and while it is easy for a religion to develop when defended by a regime, it may not necessarily expire without one. Throughout the history of Islam (as well as European Christianity), there has been a constant tension between the piety of religion and the governance of rulers, yet the two need to adapt and cooperate with each other.

The Sixth Imam, Ja'far al-Sadiq, deprived Isma'il, his eldest son, of his succession rights and installed his second son al-Kazimas as the Seventh Imam, which caused serious internal conflict. Many argued for Isma'il's succession, but this did not occur, and Ismail died in 762. His acolytes believe that he was not only the Seventh Imam but also the last Imam; Isma'il went into hiding and became the "Hidden Imam." More often known as "Isma'ilis," they are also referred to as the "Seveners."

The Isma'ilis established a complex, mystical religious philosophy, professing that the Qur'an contains both explicit and implicit meanings: The explicit meaning includes the accepted interpretation of the scriptures, while the implicit meaning includes eternal truths contained in the scriptures and teachings, whose subtle and profound significance should be sought via metaphorical and intuitive means. During the tenth–twelfth centuries, they founded the Fatimid dynasty in North Africa and established a new city, Cairo, as their capital.

The Eleventh Imam in Twelver Shia Islam, Hasan al-Askari, spent his life under house arrest in a military camp in Samarra, north of Baghdad, and was poisoned at the age of 28. There is no record of any heir, so it would have been difficult to pass on his role as Imam in accordance with Shiite principles.

But many of his supporters claim that he had a son, Muhammad ibn Hassan, who was the Twelfth and final "Hidden Imam." They profess that he will return to the mortal world as "Mahdi" when the earth is full of darkness, eradicating evil and radiating brightness and justice. This school is known as the Twelver Shiites. Since the vast majority of the 80 million Iranians and more than 21 million of the 38 million Iraqis belong to this sub-sect, when people speak of Shia Islam, they are mostly referring to the Twelvers.

The idea of Mahdi's return at the end of time is very similar to the Zoroastrian belief that Mazda will ultimately bring light and justice to the world by defeating Ahriman. It is also analogous to the concept of Messiah in Judaism as well as the Christian belief in the Second Coming of Christ. The origin of this Persian messianic concept is thus embedded in the fundamental beliefs of Judaism, Christianity and Shia Islam.

From the point of view of comparative religion, there are indeed some differences between Shiites and Sunnis. For example, because Shiites are often persecuted or oppressed, there is a "Taqiyya principle" that empowers them to conceal their beliefs when dealing with an enemy who possesses an overwhelming advantage. Strictly speaking, the Sunnis deny the validity of this principle. Nonetheless, during the Crusades in Palestine when Christians were oppressing and slaughtering Muslims of all stripes, some Sunnis may have selectively applied it—to save their own skins.

In fact, the division of Christianity into Catholicism and Protestantism during the sixteenth–seventeenth centuries was often accompanied by mutual persecution. The concept of " mental reservation" was advocated by some Catholic scholars, which meant that the faithful could outwardly submit to one another's rituals while retaining their own personal state of mind. This "mental reservation" is actually similar to the Taqiyya principle established by Shiites centuries earlier.

In terms of comparative religion, I would make another observation: In the general divide between Sunnis and Shiites, the Sunnis claim to be respectful of tradition and therefore more concerned with Sharia and al-Fiqh. In this respect, Sunni Islam is closer to Judaism, the first monotheistic faith. The Shiites are a little closer to the Christianity founded by Jesus, because both religions are more concerned with humility and sacrifice and have developed a hierarchy in the process.

This hierarchy implies that each believer does not possess a completely equal status and understanding of religion, but that some are closer to God and better able to interpret God's meaning. In Catholicism, for example, there are the pope, cardinals, bishops, priests, seminarians and then the laity.

The Shiite community has gradually developed a hierarchy, especially Twelver Shia. In general, the gulf in status between laymen and religiously trained scholars (*ulema*) is greater than that between the two among the Sunnis. For Iran's Twelver Shia, the highest echelons are the Grand Ayatollah, Ayatollah, and the Hujjat al-Islam and Grand Mullah, some of which are not precisely defined.

In addition to hierarchy, there is a similarity between Twelver Shia Imams and the Catholic Church in terms of creed. In Catholicism, the Pope is considered the representative of Jesus on earth, and therefore the Pope's edicts on religious matters never err, a dogma known as "Papal infallibility." According to Twelver Shia, the Twelfth Imam is in hiding, and his will is revealed through the highest clergy such as the Grand Ayatollah, ensuring no deviation from God's will or the Qur'anic revelations.

It is because of this tenet, as well as its emphasis on free will and consensus, that Shiites may be more likely than some Sunnis (e.g. adherents of Maliki and Hanbali fiqh) to adapt their traditions and "keep abreast of the times" when faced with real-life issues.

Sufism and Sufi Orders

Beginning with the ninth century, many newcomers to Islam had previously experienced other religions. For example, there were Muslims who had practiced Christianity or Zoroastrianism, and later many Shamanists converted to Islam. Compared with the Muslim customs of reciting a short *ayah* from the Qur'an, or repeated bowing or prostrating oneself, these faiths offered more emotive experiences that helped narrow the distance between the acolyte and their God. Therefore, some Muslims gradually began to lead an unembellished lifestyle and use meditation to achieve greater intimacy with Allah, while others employed singing, dancing and music to accompany rituals and enhance spirituality. This is how Sufism complemented dry Islamic ceremonies.

25 SHIA ISLAM AND THE SAFAVID DYNASTY

Mausoleum of Naqshbandi Sufi order's founder near Bukhara

But undergoing such a religious experience is not something anyone can achieve based upon their preferences; it often requires a teacher to guide them and indicate a specific path, the so-called "doorway." Therefore, Sufism slowly evolved into organized orders (*Tariqas*). As soon as a master teacher's reputation spread, disciples gathered around him, and naturally, an order took shape. Some masters raised funds, built mosques and handed over mosques and the mantle of leadership to a relative, thereby ensuring the continuation of a given Sufi order. So, Sufis are Muslims who believe in a particular form of worship and sometimes embrace a distinctive interpretation of God. The Sufi order represents both a gathering of Islamic mystics and a form of organization in Islamic society.

Sufism exists independently of differences or controversies between Sunnis and Shiites, and a Sufi can be either Sunni or Shiite. However the prevalence of Sufism, or the emergence of Sufi orders, has occurred mainly in Persian- and Turkic-speaking areas. Sufism is also found in the Arab world, but not as widely as in the Persian sphere.

In addition, most traditional Muslim religious scholars were concentrated in the cities and rarely encountered rural folk or the Turkic peoples of the steppes. But during the development of Islam, many itinerate Persian Sufis subsisted on alms while trekking in the countryside or across the steppes, and they had more frequent contact with plain-living Muslim farmers and nomadic shamanists. Gradually, their Sufi ways of worship propagated and extended Islam's reach, but also deviated from some orthodox rules and rituals.

This led to disputes between the ulema and Sufis. During the eleventh–twelfth centuries, a Persian scholar, al-Ghazali (1058–1111), who was well-read in traditional religious theory but came from a Sufi family, proposed a compromise that would impact all of Islamic society: Traditional Muslim scholars would recognize that Sufis were acting in accordance with Islamic doctrine, but Sufis could only base their rituals strictly upon the Qur'an, and must not deviate from *tawhid*, i.e., the basic doctrine of the oneness of God.

Turkmen Military Alliances and the Safavids' "Red Heads"

As the Turkic-speaking peoples left the steppes and entered the Persian sphere and embraced Persian-style Islam, Sufi orders with a Turkic background grew more prevalent. The founders of important Sufi orders—such as what is now the largest, the Naqshbandi order—were almost always Persians, but devoted members and lay participants were mainly Muslims from Turkophone tribes.

Around the fourteenth century, on the eastern and southern shores of the Caspian Sea, and even later in the eastern and southern parts of Anatolia, there were a pair of Persianate Turkoman tribal confederations that practiced Sunni Islam and spoke the Oghuz branch of the Turkic language. They formed tribal alliances in the late fourteenth century and gradually took control of political power. One was the White Sheep Dynasty (Aq Qoyunlu), which formed near Tabriz, and the other was the Black Sheep Dynasty (Qara Qoyunlu), which emerged near Herat in northwestern Afghanistan after the Timurid Dynasty began to decline. But they eventually went to war and the White Sheep emerged victorious.

A descendant of the founder of the White Sheep, Ismail, was a charismatic and courageous leader who unified most of present-day Iran and part of the Caucasus in 1501, and established a new regime in Tabriz, the Safavid Dynasty, named after the Safavid Sufi order headed by his grandfather.

Ismail's Safavid regime was initially quite extreme. He declared Shiite Islam to be their faith and followed a fanatical sub-sect of Shiites that required believers to denounce the first three of Islam's four Rashidun Caliphs, who were Sunni.

While the Shiite Safavids were busy establishing themselves, the Ottoman Empire to the west was firmly Sunni, and a group of Uzbeks of Mongolian descent from the southern Russian steppes to the east of Khorasan Province replaced the Timurid Khanate with their own khanate. This meant that the young Safavid dynasty had to do battle on two fronts. They did succeed in consolidating their rule, however, reorganizing the areas once occupied by the Black and White Sheep Turkmens, and basically restored the territories of the Sassanid Empire, which largely established the geographical boundaries of modern Iran.

Thanks to his pious and courageous troops of Turkic origin—the crimson-hatted *Qizilbash*—Ismail was able to achieve victories on the military front. On the one hand, Ismail was originally part of the White Sheep Turkmen ruling elite, but once he had established his regime, he had to fight or destroy the remnants of the White Sheep group in order to fortify his rule.

On the other hand, he first exploited and then fought against the Sufi order. Ismail had both a Sufi family background and ties to the *Qizilbash*, but he was determined to restrict the influence of both once firmly in power. And so, he needed once again to ally himself with a group of religious supporters, and this time his choice was the upper echelon of the Twelvers. He selected and nourished supporters in Qom, a long-time base of Shia Islam, and during the Safavid era, large numbers of clerics who hailed from the city were appointed to senior posts.

Shah Abbas the Great

The main military force behind the success of the Safavid Dynasty was the *Qizilbash*—lit., "Red heads," a reference to the crimson headgear they donned—while its main political and intellectual strength came from Shiite clergy. Toward the end of the seventeenth century a new shah emerged, Abbas the Great (r. 1588–1629), the dominant monarch of the Safavids who occupies a prominent place in Persian history. Abbas lived in an era when reforms were imperative, and he met the challenge head on.

First of all, he altered the uniform and weaponry of his army, introducing muskets and cannons. His musket corps was similar to the one previously instituted throughout the Ottoman Empire.

Then he proceeded to reform methods of governance. Persians, Pashtuns, Turkmen, Azerbaijanis, Armenians and Kurds were shaped into what was, conceptually and practically speaking, a single multi-ethnic state, and established Persian as the official language. In this system, the occupational orientation of the various ethnic groups differed. The Armenians, for example, primarily served as merchants who profited mainly from silk then fabricated in Persia's Gilan, not China.

The world-famous Great Mosque of Isfahan

In addition to reforming the military, administration, and religion, Abbas changed the perception that only Persians could serve in the government's upper echelons. This change was related to his relocating the capital from Tabriz to Isfahan in today's central Iran. He decided that the Safavid capital would eclipse all other cities, so he and his successors built many magnificent mosques, palaces and caravansaries. The architecture of Isfahan became so beautifully imposing that

Persians of the seventeenth–nineteenth centuries boasted "*Isfahan nesfe Jahan*"—"Isfahan is half the world."

Isfahan's renowned Allahverdi Khan Bridge with 33 arches

A Zurkhaneh—traditional venue for martial arts training practiced to music—in Isfahan

After Abbas the Great, the Safavid Dynasty did not produce another shah of his heroic ilk. The changing world situation caused the Safavid dynasty to fall behind and reluctantly concede the rise of the Europeans.

When discussing the gradual decline and fall of the Safavids, however, one cannot ignore Abbas the Great. Although he created a new type of administrative organization, power did not lie within that body; it could be upright and effective, or corrupt and diffuse. What was important was who headed it and how they led it.

During his reign, the shah ruled with personal charisma and extraordinary energy, supplemented by religious passion. Abbas was indeed religiously fervent himself, and in 1601 traveled on foot for 28 days to Mashhad in eastern Iran on a pilgrimage to the shrine of Imam Riza. He used these qualities to set an example for members of his dynastic administration, and with great success.

However, the administrative system Abbas created was gradually relaxed soon after his death and the Safavid Empire fell into decline.

CHAPTER 26

Persian Civilization and Iran's Modernization

Soon after the passing of Abbasid the Great (r. 1571–1629) of Persia's Safavid Dynasty, the world situation began to change rapidly and the Persian Empire entered a new era.

Firstly, the Europeans established a number of strongholds in America and Asia and were robustly operating colonies there. Second, several of the world's great powers were ruled by visionary monarchs: China's Kangxi, Russia's Peter the Great, and France's Louis XIV. Each consolidated and expanded his country's territory while enhancing his imperial primacy.

Contemporaries of these emperors included several scientists who arguably had a greater impact on future generations, such as Great Britain's Sir Isaac Newton (1642–1726) and Germany's Gottfried Leibniz (1646–1716). Newton's contributions to physics and astronomy formed the basis of our understanding of the world today; Leibniz's mathematical operations and binary algorithms laid the foundation for calculus and concepts of the Digital Age.

In the same era, Persia did not have powerful emperors who expanded their territories, nor did it have great scientists. What Persia had to contend with was no longer the ancient Greek city-states, Alexander the Great, the Roman Empire, or Byzantium in Europe. This determined that it would face great challenges in the west and north. To its east, Afghanistan, which also lay within the Persianate sphere, once invaded and occupied Isfahan, the proud capital of the Persians.

In 1722, the Safavid Empire finally came to an end, and was replaced by the Zand Dynasty from the west, with its capital in Shiraz, now the capital of Fars Province. Soon after, the Zand was overthrown by the Qajar Dynasty, which was established by Turkmen (also called Turcoman, tribes of Oghuz Turkic origin), and the capital was relocated to Tehran at the southern edge of the Caspian Sea.

For more than 100 years under the rule of the Qajar Dynasty (1789–1925), Persia had the challenge of maintaining its original boundaries and cultural traditions while facing military and economic pressure from Russia and Britain.

The Qajar Dynasty Reforms

The Qajars took the initiative to hire European military instructors to reform the army establishment and weaponry, and the ruling class gradually Europeanized its lifestyle. For example, instead of lying on a traditional Middle Eastern *divan*, they sat upright on a European-style sofa. Even the garb of the shahs transformed: Instead of turbans and baggy *sirwal* pants, they wore pointed tweed hats and narrow-legged trousers; however, they did not adopt the wigs and heeled shoes of European emperors. In fact, this attire was highly symbolic. Persia wished to learn from the West but did not seek wholesale Westernization.

The Qajars tried to reform themselves while borrowing from the strengths of Europeans. But Russia soon incorporated the northern portion of the Persian Empire in its sphere of influence, and Great Britain regarded the southern portion as its sphere of influence, given its proximity to India and Afghanistan.

In fact, Persia was now caught in the middle of the infamous nineteenth-century "Great Game" between these two countries for Central Asian dominance. Similar to what China and the Ottoman Empire faced at the time, other European powers were also laying claim to economic and political privileges, such as the right of its citizens not to be subject to Persian courts.

In addition, most Persian officials at all levels were unfamiliar with financial management, i.e., Persia lacked effective systems of auditing and taxation, or outright embezzled public funds. The central dynasty was often strapped for cash—several shahs were so profligate that they traveled to Europe in luxury, in addition to having innumerable concubines and servants in their courts—so they frequently borrowed from the West, each time making the loan conditional on granting a monopoly or the right to develop a particular piece of Persian territory.

From the late nineteenth century to the early twentieth century, the Qajars employed a Belgian as the chief of customs (and later as the minister of finance), a Swedish military officer to train the armed police, and an American as the country's financial advisor. These Westerners did have some positive effects on Persia at the time.

When it came to evolving for survival's sake, the Sunnis were more legalistic and traditional in terms of Islamic law, while the Shiite philosophical system was relatively more receptive to new technology and ideas.

Unlike some Sunni societies where there was considerable resistance to technological and social innovation due to religious conservatism, Shiites were dominant in Persia and more flexible. But Persia's prodigious clerical class, the *ulema*, was generally reluctant to dismantle old economic and social structures, and especially unwilling to relinquish their own land holdings and right to manage large land donations. As a result, Persia proved incapable of devoting adequate resources to industrial investment.

On the intellectual and cultural front, at the end of the nineteenth century there emerged an Islamic thinker who had no religious rank but was regarded as a great teacher—*al-Afghani* or "the Afghani." He was so named probably because he was born in Afghanistan, but in fact he was Persian. Afghani believed that there was no conflict between Islam and science and that the principles of consensus and analogical deduction allowed by Islamic law could be used to nurture science and technology equal to or superior to that of the West. Afghani's ideas were favored by many rulers of Islamic countries of his era. His ability to make friends, or at least gain access to these rulers, gave him considerable influence over the contemporary Islamic world. Although the formulation of his thought was inconsistent from one period to the next, he was, on the whole, an Islamist offering new insights.

Afghani had resided in Paris and influenced some overseas Persian students. When they returned home, most were dissatisfied with the situation in Persia and wanted to build a more modern country through constitutional reforms.

In the wake of the intellectual awakening and decline of the state, many bazaar merchants and Shiite clerics also actively participated in political discussions. During the closing years of the nineteenth century, the Qajar rulers were forced to relax censorship and permit the establishment of various associations among the people, and even schools for girls. This was a pioneering move at the time, both in Islamic countries and throughout Asia.

As the twentieth century progressed, robust calls for reform rang out in Persian society, many of which originated among conservative clerics. In the summer of 1905, during the *ashura*—when Hussein's slaying is traditionally commemorated on the tenth day of the first month of Islamic calendar—hundreds of stores in Tehran went on strike and many people marched to the tomb of Ali's sixth-generation grandson. In the winter of the same year, two bazaar merchants were injured by the police, which led to a large number of public protests. From then on, there was heated debate and a growing demand for constitutional government.

In the summer of 1906, a personality of holy descent was shot dead by the police as the government tried to silence a group of vehement clerics, leading to renewed street protests and a public outcry.

At this time, large numbers of merchants, mullahs (mid-level religious scholars) and citizens thronged the British legation compound in northern Tehran—reportedly reaching 14,000 at one point—to seek refuge. Bazaar merchants on the outside provided the petitioners inside with food and supplies, and Tehran's markets remained largely unpeopled for more than a month.

His hand forced; Mozaffar ad-Din Shah Qajar signed a decree agreeing to the establishment of the Majlis (legislative assembly).

Convened in October 1906, the assembly quickly formulated a constitution, and the basic system of the state was first incorporated in the 51-article Fundamental Law, which the shah approved. Within a few days of the ratification, this monarch who had reigned for 11 years, died at the age of 54. His son Mohammad Ali Shah Qajar then briefly occupied the throne (1907–1909).

Although the Majlis were divided into Westernized and Islamic factions, a constitution was soon adopted. This was an important event not only for Iran but also in world history. This constitution recognized Twelver Shia as the official religion but clearly expressed that the power of the state originated in the people (with no mention of Allah or the Twelve Imams).

The constitution required that bills passed by the Majlis must be in accordance with Sharia law, compliance is determined by a committee of five senior clerics. In addition, the constitution protected the human rights of the non-Shiite Muslim population by providing guaranteed seats in the Majlis for minority areas such as Azerbaijan, and other religious and ethnic groups such as Armenians and Jews. The constitution provided for a two-tier indirect electoral system in which the right to vote was vested in property owners.

These political reforms took place five years before China's Xinhai Revolution, without violence or bloodshed, but after peaceful demonstrations. This constitution, adopted in 1906, remained in force until Iran's 1979 Islamic Revolution.

The Pahlavi Dynasty

Soon after the bloodless revolution in Iran, Britain and Russia officially divided their spheres of influence in Iran, with Britain allocated a relatively smaller portion.

Although Britain and Russia divided their spheres of influence in Persia, the strategy of the last substantial shah of the Qajars, Muhammad Ali Shah, was to utilize Russia to offset Britain. In return, the Russians helped him train an elite cavalry known as the "Persian Cossack Brigade" in the north.

After the promulgation of the constitution, controversy erupted between radicals and conservatives. This dispute was also reflected in the upper echelons of the ulema, with senior clerics in many parts of the country taking a stand. There was even a riot in Najaf, one of the holiest cities in Shia Islam, that is now located in modern Iraq. In June 1908, the shah felt that he was ready for action and ordered the Cossack Brigade to march into the capital and bombard the Majlis. In the midst of the chaos, the shah took the opportunity to dissolve the legislative body.

World War I commenced soon thereafter, however, and Russian power withdrew from Iran. After the 1917 October Revolution, Soviet Russia had other things on its mind, not to mention Lenin's proclamation abolishing the unequal treaties of the Tsarist era. Therefore, after the war, the biggest winner in Persia was undoubtedly the British Empire.

At the time there were frequent conflicts between the two factions in Persia, and assassinations occurred on both sides. Businesspeople criticized the Democrats, and minorities were repeatedly attacked. In 1921, anti-Jewish riots took place in Tehran. Commander of the Cossak Brigade, Reza Khan, quelled the riots and then seized control of the capital, appointing himself Minister of Defense. The localities also took the opportunity to stop collecting taxes for the central government, and the Qajars henceforth lost all de facto power. The dynasty was not yet officially dead, however, and after the turmoil, the 12-year-old son of Muhammad Ali Shah was named the new monarch, while Reza Khan became prime minister.

In 1925, Reza Khan formally abolished the Qajar Dynasty, took Pahlavi as his surname and established the Pahlavi Dynasty. A military man with military and political skills, he had authoritarian tendencies and strongly nationalistic feelings. Traditionally, Muslims did not use surnames, so the adoption of this family name was in itself an important act symbolizing modernization. During the Sassanid era (224–651), the term "Pahlavi" referred to the Persian script.

After World War I, despite the shah's reluctance, Britain forced a series of unequal treaties upon Persia. It so happened that a large amount of oil was discovered there at this time, which made the series of treaties that Britain had forced Persia to sign even more favorable to the former. At the same time, the discovery of oil gave the new shah a relatively strong treasury and thus a financial foundation for reform.

Reza Pahlavi carried out a series of reforms without carefully researching his society. The first of these reforms was a secularization measure that required each family to take a surname. This was similar to what the Turkish strongman Kemal Atatürk had done, following the European example but ignoring Islamic tradition.

The second was a policy of forced Persianization, which required everyone to speak Persian and either degraded or weakened the status of minorities such as Kurds, Azeris, Turkmen, Armenians and Jews. He ignored the existence of ethnicities in the country, and that Islam—particularly Shia Islam—was the great unifier. During the Safavid era (1501–1736) Shia Islam had become the largest covenant in the Persian Empire and the basis for the majority of the population to identify with each other.

Hastily implemented, this Persianization policy destroyed social cohesion and excluded Azeris and Turkmen, among others. In addition, he treated the traditional nobility, especially the landed nobles and clerics, with contempt and denied them their original status. So, he made enemies on all sides: The West criticized him for his fascist tendencies, the man-in-the-street didn't support his secular reforms, and aristocrats and clerics who had been in power in the past yearned for his downfall.

26 PERSIAN CIVILIZATION AND IRAN'S MODERNIZATION

Imam Reza Holy Shrine in Mashhad, Iran's second largest city. Martyred in 818, Imam Reza was the Eighth Imam of Twelver Shia

In 1935, the Persian government informed all governments that Persia was now officially renamed "Iran." Iran originally signified the "Land of the Aryans."

At the time, the Nazis in Germany were zealously promoting the Aryan race as superior, and since the British, Americans, French and Soviets opposed the rise of Nazism, they were naturally displeased with Reza Pahlavi's renaming of Persia. Despite the shah's strong identification with things Persian, according to research, his family was actually of Mongolian descent. But lineage is arguably not a crucial element in determining one's cultural and ethnic identity, especially one involving a bloodline of some seven hundred years.

During Mongol rule of Persia in the thirteenth–fourteenth centuries, there was a great deal of intermarriage with native Persians, so the Mongols eventually disappeared among the Persian population. Therefore, it is impossible for almost anyone in modern Iran to accurately trace his or her bloodline over the millennia.

Amidst all the opposition and controversy, Reza Shah Pahlavi had little choice but to flee to South Africa in 1941. His 21-year-old son, Mohammad Reza Pahlavi, succeeded him as the second monarch in the Pahlavi Dynasty.

The White Revolution

The two successive Pahlavi rulers shared the same ideology and similar policies, and both wished to modernize Iran as rapidly as possible. When Mohammad Reza Pahlavi ascended to the throne, he strived diligently for the oil revenues to which Iran was entitled, and that he intended to utilize for building Iranian industry. He recruited foreign engineers and accountants at high salaries to work in Iran, so considerable achievements were recorded in the country's industrialization and overall modernization during his rule (1949–1979).

At the onset of the Cold War between the United States and the Soviet Union in 1951, Mohammad Mossadegh, a socialist politician who served as Iran's prime minister, wanted Iran to obtain a greater share of its oil revenues, so he nationalized the British oil companies in Iran, generating heated pushback from both Britain and the United States. He was assassinated in 1953, and it is widely believed that this was the CIA's work.

Thereafter, the shah chose to side with the United States during the Cold War. Interestingly, when it came to agricultural and land reform, he adopted some of the policies that Chiang Kai-shek had implemented in Taiwan, China. In 1958, the shah visited the island to see for himself how the "Land-to-the-tiller" initiative was put into practice, and upon his return to Iran, he instituted agrarian reforms that were partially inspired by the Taiwan experiment in China.

After the Nationalist (Kuomintang) government retreated to Taiwan, it divided some of the public-controlled industrial assets into shares and used these shares to redeem private land from any landowner who possessed more than a certain amount of farmland. These plots were then distributed to the landless tenant farmers, who, in addition to paying taxes to the state, also had to source fertilizers, pesticides, and farm equipment from cooperatives that were jointly operated by firms in the private and public sectors.

In 1963, Mohammad Reza Pahlavi officially declared a "White Revolution" to satisfy the peasantry's thirst for land and also to deter the "Red

Revolution" for which the communists were agitating. However, "white" as this revolution might be, it was opposed by large landowners and clerics who operated religious estates. Iran had once experienced a wave of pro-socialist thought, and some nationalist intellectuals did not want to see their country emulate the American model in terms of governance and diplomacy.

In order to subdue or suppress dissidents, the shah created SAVAK—lit., Intelligence and Security Organization of the Country—an agency that reported solely to him. SAVAK could detain, torture, and even kill his opponents with total impunity. This aroused widespread opposition that was naturally directed against the autocratic monarch.

In the eyes of the clerics, the shah intended to de-Islamize Iran and transform it into a secularized country like Turkey. In the eyes of the clergy, this would constitute a heinous crime for the clergy, and the accusation was well founded.

The shah, like any person in power, treasured his right to rule and was most reluctant to abandon it. In addition to the opposition of the common people and clergy, however, Westernized intellectuals despised his centralization of power, while leftist intellectuals were inherently opposed to imperial authority.

And so in 1979, day after day millions of people took to the streets in the major cities of Iran, chanting for the shah's execution. Seeing that the tide had turned against him, he followed in the path of his father and fled first to Egypt, the motherland of the shah's wife. He was then briefly detained in Morocco, the Bahamas and Mexico because the new Iranian government demanded his extradition. Soon afterward he went to the United States for medical treatment as his cancer worsened but remained for less than two months. His final time in exile was spent in Cairo, where he succumbed to illness in July 1980.

Revolution and Modernization, Cleric-Style

After the shah's flight abroad, Ruhollah Khomeini, the leading Shiite figure whom the shah had dealt with so harshly and had chosen exile overseas for many years, flew back to Iran from Paris. He was greeted at Tehran airport by an ecstatic crowd of several million. Not all those welcomers shared the same thinking; many were just common folk who supported the ayatollah, having heard his cassette tapes—smuggled into

Iran—filled with anti-shah commentaries about current affairs and his vision for a future Iran.

At the time, the united front strategy followed by clerics loyal to Khomeini was to concentrate their efforts against the shah, i.e., anyone keen to overthrow him was a comrade-in-arms. The National Front grouped liberal figures in politics, prominent members of the community who were sincere in their religious beliefs, Westernized intellectuals, and merchants and landowners whose interests had been harmed by the White Revolution.

Khomeini returned to the country amidst great popularity. A highly capable and decisive leader, he exploited his prestige to rapidly organize the "Council of the Islamic Revolution" and gradually excluded the National Front's liberal and democratic elements from the new regime by suppressing, sentencing, arresting or expelling those who opposed him. With lightning speed, a national referendum was held and the Islamic Republic of Iran was proclaimed.

In addition to retaining the modernized armed forces established by the deposed shah, the "Islamic Revolutionary Guard Corps" was created and placed under the direct control of Ayatollah Khomeini, now the nation's Supreme Leader.

In accordance with the philosophy of the Council of the Islamic Revolution, the clerics rewrote the draft constitution that had been formulated by Mehdi Bazargan, the liberal interim prime minister. The new constitution contained these points: Twelver Shia Islam was stipulated as the state religion; politics and religion need not—and could not—be separated; the state maintained a secular governmental structure with an elected president, governors, mayors and so forth, as well as an elected parliament, provincial and municipal councils, but in addition to elections there was to be a system responsible for the recommendation, vetting and appointment of officials; and electoral candidates must be approved by the relevant clerical councils.

In other words, the state was to be led by religion, the government was to be led by the Supreme Council of Religion, and there was to be a Council of Religion for each key ministry.

What this achieved was a system never before attempted in the Islamic world: Firstly, Islam was to be consolidated in the Iranian state, thus all levels of government must recognize God's rule and submit to His will; secondly, the state was to be Islamized, and all branches of government must have a collectively responsible body including the clergy, known as Assembly of Experts, Guardian Council, etc.

There was another key point: The concept of equality was to be realized, i.e., "The Supreme Leader as well as members of the highest religious and governmental organs shall be equal to other citizens before the law."

In short, if we were to characterize Khomeini's Islamic revolution in a single point, it was the institutionalization of Islam and the Islamization of institutions. But what *is* Islam?

In today's Iranian context, Islam is not the Islam of the Sunnis, nor the Islam of the once very active Sufis, but the Islam of the clergy professing the Twelver branch of Shia Islam. Over the centuries, scholars of Shia Islam have developed a theory and a system. The theory was based on the need for a group of Islamic scholars to explain and implement the concept of the Imamate after the Twelfth Imam went into seclusion and until his eventual reappearance as Imam al-Mahdi.

These clerics are divided into different classes. For example, a *Mujtahid* in Persian was a model Muslim jurist. Among them, there was a less formal or universally recognized title, *Ayatollah* (a Persian borrowing from the Arabic for "sign of God") denoting an authority on religious law and its interpretation. After Iran's Islamic Revolution, the appointment of ayatollahs became more institutionalized and formalized. In other words, whoever holds de facto power can appoint an ayatollah.

Originally, ayatollahs could emerge throughout Shia Islam, including in Iraq, Iran, Afghanistan or Pakistan. But after Iran's revolution, a "Grand Ayatollah" position (*Ayatollah Uzma*, "Great Sign of God") was created, i.e., the head Ayatollah. They had a creed: In religious matters, decisions of the Grand Ayatollah, concluded after consulting with other senior clerics, would represent those of the Twelfth Imam, unless and until Mahdi himself emerged from occultation to save and transform the world.

Before Ayatollah Khomeini's victorious homecoming in 1979, there was a highly respected Iran-based ayatollah, known as "Hukumat-e Eslami: Velayat-e Faqih," a term that had come to signify "regent." When Khomeini became Iran's Supreme Leader under the constitution, he stripped this religious scholar of his honorary title, an unprecedented move. Evidently, Khomeini, a revolutionary leader of Islamic scholarly origin, was an exceptionally decisive, unpredictable and ruthless political figure.

The Iranian Islamic Revolution need not have resulted in mutual hostility with the United States. But in 1979, in an unanticipated move, Iranian students broke into the US Embassy in Tehran, took more than 50 diplomats and staff as hostages, and detained them for 444 days. This earned the deep resentment of virtually all Americans and created a stalemate between the United States and Iran that has yet to be broken.

Khomeini died in 1989, and when he did, a frenzy ensued among millions of mourners. The crowd clamored for a small piece of his coffin as a holy relic, so his coffin eventually had to be transported by helicopter to the cemetery.

His successor to the post of Supreme Leader, Ayatollah Khamenei, is also a man of strong leadership character. It has been more than 40 years since the Islamic Revolution in Iran, and it is undeniable that the president and other government officials have been elected on time and in accordance with the constitution several times over the past four decades. Whether or not this involved electoral fraud is, however, a matter of debate. But there is no doubt that the 12-person Guardian Council is the ultimate decision maker as to who can become a candidate.

Currently Russia regularly deals directly with Iran, as does Syria, while China and Turkey do so less frequently, but most other countries are either sanctioning the Islamic Republic or maintaining a safe distance. In 2018, under President Trump the United States abruptly withdrew unilaterally from the nuclear deal known as the Joint Comprehensive Plan of Action—agreed between Iran and the P5+1 (permanent members of the United Nations Security Council plus Germany) after more than a decade of discussions—thereby renewing tensions between the United States and Iran.

Since Biden took over the presidency, the United States, with varying degrees of support from the other signatories of the nuclear deal, has engaged in indirect but intensive negotiations with Iran on the resumption of the nuclear deal. Albeit an outwardly hardline stance, the new Iranian administration installed in 2021, supported by the top leader Khamenei, would most likely agree to reactivate the signed deal in exchange for lifting various sanctions imposed on Iran. The reason for Iran's negotiable "hardline" position is the discontent of the ordinary citizens, who may not oppose the polity of the Islamic Republic per se but are angry at the hardships brought by the policies of Iran's leaders in the past two decades.

Only history can tell whether the Islamic Revolution will take Iran, a country with a remarkable ancient civilization, in a more modern direction or hinder its modernization.

Based upon several trips to Iran and my conversations with Iranians, especially intellectuals, I have found that most are not discouraged, nor are they opposed to Islam, but they are generally unhappy with the outsized influence of the clergy. Both Pahlavi shahs were eager to modernize, secularize and Westernize Iran, but neither father nor son was willing to abdicate. Today's Islamic Republic of Iran also yearns to modernize and has accomplished much, otherwise, there would be no need for the six nations to ink a nuclear deal with it.

The author and students at Tabriz Islamic Arts University

In any case, reality will force the Islamic Republic of Iran to modernize economically and militarily. But the current system of governance naturally generates a two-tier society as in the past—comprised of an aristocracy and commoners—except that the former have been replaced by a nepotistic clerical class.

It is gratifying to note that while Iran is a state governed by Sharia, the University of Tehran, which was established during the Qajar Dynasty, boasts a history of more than 100 years, and is currently the most prestigious and academically robust institution of higher learning in the country, and possesses a student body in which sixty percent are women. Although many Muslim-majority societies do not encourage girls to study, in this respect Iran differs from Saudi Arabia and most recently, Afghanistan under the Taliban.

One of the arguments between Khomeini and Iran's last shah was whether women could stand for election or vote. The shah initially said yes, while Khomeini opposed both. Now I can only say that after all, a society's functioning and evolution have their own peculiar logic.

The West and Persia confronted one another some 2,500 years ago via Greece and Persia, and some 1,500 years ago as Byzantium and the Sassanid Dynasty. I wonder how and when the Western world and Iran will open their hearts to each other? Can a cleric-led Iran achieve a modernization that can stand up to objective scrutiny?

PART VII

Caucasus

CHAPTER 27

Ethnographic Museum on the Border Between Europe and Asia

In 1953, when Soviet dictator Stalin died his most trusted secret service chief, Lavrentiy Beria, was executed. As a junior high school student in Taipei, I read in the newspapers that neither of them was Russian. They were Georgians from the Caucasus. And I soon learned that Anastas Mikoyan, another important statesman of the Soviet Union, was an Armenian raised in this region that lies between the Black Sea and Caspian Sea.

In 1963, when I was a graduate student at Stanford University, I came to know two fellow graduate students from Turkey who were undergraduates at Middle East Technical University in Ankara. One was of Turkish descent and the other Armenian. They shared a rented-room and a jalopy, but they had different versions of what befell the Armenians during World War I.

In 1973, when I was teaching at the State University of New York at Buffalo, I became acquainted with several Iranians. They all spoke Farsi, but one was an Azeri from the north, and an older postdoctoral student was an Iranian citizen who claimed to be Armenian. In order to clarify the relationship between Armenia, Azerbaijan, Georgia, Turkey, Iran and the Soviet Union, as well as the different ethnic groups in the Caucasus, I consulted the *Encyclopedia Britannica* and got a preliminary understanding of the human geography and history of the Caucasus.

In 1992–1993, Georgia, which had just gained independence from the Soviet Union, was in the midst of a civil war due to the outbreak of an independence movement in the Abkhazia region.

In 2003, a large crowd of Georgians, led by a young American-educated lawmaker, marched into the Parliament during its opening session with red roses in hand to expel the president and seize power. This was what the Western media hailed as the bloodless "Rose Revolution." The former Minister of Justice who led the movement—Mikheil Saakashvili—then took over the presidency of Georgia.

By 2013, the whimsical and combative Saakashvili had lost popular support and was accused of corruption and abuse of power. He fled to Poland as a refugee and entered Ukraine the following year, where he obtained Ukrainian citizenship with the help of President Petro Poroshenko, and was appointed governor of Odesa. Soon after, he was sentenced in absentia by a Georgian court, and his Ukrainian citizenship was also revoked because of a disagreement with Poroshenko.

In the spring of 2018, Saakashvili was forcibly deported to Poland. Since the Georgian government requested Poland to extradite him in order to serve his sentence, he left Poland for Ukraine, where he maintained a high profile by criticizing Poroshenko in the media, and even organized anti-Poroshenko demonstrations.

Human affairs are liable to change, or as the graphic Chinese adage has it, "White clouds morph into grey dogs." The political map, population distribution and social institutions of the Caucasus have undergone astonishing changes over the last half century.

The term "Caucasus" is not new to most people, but what is the region's historical background? At present, what is its status in terms of demographics, languages, religions and politics? What impact will the Caucasus have on the international landscape in the future?

THE CAUCASUS: GEOGRAPHY AND CULTURE WITH A DIFFERENCE

The Greater Caucasus, the mountain range that stretches between the Black Sea and the Caspian Sea (the Lesser Caucasus lies to its south), forms a section of the boundary between Europe and Asia. The northern foothills are considered European, while the southern ones are deemed Asian. The entire mountain range stretches over 1,000 kilometers from northwest to southeast, with many peaks, the highest of which is Mt.

Elbrus at 5,642 meters, the highest mountain in Europe. There are 14 other peaks in the Greater Caucasus exceeding 5,000 meters above sea level, while the highest peak in the Alps, Mont Blanc in southern France, falls short at 4,807 meters.

The Greater Caucasus: The author at the southern foot of the range in Georgia, with Russia to the north

The northwestern edge of the Caucasus lies at on the southeastern coast of the Black Sea, bordered by the Crimean Peninsula. The Black Sea's key port is Russia's Sochi, which hosted the 2014 Winter Olympics. The eastern edge of the region borders the western coast of the Caspian, whose main seaport is Baku, the capital of Azerbaijan.

There are more than 200 glaciers in the Caucasus Mountains, but few passes are easily accessible. The gently sloping northern foothills of the range are bordered by the Kuban Steppe and feature a temperate climate, while the southern foothills are quite steep and bordered by Turkey and Iran, with a largely subtropical climate. There are peaks, plateaus, plains, deserts and even lowlands on the northern and southern sides of the entire mountain range, as well as lakes, rivers, wetlands, forests and steppes. Therefore, the Caucasus has a wide variety of flora and fauna, and is suitable for hunting, animal husbandry and farming.

There is a myth among the inhabitants of the Caucasus that after creating the earth, the Creator found some of it too plain and uninteresting, and so decided to distribute some beautiful mountains, waterways, flowers and trees across the land. He placed all this magnificent and beautiful scenery in a big sack and was about to fly to the heavens and scatter them when Satan—who had evil intentions and did not want the earth to be too impressive—secretly slit a hole in God's sack. When God flew over the Caucasus, all those mountains and rivers tumbled out between the Black and Caspian Seas!

Mythology aside, many scholars believe that the Caucasus was one of the earliest cradles of human civilization, not far removed in time from Mesopotamia. Archaeological evidence suggests that the Tocharians, who arrived in China's Xinjiang via the northern coast of the Black Sea about 4,000 years ago, and the Aryans, who entered the Iranian plateau and the Indian Peninsula about 3,500 years ago, both traveled east through the Caucasus while skirting the southern coast of the Caspian Sea.

About 3,000 years ago, nomadic tribes such as the Scythians coming from the steppes north of the Black Sea invaded the Caucasus speaking Indo-European tongues, while the early inhabitants of the Caucasus spoke a variety of Caucasian languages that were very different from each other and had nothing at all to do with Indo-European languages.

Anthropologists have recently confirmed that the earliest Homo erectus ("upright man") skeletons on the Eurasian continent were found in Georgia. They are approximately 1.8 million years old, however, this does not necessarily prove that the Caucasus was the first place where modern Homo sapiens appeared. Today, most scientists agree that Homo erectus, Neanderthal and modern Homo sapiens evolved gradually from primitive humans in eastern Africa, and left Africa for Eurasia about 2 million, 300,000 and 100,000 years ago, respectively.

When it comes to early humans in the Caucasus, I believe that the commonly employed term, "Caucasian race," requires some explanation.

In the second half of the nineteenth century, many European scholars were keenly interested in the study of human races. In 1870, several scholars in physical anthropology at Germany's University of Göttingen proposed a simple classification of human races: Caucasian, Mongolian and Black, commonly known as White, Yellow and Black, based on characteristics of the skull, cheekbones, eye sockets, nose, hair and skin color.

These denominations were quite unscientific, and failed to point out physiological differences in the three races. Even if they do suggest differences in appearance, clear criteria for the differentiation are still missing. For example, many ethnicities in Central Asia, South Asia, West Asia, Southeast Europe and North Africa would be difficult to categorize accordingly.

Racism was prevalent in Europe during the colonial era, and most people embraced the misconception that white people are "superior." These Eurocentric prejudices spread throughout the world because of Europe's might at the time. Even in China, the respected scholar and social activist Liang Qichao (1873–1929) wrote that the white race was superior to all other races; among whites, the Teutons were the most superior; and among the Teutons, the Anglo-Saxons were the most superior. This statement was consistent with the reality that the British Empire was then the world's greatest power. But were he alive today, he would certainly not make such an assertion.

Over the past half century, human genetic research has progressed in leaps and bounds, and there is now a wealth of data concerning visible and invisible physical characteristics. As a result, excepting an ignorant minority or persons with racist biases, "Caucasian" is no longer in wide use, and scientists typically do not employ the term.

While there is a degree of blood ties—i.e., specific genes that are shared—among certain ethnic groups, culture and psychology are also important factors. Thus, it would seem that the designation of the population native to the Caucasus as the standard for the "Caucasian race" is an undeserved appellation!

A Virtual Museum of Peoples and Tongues

At 400,000 square kilometers, North and South Caucasus cover an area twice the size of Guangdong Province of China, but their population of less than 30 million is just one-third that of Guangdong. Yet more than 100 languages are spoken by the almost 40 ethnic groups who inhabit the northern and southern sides of the mountain range.

The languages of the "white" peoples of Europe, Asia and Africa are generally categorized as either "Indo-European" (e.g., Romance, Slavic, Iranian languages) or "Afroasiatic" (e.g., Hebrew, Arabic). However, because of the high mountainous barrier, the languages spoken by the indigenous peoples of the Caucasus are not mutually intelligible and do not belong to any language family. Therefore, linguists have little choice but to refer to them collectively as "Caucasian languages" when many of them are language isolates.

The North Caucasus is now a territory of the Russian Federation, and divided into several autonomous republics and oblasts. Roughly speaking, the early Caucasian-speaking inhabitants of the region included several ethnic groups of the Dagestan Republic in the east, Chechens and Ingush in the center, as well as the formerly widespread Circassians, who now live mainly in the western part near the Black Sea. The Ossetians, who are not considered "indigenous," speak an ancient Iranian language and dwell mainly in the central Caucasus Mountains. Of course, there are also many Russians, Ukrainians, Tatars and Mongolians in the North Caucasus.

In fact, Russian has been the main language of life and work in the Caucasus for almost a century and a half, and the two main religions in the North Caucasus are the Russian Orthodox Church and Sunni Islam.

In recent years, terrorists hailing from Chechnya and Ingushetia, both constituent republics of the Russian Federation, have been the source of many casualties and headaches both to their inhabitants and the central government.

By the mid-nineteenth century, most of the Circassians, who were known for their tough, war-like men and beautiful, capable women, had been killed or banished to various parts of Eurasia. Historically, many of the key leaders of the Mamluks (Arabic for "possessed," i.e., slave) who ruled Egypt during the late twelfth to early nineteenth centuries were "military slaves" of Circassian origin. Many Ottoman sultans, government and political leaders and wealthy merchants preferred to take Circassian women as wives or concubines, so much so that some fashionable Turkish ladies today proudly claim Circassian ancestry.

The Dagestanis in the eastern part of the North Caucasus are also known for their warrior prowess, and their sabers are both trenchant and lovely. While traveling in Russia, I didn't chance upon a Circassian woman, but I did purchase a fine dagger that is the envy of many.

As for the South Caucasus, also known as Transcaucasia, the most famous indigenous people are, of course, the Georgians. Already civilized some 3,500 years ago, they adopted Christianity in the middle of the fourth century, and created an alphabet in the fifth century that is still in use today.

The Abkhazians, who have frequently been in the news for the last decade, reside mainly in northwestern Georgia, speak a Caucasian tongue different from Georgian and are effectively independent.

The Adjarians, who border Turkey in the southwest corner of Georgia, speak another Caucasian language, are mostly Muslim and also enjoy de facto autonomous status.

An old monastery in the Georgian countryside

Gudauri: A small Georgian town where Christianity and Islam coexist

The main Indo-European-speaking peoples in the Caucasus are the Armenians. They migrated from Asia Minor to the Caucasus about 2,000 years ago and became the world's first officially Christian kingdom in 301 CE. Today, the Armenian Catholic Church and the Ethiopian Orthodox Church both have an outpost within Jerusalem's Old City.

The Armenian script was created about 406 CE, slightly before the current Georgian script, and has been in use ever since. Both predate the appearance of the Russian Cyrillic alphabet by about 600 years.

It is worth noting that Christianity was practiced in Georgia around the same time as in the Roman Empire, and the Georgian Church is thus considered an early Christian church. But after Russia took control of Georgia in the early nineteenth century, the Georgian Church became organizationally subordinate to the Russian Orthodox Church.

Another branch of Indo-European speakers in the South Caucasus is the Ossetians, whose South Ossetia has been the flashpoint for conflict between Russia and Georgia in the last decade or so. They speak an ancient Indo-European tongue, and some scholars believe that they share similar ancestors with today's Kurds.

Young seminarians at Etchmiadzin, birthplace of the Armenian Church

An old church in the Armenian countryside

The Caucasus region is highly inaccessible due to its mountainous terrain, and tribes and communities have rarely interacted. Even discounting its myriad invaders over the centuries, the region's jumble of languages would be very complex due to its topography. When the Roman army conquered the Caucasus 2,000 years ago, it reportedly employed more than 80 interpreters to deal with the locals.

Today, of course, the Caucasus is home to the most recent invaders, the Russians, the Mongols who preceded them, and even earlier Turkic ones. Other more ancient conquerors include the Greeks, Romans and Byzantines of Europe, and Assyrians, Medes and Persians from Asia. All stationed their troops and established administrative districts in the Caucasus. It can be said that the Caucasus has historically been a place of confrontation between the East and West. Today, the eastern and western parts of Georgia have long been dominated by opposing forces from Asia Minor and the Iranian plateau, and its capital, Tbilisi, has been devastated by war 29 times!

CHAPTER 28

Musical Chairs in the Caucasus

In the first half of the seventh century, Islam flourished in the Arabian Peninsula, thus altering the course of history in North Africa and West and Central Asia. In the Caucasus, the Arabian empire supplanted the Persian Sassanid empire and continued confronting the Byzantine Empire, bringing an entirely new player to the region.

THE TUJÜE MAKE THEIR ENTRANCE

At the end of the sixth century, the Tujüe (Turkic) Khanate, which originated on the Mongolian plateau, split into two khanates, the Eastern and Western. A branch of the Western Turkic Khanate advanced westward, while a confederation of Turkic tribes established the Khazar Khanate north of the Caspian Sea. It gradually extended its power into the North Caucasus and present-day Ukraine.

In the eighth century, the Khazars profited from their position along the east–west trade route. Being located between two empires—the Christian Byzantines and the Muslim Arabs—they preferred not to side with either, and their ruling elite opted to adopt Judaism instead. The khanate remained in power for nearly two centuries, the sole regime in history not founded by Jews to designate Judaism as its state religion. It was subsequently wiped out by other Turkic tribes, and later still by Mongols and Slavs. Many of the descendants of the original Khazar tribes, known to Russians as Kumyks, still inhabit the eastern part of the North Caucasus.

From the eighth century onward, many of the Turkic peoples who had occupied the steppes of Central Asia converted to Islam and crossed the Syr Darya east of the Aral Sea into what had previously been the Persian cultural sphere, and is now Uzbekistan. From the tenth century onward, many Turkic tribes crossed the Amu Darya southward into present-day Afghanistan, Turkmenistan and Iran.

One of the most powerful, the Seljuk Turks, penetrated farthest westward. They founded a vast kingdom in Persia in the eleventh century. In 1071 CE, at the Battle of Manzikert in Byzantine's Armenia (today's eastern Turkey), they crushed the Byzantine army and captured their Christian emperor Romanus IV.

This marked the penetration of large numbers of Turkic groups—who had previously occupied the northeastern part of the Persian cultural sphere—into Asia Minor, which then constituted the heartland of the Byzantine Empire.

Monument to Nizami Ganjavi, one of the most outstanding poets of the Islamic world, born in the twelfth century in Ganja, a small town in central Azerbaijan

The present-day Azeris were originally a Turkic tribe that entered the Caucasus along with the Seljuks. By the twelfth century, their upper class was Persian-speaking, and one of them, a poet named Nizami Ganjavi, grew up in the western part of present-day Azerbaijan. He penned the *Khamsa* (lit. Quintet), five epic poems in rhyming couplets of Persian that have become literary treasures of the Islamic world, especially among speakers of Iranian languages. One of these poems relates a love affair between Sassanian Prince Khosrow and Shirin, an Armenian princess. This saga has been the subject of countless Persian miniature paintings for centuries.

At the beginning of the fourteenth century when the Mongols controlled much of eastern and central Asia Minor (Anatolia) and the Seljuk Turkic Sultanate weakened and divided, Osman Gazi (1258–1324), the leader of a small principality located in the northwest corner of Asia Minor gradually expanded his territory and established a state of his own. After Osman, ten generations of Ottoman rulers—the name derived from Uthman, the Arabic form of his name—continued to rule for 250 years, and all were diligent administrators and robust warriors gifted in both intellectual and martial arts.

By the mid-sixteenth century, the Ottoman Empire had reached the peak of its power. Its territory included Asia Minor (modern-day Turkey), part of Central Europe (Hungary, Romania, the Balkans), North Africa (the Maghreb, Egypt), both the western and eastern parts of the Arabian Peninsula, the western coast of the Persian Gulf, the Levant (Palestine, Syria) and Mesopotamia. The northeastern frontier of this powerful empire was located in the western part of present-day Georgia.

THE PERSIAN RENAISSANCE

In the middle of the thirteenth century, the Mongols, led by Hulagu Khan, son of Genghis Khan's fourth son, Tolui, conquered Iran and the South Caucasus and established the Ilkhanate, with its capital in Tabriz on the southern edge of the Caucasus. During this period, Perso-Islamic civilization suffered great damage.

The Mongol army led by Batu, the son of Genghis Khan's eldest son Jochi, reached the Caucasus before Hulagu's troops. Batu's forces occupied the entire southern Russian steppe, including the plains and wetlands of the Kuban River valley north of the Caucasus Mountains. The Mongols soon integrated with the Turkic-speaking peoples who had already been grazing and trading in the area for a long time, and they also adopted Islam. The Orthodox Russians referred to this amalgamated people as Tatars.

Interaction and strife between the Russians and Tartars persisted more than two hundred years. In the sixteenth century, however, the Russians defeated the Tartars and consolidated their control over the middle reaches of the Volga River, and thus found themselves adjacent to the North Caucasus.

The Mongol rulers of Persia soon converted to Islam, marking a rejuvenation of Persian culture.

In the early fifteenth century, Timur, a self-proclaimed Mongol but Turkophone soldier from Samarkand in Central Asia, occupied all of West Asia, including parts of Asia Minor and the South Caucasus. His son made Herat in western Afghanistan his capital, and the Timurid Empire adopted Persian as its court language. They built many mosques in Central Asia and West Asia, established madrassas, developed science, promoted literature and emphasized the arts, thereby fueling a Persian Renaissance.

The beginning of the sixteenth century saw the fall of the Timurid Empire. Arising in its place in Central Asia was the Uzbek Khanate (Abulkhair Khanate) founded by Turkified Mongols who came south from the middle reaches of the Volga River, while in West Asia, Persianized Azeris and Turkmens established the Safavid Dynasty.

Since the Uzbeks were never Persianized, Central Asia today is primarily a Turkophone world, while Iran, Afghanistan and Tajikistan remain part of the Persian cultural sphere.

During the sixteenth–seventeenth centuries, the Safavid Dynasty established Iran as a Shiite Islamic empire with a well-developed military, commercial, literary and artistic presence. The northwestern frontier of this empire lay in the eastern part of the Caucasus, which included the present-day Republic of Azerbaijan, and the Russian Federation's Republic of Dagestan. In the eighteenth century, the border between Persia and the Ottoman Empire stabilized, while the border between Persia and Russia changed repeatedly due to war.

I bought a world-famous Tabriz carpet woven in northern Iran's Tabriz that almost borders on Azerbaijan. I took the opportunity to acquaint myself with the site where the Ilkhanate and the Golden Horde battled over this ancient city in the fourteenth century, and where the flags of the Turkish Ottomans and Persian Safavids were raised and lowered alternately during the sixteenth century.

The Russian Long-term Strategy

During the thirteenth–fifteenth centuries, the loosely organized Russians lived in a vast forested area where they were ruled by a mixture of Mongols and Tatars. Beginning in the fifteenth century, the Russians gradually broke away from their control, and with the Grand Principality of Moscow as their base, expanded in various directions.

At the outset of the eighteenth century, Peter the Great (1682–1725) relocated the capital of Tsarist Russia from Moscow to St. Petersburg, a newly built city reclaimed from inhospitable swamplands on the Baltic Sea coast just 165 kilometers from Finland, in order to learn from Western Europe. But this talented, strategically oriented monarch and his more talented female successor, Catherine the Great (1762–1796), in no way neglected to expand their territories eastward and southward, seeking out warm-water ports.

With the Afghan Pashtun's siege of Isfahan—the Safavid Dynasty's capital—marking the end of the Persian Empire in 1722, a number of minor monarchs in the Caucasus took the opportunity to forcefully establish a state, and they were subsequently attacked by the declining empire's rulers. The leaders of these small khanates turned to Russia for help. It was a case of chasing away a wolf at the front door, while letting in a tiger at the back!"

During the Russian invasion of the Caucasus, in addition to the regular army and administrative officials commanded by the nobility, the Tsar was served by a group known as the Cossacks. The Cossacks were a motley community of soldiers, thieves and peasants not necessarily related by blood. In fact, the Cossacks were not a "people" per se. They were mainly composed of lower-class members of Russian, Ukrainian and Polish societies. Having gained new land through war, they settled and cultivated them. They practiced self-rule, but remained loyal to the Tsar in St. Petersburg.

Many Russian literary works highlight the adventurous spirit and romantic lifestyle of the Cossacks as they pioneered new territory for Imperial Russia. Perhaps best known in the West is a novella inspired by Russia's military campaign in the Caucasus, *The Cossacks*, authored by Leo Tolstoy who served as a soldier there in the 1850s.

By the end of the eighteenth century, Russia had already annexed most of the North Caucasus and placed the Circassians, Ossetians and the Kumyks and Nogais (both Turkic peoples) under Russian rule. By the mid-nineteenth century, thanks to various wars waged against the Persian and Ottoman Empires and treaties negotiated with them, most of the South Caucasus had also been incorporated by the Russians, and modern-day Georgia, Armenia and Azerbaijan were formally part of Tsarist Russia.

At the beginning of the twentieth century, a monk from a Georgian seminary, born Ioseb Besarionis dze Jughashvili, changed his name to Josef Stalin, converted to Marxism and advocated proletarian revolution in Transcaucasia along with his companion Lavrentiy Beria, who would later serve as Stalin's infamous secret police chief.

When the October Revolution came, a wave of nationalism in Europe swept through Transcaucasia, and in 1918, Georgia, Armenia and Azerbaijan—each home to different ethnic groups, religions and spoken languages with different scripts—each successfully fought to form an independent republic.

In 1922, with the Bolshevik's Red Army looming at their borders, these three republics were abolished, and were instead recast as the Transcaucasian Socialist Federative Soviet Republic. The first Commissar of Nationalities in the USSR's People's Commissariat of Nationalities was in fact the former seminarian from Georgia, Josef Stalin.

In 1936, under Stalin's leadership as General Secretary of the Soviet Union's Communist Party, the new constitution of the USSR abolished the Transcaucasian Soviet Socialist Federal Republic and revamped Transcaucasia into three separate republics within the Union of Soviet Socialist Republics—Georgia, Armenia and Azerbaijan. The North Caucasus, however, was fully incorporated into the Russian Republic as a frontier region.

In 1943–1944, when the Germans attacked the Soviet Union's Volga region, the Soviet authorities suspected the Chechens and Ingush of the North Caucasus, as well as the Crimean Tatars, of being sympathetic to Germany, and exiled them en masse to Central Asia and Siberia. After Khrushchev's blunt critique of Stalin's cult of personality in 1956, they were allowed to return to their homeland, but they did not receive any compensation, and naturally, they could not gain repossession of their houses and assets.

This saga of mass killing and deportations certainly strengthened the control of Tsarist Russia and the Soviet Union in the North Caucasus, but they are also the reason why the region remains a well-spring of terrorism in the twenty-first century.

In the early 1980s, shortly after the Soviet Union dispatched troops to Afghanistan, I read an article in an American journal on international affairs. It pointed out that the Soviet Union, although superficially strong, lacked cohesion because its territory was too vast and populated by a surfeit of ethnicities. The article concluded that, given the right conditions, the Soviet republics would become independent one after another, and that there would be no peace post-independence. In terms of the Caucasus, this inference appears fairly accurate.

CHAPTER 29

North Caucasus: Russia's Southern Frontier

Beginning in the sixteenth century when the Russians entered the midstream region of the Volga River and occupied Kazan, they progressed eastward and southward for more than 100 years. Despite its vast territory and abundant resources, however, Russia's location and climate hampered communications with the outside world. Although Tsarist Russia's capital was relocated to St. Petersburg on the Baltic Sea at the beginning of the eighteenth century, the motivation to look southward for warm-water ports and access to places across Europe and Asia remained strong.

One reason for the ongoing confrontation between Russia and Britain in Central Asia in the nineteenth century—dubbed the "Great Game"—was the desire of Imperial Russia to gain dominant access to the lands of Afghanistan, Pakistan and India, and thus gain access to a port near the Indian Ocean.

The southern frontier of the Russian Federation today is in the North Caucasus (Ciscaucasus), which includes two important ice-free ports: Sochi on the Black Sea's southeastern coast, at about 44 degrees north, from which Russia can readily enter the Black Sea and then cross the Bosphorus and Dardanelles to the Mediterranean; and Dagestan's Makhachkala on the western coast of the Caspian Sea, at about 43 degrees north, which provides access only to the periphery of the Caspian Sea and no entryway to other seas.

Therefore, although Russia's long-cherished wish for a warm-water seaport has been fulfilled, its inherent geographical disadvantage hampers it from becoming a fully integrated economic power like the United States, China or India.

Unique Peoples of the North Caucasus

In the course of their southward expansion, the Russians first encountered the nomadic peoples of North Caucasus, including the Kalmyks, who are of Mongolian descent, and the Turkophone Kumyk and Nogai peoples. Later, Russian forces gradually came into contact with the native Caucasian peoples residing in the area where the Caucasus Mountains and flatlands meet, and this led to protracted conflicts.

Prior to the eighteenth century, several major religious shifts occurred among different ethnicities throughout the Caucasus. The first two eventually led to Christianity becoming one of the principal faiths, mainly due to the influence of two Christian states, the Byzantine Empire and the Kingdom of Georgia.

There were three subsequent waves of Islam, first in the eighth century when the Arab Empire entered the region and introduced Islam; during the tenth–fourteenth centuries when the Mongols and several Turkic-speaking tribes, who had already converted to Islam, swept across the region in large numbers and powered the expansion of Sunni Islam; and finally in the seventeenth century when the Ottoman Empire led a wave of conversions.

The Ottomans had footholds throughout the Caucasus, on the flatlands, mountains and coastline. Their influence spread forcefully, so that even the indigenous peoples of the North Caucasus, who had long adhered to traditional nature worship, converted to Sunni Islam.

The native dwellers of the North Caucasus were trapped among towering mountains and precipitous ridges since early times and had little contact with the outside world, thus creating a strong cohesive force arising from a shared sense of "homeland." They were composed mainly of tribes, each of which included patricians, freemen and fellow tribesmen who were slaves.

Neither Christianity nor Islam has changed the custom of the mountain people to make their clan members the object of their allegiance. Some customs that are not permitted by Christianity and Islam, such as blood revenge, are still part of their sense of honor and shame. If a woman violates the customs of her tribe and marries or elopes with a man of another tribe or even a different ethnicity, males of her tribe must retaliate. If one of their own is killed or seriously injured by the other party in a violent conflict, they must try to kill or seriously injure a member of the offending group, or exact a similar degree of revenge. Such blood feuds were common in pre-twentieth-century North Caucasian society.

Another tradition in North Caucasian society is the system of democratic consultation among tribal elders. This is similar to clan councils in China's rural villages, which are composed of highly respected elders of several families who gather to decide on clan affairs through discussion.

The Caucasian tradition is somewhat unique, however. For example, in meetings the elders speak first and etiquette dictates that they may not be interrupted. If the elders speak at great length, the gathering may last several days until the family hosting the assembly is overwhelmed. To resolve the problems of food and accommodation this poses, such clan get-togethers often arrange to "move house."

Circassian Traumas

As the Russians crossed the Kuban River and continued southward into the northern foothills of the Caucasus Mountains, the indigenous people they most frequently encountered were the Circassians. Scattered throughout the northwestern part of the North Caucasus, their population must have topped one million when the Russians encroached upon their land in the early nineteenth century.

Intriguingly, this ancient people has been a prominent part of the history of the Middle East.

Circassian men were physically robust and fierce fighters, while the women were known for their alluring beauty. As a result, many Arab countries recruited non-Muslim Circassian men as slave soldiers—Islamic law forbids enslaving a fellow Muslim—or Circassian women to serve as odalisques at the court.

Among the Mamluks who ruled Egypt after the thirteenth century, there were a large number of soldiers of Circassian origin, several of whom became sultans of the Mamluk Dynasty after converting to Islam. There were innumerable Circassian concubines in the royal harem, and several Ottoman sultans were mothered by Circassians.

At the beginning of the nineteenth century, there was a growing exchange between Circassian tribes and the Ottoman Empire. The Northwest Caucasus, where the Circassians had lived for generations, was close to the southeastern coast of the Black Sea, so it was nearly always easy to reach eastern Anatolia by sea, and even Istanbul via the Bosphorus Strait.

When the Russians invaded the hinterland of the Northwest Caucasus, the Circassians looked to two countries for assistance: Britain and the Ottoman Empire. The latter was in decline by the nineteenth century and no match for the Russians. Britain was not keen to see Russia occupy so much territory and obtain a warm-water port, so the British sent diplomats and others into the Circassian region as merchants, both to spy and to help the locals buy arms.

Eventually the Circassians were driven by the Russians to the peak of the Caucasus Mountains and forced to abandon their lands in the hills and in the plains. By this time, most of Dagestan in the eastern part of the North Caucasus was already occupied by Russia.

A Sufi leader known as Imam Shamil organized an army to resist Russia, and the Circassians agreed to join Shamil's jihad against the Russians. He exercised power mainly in the eastern part of the Caucasus Mountains, namely Dagestan, Chechnya and Ingushetia. He ruled the country strictly by Sharia and had strong personal charisma and appeal, which for a certain period made him quite successful in resisting Russia. However, Russian society and its military organization were much stronger than those of the indigenous peoples of the Caucasus, so their fate became all too obvious after the middle of the nineteenth century.

At this time, a confederation of tribes formed in the western part of the Caucasus Mountains, its make-up dominated by Circassians. Comprising ten chiefdoms and three democratic tribes, the confederation designed a flag to strengthen its identity and gain international support. This political alliance was clearly disadvantaged vis-a-vis the Russian army and the Cossacks, and when Imam Shamir was finally forced to surrender in 1859 (on condition that the lives of his family members be spared), the Circassians were faced with the choice of surrendering or continuing their struggle.

In the end, some of them accepted the Russian terms and agreed to cease fighting and relocate to the plains north of the Kuban River, where Russia wanted them to dwell, while others fled to the high mountains to continue their struggle. One of the tribes that continued resisting was called Ubykh, an endonym used among speakers of the Ubyx dialect of Circassian. Their leader resisted Russian occupation with determination all his life, and after the old leader passed, his son took up his mantle.

In 1864, however, even this last source of resistance, the Ubykh tribe, could not fight on. So, at a site on the Black Sea coast they signed a pact with the Russians that permitted Circassians to proceed to the Ottoman Empire (today's Turkey) by boat, while the remainder were forced to relocate to places designated by the Russians. The Russians also demanded that the mountainous areas of the tribe, which had previously been used as their base, be cleared and vacated. This was the final victory of the Russians in the North Caucasus war and the beginning of doom for the Circassians.

Why do I label this "the beginning of doom"? Because although during their struggle against the Russians the Circassians had suffered heavy casualties, the nation remained largely intact. However, after several generations of tsars, Imperial Russia was determined to seize the entire Caucasus region, and there was no room for any native people to stand in the way.

The Cossacks, who served the Tsarist government, were also eager to move south and take over more of the fertile southern Caucasus Mountains, so the native Circassians were expelled and massacred in large numbers. Although there is no record of the exact number, the evidence available today suggests that 300,000 to 400,000 died.

The Circassians who fled to Ottoman territory numbered nearly 100,000, and further dispersed throughout the Balkan Peninsula, Syria and Palestine. There are still communities of Circassian descent in Jordan and Israel today. Because Caucasians spoke so many languages, it was difficult for outsiders to distinguish between them; the Ottomans called the tribes that spoke Ubyx and tribal populations that spoke similar languages "Circassians." Members of the Circassian diaspora, who are now scattered throughout the region, also use this name themselves.

In the Russian Federation today, persons who qualify as Circassians probably number less than 100,000. In the Soviet era they were given three different names (the Cherkes, Adyghe and Kabardinian) and assigned to three different administrative districts. This was clearly a strategy of ruling by division.

In short, a people that originated in the North Caucasus played a role in writing Middle Eastern history during the eleventh–twelfth centuries, and still had a population of about one million by the nineteenth century, in the wake of a millennium of change is now scattered throughout the Middle East, and has no place to call home aside from a few small administrative districts in the Russian Federation, whose names have been designated by the Russians.

CRIMEAN WAR: CAUSES AND CONSEQUENCES

From the eighteenth century, when Catherine the Great began to focus on the expansion of Russia into the Black Sea region, the Crimean Peninsula was incorporated into Russia in 1783. Through the continued efforts of Tsars Alexander I (1801–1825) and Nicholas I (1825–1855), the North Caucasus near the Crimea gradually came under Russian control. Meanwhile, the Ottoman Empire was in decline and no longer fit to rival Russia.

Around 1850, the British formulated an unambiguous foreign policy—counter Russian expansion in the Black Sea, and curb its arrogance. The immediate goal was to prevent Russia from basing a navy in the Black Sea, and this was the real cause for the Crimean War that followed shortly afterward. It was a geopolitical decision.

The fuse that ostensibly ignited the Crimean War was a struggle over administration of the Christian Holy Land in Jerusalem. At that time, the whole of Palestine (including Jerusalem) belonged to the Ottoman Empire. France thought that as the most powerful Catholic nation in the world, it was the representative of Catholicism throughout the world, and therefore the Church of the Holy Sepulcher where Jesus was crucified and buried should be under their management. The Russians, on the other hand, figured that since they represented all Eastern Orthodox Christians, including Greeks, Serbs, Romanians and Bulgarians, administering the church in the Holy Land was their brief.

And that's how it happened: A massive conflict—the Crimean War—erupted between the Ottomans, French and Russians over the trifling matter of... a key to a church portal.

In this war, Britain and France joined hands to help the Ottoman Empire battle against Russia, and the trio defeated Russia in 1856. The topic of this chapter is not the Crimean War, so we will not go into details of the conflict. However, since Crimea is a neighbor of the North Caucasus, and the Russian-waged war in the North Caucasus—and thus the very fate of the North Caucasus—were then at a critical juncture, I'd like to insert a commentary on the Crimean War (1853–1856) here.

The war ended with Russia's defeat and the loss of its right to a Black Sea navy. Or as the British put it back then, the war prevented the sea from morphing into a "Russian lagoon."

On the one hand, this resulted in the loss of Russia's control over part of the west coast of the North Caucasus, and slightly prolonged the native population's campaign of anti-Russian resistance.

On the other hand, defeat in the Crimean War made the reform-minded Tsar Alexander II determined to undertake radical changes in Russia, relieving systemic conflicts and stabilizing a society in turmoil. One of his most important reforms was the abolition of serfdom, a crucial event for Russian society. The failure of the Crimean War could in some way be considered a blessing in disguise, for otherwise, it is inconceivable that the Russian Empire, which still needed a large number of serfs to produce food, would soon industrialize and become a strong socialist state like the Soviet Union.

Soviet Era: Policy Toward North Caucasus

Defeat in the Crimean War pushed Tsarist Russia to pay more attention to gaining control of the Caucasus region, until it was completely annexed.

After the Bolshevik Revolution of 1917, several different republics were formed within the Caucasus. After the formal establishment of the Soviet Union in 1922, however, the Transcaucasian Socialist Federative Soviet Republic was founded, grouping Georgia, Armenia and Azerbaijan.

Once Josef Stalin, who was born in Georgia, gained absolute dominance over the Soviet Union in 1936, the new constitution of the Soviet Union dictated the dissolution of these Transcaucasian republics and the establishment in the South Caucasus of three separate socialist republics: Azerbaijan, Georgia and Armenia. They would have the same status as Russia, Ukraine and Belarus. In the North Caucasus, several Ethnic Autonomous Regions were created. As mentioned above, each republic and autonomous region housed a number of cross-border ethnicities within its borders, making it difficult for these administrative units to function properly according to the principle of ethnic autonomy.

At the outset of World War II, the Nazi army launched a heavy attack on Stalingrad (now Volgograd) on the lower Volga plain, placing the North Caucasus in what the Soviet government considered a hazardous zone. Stalin and his trusted aide Lavrentiy Beria, surmising that the peoples of the North Caucasus might sympathize with the Germans and oppose the Soviet regime, dispatched troops to resettle the Crimean-based Tatars, highland Turks and the Chechens and Ingush in Central Asia. Such hasty deportation birthed intense resentment and indelible trauma among these peoples.

The North Caucasus after the Second Chechen War

In the late twentieth century, following the success of Iran's Islamic revolution and the huge petrodollar benefits afforded Saudi Arabia, an Islamic renaissance emerged among Muslims worldwide, Sunni and Shia alike. One consequence was that a significant number of Muslims became more devout and even tended to embrace the fundamentalist tenets of Saudi Arabia's Wahhabi sect.

Muslims in the Soviet Union and later in the Russian Federation, particularly in the Caucasus, also came under the sway of Wahhabism. Before Al-Qaeda's 9/11 watershed terrorist attack against the United States in 2001, rebel regimes based on religious extremism had already emerged in many places such as the Philippines, Afghanistan and Nigeria. Chechnya in the North Caucasus also experienced war in 1991, and in 1999 rebels there led by former Soviet military officers declared independence from the Russian Federation.

In the wake of the 9/11 attacks, a number of terrorist groups materialized, all claiming to be waging jihad or Holy War. Such terrorist groups surfaced in Chechnya, Ingushetia and Dagestan in the North Caucasus. In some areas, they governed in the name of Islam, and involved former military officers with combat experience.

Putin's policy of forceful military offensives, undertaken after he became president, largely stabilized the situation in 2003 and installed a pro-Moscow Chechen, Sergei Kadyrov, as Head of Chechnya Republic. However, sporadic military operations continued, and terrorist attacks occurred from time to time. This low-intensity exchange of fire continued for several more years until 2009, when it officially ended.

In 2004, when increasingly serious terrorist attacks were occurring in Chechnya, the most large-scale, lethal terrorist event in Russian history transpired at School Number One in the city of Beslan in the Ingushetia Autonomous Region, where more than 1,200 persons were taken hostage by a gang of organized terrorists. Three days later, Russian forces launched an attack that ended the Beslan School Siege with the deaths of more than 300 hostages—including 186 schoolchildren—as well as all the terrorists.

The spillover effect of this terrorist operation led to sporadic terrorist incidents on the part of other small terrorist groups in Chechnya and Dagestan, and occasional terrorist events continued for several more years.

But in the last decade the Russian government has been determined, on the one hand, to fight terrorism without mercy and, on the other, to actively step up the region's economic development, especially to use the 2014 Winter Olympics as a turning point to build a more peaceful social environment in the North Caucasus. Travelers can now enter and leave the region, although they may have to obtain a border pass.

Sochi, a Black Sea port city, has been a popular vacation destination for Russians since the nineteenth century, and its beaches are once again gaining popularity among tourists. As for Grozny and other regions of Dagestan, tourism is gradually being developed.

The history of the North Caucasus, which has endured for 3000 years, appears to be entering a new phase.

CHAPTER 30

The Post-Soviet South Caucasus

Dissolution of any great empire always has its aftermath.

The ending of Tsarist Russian Empire in 1917 and the collapse of the Soviet Union in 1991 successively led to altered political affiliations as well as ethnic strife in South Caucasus.

In fact, the root cause of the tumultuous changes in this area can be traced back to the decline of the Ottoman Empire beginning in the seventeenth century and its eventual demise in 1922, in the wake of World War I.

The splitting of Transcaucasia in 1918 into three republics, Georgia, Armenia and Azerbaijan, which resembled nation-states, was the immediate result of October Revolution and the end of the Tsarist rule of this area. Within a few years, however, they all reverted to Moscow under the aegis of the Union of Soviet Socialist Republics, i.e., the Soviet Union.

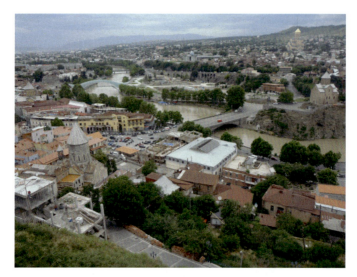

Tbilisi, capital of Georgia

Georgia and its "European Complex"

In June 1991, I attended my daughter's graduation ceremony from Harvard University. Recipient of an honorary doctorate and invited speaker that day was (the then still) Soviet Union's Foreign Minister Shevardnadze. The former KGB general and First Secretary of the Communist Party of Georgia and a member of the Soviet Politburo was warmly applauded by the American elite in the crowd. Although he was cheered in Boston, just two months earlier his homeland had declared independence from the Soviet Union under the leadership of a longtime political dissident who happened to be a professor of English literature.

Immediately after independence, Georgia was plunged into the chaos of civil war. The nationalist professor, President Zviad Gamsakhurdia, mobilized the army to suppress independence in Abkhazia, but was forced to flee to the Russian Federation's Chechen Republic due to his brief but poor spell of governance.

In 1992, Shevardnadze, temporarily idled in the wake of the Soviet Union's collapse, was put forward by hometown supporters as the new head of Georgia. But the new president, despite his administrative experience, was not only unable to prevent the continuation of the civil war, but was also the target of some 19 assassination attempts! He escaped with his life, but Mikheil Saakashvili, a young American-educated lawmaker whom Shevardnadze had promoted, led a throng of people—roses in hand—into the government headquarters in 2003 and threw Shevardnaze out. This was the famous bloodless "Rose Revolution."

Many Georgian leaders and elites would love to join the North Atlantic Treaty Organization as soon as possible in order to become a "European state" within Asia, like Israel. Paradoxically, Georgia has desired to enter Europe on Russia's coat-tails since the nineteenth century, thus freeing itself from Persia and the backward Ottoman Empire that had ruled it in turn for centuries. Yet twenty-first-century Georgia is still outside Europe looking in, not one iota closer to EU membership than Turkey.

In 2008, Georgia and Russia broke off diplomatic relations due to the conflict in South Ossetia. But Georgia, a small country with a population of just a little over 5 million, faces problems that go far beyond its powerful former suzerain. Given Putin's machinations, Georgia cannot escape from Russia's sphere of influence no matter how much it thrashes about. In recent years, Georgia has seen a widening gap between the rich and the poor, corruption and abuse of power by officials and low internal cohesion. It has several de facto independent autonomous regions in its territory, including South Ossetia, Abkhazia and, less frequently noted in the press, Adjara. There are 250,000 ethnic Georgian refugees expelled from Abkhazia residing near Tbilisi. In addition, there are about 300,000 Armenians and 300,000 Azeris near its borders with two neighboring countries. In 2022, as many as 100,000 Russian men are said to have entered Georgia in order to doge the military call-up due to Russian's war against Ukraine.

These problems constitute a major obstacle to building a state with a predominantly Georgian population. More seriously, national unity is not what the average Georgian has in mind. Like many other parts of the world that have not been baptized by modernity, the average Georgian owes allegiance only to his family and the region in which he lives, and has no special sense of identity with the state. For example, most residents of Gori, Stalin's hometown, are still proud of their countryman-made-good, and many volunteer to guard the Stalin Memorial in the city.

Speaking of nationalism, I should add a note or two. Saakashvili, the leader of the above-mentioned "Rose Revolution," was the president of Georgia for several years. But he made so many enemies that he was accused of corruption and abuse of power, and had to flee the country for Ukraine to escape prosecution.

With the support of Ukrainian President Petro Poroshenko, he was granted Ukrainian citizenship and Poroshenko appointed him Governor of Odessa in 2015. Soon after, the two publicly fell out, with Saakashvili attacking Poroshenko and Ukrainian prosecutors accusing Saakashvili of helping Russia fight Ukraine. In 2017, Saakashvili was stripped of his Ukrainian citizenship, but he continues to be at odds with Poroshenko.

Thanks to a change of president—former comedian Volodymyr Zelenskiy was elected in 2019—Saakashvili regained his Ukrainian citizenship. But he did not stay there long. Instead, he secretly snuck into Georgia and was imprisoned. Later, he admitted that he had fathered a daughter with a Georgian singer. So this hyperactive Georgian politician seems unable to stay away from the headlines!

During the 2008 Beijing Olympics, the relationship between Georgia, South Ossetia and Russia dominated much of the world's news. For reasons known only to those who had dealt with this issue, Georgia dispatched troops to South Ossetia, an autonomous region, but in reality its status was tantamount to that of an independent state with pro-Russian sympathies. The resulting attack by Russian troops on Georgia naturally aroused sympathy in the West. For a while, Georgia may have felt as if it were part of Europe.

Meanwhile in South Caucasus, there seemed to be signs of positive interaction between Turkey and Armenia, which had been feuding for 100 years: Turkey's President Abdullah Gül accepted an invitation on the part of Armenian President Armen Sarkissian to attend a World-cup qualifying soccer match between the two countries. The game in Yerevan ended years ago, yet it is still unclear which of the two countries won or lost on the strategic front. But given that the EU has yet to embrace Turkey despite such fence-mending efforts, it would appear that Georgia's dream of joining Europe will remain just that.

Azerbaijan and Black Gold

Although Georgia could not have become a state based upon a single ethnicity, Armenia and Azerbaijan became largely monoethnic after the collapse of the Soviet Union through war and ethnic cleansing.

Baku, the capital of Azerbaijan, was the global center of the petroleum industry in the early twentieth century, and home to many moneyed Europeans—such as the Nobel brothers—whose mansions still dot the city

Historically, Azerbaijan has been ruled by Persia and Russia, but the discovery of petroleum in Azerbaijan in the early twentieth century attracted an influx of European and American investments. The Rothschild family, European tycoons, owned many assets there. Before World War I, Azerbaijan accounted for half of the world's oil production. In recent years, due to its rich oil reserves (perhaps exceeding Iran's, statistically speaking) droves of international energy companies have located themselves in the capital Baku, making it the picture of prosperity.

Azerbaijan has had just two presidents since independence in 1991, Haydar Aliyev and his son Ilham. Prior to the Soviet Union's dissolution, the elder Aliyev was General Secretary of Azerbaijan's Communist Party and a Soviet Politburo member. Their foreign policy has been to maintain close ties with Turkey (both languages belong to the Oghuz branch of Turkic tongues), woo Georgia and robustly resist Armenia, but maintain as much distance as possible from both the United States and Russia. The oil pipeline from the Caspian Sea to the Mediterranean was completed under the elder Aliyev.

Although per capita income has increased rapidly in recent years, the quality of the people and the social atmosphere have seen little progress. On the whole, Azeri society lags behind that of Georgia and Armenia.

Armenia and a Twentieth-Century Massacre

The Armenians have a distinguished history, and at their height their territory was much larger than it is today. Many of the intellectual elite and merchants of the Ottoman Empire were Armenians. In the first half of the nineteenth century, Greece, also a Christian country, gained independence with the aid of Britain and France, and this led many Armenians to dream of independence from the Ottoman Empire under the aegis of Tsarist Russia.

Before World War I, Russia and the Ottoman Empire clashed several times, and the Ottomans ceded a large part of the territory inhabited by Armenians to Russia. During World War I, many Armenians were pro-Russian and thus were targeted for retaliation by the Turkish-speaking, Muslim Ottomans as their empire faced dismemberment. Armenians were slaughtered throughout Asia Minor, and driven on foot to the Syrian desert, which was then still part of the Ottoman Empire. Although officially denied by Turkey to this day, the Armenians and their supporters in Europe and America say that more than a million people perished in this massacre.

The Armenians are indeed a people who have endured great suffering. Since the Middle Ages, they have been known for their commercial acumen, similar to the Jews in Europe and North Africa. While ruled by Arabs, Persians, Ottomans and Russians, they fled on several occasions to save their lives.

The Republic Square in Yerevan, Armenia

Millions of ethnic Armenians live in North America, Western Europe, the Middle East and Russia, most of them well-educated and many of whom possess considerable political and economic influence in the countries of their abode. After Armenia's independence in 1991, the Armenian diaspora strongly encouraged Armenia to take over the formerly autonomous oblast of Nagorno-Karabakh within Azerbaijan. This led to a war between the two newly independent neighboring states and a high death toll on both sides.

Since this war was fought during roughly the same period as the war of Bosnia and Kosovo amid accusations of ethnic cleansing by the Serbians, it largely escaped the attention in the international press.

Thirty years later, after several rounds of clashes and cease-fire agreements, the two countries fought again over the same issue in 2020, and this time the Armenian forces were nearly devasted. The Nagorno-Karabakh dispute is under Russian's arbitration and the war zone is temporarily occupied by Russian peace-keeping troops.

Awkward Transcaucasia

My Armenian friends tell me that based on their past experience as neighbors, classmates and colleagues, Armenians are more willing to befriend Azeris than the "arrogant" Georgians. For their part, it's also said that

Georgians are more willing to associate with Azeris than with the "cunning" Armenians. Regardless of who likes or dislikes whom, the three countries of the South Caucasus are in a constant state of conflict and crisis. Behind this are thousands of years of historical grudges, plus the reality of contemporary competing political interests among various international parties. Today, virtually any territorial claim of any ethnic group living in the Caucasus, or any accusation against another ethnicity, can find its historical basis.

The population of the Caucasus is divided into a kaleidoscope of linguistic groups and ethnicities, all of which have historical baggage, and none of which have experienced the baptism of modernization. Extremism, corruption and malfeasance and homelessness are widespread and not limited to any single people or country.

There is no doubt that all three countries of the South Caucasus (also known as Transcaucasia) are in the process of transformation. In fact, be it socialism or capitalism, democracy or autocracy, all need to be practiced within a certain social and cultural tradition. The democracies practiced in Western countries and the civil society they have been promoting in recent years have not yet found suitable soil to take root in the Caucasus. The concepts of nationalism and nation-states once practiced in the West still resonate strongly in this ancient museum of peoples.

Even without geopolitical rivalries among the major powers, the Caucasus is unlikely to settle down, become democratic or prosper in the near future. Currently, the United States, Western Europe and Russia are engaged in a "new Cold War" over the South Caucasus. But let it not be forgotten that real stakeholders include Turkey and Iran, the two major regional powers.

CHAPTER 31

South Caucasus: International Machinations

Quite a few years ago, Michelle Yeoh and Pierce Brosnan co-starred in a Baku-based James Bond spy flick entitled *Tomorrow Never Dies*, which was about the bizarre plots hatched by certain countries in their rivalry for oil in the Caspian Sea region. I went to see the movie because I was interested in the Caucasus.

But I left the cinema wondering, "In the future, what will *really* transpire?".

Since the Russian-Georgian war in 2008, media has widely reported on the importance of Georgia to the West, and one focal point of media attention has been the huge Baku–Tbilisi–Ceyhan (BTC) oil pipeline that runs from Baku to Ceyhan, a Turkish seaport in the northeast corner of the Mediterranean. There is also a very large gas pipeline from Baku to Turkey's Erzurum via Tbilisi, known as the South Caucasus Pipeline or BTE.

Analysts believe that these two pipelines give Georgia great strategic value, and therefore the United States and Europe will ensure that Russia does not take the opportunity provided by Saakashvili's reckless military campaign in South Ossetia to drag Georgia back into Russia's sphere of influence again. What has happened shows that by its military actions Russia managed to separate South Ossetia from Georgia, while pushing Georgia even closer to the West.

This analysis certainly has some merit. The route south to the Mediterranean through Tbilisi, for instance, is quite convenient for countries such as France, Italy and Spain.

But if we are talking about oil and natural gas, then take a good look around the Caspian Sea. In fact, Russia, Kazakhstan, Turkmenistan and Iran are all major oil and gas producers with stakes in the Caspian region, and there are currently dozens of oil companies from more than a dozen countries exploring and extracting oil in the area. There are also many oil and gas pipelines—on-stream and proposed—for transporting these raw fossil fuels in various directions.

Therefore, although the pipeline through Georgia has strategic value, it is not absolutely key. In my opinion, energy is not the main reason why the Americans, Europeans and Russians are jousting over Georgia, and its future development will not be dictated by energy.

Geography (primarily) determines historical development, while history and geography together shape culture; culture inevitably impacts political and economic development. Economic power is the foundation of military power, and both are the backbone of diplomacy. From another perspective, diplomacy is an extension of internal affairs, i.e., a given country's foreign policy and diplomatic measures inevitably reflect the political situation of that country. I assume these are objective "laws" that we can all embrace.

Below, I will explore the evolving geopolitical state of affairs in the South Caucasus from this perspective.

Maneuvers of the Turks, Iranians and Russians

Both Turkey and Iran were once the center of great and powerful empires, richly experienced in dealing with different ethnic groups and religions internally, and contending with countries of different strengths and weaknesses externally.

The slogans that recall China's decline in the nineteenth and early twentieth centuries and still make the Chinese people's blood boil, such as "Resist the Mighty Outside while Eradicating Traitors Inside," and expressions like "ceding land, making forced reparations, forfeiting power and undergoing national humiliation," are also applicable to these two Middle Eastern countries that have never known colonization. For them, one of the "mighty" was their old neighbor, Russia. But times have changed, and in recent years, the "mighty" in the minds of Turks and Iranians is primarily the United States.

Since the collapse of the Soviet Union, Turkey, Iran and Russia no longer share a border. Naturally, it's advantageous to Turkey and Iran to have the three South Caucasus countries serve as a buffer. Nor is it a bad thing to deal with Russia since it no longer represents the colossal Soviet Union; the ability to invest in or trade with Russia, or obtain technology transfer from Russia, allows them to reduce dependence on the United States and Europe, and is therefore beneficial to Turkey and Iran.

However, the sudden decision by Georgian president Saakashvili to dispatch his troops into South Ossetia in 2008 crossed a Russian red line, and caused Russia to once again station its troops in the South Caucasus, which was decidely *not* a good thing for Turkey and Iran. In response, Turkey and Iran have tightened their ties with the three key South Caucasus countries—Georgia, Armenia and Azerbaijan—to prevent them from being drawn back into the Russian orbit. No other players are better equipped than Turkey and Iran to balance the disputes and untangle the knots between these three countries.

Turkey's stated goal had for many years been to join the European Union. But the EU seems unwilling to embrace it, so many a Turk decided Turkey should "Look East." Some of my more Westernized Turkish friends have even lost patience with Europe and are no longer as interested in joining the EU—though they still long for European-style freedom and democracy, and do not identify with the Turkey's current authoritarian president, Recep Tayyip Erdogan.

The group now in power in Turkey is not the deeply Europeanized Istanbul elite, but the devout Muslims who mainly represent Anatolian small- and medium-sized businesses. They know and feel more attached to eastern Turkey than the "secularists" who reside west of the Bosphorus.

Because of the "Kurdish problem" in the southeast, which has plagued Turkey since the insurgency in the 1980s, and the war in Syria, which profoundly affected Turkey's security and sovereignty, Turkish policy in recent years tended to skip over the Caucasus and aim more at Central Asia; the firms and cultural institutions have made significant investments in Turkic-speaking countries such as Kazakhstan.

As it seeks to navigate its way between Russia and the United States, current and future Turkish administrators will be in a difficult position. Nonetheless, "Looking East" is a must. Ideally, Turkey should try to diminish the tendency of its Kurdish and Armenian communities to identify more strongly with their ethnic roots than the country in which they and their forebearers have called home, for this is a sword dangling over Turkey's head. It would then be better positioned to deal with the complex situation involving neighbors such as the European Union, Egypt, Iran, Saudi Arabia and Israel, as well as more powerful players such as Russia and the United States.

It's been 42 years since Iran's Islamic Revolution. What Iran really wants—and needs—to do is modernize. But Iran faces a dilemma: It is difficult to break sanctions and modernize without normalizing relations with the United States and Europe, which is why Iran signed a limited nuclear agreement with six countries in 2015; but yielding in order to establish good relations with the United States and Europe would cause the current regime to lose its special status within the Islamic world, and possibly threaten the legitimacy of its rule within Iran itself.

In any case, if Iran's religious regime does not reduce unemployment, increase government efficiency and improve the lives of its people, it will sooner or later have to face problems it does not want to see. The widespread demonstrations in the fall of 2022 by the young in Teheran and later by the whole population in most of the country was a reminder of this to the clerics in power. Even though the demonstrations were suppressed by brutal force, there is no way the Iranian government can diminish the anti-cleric sentiment.

Russian, American and European rivalries over Georgia, Crimea and, more recently, Ukraine, have drawn Iran more support from its traditional enemy, Russia. Iran recently took advantage of this new situation by agreeing to renegotiate the nuclear deal signed with "P5 + 1" (5 permanent members of the UN Security Council plus Germany) in 2015 and scratched by the Trump administration of the United States in 2018. Its strongest wish and public demand is the relaxation of the sanctions imposed on it by various countries over the years.

Russia is abundantly experienced in dealing with Turkey and Iran, and geography dictates that they will always be in the same neighborhood. In the foreseeable future, a spirit of good neighborliness will likely dominate in Russia's treatment of these two regional powers. After all, only a fool or a madman would bicker with his neighbors while dealing with a pair of big-time foes striding fiercely toward his doorstep. Russia's best strategy in the Middle East and the Caucasus is to bring its neighbors by its side to help resist those two, the United States and the EU, its war in Ukraine notwithstanding.

What the United States, EU and Russia May Envision

Regarding the issue of the civil war in Syria, which has troubled various global powers in recent years, in terms of willingness to pay a certain price for it, there have been Russia, the United States and the European Union in descending order. In terms of the stakes for the ongoing war in Ukraine, the order becomes Russia, the European Union and the United States. But in terms of power that could be exerted in the conflict, the order would be the inverse, i.e., the United States, then the European Union and Russia last.

From a global perspective, in addition to environmental pollution, international crime and the financial crisis, the trio face two shared challenges: How to respond to the expansion of radical Islamism and the rise of East Asian countries, especially China's. From the point of view of culture and values, save for the Tsarist nationalism espoused by Putin & Co., there are now no irreconcilable fundamental differences between Russia, the United States and the EU, only conflicting interests. Therefore, whatever the sharp contradictions between them, there will no longer be a struggle like the one that took place 60 years ago.

For the United States, the current situation in the Caucasus, Ukraine and the Middle East is an opportunity with more positives than negatives. Its strategic design to enter Eastern Europe and Central Asia, the interests of its own energy and military-industrial groups, and the promotion of American values can be mutually reinforcing and function as an integrated whole within this large region.

But the American elites, whether Democrats, Republican or unlabeled, must deal with America's middle class whose standard of living has not improved in 20 years, and must meet the need to upgrade domestic infrastructure, improve education and increase investment in health care.

In recent years, the mainstream American elite has perceived China as a new challenger alongside the older foe of Russia, so it is inevitable that defense spending will increase. This leaves the United States with two options: Lower its posture and settle for being the most powerful country, if not the global hegemon; or take a gamble and apply both military and economic pressure on Russia and China simultaneously, risking the prospect of Russia and China embracing each other. In the coming decades, what matters to China the most is its modernization efforts and reaping tangible economic benefits westward along the Silk Road, which represents an ancient passageway for East–West cultural exchange.

In terms of issues related to the South Caucasus, Ukraine and the Middle East, the interests of the EU and the United States are virtually identical, so Europe will certainly move in concert with its ally across the Atlantic.

But since European countries are physically close to Russia and are also impacted by the flow of refugees from the Middle East, North Africa and in the near future, a huge influx of Ukrainians, the Europeans do not wish for the United States to get too tough on Russia, nor do they want to see the Americans push the problem, such as energy costs, onto European shoulders.

The war in Ukraine aside, the EU's main focus over the next few years will be on Brexit and assimilating recurring refugee flows. Given that, to expect twenty-first-century Europe to accomplish great things is hardly realistic!

In the wake of the Soviet Union's collapse, the Russian nation's self-esteem built up over the centuries was badly bruised, and its actual geopolitical interests profoundly damaged. So, during years of careful consideration, Putin has built a domestic consensus, clenched his teeth, given Georgia and Ukraine a lesson and refused to yield to the United States regarding these former Soviet Republics.

However, Russia will not take the initiative to make too much of a fuss, as long as it can regain its voice in the South Caucasus, keep Crimea and prevents NATO from placing military bases on its doorstep. The decision to invade Ukraine, Russia's largest neighbor in Europe and also near kin, must have come as a surprise. But I double it was the sheer gamble or gambit by Putin alone.

Before the Georgian and Ukrainian hostilities, or at least when Putin first became president at the turn of the twenty-first century, Russia could have chosen to deepen cooperation with the EU, play by the European rulebook and gradually join the West while resolving its own internal problems. This was the cherished dream of Tsar Peter the Great three hundred years ago, and it remains the wish of many Russians today.

But the recent repeated offensives by Europe and the United States against Russia have given Putin an opportunity to unite internally. His policy orientation will lead to a rise in Russian nationalism and a renewed emphasis on its character as an "oriental" and "authoritarian" state, resulting in a future in which Russia's political ecology and cultural orientation will differ from that of the West.

Such a development may not be overly disadvantageous for certain Western countries, since a Europe including Russia would no longer be dominated by Germany, France, Belgium, Italy and Spain, nor would such a Europe be so easy for the United States to manipulate. But for the three small countries south of the Caucasus Mountains (as well as Ukraine and the Baltic States) that wish to escape Russian influence, the significance of such a development is not difficult to foresee.

Whatever happens to the war in Ukraine, the fundamental problems for Russia are still "domestic" in nature. For example, how to cope with an aging population? What about Russia's sparsely populated "Far East"? How to energize the economy monopolized by the oligarchy that has prospered under Putin?

Perhaps most important to Russia, Europe, the United States and, indeed, the world is whether the average Russian is willing to live a life once envisioned by Peter the Great, or to pass through this world in a lifestyle so different from that of an average citizen in Western Europe?

PART VIII

Turkish March

CHAPTER 32

Westward Migration of the Turkic-speaking People

The Turkic people are believed to have originated in the upper reaches of the Yenisei River, located in present-day northwestern Mongolia. Their language was similar to those of the Dingling, Tiele and Rouran, all nomadic peoples mentioned in ancient Chinese historical texts. Conflicts and wars occurred frequently among them, and alliances forged between them were fragile and subject to rapid change. Before the Turkic-speaking tribes united, they were enslaved by the Rouran and dubbed "blacksmith slaves" due to their superior ironwork. In 552, the clans comprising the "blacksmith slaves" joined forces to establish a nation of their own, one which expanded into an empire over the next few decades.

The vast territory of the Turkic nation was divided into the eastern and western parts, each ruled by a Khagan. The Eastern Turkic Khanate maintained close relations with several dynasties in China's Central Plains, and the founders of the Sui and Tang were even granted titles by Turkic rulers. During this period, Tang Dynasty royalty and generals of Han ethnicity who were based at the northwestern frontier often intermarried with members of the Turkic khanate's ruling class. So much so that Li Shimin, Emperor Taizong of the Tang Dynasty, was at least half Turkic.

Master horsemanship was a key aspect of the culture of steppe nomads. Domesticated around six thousand years ago, horses were originally treated as a source of meat. Later, humans realized that horses not only could carry heavy loads, they were also blessed with sharp hearing and superior memory—hence the Chinese adage that "an old horse knows its way." With its long neck, a horse can see far and wide, while its speed proves useful on the battlefield. Cavalry became a huge military advantage for the nomads.

The Turkic people possessed another equine-related asset: they could use a double-curved bow, made of layers of sinew, birch and horn, while on horseback. The arrows released from these double-curved bows featured high speed and great penetration power, similar to the English longbow. However, due to its length—about 1.8 meters, the height of a grown man—the longbow required that the archer place both feet firmly on the ground.

FROM THE YENISEI RIVER TO THE DANUBE (552–1529)

While the Eastern Turkic Khanate maintained ties with the Sui and Tang Dynasties, gradually switching allegiance to them and merging with the local population, it eventually lost contact with the Western Turkic Khanate.

Meanwhile, the Western Turks moved westward to the Aral Sea, which was fed by the Syr Darya in the north and the Amu Darya in the south. At first they resided north of the Syr Darya, while agricultural Sogdians occupied the southern region. Later on the Turks crossed the Syr Darya; some voluntarily became soldier-slaves, while others were sold to serve as house-slaves of the local settlers.

Afterward, the Turks ventured south of the Amu Darya, thereby entering the Persian realm as well as approaching Baghdad. During the tenth–eleventh centuries, it was the capital of the Abbasid Caliphate, which was nominally ruled by the Abbasid family, clansmen of the Prophet Muhammad. Baghdad was also the political and cultural center of the Islamic world and one of the four great capitals of the era, along with Cordoba in Spain under the Moors, the Byzantine Empire's Constantinople and Kaifeng City in Song Dynasty China.

In the late tenth century, a portion of the Oghuz Western Turks had broken away and banded together under the leadership of the Seljuk clan. They first settled in Bukhara, a major city between the Syr Darya and Amu Darya on the Silk Road, and it was there that the Seljuks converted to Islam. Then they crossed the Amu Darya, moved southward along the east coast of the Caspian Sea and entered the Islamic heartland. Tughrul, leader of the Seljuks, led his army into Baghdad in 1055 and seized power from the Shiite Buyid Dynasty who ironically were the real power behind the Abbasid family, hereditary head of the Califate of Sunni Islam.

The Abbasid Caliph appointed Tughrul "Regent of the Empire" and bestowed him with the title "King of the East and the West." From then on, the Caliph was reduced to a figurehead in the hands of Tughrul who went on to found the Seljuk Dynasty.

In 1066, 11 years after the Seljuks conquered Baghdad, the Duke of Normandy, originally from Norway, crossed the English Channel. This was somewhat analogous to the less refined Turks capturing the highly civilized Persian territories.

Just five years later, the Seljuks defeated the Byzantine army at Manzikert (today's Malazgirt) in eastern Asia Minor (Anatolia, the Asian side of modern Turkey), and captured the Byzantine Emperor. Thereafter, the Seljuk Turks poured into Asia Minor, fighting as *Gazi* (warriors of the Islamic faith) and encroaching step-by-step on the central part of Asia Minor, which was then the most critical piece of territory within the Byzantine Empire. By the middle of the twelfth century, the Turks had established many principalities on what is now the Asian side of Turkey.

The leader of the Seljuks proclaimed himself "Sultan" and made Konya, a city in south-central Asia Minor, the capital of the new Seljuk Sultanate of Rum. It had been nearly 400 years since the Seljuk Turks left the Asian steppes north of Syr Darya, and over 600 since they set out from Mongolia, the cradle of the Turkic peoples. In the process, the Seljuk Turks were steeped in both the Islamic and Persian cultures, and intermarried with Sogdians, Persians, Arabs, Armenians and Greeks, but continued to speak their own Turkic tongue.

The Seljuk Sultanate of Rum (derived from Rome, meaning Europe) and other principalities founded by the Turks in Asia Minor continued to expand ceaselessly, partly out of Islamic zeal, and partly due to the logic of war intrinsic to steppe nomad culture. The Turks defeated local lords one by one and transformed them into vassals. Meanwhile, via administrative power, religion and intermarriage, the Turkic Oghuz language, albeit enriched by Persian and Arabic vocabulary, gradually displaced Greek as the lingua franca of Asia Minor.

In 1243, as the Turks marched westward largely unhindered, another group of Mongolian steppe people, led by Genghis Khan's grandson Batu, entered Asia Minor. His invincible army occupied a large part of Asia Minor and vanquished the Seljuk Sultanate of Rum. The Seljuk

Dynasty, preoccupied by the Mongols, had failed to pay sufficient attention to some lords in its territory, and many local tribes thus won their independence.

One group of Turks migrated to an area very close to Constantinople (today's Istanbul), the capital of the Byzantine Empire. In 1299, their leader Osman Bey founded a small principality. The first two leaders of the kingdom dared not take the title "Sultan," but as their realm expanded, especially after they seized many territories of the Byzantine Empire to the west and conquered other Turkic principalities in the east, later rulers did claim the august title. This minor principality was to become the Ottoman Empire.

The subsequent leaders of the Ottoman Empire were savvy war-makers who also excelled at governance, and the Empire's power reached its peak under Suleyman the Magnificent (1520–1566). In 1529, he led his army to the Danube and laid siege to Vienna. The powerful Sultan with a thin face and narrow nose was regarded as Europe's greatest ruler of his era. Ironically, he may not have been aware that the shepherds who lived along the upper reaches of Yenisei River, with their round faces, flat noses and Turkic tongue, were actually his ancestors.

From Principality to Empire (1299–1566)

Osman Bey, founder of the Ottoman Empire, was a lucky man. His principality was situated just opposite of the Byzantine capital, a different empire with a different religion. When the Mongols conquered the Seljuk Sultanate of Rum, many local lords sought independence and after the Mongols retreated these lords fought among one another, allowing Osman to focus on his primary enemy to the west, the Byzantine Empire. Ironically, the Ottomans became intimately involved in the internal affairs of its neighbor when the Byzantine Emperor sought the help of Orhan, Osman's son, in launching a war against a political enemy. The emperor's daughter was consequently married off to Orhan.

Henceforth, several Ottoman Sultans married the daughters of Christian rulers. Other people in the Ottoman Empire, from nobles to civilians, also married European Christians, and it was only reasonable that over time the Ottomans came to think of themselves as European.

Osman Bey had founded his small principality around 1299. After over a century of territorial expansion, his descendants occupied much of Europe, and the capital was relocated from Bursa in northwest Asia Minor to Edirne (formerly Adrianople) on the Balkan Peninsula.

Then, a powerful figure of Mongol descent who spoke a Turkic language appeared in east Asia Minor. His name was Timur. Based in Samarkand, an important city in modern-day Uzbekistan, Timur conquered what is now Afghanistan to the south and then sacked Delhi in India. He marched westward to the Persian Gulf, entered Ankara and ravaged western Anatolia. In the eleventh century, the Turks had once captured the emperor of the Byzantine Empire, but this time it was Timur, a Turkified Mongol noble, who reversed the roles and took the Sultan of the Ottoman Empire prisoner in the fifteenth century. As a result, the Ottomans had to delay their final onslaught against the Byzantine Empire and first face their strong enemy from the east.

Several generations later, an army led by 21-year-old Mehmed II captured Constantinople in 1453 and the emperor of the Greek-speaking Byzantine Empire—considered the continuation of the Western Roman Empire with its capital in Rome—expired on the city ramparts. He was thus the 95th and last emperor of the Empire.

The fourth Sultan after Mehmed II was Suleyman the Magnificent, who reigned between 1520 and 1566. He was the most powerful and illustrious Sultan in the history of the Ottoman Empire. To the west, he led his army to lay siege to Vienna in 1529, and to the east, he conquered Baghdad in 1534. Before his rule, the Ottoman Empire had incorporated Egypt, Syria and the west Arabian Peninsula including the holy cities of Islam, Mecca and Medina. From 1517 to 1924, the Sultans of the Ottoman Empire were also the Caliphs of the Islamic world—successors to the Prophet Muhammad.

The Ottoman Empire possessed a superior geographical position. It could expand westward without fearing too many enemies to the east. The Battle of Kosovo was a decisive event in the fourteenth century. In this battle, the Ottoman Empire defeated the allied forces of Serbia, Bulgaria and Albania, and thus took control of the entire Balkan Peninsula. Following the Battle of Kosovo, the Ottoman Empire began its attack on Constantinople.

The Ottoman army that laid siege to and occupied Constantinople was by no means an all-Turkic Muslim force. Many of the artillerymen were Roman Catholic Hungarians, and the cavalry was composed of Serbians who were adherents of Eastern Orthodoxy.

As noted above, the first dozen or so Sultans of the Ottoman Empire were all savvy war-makers who also excelled at governance, but the success of the Empire should also be attributed to the institutions at work.

Firstly was the zeal engendered by religious belief. Warriors who fought to expand the domain of Islam were designated as *Gazi*, a prestigious title that engendered a sense of honor and strengthened emotional loyalty to the Empire.

Next was the *devshirme*. This was an innovative system created by the Ottoman Turks, in which Christian male teenagers were trained as personal slaves of the Sultan, and then placed in the palace guard, army or government bodies. Throughout Islamic history, excepting in Persia and India, most populations under Islamic regimes included Jews and Christians, and according to the Prophet Muhammad and the Quran, they were to be protected. Although not Muslim, they were monotheists who believed in holy scriptures recognized by Islam, so they were called "People of the Book." People of the Book should never serve as slaves—so long as they paid a head tax. To deal with this dilemma advantageously, the Sultan's scholars pronounced an innovative if far-fetched interpretation: if a Christian's head tax were refunded, he would no longer be afforded protection and could be enslaved.

In practice, healthy and intelligent Christian boys of 10–18 years old were selected from Europe or Anatolia (Asia Minor) and sent to a farm where they converted to Islam, learned the language and received an excellent education. As adults, they were singularly loyal to the Sultan, in contrast to the tribalistic Ottoman Turks who frequently fought among themselves, which inhibited the exercise of central authority.

This system for generating *devirshirme* may have been incompatible with Sharia, but it markedly increased the numbers of Christians who were competent and devoted to the Sultan. Upon adulthood, many encouraged family members to convert to Islam and even join their ranks.

The most famous soldier-slaves were the Janissary Corps, powerful in combat and fiercely loyal to the Sultan. During the expansion phase of the Ottoman Empire, these troops were invincible and the only standing army in Europe, and possibly worldwide.

The third institution that served the Empire well was the *millet* system. This was also a creation of the Ottoman Turks, although it complied with Islamic tradition. The Sultan did not classify his people based on race or language; instead, citizens were allocated to a specific *millet*—a confessional community—according to their religious beliefs.

Regardless where they lived in the Empire, all Muslims, Jews, Armenian Christians and Greek Orthodox Christians were members of their respective *millet*. In each *millet*, the appointed leader was responsible for collecting taxes that were handed over to the central government. That said, the *millet* effectively practiced self-management in the areas of religious affairs, education, marriage, the distribution of property, litigation, internal conflict resolution and so forth. However, the *millet* could not maintain its own military because all armies belonged to the Sultan.

Another Ottoman convention was the *timar* system, which stipulated that all land was the property of the Sultan and could not normally be traded nor inherited. The Sultan would award war heroes with tracts of land, but their descendants could only inherit the estate with his permission. This militated against the growth of a landlord class or large families who could amass wealth and manpower to resist the central government. This system played an important role in maintaining the rule of the Sultan and the royal families of the Ottoman Empire, while alleviating confrontations between farmers and landlords.

Finally, the hereditary system of the Ottoman Empire should not be overlooked. It is hard to judge whether the system is good or bad. Perhaps it had its advantages during the Empire's formative period, but negative ramifications were felt later. It took the Ottoman Turks a millennium to travel thousands of kilometers west across the steppes and merge their bloodline with the Persians and Greeks, but they always maintained the basic governance system of a steppe people, and therefore did not apply the practice of primogeniture.

In a word, the hereditary system of the Ottoman Empire was quite similar to that of other steppe peoples, including the Mongols who founded the Yuan Dynasty: when a ruler died, the throne passed to a brother or one of his sons or nephews, but his specific successor was to be selected in a *kurultai*, or a grand clan meeting.

Fortunately, during the first 150 years of the Ottoman Empire, talented men inherited the throne. However, Mehmed II (1451–1481) feared that his brothers might rebel when he left the capital to make war. Therefore, he and subsequent Sultans tried different ways to ensure that their siblings could not pose a threat. For example, the Sultan would give imperial concubines—odalisques—to his brothers so that they might lose themselves in carnal pleasure, or even confine them to their palaces, to bar them from exercising political influence. One of the Sultans even bribed several Sharia judges to concur that it was necessary to poison his male siblings for the stability of the Sultan, and he duly executed all his brothers when he ascended to the throne.

FROM BRAVE ARMIES TO CONNIVING COURTIERS (1566–1699)

Suleyman the Magnificent (1520–1566) was the greatest and most illustrious Sultan in the history of the Ottoman Empire. During his reign, the territory of the Ottoman Empire comprised all southeastern Europe; Anatolia (Asia Minor) and the Caucasus; western and northern parts of the Black Sea region, including Crimea; the entire "Fertile Crescent" (today's Iraq, Syria, Lebanon, Israel, Palestine and Jordan); the western part of the Arabian Peninsula including Medina and Mecca, and its eastern part (the Persian Gulf countries) and Egypt and North Africa (today's Libya and Tunisia).

As such, under Suleyman the Magnificent the Ottoman Empire was the undisputed leader of the entire Islamic world.

Following the conquest of Egypt in 1517, however, the Ottoman realm had actually begun to contract. As long as the empire kept expanding, new *timar* (temporary land grants) could be awarded to those who distinguished themselves in battle; new territory ensured better allotments and greater loyalty. But while territorial expansion slackened, demand for a wealthy lifestyle among descendants of *timariat* did not.

In addition, the Portuguese discovered a new route in 1498 that began to shift the center of global commerce from the Mediterranean to the Atlantic. Ships could now sail to the Indian Ocean via the Cape of Good Hope and eventually reach China, the world's richest country. As a result, the Mediterranean and the Silk Road gradually became less important. Since the Ottoman Empire had relied on taxes collected from trade with Europe at the end of the Silk Road as well as the southern and eastern Mediterranean, the altered trade routes reduced tax income. As the Sultan's revenues decreased, his armies became less powerful and new territory could not be acquired. A vicious cycle thus ensued, whereby the lack of new land meant little growth in the taxable population, hence a further long-term drop in the Sultan's revenues and an increasingly anemic war chest.

From the sixteenth to the seventeenth century, the Ottoman Empire's main rival was the House of Hapsburg in Austria, but in the east, the Safavid Empire founded by Shiite Persians also caused trouble. In general, the Renaissance fortified Europe in many respects; although the Ottoman army once again surrounded Vienna in 1683, it ultimately retreated in failure. This marked the end of the Ottoman Empire's period of superiority over its old enemy, and its offensive posture gradually became a defensive one.

During this period, the top levels of the Ottoman Empire became extravagant and dissipated. Conservative bureaucrats, and the clergy—and the Janissary Corps under the latter's influence—united to hinder the push for reform. Wrangling within the court became increasingly fierce, and conniving courtiers, harem beauties and fawning literati all played their bit parts. The conflicts between the Sultan and his brothers often reflected the competition between their mothers within the harem, as well as the internecine power struggles among the ambitious families behind these women.

In the sixteenth century, there were a total of five Sultans. In the late sixteenth century, Mehmet III executed his 19 brothers by using a loophole in the law during his reign. The succession of the Sultans took place even more frequently in the seventeenth century, with eight Sultans enthroned in total.

If the Ottoman Empire had had only one enemy, such as the House of Hapsburg, the Ottomans might have been able to contain it even as the former grew stronger over time. But a new rival, Russia, rose in the north. After the Grand Duchy of Moscow threw off the shackles of Mongol rule in the fifteenth century, Russia gained strength and embarked on outward expansion that resulted in contact and conflicts with the Ottoman Empire in Eastern Europe, Crimea and the Caucasus.

In 1683, the Ottoman army launched its final attack against Austria and surrounded a weakly defended Vienna. Nonetheless, the commander-in-chief underestimated his enemy, and the Ottoman army was forced to evacuate when Polish reinforcements arrived. Henceforth, the Ottoman Empire had to fight against countries such as Austria, Poland, Russia and Venice on several fronts simultaneously, and was ultimately constrained to sign the Treaty of Carlowitz, a humiliation because it was the first treaty that required the empire to cede territory.

Although toward the end of the seventeenth century several Sultans attempted to revitalize their empire, most were capricious and cowardly. There were some well-known loyal figures, such as the Koprülü family several of whose members served as Grand Vizier, but officialdom was dominated by corruption and misuse of the law. Famously, *timar* land allocation certificates—once exclusively awarded for outstanding military performance—were issued to women in return for bribes.

In the eighteenth century, the Ottoman Empire fell from its vaunted position as the premier continental power to become the "sick man of Europe." The sunset of this powerful Empire was inevitable.

CHAPTER 33

The Road to Republicanism

The Ottoman Empire occupied Mecca and Medina in 1520 and the Turks gradually become coffee lovers. Introduced from Ethiopia to Yemen and then to Mecca, coffee spread throughout the Islamic lands via haji as they returned home from their pilgrimage. When the Ottoman Turks took over management of the Holy Lands, they monopolized coffee distribution and reaped huge benefits.

Today's "Turkish coffee" (*Türk kahvesi*) refers to a powder, made from finely ground, roasted coffee beans, that is boiled in a small pot and drunk unfiltered. When fully imbibed, the thick and aromatic brew leaves a small pile of bitter coffee grounds at the bottom of the cup. During the sixteenth and seventeenth centuries, coffee houses were a common sight in Istanbul, Asia Minor and across the Middle East. There were no newspapers and no radio broadcasts at the time, so men went to the coffee house to palaver and exchange news. Fearful that people mingling in cafés might engender social unrest, from time to time the Sultan would order them closed.

Most visitors to Turkey will remember several famous mosques, many built by master architects in the sixteenth and seventeenth centuries. One who deserves a special mention is Mimar Sinan (Sinan the Architect). Born to a Greek family in Anatolia, the heartland of modern Turkey, as a child he helped his father do masonry work, and he was later recruited into the Janissary Corps. He was an army engineer responsible for building bridges, roads and bunkers, but Sultan Suleyman foresaw his talent and ordered him to design and oversee the construction of a large mosque. Eventually Sinan was designated chief royal architect and headed hundreds of projects. The most famous mosque in Istanbul—Suleymaniye Mosque—was designed and built by him, but experts consider the Selimiye Mosque his masterpiece. It is located near present-day Bulgaria and Greece in Edirne, the former capital of the Ottoman Empire, and was completed when the master architect was 84 years old.

In his memoirs, Sinan stated that his greatest glory and joy in life was to be at the Sultan's side and hear him speak, even though at times the Sultan was astride a horse as Sinan followed humbly on foot.

From "Study the Barbarians" to "Reform and Adjustment" (1699–1839)

Just as the Ottoman Empire reached its peak, and its upper class descended into debauchery and corruption reigned in officialdom, the outside world was experiencing momentous change. Gold and silver from the Americas stimulated business and trade, and led to the monetization of economic activity. The Ottoman Empire also quietly entered the era of monetary economics, and taxes and salaries were no longer paid in goods but in currency. To maintain its massive expenditures, the government frequently issued defective gold and silver coinage, which caused inflation; inflation in turn lowered the living standards of officials and soldiers. Many people engaged in part-time work or used whatever means necessary to get their relatives on a government or army payroll.

Even members of the Janissary Corps engaged in other trades in order to make a living and gradually neglected their military duties. Several Sultans minted currency to cover the costs of wars abroad, but their armies were easily defeated and the inflation engendered caused even greater social discontent. The once invincible Janissary with their glorious battlefield history were now repeatedly defeated and criticized, and therefore they allied with the clergy to resist reform, and repeatedly fomented trouble.

These phenomena constituted a great misfortune for the Ottoman Empire. Not so long before, the European countries had emerged from the Middle Ages, and if the upper classes of the Empire had been determined to innovate, the gap between the two might not have grown so wide. But due to resistance from conservatives, high-placed officials who supported the reforms were often unable to implement it. In order to uphold the authority of the clergy, for example, the conservatives were opposed to the printing press and forbade Muslims to open printing shops.

Even so, in the eighteenth century, some imperial family members and officials keen to revitalize the Empire persuaded the Sultans to learn from European experts and introduce advanced technology from the West, especially for the military. Sultan Mahmut I, who reigned 1730–1754, employed a French convert—who took the name Humbaraci Ahmed Pasha—to serve as his advisor. As a result, a military academy and the howitzer (*humbaraci*) troops were established.

Sultan Selim III (1789–1807) also showed himself to be an eager reformer. He established a new army and adopted European methods to train his soldiers, but the Janissary Corps overthrew him and installed a new Sultan. A reform-minded *Bey*, a lord with considerable local power, appeared on the scene determined to reinstate the Sultan, but Selim III was assassinated within the palace before he could formally return to the throne.

Whatever the result of these see-sawing attempts at internal rejuvenation, much of the eighteenth century was a period of encroachment on the Empire. Due to Peter the Great's successful push for reforms, Russia became much stronger and more ambitious for territory. In 1783, Catherine the Great wrested the Khanate of Crimea from Ottoman control. From then on, the Ottomans not only lost much territory around the Black Sea, but also experienced disaffection among the Eastern Orthodox communities (*millet*) within their own borders.

Meanwhile, in the Arabian Peninsula, the religious leader Muhammad ibn ʿAbd al-Wahhab, who advocated a brand of fundamentalism known today as Wahhabism, agreed to a mutual support pact in 1744 with a tribal leader, Muhammad bin Saud, who dreamt of unifying Arabia; they married each other's daughter to consolidate the alliance and ensure that political and religious dominance stayed within their families. They vowed to expel the Ottoman Turks, who did not conform to the Sharia—for they permitted alcohol and revered Sufi mystics—from the Arabian Peninsula. Thus the Ottoman Empire's hold on the heartland of Islam was in peril.

As the eighteenth century came to an end, Napoleon invaded Egypt. Administrative power in Egypt was eventually assumed by Muhammad Ali Pasha who led an army from Albanian to land in Egypt, and control of Egypt remained in the hands of his descendants until 1952, henceforth rendering Egypt de facto independent of the Ottoman Empire.

Under the leadership of its bureaucrats, the Ottoman Empire formally introduced the French military system when the French Revolution ended in 1799. Printing houses were established, newspapers launched, translation bureaus founded and books printed in European languages. Large numbers of students were dispatched to advanced countries, and business and industrial activities were encouraged in the hope that these measures would rejuvenate the domestic economy.

In the nineteenth century, Austria, Russia, Great Britain and France all invaded the vast Empire. European powers eagerly provided loans to the Ottomans, and negotiated tariff agreements and most-favored-nation status and other unequal treaties that were disadvantageous to the declining Empire. Based on their claim that the Ottoman legal system was "backward," they also obtained extraterritoriality for their own citizens and devotees of certain religions who resided on Ottoman lands, thereby exempting them from trial by the Ottoman authorities. For example, Russia announced that it would protect Orthodox Christians; Roman Catholics were under France's aegis; and a new *millet* whose existence the Sultan was forced to recognize—Protestants—would enjoy the protection of Britain. Only Jews initially had no benefactor, and thus they were strongly loyal to the Sultan throughout most of the history of the Empire. But at the end of the nineteenth century, a fortified Italy took the Jewish *millet* under its wing.

Around 1820, the governments of Britain, France, Austria and other countries, as well as European literary giants Honoré de Balzac and Lord Byron, encouraged the Greeks to seek independence. Byron even went to Greece, fought against the Ottoman army in guerrilla warfare, and wrote poems about the Greeks' heroic deeds in the face of oppression.

The Ottomans, of course, couldn't tolerate Greece's independence, because the Greek land seized from the previous Byzantine Empire constituted a crucial part of the Ottoman Empire, territory-wise and symbolically. The Sultan sent the elite Janissaries to suppress the independence movement but they were defeated, and the Greeks won their independence in 1821, the first nation to free itself of the Empire. Five years later, Mahmud II dissolved the humiliated Janissary Corps.

The people realized that the Ottoman Empire's very existence depended upon learning from Europe. Of course, first and foremost, their desire was to learn about things military, but others called for deeper reform. Keenest on reform were the bureaucrats in the imperial government, grandly referred to as the "Sublime Porte," especially diplomats who had served abroad. In the Ottoman Empire, no social class could serve as a counterbalance to the Sultan; since the bureaucrats lacked the power to carry out reform on their own, they often used the threat of looming interference by foreign powers to coerce cooperation from local notables.

Mahmud II died in 1839 and the new Sultan, Abdülmecid I, was just 16 years old. Although he did not grasp the machinations of politics, he had a kind heart and desired that his subjects live happily. With the support of his mother and the guidance of the Ottoman bureaucrats, in 1839 he issued the famous Edit of Gülhane declaring that it was necessary to implement "new rules" in order to revive the Empire. The edict laid down the radical principles that all subjects of the Empire were equal, regardless of religious belief or ethnicity, and that no one should be punished without a trial. This top-down reform was known as *Tanzimat* ("reform and reorganization"), and lasted for 39 years.

From Reform to Revolution (1839–1908)

The goal of *Tanzimat* was to establish a society ruled by law and possessing a modern economy. Some of the Ottoman elite realized that these two goals were interrelated, so a dizzying set of tasks—developing education, launching newspapers, establishing courts, ending bribery and constructing railways, post offices and a telegraph network—all became priorities.

Initially, perhaps the most visible expression of *Tanzimat* was the new apparel from the Sultan down to officials at all levels. Men abandoned their robes that touched the ground, and switched to western-styled, knee-length coats with buttons. The turban was also exchanged for the *fez*, a round red cap, symbolizing the equality of all male subjects before the Sultan. In addition, the army abolished flags with different animal patterns and adopted the design of a crescent moon and a star against a red background, which became the design of Turkey's national flag today.

Tanzimat initiated the process of secularization. All Islamic charitable foundations (*vakif*), originally controlled by the clergy, must now accept state supervision. Even the *Sheyhulislam*, the Chief Imam of Islam, was assigned an office and virtually became a civil servant.

During the 39 years of reform, the Ottoman Empire experienced two wars with Russia and ensuing crises.

With help from Britain and France, the Ottomans defeated Russia in the Crimean War (1853–1856), and under the Treaty of Paris, Russia renounced some territory it had seized. Britain, France and other countries undertook to guarantee the independence and territorial integrity of the Ottoman Empire, and the latter agreed to adhere to "Europe's political, cultural and economic path." However, these same countries refused to accept the Ottoman Empire as an equal party to the accord, on account of its different legal system.

Officials of the Sublime Porte took advantage of this situation, and immediately urged the Sultan to issue new edicts, so as to further promote Westernization and secularization. The government reiterated that under the rule of the Sultan, Muslims and Christians were equals, and promised to set up banks, expand roads and ameliorate industry and commerce. In 1858, the government promulgated a new criminal law, and a land law that permitted private ownership.

In 1875, after two decades of incessant foreign borrowing, the Ottoman government declared bankruptcy and announced that it would henceforth pay only one-half the interest owed on all debts. Unquestionably, the health of the "sick man of Europe" was deteriorating.

During 1875–1877, Christians in parts of the Balkans revolted out of dissatisfaction with autocratic rule. The government sent troops that carried out a bloody suppression, and the French and German consuls were killed in the chaos, which almost resulted in military intervention by the major powers.

Tanzimat brought two profound changes to Ottoman society. Firstly, a new-fangled, westernized comprador class came into being due to increased European trade, the rising status of non-Muslim communities and the impact of students returning from overseas study. Most of these people did not have a vested interest in the old social order, and many were Christian.

Secondly, because of the weakening of the Empire, Muslims were deeply dissatisfied with the Sultan and his bureaucracy. Many intellectuals from the lower and middle classes joined the Young Ottomans, an organization that was initially established by the elites, but the former gradually grew dominant. They critiqued domestic politics in newspapers at home and abroad, and even engaged in underground movements to overthrow the Ottoman system. Unable to compete effectively with the Christian merchant class, Muslim subjects increasingly joined the government or military, attended Islamic theology schools (*madrassas*) or aspired to join the professional clergy (*ulema*).

In 1876, in a move to placate the demands of persistent protesters in the capital, Sultan Abdülaziz appointed a group of popular reformists to key posts, including the *Grand Vizier* (Prime Minister) and *Sheyhulislam* (Chief Imam). But the *Sheyhulislam* quickly assented to the Sultan's ouster and the ministers forced him to abdicate; he slit his wrists and died two days later. The new Sultan, a nephew of Abdülaziz once imprisoned by him, served less than three months before he was deemed mentally unfit. The reformists dismissed him and invited Abdul Hamid II, his younger brother, to ascend to the throne. He supported the proposed constitution drafted by the reformists, and it was officially introduced at the end of 1876, and soon followed by parliamentary elections—a major first in Ottoman history.

In 1877, the Russians began a two-pronged attack on the Ottoman Empire from the Caucasus and the Balkans. By early 1878, their troops were closing in on Istanbul and pressing the Ottomans to grant independence to Romania and Serbia, and make Bulgaria—its territory already expanded with the help of Russia—fully autonomous. Russia itself also seized large tracts of land. But Britain and Austria were unwilling to see Russia grow stronger. When Germany's Chancellor Bismark proposed holding the "Berlin Conference" in 1878, countries such as Britain and Austria induced Russia to participate. In the end, Russia made some concessions, and Britain obtained Cyprus as a reward for speaking up for the Ottoman Empire, but incredibly, the latter lost nearly forty percent of its territory.

Historically, the period of "reform and reorganization" from 1839 to the introduction of the constitution in 1876 was a transitional phase that sowed the seeds of modernization. But from the perspective of those who lived it, the *Tanzimat* era was full of setbacks: the voice of resistance to the reforms was loud and persistent, and reformist policies were not properly implemented. Meanwhile, officials, regardless whether "reformists" or "reactionaries," were generally inept and worse yet, grafters.

Claiming that the Empire was in grave danger because the Russian army was nearing Istanbul, Sultan Abdul Hamid II announced the dismissal of parliament in 1878. This "recess" was to last three long decades.

His opponents accused him of implementing thirty years of reactionary and brutal dictatorship. In fact, Abdul Hamid II not only ruled the

Empire with a strong hand, but was also determined on reform. He appointed and dismissed officials at will, and many opponents were exiled. He practiced strict censorship and maintained an omnipresent network of spies, including coffee houses. At the same time, inspired by the European model, he also earnestly promoted education, vigorously developed the economy and strengthened the armed forces.

Opposition to Abul Hamid II found its origins in two key areas: the growing sense of nationalist sentiment among the Empire's non-Turkic ethnic groups, and intense dissatisfaction of Western-educated Ottoman youth toward autocratic rule. In order to unite the Muslims within the Empire and to resist the West and Russia on the spiritual front, Abdul Hamid II publicly supported "Pan-Islamism" and emphasized his role as the Caliph of Muslims worldwide.

No doubt in so doing he wished to fortify his own position, and perhaps to maintain the independence and well-being of the Empire too. But once social change is unchained, it enters an irreversible historical process. Those who wish to forestall the process will only become victims in one form or another. Abdul Hamid II realized his uncle's suicide was a tragedy for the nation and tried hard to avoid the same fate.

In July 1908, an underground organization, the "Young Turks" (formerly the "Young Ottomans") incited young army officers stationed in Macedonia to launch an armed uprising. Then a group of Muslim civilians occupied the armory, triggering riots across the country. Even the Sultan's most trusted Anatolian troops opted to support the uprising. On July 23, Abdul Hamid II was forced to declare that the constitution, suspended for 30 years, was once again in force. The following day, major newspapers in the capital published an official announcement that the country would hold parliamentary elections; constitutional monarchy had come at last to the Ottoman Empire.

Just one year after the reinstitution of the constitution, Abdul Hamid II was relieved of his post. He had spent three decades promoting a new educational system and constructing a modern army, laudable actions which were nonetheless tantamount to digging his own grave.

CONSTITUTIONAL MONARCHY TO REPUBLIC (1908–1923)

After the constitution was restored, parliamentary elections were held and the Young Turks found themselves in power. Their primary concern was the independence and unity of the Ottoman Empire; they reiterated "all citizens are equal" and proposed that loyalty for the Sultan should now be directed to the Motherland. These grand concepts were clearly influenced by the French revolution, but the reality on the ground was utterly different; through their actions, the European powers and the Christian *millets* in the Empire rejected them outright.

Soon, conservative Islamists rebelled in barracks throughout the capital. The forces of revolution and counter-revolution faced off, while the Young Turks split into liberal and nationalist camps. The latter allied with the new army, and they launched a harsh crackdown on their opponents and imposed a curfew in the capital. But their behavior was even more violent than that seen under the Sultan, and this brought the conservatives and their supporters into the capital where they launched a coup. The Young Turks were forced out of power.

Following the French occupation of Tunisia in 1881, despite the declaration made at the Berlin Conference concerning the "respect for the territorial integrity of the Ottoman Empire," Britain took over Egypt in 1882 and Italy invaded Libya in 1911. The Ottoman government sent troops to resist the Italians, but the situation was not favorable to the Empire.

In 1912, the Balkan countries including Serbia, Montenegro, Bulgaria and Greece attacked the European side of the Ottoman Empire. The Ottoman army retreated, again and again, losing almost all its Balkan territory. When Bulgaria besieged Edirne, Britain and France suggested that the Ottoman government abandon the city, the former capital of the Ottoman Empire and home to the superb Selimiye Mosque, and in return they would mediate. But while the Ottomans hesitated, the Bulgarians occupied the city. The Young Turks took this opportunity to mount a coup and regain power.

In 1914, the First World War broke out. In the Ottoman Empire, opinions diverged: some favored neutrality, some supported Britain and France, yet others supported Germany and Austria. The German Kaiser repeatedly made amicable gestures to the Sultan and to Muslims worldwide. Given the Empire's traditional hostility toward Britain, France and Russia, the principal leaders of the Young Turks opted to ally with Germany, and requested that German officers command the Ottoman troops, in the hopes that they could leverage Germany's military to recover lost territories and abolish extraterritoriality. This proved to be a monumental misjudgment that sealed the Empire's fate.

The First World War lasted four years during which the Young Turks were utterly incapable of reversing the Empire's downward spiral. During 1915–1917, the Ottoman army, initially numbering more than 600,000 troops, found itself fighting on four fronts: British and French troops approached Istanbul from the west; Russian forces pierced Anatolia from the east; British troops entered Iraq and the French army landed in Syria.

Meanwhile, back home, many in the Greek and Armenian communities had sympathy for the Entente countries. So the Young Turks carried out a mass deportation in 1915, during which large numbers of Armenians (and Greeks and other Christian minorities) were killed outright by mobs or soldiers, succumbed during the merciless trek eastward or were driven by the army into the Syrian Desert where they perished.

In the autumn of 1917, the October Revolution broke out in Russia and it withdrew from the war, giving the Ottomans a chance to catch their breath. But the entry of the United States into the war spelled doom for Germany and its ally, the moribund Ottoman Empire.

Sultan Mehmet V died in the summer of 1918, leaving the bitter business of surrender—and abdication—to his younger half-brother, Mehmet VI. The Young Turk cabinet ministers resigned in October, and the new Sultan appointed a liberal prime minister, and tasked him with seeking a truce. Soon thereafter, the government signed an armistice with Britain that amounted to unconditional surrender.

British and French troops immediately entered Istanbul and established a military administration. While Britain and France advanced on land, Greece and Italy landed from the Aegean Sea and the Mediterranean, respectively. The Greek army marched quickly onward after occupying the Aegean coastal area, and posed a threat to the heartland of Anatolia.

At this critical juncture, the imperial government designated General Mustafa Kemal—now a legendary war hero—to serve as Military Inspector, and charged him to supervise the disbanding of the Ottoman troops. He left the capital and arrived in the Samsun region along the southern coast of the Black Sea. He had earlier taken part in the Young Turks when it was an underground organization, but had never held important positions as his views diverged from those of the principal leaders. At this point, indignant over the Greek invasion, he resigned from the army to coordinate branches of the "Association for the Defense of Rights" that had sprung up spontaneously across Anatolia in preparation for a war of national liberation.

The 1919 Peace Treaties of Paris had virtually dismembered the Ottoman Empire. Macedonia, Iraq (including Kuwait), Syria (including Lebanon), Palestine (including Transjordan) and the western parts of the Arab Peninsula were amputated, leaving just a large swathe of Anatolia, the capital Istanbul and small neighboring pieces of European territory to the Ottomans.

The Treaty of Sèvres, signed by the Ottoman government in 1920, stipulated the loss of more Anatolian territory, as it mandated an independent Armenia and autonomy for the Kurds. The two channels connecting the Black Sea and the Mediterranean were to be managed by an international agency, and Izmir, a major city along the eastern coast of the Aegean Sea was to be governed by Greece. In addition, extraterritoriality was fully reinstated; the Ottoman Empire had fragmented and now existed as a state in name only.

In accordance with the principle of national self-determination, several ethnic minorities became independent or autonomous. Ironically, the main population of the Ottoman Empire—Turkish-speaking Muslims—did not have a homeland to call their own, because even Anatolia only became their "home" when their ancestors from Central Asia migrated there in great numbers after the twelfth century. The Ottoman Empire had been a multi-ethnic, multi-religious military conglomerate ruled by the Sultan in accordance with Islamic law. It was distinguished by religion, but there were no clear boundaries between ethnicities, and territory had never been assigned to a specific ethnic group.

Kemal decided to undertake a national war of independence with the goal of building an independent Turkish nation where Muslims, including descendants of Turkic, Kurdish, Circassian, Arabian and Laz peoples, could live in their own "national homeland" located in Anatolia and Thrace. On this point, Kemal fused the Western ideas of "nation" and "ethnic group," while carrying over the old Ottoman concept of "*millet*." He believed that all Muslims living within the territory of Turkey belonged to a Muslim *millet* and therefore constituted a nation composed of different "Islamic elements."

The first step, of course, was to free their homeland from foreign occupation. During the three-and-a-half-year war, Kemal won trust and even reverence from the majority of the Turks, while exploiting his military talent, diplomatic strategy, organization skills and charisma to maintain the neutrality of countries such as Russia and Bulgaria.

This allowed him to focus his energy on driving out the foreign occupiers. In September 1922, the national army led by Kemal marched into Izmir and the Greek army retreated in defeat. Not long afterward, his army recovered all lost ground in Anatolia.

During the war to expel the foreign interlopers, a new nation was also in the making. In 1920, after an indefinite recess of the Empire's parliament to protest against the British occupation of the capital Istanbul and the ensuing arrest of parliament members, a new Grand National Assembly of Turkey was held in Ankara, at which Kemal was elected Assembly President. In 1921, through the basic organic law the government defined its sovereignty and administrative areas, and established the state organs. Kemal's broad-mindedness, military strategy and ability to assess the overall situation with lucidity were fully exhibited during this period. Mindful that the common people still admired the Sultan and were proud of his status as Caliph, Kemal argued he had to establish a new country, for the Sultan in Istanbul had become a prisoner of the occupying infidels.

After the Turkish war of independence, the United Kingdom invited the concerned countries to discuss the "Turkey issue" at Lausanne. Given that Turkey then consisted of "one country and two regimes," the British deliberately sent the invitation letter to both Istanbul and Ankara. This move gave the Ankara government a good excuse to take actions that it saw fit, and the Grand National Assembly of Turkey passed a resolution abolishing the position of Sultan prior to the Lausanne conference. But the politically disenfranchised Sultan was to retain the position of Caliph.

In the middle of one November night in 1922, the Sultan escaped through a palace side-gate with his young son, and boarded a British warship bound for Malta. The ignominious flight of Mehmet VI, last Sultan of a dynasty with a grand history of over 600 years, marked the end of the Ottoman Empire.

CHAPTER 34

Toward a Modern Republic

In 1881, Mustafa Kemal was born in Salonika (present-day Thessaloniki, Greece's second city), then an important port on the Aegean Sea. His grandfather was a primary school teacher who could recite the Quran. His father, formerly employed in customs, ran a lumber business that failed due to social unrest, after which he became gravely ill. Kemal lost his father at the age of seven, and at 12, without telling his mother, he took the entrance exam to the Salonika Military School, and passed it. He left home to study at Monastir Military High School in west Macedonia when just 15, and attended the Ottoman Military Academy at 18, majoring in infantry. Thanks to his exemplary performance during a brief period of military service upon graduation in 1902, he was admitted to the Ottoman Military College in Istanbul and obtained the rank of captain in 1905. As a new-age officer with a solid education received during the reign of Sultan Abdul Hamid II, he was adept at military strategy, good at French, chemistry and mathematics, and also loved literature.

A Fitting Hero for His Era (1919–1938)

One's character aside, external factors also figure in the emergence of a great political figure. Mustafa Kemal, the founder of the Republic of Turkey, emerged when the time, place and social conditions were particularly favorable to his rise.

Around the time of the famous "Young Turk Revolution" of 1908, Kemal served the army in Syria, Macedonia and Libya, and became acquainted with politically aware officers, many of whom were Young Turks. In 1909, troops stationed in Macedonia were transported by train to Istanbul where they quelled a counter-revolutionary coup. Their commander was General Shevket, destined to become prime minister a few years hence, and his aide-de-camp was Kemal.

After the revolution, three Young Turk leaders in the Committee of Unity and Progress, with Enver Pasha the most powerful, controlled the imperial government. He was an elder schoolmate of Kemal who attended the same military high school and academy. But they were not close and their vision of nationhood differed. Enver's wife was an Ottoman princess, and he resolutely defended the Ottoman royalty, pushed for an alliance with the Germans against Britain, France and Russia, and advocated that German officers should command the Ottoman Army. Initially, Kemal was not against the Sultan, but he adamantly opposed handing the command of the army to the Germans.

When World War I broke out, Kemal was a military attaché stationed in Bulgaria. After Kemal's repeated requests, in early 1915 the imperial government transferred him back and assigned him to form a division southwest of Istanbul. Meanwhile, the British Army approached, threatening the capital city of the Empire. Under lieutenant colonel Kemal's command, the 19th division withstood the fierce attacks of the British army on Gallipoli Peninsula, and heroically reversed the situation. For this he was dubbed "Istanbul's Savior" and became a household name.

Enver turned envious and defensive, and after Kemal was designated brigadier general in early 1916, he was immediately transferred to Diyarbakir in southeast Turkey, a city populated mainly by Kurds. But Kemal also performed well on the eastern front. After a quick battle, two cities were recovered from the Russian army. Subsequently, he was dispatched again to Syria where he did not achieve any victories, but he fought well and oversaw an orderly retreat. With these successes, Kemal had established himself as an intelligent and courageous general who could lead the Ottoman Army and command the respect of civilians.

Dissatisfied with the tasks assigned to him by Enver, Kemal resigned from the army and returned to Istanbul where he very publicly criticized the triumvirate dominating the Committee of Unity and Progress—the so-called "Three Pasha," including Enver—that effectively ruled the nation. Luckily for Kemal, in late 1917 Mahmet Vahdettin, heir to the throne, was invited to visit Germany. Kemal was assigned to accompany him, an ideal chance to get to know the future Sultan who was no fan of the Three Pasha.

In July 1918, Sultan Mehmet V died and his younger brother Vahdettin ascended the throne as Mehmet VI. The next month Kemal was appointed army commander and sent to the Syrian front. On October 30, representatives of the Ottoman Empire signed an armistice with the Allies, while the Three Pasha escaped on German warships.

The allied forces of Britain and France entered Istanbul and established a military government. There is one intriguing detail to note: General Franchet d'Espèrey, the French commander in the Near East, entered Istanbul astride a white stallion on February 8, 1919, with cheers from the Greeks, Armenians and European residents, as had Mehmet "The Conquerer" upon his entry to Byzantine Constantinople in 1453, and Napoleon when he arrived in Egypt in 1798. This triumphal symbolism inflamed Turkish Muslims, and fanned the desire for independence that culminated in the birth of the Republic of Turkey three years later.

Kemal resigned from the military and returned to Istanbul in late 1918. He rarely showed his face in public, and some assumed he was downcast out of concern for his country and people. But according to the memoirs of his contemporaries, Kemal accepted interviews with foreign newspapers and met with many important personalities, including numerous calls on the Sultan. The energetic Mehmed VI was also very busy as he struggled to maintain the Ottoman's hold on the throne that had endured over six centuries.

Despite the opposition of the British occupiers, Mehmet VI insisted on assigning Kemal to supervise the army's demobilization in the east. Indeed, if the British had forbidden Kemal to leave the capital, Turkish history might have been radically different. But Kemal did depart and arrived on May 19 at Samsun, on the southern shore of the Black Sea. Meanwhile, the previous day the Greek army had landed in Izmir, an important city on the eastern shore of the Aegean Sea, under the cover of the Allies' warships.

Kemal immediately took advantage of his location to effect the very opposite of "demobilization." He liaised with branches of the "Association for the Defense of Rights" throughout Anatolia, and undertook preparations for war. This marked the beginning of an armed struggle for national liberation that would last three-and-a-half years, and culminate in the founding of the Republic of Turkey.

By offering specific details of Kemal's actions in the run-up to the birth of the republic, I wish to demonstrate that major turning points in history are sometimes the result of random factors, and they can also be the result of conscious choices made by key actors.

The Chinese are known for their assiduous study of the past, but mastery of principles behind history—and the ability to apply them to the present—is not unique to the Chinese. It requires both wisdom and courage to take decisive actions that shape history. In the founding of modern Turkey, Kemal and his colleagues proved their wisdom through actions at critical moments of a historical transition.

Having migrated from Central Asia to Eastern Europe, the Turks built a vast multi-ethnic and multi-religious empire touching on the continents of Asia, Europe and Africa. The Ottoman Empire and the previous Seljuk Dynasty endured more than eight centuries. Until the collapse of the Empire, God had indeed been very kind to these people.

World War I ended with the European powers literally dismembering the Ottoman Empire, leaving the ethnic Turks to their own devices in Anatolia and Thrace. In response, the Turkic Muslims founded branches of the Association for the Defense of Rights throughout Asia Minor, in order to give voice to their protests as the World War I victors sought to further slice up the "sick man of Europe." Although already largely powerless, the Sultan unexpectedly insisted on dispatching Kemal to demobilize the army in Anatolia, and it was at this juncture that Kemal landed in Samsun to rally and mobilize these local chapters that offered him a solid foundation for a united front and armed struggle.

Fortuitously, the Imperial Parliament in Istanbul adjourned indefinitely. Arguing that the enemy had occupied the capital, Kemal launched his Republican People's Party in Ankara where the Grand National Assembly was now seated. The British colonialists, past masters at "using locals to fight locals," sent formal letters of invitation to the Lausanne Conference to both the imperial government in Istanbul and the republican government in Ankara. This provided the impetus for Kemal and his partisans to formally depose the Sultan—still revered by the masses—on the grounds that he was a prisoner of the infidels.

If the Ottoman Empire had not experienced slow dismemberment over the preceding century, the Turks would have had little reason to launch a national war of liberation for a homeland of their own. Unlike the European powers, the United States, which had no colonies in Turkey, proposed "national self-determination" as the new, post-war standard for the world order. Kemal adroitly borrowed this modern term in order to claim legitimacy for his emerging republic.

When the Kemal government signed the Treaty of Lausanne in July with representatives from the major powers Great Britain, France, Greece and Italy, it was the equivalent of a "birth certificate" for a modern state, stamped and pre-approved by the West. It was a true victory for the Ankara-based government, and Kemal and his supporters knew they should strike while the iron was hot: on October 29, 1923, the Republic of Turkey was proclaimed.

Kemal and his followers were determined to disentangle themselves from the disastrous regime of the Young Turks. They would not lose themselves in nostalgia over the lost Empire; their energies would be directed to constructing a new republic. This new nation would be independent, devoted to developing a modern economy, and one in which social reforms would be carried out comprehensively, and old ethnic conflicts resolved.

The diplomatic strategy of the Ankara government was clear and effective. Kemal signed a Treaty of Peace and Friendship with Stalin in 1921 to stabilize the situation in the east, and maintained amicable relations with Bulgaria to prevent problems in the Balkans. Before World War II, Turkey drew praise from liberals in the West for its anti-Fascist stance. Turkey did not want the West to treat it as a semi-colony, nor did it regard the Soviet Union as its "big brother."

Regarding ethnic minorities, the Republic of Turkey applied the principle of resident jurisdiction: all Muslims born on Turkish soil were Turkish and owed loyalty to Turkey, but those persons of Greek or Armenian extraction were still treated under policies similar to the *millet* system in vogue under the Ottomans. Categorizing residents primarily according to their faith was no doubt expedient at the time, but it hindered a true sense of citizenship and belonging that eventually became problematic. In particular, it left groups such as the Kurds feeling in danger of losing their cultural and linguistic identity.

In terms of social reforms, the Kemal government unleashed a storm of radical change across the country amounting to nothing less than a "cultural revolution." In less than a decade, several wrenching reforms were passed into law and enacted: the secular constitution no longer recognized Islam as the state religion; the Islamic Caliphate was abolished; the Arabic-based Ottoman script was discarded in favor of a 29-letter Romanized alphabet that was announced and implemented in just a few months in late 1928; Sufi lodges (*tekkes*) were closed and their properties confiscated; the office of *Sheyhulislam* came under the government's control; *madrasa* were shuttered and citizens were required to register a surname of their choice. Mustafa Kemal himself was bestowed by the Grand National Assembly with the surname "Atatürk," meaning "Father of the Turks."

For all revolutionary regimes, economic development is a crucial but daunting task. Under Atatürk, Turkey developed a mixed economy. On one hand, the government developed infrastructure and built basic industry; on the other, private firms received subsidies for carrying out the development. The ruling party itself was divided: some advocated for state capitalism, while others believed that only free capitalism can create a healthy economy, so the government's role should be temporary. Balancing these two claims, Atatürk adopted a pragmatic approach.

But it wasn't all smooth sailing for Atatürk's policies. In 1930, the Turkish economy was impacted by the recession in the West and the common people lived a hard life. In order to implement multi-party politics, Atatürk asked a good friend to organize a "loyal opposition" dubbed the "Free Republican Party." Supporters of the two parties clashed violently at campaign rallies, while the share of votes garnered by the newly formed opposition turned out unexpectedly high. This democratic experiment ended with the self-initiated dissolution of the "Free Republican Party."

In the same year, a rural Sufi clergyman called for designation of Islam as state religion and restoration of the Caliphate. When a reserve officer was sent to investigate, the clergyman chopped off the officer's head as the crowd cheered him on.

These two developments made Atatürk understand that a successful government must deliver concrete benefits to the people, and it must ensure that the people understand the nature and goals of government policies. He also recognized that it was only natural for those who lack security to seek it in their traditions, and to take comfort in religious faith. Armed with this realization, Atatürk traveled widely and gave speeches in which he advocated channeling religious fervor into patriotic sentiment for the new republic.

Ominously, Kemal Atatürk did not appear at the celebration marking the 15th anniversary of the founding of the Republic on October 29, 1938, and his death was announced on November 10.

When Kemal Atatürk first set foot in Ankara, Turkey was still a semi-feudal agricultural society. When the Greek Orthodox Christians were forcibly repatriated in 1924, the newly established Republic of Turkey suddenly found itself without sufficient plumbers and shoemakers; Atatürk personally selected and dispatched a group of youths to Paris for training in how to tailor a suit. Yet by the time he left his people, Turkey already possessed a basic industrial foundation and a workforce experienced in various technologies. Crucially, the great majority of citizens identified themselves as "Turkish."

The Atatürk Era—without Kemal Atatürk (1938–1980)

The day following the announcement of Kemal's death, the Grand National Assembly unanimously elected Mustafa Ismet Inönü the second president of the Republic of Turkey. Inönü's anointment signified, however, the end of strongman politics, because he lacked his predecessor's heroic aura and charisma. The Republican People's Party held an extraordinary meeting and announced that Kemal Atatürk would henceforth be regarded as the founder and "Permanent Leader" of the party, and Inönü as "Standing President." Turkey had entered an era dominated by what has come to be termed "Kemalism."

The "Kemal Atatürk Doctrine" was passed at a national meeting in 1931, and included the "Six Fundamental Pillars" compiled by the Republican People's Party from Atatürk's previous speeches. The six arrows in the emblem of the Republican People's Party represent those pillars: republicanism; patriotism; populism; statism; secularism and reformism. These principles were incorporated in the Turkish constitution in 1937 and thus represent state ideology, and to this day each pupil in Turkey is required to memorize them. Generally speaking, the Kemal Atatürk Doctrine was a summary and a continuation of the reform policies of the Young Turks, not a negation of the past.

Prior to World War II, Turkey strived for independence in foreign policy. The government firmly opposed Fascism due to concerns about Italy's dominance in the eastern Mediterranean. However, Turkey maintained a neutral stance in World War II because its experience in World War I showed that the country could ill afford to offend any major combatant.

At the end of World War II, İnönü proposed changing the political system to accommodate the new world order—based on capitalism and democracy—and to facilitate Turkey's modernization. He suggested lifting the ban on political parties and permitting the birth of a multi-party system. In 1946, the first nationally contested election was held in Turkey, and the newly established Turkish Democratic Party lost despite performing well. But in 1950, the Turkish Democratic Party scored a stunning and comprehensive victory over the Republican People's Party founded by the very Father of the Republic.

This marked a historical turning point. The lower-middle class, long marginalized, discovered that it could play a key role in democratic elections. This had a huge influence on successive political parties, and in particular, the content of their campaign platforms; most maintained they represented the "common people." Gradually the Republican People's Party positioned itself as center-left, while other parties—albeit with similar politics—claimed to be center-right and found relative success among certain sectors of the electorate.

The opposition party's victory in 1950 ushered in three decades of chaotic politics, ending with a final military coup in 1980. The multi-party system birthed a bevy of politicians and parties; some lawmakers switched affiliations, and some parties changed their monikers or restructured, but stability suffered. No government held power for long. Some were voted out, the army dissolved some, and others were forced out of office by scandal. People became accustomed to corruption, currency depreciation, trade union protests and riots. The sole source of stability was the military, which claimed to be the faithful disciple of Atatürk, defending the secular constitution by "supervising" the politicians.

Turkey's military declared martial law and rewrote the constitution after the three coup d'états in 1960, 1971 and 1980, but always returned to its barracks within a year or two. Senior officers intensely despised leftists and political Islamists, so they repeatedly cracked down on the left and often banned Islamists from participating in elections. The political attitude of senior military officers stemmed partly from their acceptance of Kemalist doctrine since childhood, and partly because their special social status facilitated personal and commercial relations with the grande bourgeoisie and secular elites. They hoped that Turkey could downplay its Central Asian origins and find acceptance in the West, but they often hesitated when they actually found themselves getting closer to Europe.

In foreign affairs, Turkey abandoned Atatürk's neutral diplomacy and was completely absorbed into the Western camp after World War II. Turkey not only accepted assistance from the United States, it sent troops to fight in the Korean War, participated in the Baghdad Pact and became an active member of the North Atlantic Treaty Organization (NATO).

Geopolitics and Changes in Social Structure (1980–2014)

The modernization of Turkey, carried out in a top-down, authoritarian manner in which Europe served as a role model, has a history of some two hundred years. During the 1980s, the influence of authoritarianism was somewhat diluted due to the development of party politics and a market economy, and this set the tone for Turkey's political and economic trends from 1980 to 2014. During this period, three significant events occurred in Iran, the Soviet Union and the United States, respectively, and below we look at how they combined with domestic factors to alter Turkey at home and in the international arena.

The Islamic revolution in Iran in 1979 sharply reminded the West that a reliable Turkey is crucial, and that its all-too-frequent military coups threatened its hard-earned stability. In fact, the 1980 coup was the last one to date, although pro-Islamist voices are growing louder and Turkish politics are extremely contentious. One reason for the relative calm was the formation of the five-member National Security Council in 1961, which was chaired by the president and included four senior military professionals. At the outset, at least, this represented a form of "military tutelage."

Turkey had long used subsidies to protect and promote domestic industry, such as the policy of import substitution. The Turkish elites and most talented workforce live near Istanbul, and industry is concentrated in the Sea of Marmara region surrounding this metropolis, so Europe was Turkey's main foreign trade partner. The call to join the European Community (later the EU), came mainly from the elites in this region.

Prior to the 1980s, Turkish industry was limited by high costs, poor competitiveness and small overseas markets, largely due to dependence on subsidies and politicians who pandered to the unions. During the Iran–Iraq war (1980–88), government policy promoted a market economy and increased competitiveness, and SMEs in the east benefited, earning the nickname "Anatolian Tigers." Lifted by strong demand from their warring neighbors, total Turkish exports skyrocketed from $2.3 billion in 1979 to $11.7 billion in 1988.

Turkey's "secular" class continues to be dominated by the top elites who live mainly in Istanbul and other big cities. Radical secularization began in Atatürk's time, but a variety of religious views have managed to coexist. Religious traditions have been preserved in most small and medium-sized cities in Anatolia and the rural regions, so the SME entrepreneurs in the eastern region have an obvious Islamic coloring. They set up the "Independent Industrialist and Merchant Federation" (MSiAD for short in Turkish) to contrast with the "Turkish Industrialist and Merchant Federation" (TSiAD) controlled by large secular entrepreneurs and businesspeople. In Turkish, the first letter of "Independent" and "Muslim" are both "M," so everyone understands that MSiAD stands for "Muslim" Industrialist and Merchant Federation. In fact, both secularists and Islamists are pro-modernization; it is their *visions* of modernization that differ.

With strong industrial development and growing exports, implementation of a free economy has also created an imbalance in income distribution. According to World Bank statistics, Turkey's income inequality ranks quite high, globally speaking. The rise of SME entrepreneurs in the east and rising social inequality later became a key factor driving the victory of the pro-Islamist Justice and Development Party (AKP in Turkish) in 2002.

The disintegration of the Soviet Union and globalization advocated by the West offered another opportunity for the development of Turkey's economy, as it did for China. The Anatolian Tigers expanded their markets in the Soviet Union, especially the Caucasus and Central Asia. Even large Istanbul-based firms like Koç and Sabanci recorded rapid expansion in Russia, the Balkans and Saudi Arabia, and have transformed into multinationals. This new development has made many Turks wonder: Is joining the European Union Turkey's "only" option?

Meanwhile, Turkey's pro-Islamist parties mellowed. Having been banned and restructured many times before by the military or court order, they moderated their policies and language to avoid antagonizing the military and the secular parties. They publicly praised the great secularist Atatürk, and agreed not to impose Islamic law (*Sharia*) or alter the existing secular judicial system.

Even so, the AKP did not come to power easily. In the autumn of 2002, it won the election and received enough votes to organize a cabinet, but party leader Recep Tayyip Erdogan could not contest the elections personally, as he had a criminal record—he had been briefly jailed for "inciting religious hatred" for reciting a poem at a political rally that compared a mosque's minarets to bayonets. The AKP chose Abdullah Gül to serve as Prime Minister, but he later resigned in favor of Erdogan who made his triumphal return to election politics thanks to a constitutional amendment.

Of humble beginnings, Erdogan did not attend university, does not speak a foreign language and only received a few years of religious education. However, he is charismatic, a rousing public speaker and has a knack for problem solving that he amply demonstrated as Mayor of Istanbul. The AKP has won three consecutive elections under his leadership ever since he focused on improving the people's livelihood. Over the last decade, the economy has made great progress and maintains a high growth rate.

Besides improving the economy, Erdogan also reshuffled the National Security Council at the behest of the EU, assigning civil servants to take charge of the Secretariat in order to reduce military influence. Meanwhile, his government carried out a large-scale investigation over several years that has resulted in the jailing or prosecution of more than 100 senior military officers (including the former Chief of the General Staff, commander of the armed forces), police officers, judges, politicians, journalists and academics. Dubbed "Ergenekon" (a reference to a mythical site in the Altay Mountains, homeland of the Turkic peoples), this ultranationalist organization allegedly planned terrorist attacks and even hatched a plot to overthrow the government. The ongoing investigation caused huge controversy in Turkey, not least because of its deleterious impact on freedom of the press. The 9.11 event in the United States and wars in Afghanistan and Iraq have made Turkey more strategically indispensable than ever. The West, and the United States in particular, recognizes that Turkey is its most valuable friend in the Middle East and the Islamic World. Some argue that it may actually be preferable for Turkey to remain in the Islamic World—rather than entering the EU—where it can serve as a role model for other Muslim societies. Ironically, despite its progress toward modernization and constitutional democracy, the dream of "leaving Asia and entering Europe," cherished by several generations of Turks, many of them devout Muslims, looks increasingly unattainable.

Of course, the assessment of Western countries is based on their own perceived interests. But as a nation with a population of nearly 80 million and one thousand years of glorious history played out both in Europe and Asia, Turkey also needs to clarify its positioning for its own future.

Based on its Eurasian location and history, Turkey's future development must take into account both East and West. Turkey is currently the 19 th largest economy in the world, the result of a fusion of statism with a market economy; it is hard to imagine that Turkey would choose to give up either. A form of democracy has been implemented, the hard-won result of conflicts and compromises between elites and the working class, soldiers and politicians and secularists and Islamists over eighty years. But the foundations of political democracy are still not solid, and cannot be so long as the contentious issue of Kurdish autonomy remains unresolved.

Turkey's development is instructive for the developing world, especially for Muslim countries. But two questions remain unanswered: 1. Is Westernization the sole route to modernization? 2. Or, can a country modernize while remaining within Islam's cultural sphere? Turkey, as well the world, awaits the answers.

CHAPTER 35

European Turkey: The Bosphorus and Edirne

LIVING IN BOTH EUROPE AND ASIA

In 2009, after a short delay due to celebratory activities in Beijing and procedural problems on the Turkish side, I arrived in Istanbul on October 4, the only city in the world that straddles the Eurasian continent. This was my fourth visit.

At the invitation of the Turkish government, I was to be a visiting professor at Boğaziçi University (Bosphorus University) for one semester, and I hoped to take this opportunity to tour Turkey and its neighbors. I would be teaching two courses: "Modern Biomedical Engineering and Quality of Life" for graduate students in biomedical engineering, and "China and the Silk Road" for third-year undergrads in the History Department.

As one of the finest tertiary institutions in Turkey, it recruits the best students in Turkey every year via the national entrance exam. I thought they would all be smart and hard-working, but in fact, students from Peking University and Tsinghua University, while unable to follow lectures in English, are just as smart, and probably work harder.

The main campus of the university is in Europe, overlooking the Bosphorus from the three-story, white wooden building where I lived, just twenty steps from the famous Rumelihisarı or European Fortress. Fatih Sultan Mehmed II constructed the fortress in 1452, and a year later, he sacked Constantinople proper, thereby ending the Eastern Roman or Byzantine Empire that had outlived the fall of the Rome-based Western

Roman Empire by nearly a millennium. Today, the fortress has been transformed into a national museum for people to savor this victory of the Ottomans.

I rearranged the furniture in my apartment so that I could see not only the suspension bridge over the strait in the distance from the front window, but also the wider strait and the Asian coast from the window in my study.

The Biomedical Engineering Department was located in Asia, and my office there offered a marvelous view of Rumelihisarı and even of my residence, all of which was very pleasant. That said, I spent most of my time on the European side, using the History Department's office if I needed to print out or photocopy something, or ideally, working from my apartment.

When you think of Istanbul, images of towering Ottoman minarets, majestic mosques, bazaars filled with all variety of wares, women scurrying by in austere black robes, bearded men sipping strong Turkish coffee (Türk kahvesi) at a café or seated on short stools on a narrow sidewalk may come to mind. Such vignettes can still be seen for miles around Topkapı Palace, where the Ottoman rulers and their royal relatives, court officials, courtesans, eunuchs and Janissaries (elite army corps) lived, worked, prayed, played and conspired. One Sunday I spent a whole afternoon in the environs of the palace's Sublime Porte (*Bab-ı Ali*) and forked out 15 lira for a beaded curtain.

To make up for my outlay of 15 lira for the curtain, I decided to walk across the Golden Horn to the more prosperous part of town. In the twilight on the Galata Bridge, anglers constantly cast their carefully baited fishlines, while the mostly empty buckets at their feet were hungry for the last catch of the day. Once I reached Karaköy, the north shore of the Golden Horn, I ascended the steep steps to the 1,500-year-old Galata Tower, where there are several souvenir stores and a restaurant that hosts performances by whirling dervishes, and then proceeded across Istiklal Caddesi (Independence Street) to a bus stop in Taksim, the bustling heart of Beyoğlu.

Driven by curiosity, this less-than-2000-meter trek of mine took over an hour. But in that time, I experienced nearly 2,000 years of history, which is what makes Istanbul so fascinating, and so geographically, socially and ideologically complex and unique.

I had been interested in Istanbul for many years, but my real contact with it came at the end of January 2004, when I had the opportunity to spend five days there during the Lunar New Year. I'd just finished reading Orhan Pamuk's novel that takes place in the late sixteenth century, My Name is Red, and wanted to see for myself both the city where it was set and the author. Unfortunately, there was a snowstorm and I was suffering from back pain, but this did not disrupt my trip. I still managed to hit the celebrated tourist sites and even dined with this novelist—winner of the Nobel Prize for Literature two years later.

Between 2004 and 2009, I visited Istanbul three times and spent a total of 30 days in the metropolis. Those 30 days proved to me that Istanbul is the most interesting city I have ever visited, whereas until then I had always found Paris the most charming. Despite my love of France and my numerous trips to Paris since 1963, the climate in Istanbul is more pleasant, the landscape more beautiful and the culture more profound. It always engenders a strong powerful clash between history and contemporary reality, and this makes visitors feel welcome.

As to why I feel more welcome in Istanbul, let me explain. Because I speak French, I don't encounter the same hassles in Paris as foreigners who have trouble communicating with the locals, who famously expend little effort to please tourists. In Istanbul, which is just as bustling as Paris, foreign tourists often cannot read signs written in Turkish or speak a word of the local language, but the Turks are usually eager to help out. In Istanbul, and other cities in Turkey too, I could feel real warmth and hospitality from the bottom of their hearts. Once we asked for directions, passers-by formerly in a rush patiently indicated the route to take, and sometimes even accompanied us part of the way.

"Welcome to Turkey!" was a frequent enthusiastic refrain wherever we went. Shopkeepers and taxi drivers would usually round down to a whole number when they encountered tourists who couldn't count their change. Hotel guards, subway station staff, waiters and even police officers were usually very gracious about serving tourists. I've heard that the Turks are less gracious and can get more heated when it comes to soccer and politics, so I diplomatically avoided these topics.

The Turkish language is spoken with a rapid-fire quality, but it's also pleasant to the ear. I found that Turks tend to speak at a lower volume when eating than Chinese or Americans, and most of the Turks I know normally speak softly. Their elegant demeanor conveys an agreeable and natural style.

Turkish drivers often "rewrite" traffic rules themselves, but not as casually as their Indian and Chinese counterparts. Drivers in Turkey have a more amicable relationship with one another and generally don't get annoyed or angry.

Because there are many more pedestrians than drivers on the streets of Istanbul, the former are definitely worth mentioning here. Generally speaking, Istanbul's pedestrians are skillful judges of the approximate speed of oncoming vehicles. For them, traffic lights and crosswalks are mere references, and they decide when and where to cross according to their own convenience—as if all Istanbul motorists possessed superb reflexes and could brake on a dime.

Now that I know how to take buses in the area, I can't resist sharing my insights with you about the local bus scene. Since many bus routes share the same stop, it's not practical to queue up at the curb. Every time a bus stops, I observed what I'd dub the "victory of civility over chaos." Although you couldn't be sure exactly where to stand while waiting, it appeared that each passenger who intended to board did so in a timely fashion. In my many "self-funded studies" of the sociology of public transportation in Istanbul, for which I paid 1.5 Turkish lira on several occasions, I never saw any pushing or elbowing.

Built in the sixteenth century, Edirne's Selimiye Mosque is very elegant, with a Byzantine dome structure and four slender Ottoman minarets

A Visit to Architect Sinan's Chef-d'oeuvre

Edirne is 250 kilometers northwest of Istanbul, bordering Greece and Bulgaria. A major Greek city known as Adrianople since the second century, it was taken by the Ottomans in 1361 and became their capital until 1453 when a much bigger prize, Constantinople, fell in their hands.

At this point, the Ottoman Sultan formed an elite army with Christian captives from Adrianople, the Janissaries (*yeniçeri*, lit. new soldier), under his direct command. Every member a personal slave of the Sultan, the Janissary Corps—eventually recruited via child levy among non-Muslims who were converted to Islam for the purpose—was the first standing army in Europe and responsible for many Ottoman victories for more than 400 years.

My interest in Edirne, however, lies mainly in a gem of Ottoman architecture, the Selimiye Mosque.

Equipped with a great deal of gusto and one magical Turkish word, *Selimiye*, my wife and I took an early morning bus-ride on our first Saturday in Turkey to visit Edirne, just seven kilometers from the Greek border. The 3-hour ride from Istanbul to Edirne was a delight; the US$12 ticket with reserved seating included free black tea and snacks served by a male waiter wearing a black-tie.

The bus stopped at the Edirne bus terminal on the city outskirts. Passengers were supposed to be transported, free of charge, to their destinations by a fleet of minibuses. It was at this point that our Turkish word came into good use. Mouthing *Selimiye* repeatedly, we were led to a waiting minibus. It meandered through residential areas, making me anxious about where we were actually going. At long last, however, the driver signaled for us to disembark.

As soon as our feet touched the ground, we saw a huge mosque, partially obscured by tall trees, in the middle of a broad boulevard.

Selimiye Camii is widely considered the masterpiece of the foremost Ottoman architect, Mimar Sinan (1491–1588). The equal of the best Renaissance architects in Europe, Sinan was born into a Christian family in Anatolia and taken at a young age to become a member of the Janissary Corps, and later served as an army engineer. He was spotted by Sultan Suleiman I, the greatest and longest reigning of Ottoman sultans, for his talent in design. Often running alongside the Sultan's horse during military campaigns, Sinan was entrusted to design the *Süleymaniye Camii* in

Istanbul. Later he was given the task by Sultan Selim II, Suleyman's son, of designing a mosque in Edirne to be named, of course, *Selimiye Camii*.

Viewed from the exterior, it features a huge Byzantine dome structure, supported by a group of smaller domes and accompanied by four Ottoman-style slender minarets, each with three balconies. Laid out on an octagonal plan, the interior is very spacious and light. The decorative elements are artful yet not ornate. Non-imposing dignity and non-flamboyant elegance are the two qualities I perceived in this great mosque. Sinan, who lived to the age of 97, designed and supervised the construction of his masterpiece when he was already in his 80s.

If we had seen nothing more than this mosque, it would have been worth the trip already. But we got much more than we anticipated.

There is also a small museum full of Islamic art pieces and historical documents. A sixteenth-century caravanserai, also designed by Sinan, it is now a quaint hotel; just the kind of place where we could have a cup of Turkish tea and give our feet a rest.

While taking our afternoon promenade on the streets of Edirne, I noticed an interesting phenomenon: A higher percentage of people with Asiatic facial features in this westernmost European city of Turkey than in any other Turkish city I had visited.

On the return bus-ride, an idea suddenly flashed through my mind. I faintly recalled that the Ottoman Sultans had garrisoned soldiers in Edirne, and resettled many civilians there too, in order to strengthen this European foothold and their new capital. Indeed, the Ottomans started as a *ghazi* state and the first two rulers did not call themselves *Sultan* but used the title *Ghazi*, meaning "frontier warrior for Islam." We were now seeing the results of a deliberate emigration policy implemented some 650 years ago, on the faces of people in Edirne!

CHAPTER 36

Anatolian Turkey: Trabzon and Konya

GREEK CHURCH, TEA PLANTS AND A WEDDING PARTY

When I was in graduate school at Northwestern University outside Chicago, there was a light-hearted T-shirt that read: "Three years ago, I cudn't spel ingineer, now I is one." I can now truthfully say: "Three years ago I couldn't spell Trabzon, and now I am writing about it."

Deep in the mountains southwest of Trabzon, over a high cliff, perches the Greek Orthodox Sumela Monastery, a sanctuary founded in the fourth century. It has stood there through the Byzantine, Seljuk, Ottoman and Turkish Republic periods, occasionally vandalized but usually under protection, in disrepair but never ruined. The complex was renovated in the twentieth century, and it was a little disappointing to see an obvious difference in style between the remaining old structure and the replacement.

For the ancient Christians, it was probably their religious fervor that inspired them to paint the frescoes. To me, to build a monastery in such a secluded place probably reflected not only a devotion to their God, but a common human desire to lead a life without tumult.

How else could one explain so many Chinese poems and paintings on the theme of solitude and tranquility in the mountains? There in the deep mountains near Trabzon, I experienced the same sentiments as expressed by poets in ancient China. But a poet I am not. How I wish Wang Wei (701–761) could have come to Trabzon and crafted some poetry in this monastery!

Mind you, this wasn't entirely impossible since his Tang Dynasty contemporary and travel writer, Du Huan, went as far as Palestine, Egypt and Morocco.

Christian monastery built in the fourth century near Trabzon, Turkey

Aboard a minibus marked "Ayasofya" in Turkish, my wife and I were taken to a small hill just outside Trabzon. This Haghia Sophia—sharing the same name as the more famous but much larger and grander church in Istanbul—was constructed in thirteenth century by the ruler of a Greek kingdom that had split from Byzantine Empire after the Fourth Crusade caused many Byzantine nobles to leave Constantinople. The kingdom was already surrounded by the encroaching Seljuk Turks. Although it is a Byzantine-style Christian church, some of the stonework has interlocking geometric patterns in the Islamic Seljuk art style. Cross-cultural borrowing happened in this case in spite of religious and political hostilities between the Muslim Turks and the Christian Greeks at the time.

In fact, this kind of borrowing is also noticeable in the opposite direction: the adoption of the Byzantine dome structure in almost all

Ottoman mosques. The most illustrative example is the Blue Mosque, which features five main and eight secondary domes. Also known as the *Sultan Ahmed Mosque*, it was built after the Ottomans had mastered the art of architecture and stands next to the Hagia Sophia (lit., Holy Wisdom). The latter was repurposed and renamed in 2020 as the Hagia Sophia Grand Mosque.

With the Black Sea to the north generating moisture and mountains to the south blocking it, the Trabzon area has the highest annual rainfall in Turkey. It is therefore surrounded by lush green vegetation on all sides except the north. Besides dense forests, much of the vegetation comprises tea plantations.

In a small village about 100 kilometers east of Trabzon and 50 kilometers from the coast, a man in his forties struck up a conversation with us while we were having our photo taken with a group of local residents who were hanging around a roadside cafe. He works for the state-run tea company Çaykur (pronounced *chai-kur*, as tea is called "chai" in Turkey), and took us on a tour of a nearby factory that processes organic black tea and introduced us to the factory's general manager, who explained how Turkey became a major tea producer. I shared with our hosts that the beverage is known as "tea" or "té" in Western Europe because the Western Europeans who came to China's southeast coast in the sixteenth century learned from the locals as "te" or "de"; whereas the Central Asians, Indians, Persians and Arabs long before that borrowed the name "cha" (or "chai") from the Northern Chinese.

Afterward, this amiable and kind man offered to take us to another plant that processes green tea! Our decline to this second invitation, however politely made, seemed to have hurt the feelings of this over-zealous host.

Of course, we prefer over-zealous hosts to hostile locals. At a wedding party which we ran into in a town near a beautiful lake, we met neither kind, which is what we liked the most. Men and women formed separate lines to dance to a loud blast of folk music. One man noticed us and offered some sweets to us with just a nod and a smile. A pretty little girl on her daddy's shoulders kept peeking at us, but he did not acknowledge us.

When the neighboring minaret broadcast the muezzin's call for prayers just before dusk, it competed with the dance music, but no one stopped dancing. We walked over to the mosque where a few people were performing their ablutions or simply removed their shoes at the entrance and entered to pray.

At this point, my mind switched back to the cute little girl at the wedding party. Which sound system would she choose to listen to when she grows up? As I was casting my last glance at this small town whose name I can't even spell, I sincerely wished that she would not have to choose between dance and prayer but would be free to do both.

Checking out Rumi's Roots

Although I don't know Turkish and most Turks don't speak English or French, my experience in Trabzon convinced me that I could visit Turkish cities without a personal guide and even enjoy it.

And so one Friday night in November 2009, emboldened with such confidence, I flew to Konya, the ancient capital of the Seljuk Rum Sultanate, and checked into what the guidebook described as "the most famous hotel in Konya."

The next morning, I picked up a local map from the hotel desk and asked directions to the *Mevlâna* Museum, Konya's principal tourist draw. Alas! My high-level misreading of the map eventually led me to an unfamiliar street with just one barbershop open. Map in hand, I pronounced "Mevlâna Museum" in my awkward Turkish. The barber motioned for me to follow a young man who led me less than 50 meters down the street, stopped, muttered something and then walked away, smiling.

Amidst my puzzlement, a minibus drove by. I realized that this unmarked place was the place where locals caught the minibus. But I didn't dare stop the minibus for fear of getting the wrong one, so I went back to the barbershop and asked the owner to show me where I was on the map.

Onlookers regarded us with curiosity. I quickly realized that "Where are we on the map?" is not something that can be expressed by hand gestures, and only serves to confuse. But the old barber was not affected. He led me out of his shop to his car nearby and courteously opened the door for me.

Konya's iconic Mevlâna Museum

For the next 15 minutes, we didn't say a word, just smiled occasionally. The barber stopped the car when I spotted the green-tile minaret of the *Mevlâna* Museum. These two persons who didn't share a common spoken language had known each other for 30 minutes, traveled together for a few thousands of meters, one grateful for being helped, the other content for aiding a visiting stranger, said their goodbyes... all without a hitch.

Jalal al-Din Muhammad (1207–1273) lived in the territory of the former Eastern Roman Empire called "Rum" and is therefore known to Westerners as "Rumi." Rumi grew up in present-day Balkh, Afghanistan, to Persian-speaking parents. Rumi's father founded an Islamic Sufi order and moved with his family and followers to Konya, ruled by the Seljuk Turks, in order to escape the Mongols. Later, the Mongols occupied Central and Western Asia and took control of most of Anatolia, forcing the Seljuk rulers of Konya to become their vassals.

Rumi succeeded his father as an elder of the order—Mevlânâ means "our leader" in Persian—at the age of 24. He believed that music and dance could bring people into a state of ecstasy of "universal love" and liberate them from the anxiety and pain of everyday life. This approach to religious understanding has given thousands of Muslims a deep sense of existential reality and spiritual fulfillment that traditional Islamic rituals would not have allowed them to experience.

Rumi's *Masnavi*, a collection of some 25,000 mystical poems, was completed shortly before his death. The residents of Konya, including Christians and Jews, mourned him deeply. His son and disciples founded the Sufi Mevlevi Order, and his name became synonymous with Sufi poetry to readers around the world.

Today, the *Mevlâna* Museum, an extension of the Mevlevi Order, houses Rumi's tomb, as well as his manuscripts and other relics. I stayed in the ceremonial hall for a long time, imagining the religious rituals of 700 years ago.

The order is known in the West as the home of the "whirling dervishes," a name derived from a unique dance ritual called the Sema.

In the evening, I watched a wonderful sema performance at the newly built *Mevlâna* Cultural Hall. The whirling dervishes were clothed in white or black robes and red conical hats. Musicians played instruments and chanted lines from the Qur'an in accompaniment. The dervishes extended their arms at shoulder height, one palm facing the sky and the other facing the ground, and spun around at length to the beat of the languorous and elegant music, in an attempt to achieve a state of unity with God, which is the ultimate goal of the dance ceremony.

When I first observed the Sema in Istanbul in 2006, I did not understand the meaning of the various parts of the ritual and therefore did not pay much attention to the religious aspects of the dance ceremony. This time, the Sufi dancers in the Konya hall were not just performing, but were fully engaged in the ritual, completely absorbed in their personal religious consciousness. This experience made me, as a non-religious person, strongly aware that human beings need spiritual fulfillment, and that this religious ritual provides that fulfillment in a mysterious way.

However, Sufism is still controversial in the Islamic world. Sufi poets often use wine and beauty as metaphors for God in their poetry, which traditional Muslims either abhor or despise (*see Chap XXIII, Persian Poetry and Painting*). The Sufi quest for the state of unity between man and God, and the cry "I am God, God is me"—emitted by some Sufis in exaltation—are strongly condemned by conservatives such as the Wahhabis, who contend that these practices violate the fundamental Islamic tenet that "There is no God but God" (*La ilaha ill-Allah*).

Doctrine aside, in many countries, including Turkey, Sufis represent an important social and political force because the members of these communities are well organized and often support each other as colleagues and neighbors.

I spent all of Saturday afternoon strolling through the streets of Konya, observing the residents who are notable for their piety. I didn't know much about the relationships between people in this part of the world, but I was struck by the courtesy and amiability of most people in this ancient capital of the Seljuk Khanate.

Turkey, currently ruled by a moderate Islamic party, has robustly promoted Konya as a tourist destination and a center of Islamic culture. This is not as controversial as other policies of the Turkish government, because even the most secular members of society consider Konya a distinguished political and cultural center in Turkish history. I'm glad I visited.

Chapter 37

Emergence of Neo-Ottomanism

Hagia Sofia Grand Mosque in present-day Istanbul, built in the middle of the sixth century, was the most representative religious structure of the Byzantine Empire. After the Ottomans seized Constantinople in 1453, this Greek Orthodox church was transformed into a mosque and surrounded by four minarets. After the establishment of the officially secular Turkish Republic, it was converted into a museum in 1934. In 2020, the current government announced the reversal of the 1934 decision and restored it as a functioning mosque

The 2002 national elections were a turning point in Turkish history: The Justice and Development Party (AKP) won a majority of seats in the National Assembly and became the first Islamic party to gain power in 80 years.

The soul of the AKP is Erdogan, who served as prime minister for eleven years and then president for two terms and will contest a third in 2023. During this period, he has engendered countless domestic political storms and international controversies, but his leadership within the party has strengthened, leading the AKP to successive election victories.

As a result, Erdogan himself has taken a leading role in the future of Turkey. This phenomenon is important for Turkey, the Middle East, Central Asia and Europe. The reasons for this are Erdogan's charisma and ability, changes in the international situation and certain social realities in Turkey proper.

Let's start with the man himself. Erdogan came from a grassroots background, working as a street hawker in Istanbul's hardscrabble Kasımpaşa when he was a teenager and studying at an Imam Hatip religious vocational high school, and later becoming a semi-professional football player. His speech and demeanor are popular with the lower and middle classes; he is generally firm, confident, and sometimes talks tough with foreigners, as most Turks expect from their leader. In addition, he is a natural politician who has a long history of enlisting allies and combatting opponents.

Now, let's talk about the international environment. Since the end of the Cold War, Turkey's immediate environment has changed dramatically. Although it remains a strong ally of the United States and has the second largest armed forces in NATO, geopolitical and commercial relations in the Greater Middle East have undergone fundamental changes. Turkey's relations with Russia have improved markedly, while its cultural and commercial ties with Iran have increased, and it has gained greater influence over the three South Caucasus countries, the five Central Asian states as well as in the east Mediterranean region. This has made many Turks realize that after all, Turkey is a major Muslim country in the Greater Middle East.

Then came the transformation of Turkish society. The Kemalists ruled Turkey for eighty years, and most of the social elite, a large part of whom lived in or near Istanbul, believed that Westernization and secularization were Turkey's destiny. Ironically, this elite consisted of two groups of people who were mutually suspicious and even often hostile: The military, who had strong nationalist tendencies, and the intellectuals, who believed in modern Western liberalism and opposed military domination.

On the other hand, many members of the lower and middle classes of Turkish society, most of whom lived in its Asian part, Anatolia, have never been truly Westernized or fully secularized. They feel that the elite did not take Islamic faith and Ottoman cultural tradition seriously enough. Among the large population of practicing Muslims are members of the AKP, which is primarily politically active, and the Gülen movement, which was primarily active in the social and cultural sectors.

During the first decade of the twenty-first century and early years of the second, the most influential religious community in Turkey was the social movement founded by the Islamic scholar Fethullah Gülen, which has no official name but is known to its members as *hizmet* ("service society") or *cemaat* ("congregation") in Turkish. Gülen says he was influenced by the nineteenth-century Kurdish Sunni Muslim scholar Said Nursi, and by Rumi (see Chapters 25 and 36), the renowned thirteenth-century Persian-language Sufi poet and inspiration for the Mevlevi Order founded after his death, also known as the Order of the Whirling Dervishes.

Gülen has been influential in advocating a "cultural Islam" (as distinct from a "political Islam") that advocates fraternity, tolerance, hope, dialogue, participation and mutual respect. He has resided in the United States since 1999, from where he has promoted science, market economics and multi-party politics, and emphasized mutual adaptation between Islam, modernity and education.

Prior to its official designation in Turkey as a terrorist organization in 2016, the Gülen movement—once reportedly numbering several million members—had established a loose and discrete organization comprised of hundreds of schools in Turkey (and nearly one thousand worldwide), charities, real estate trusts, employers' federations, student groups, cultural associations and mass media including the very popular Turkish daily, *Zaman*, that was closed down by government order after the failed coup in 2016.

Regarding the Gülenist movement, there are radically different opinions in Turkey and abroad. Now outlawed in Turkey proper, some see it as a secret society that excels at camouflage, some perceive it as a body designed, organized and directed by the United States, while others view it as visionary, i.e., the future shape of Islam and a model for Islamic society.

Economically, small and medium-sized enterprises, primarily in Anatolia, did not benefit from government business policies prior to the rise of the AKP, but in recent years they have demonstrated geographical, cultural and technological advantages in trade with Iran, Egypt, the Caucasus and Central Asian countries, boosting their self-confidence and increasing their profits. These firms, which are beginning to flourish, have in turn greatly increased their success in bidding for many of the infrastructure projects launched since Erdogan's AKP came to power.

It can be said that the voter base of the AKP consists of devout Muslims in the hinterlands of Anatolia, especially the population associated with small and medium-sized businesses. These firms and the omnipresent charitable funds (*vakıf*) they manage that are commonplace in Muslim societies are thus the main contributors to the AKP.

The solid backing of the Gülenists, including their affiliated television, newspaper and radio stations during the first decade of the twenty-first century, was crucial to the AKP on the interrelated levels of financial backing and votes. Bluntly put, without their support, Erdogan and the AKP might not have been able to come to power in the first place.

In the first few years after he became prime minister in 2003, Erdogan placed sympathizers of the AKP, including Gülenists, in the military, police, intelligence and court systems, and then ordered personnel from these key departments to investigate secularists who were opposed to his administration.

In 2010, Turkish officials began investigating a secret coup allegedly hatched by military personnel in 2003, under the code name "Operation Sledgehammer" (*Balyoz Harekâtı*). Hundreds of senior military officials, including former chiefs of staff and commanders of the army, navy and air force, as well as police officers, judges, academics and cultural figures, were indicted, most were sentenced, and many active-duty military officers were forced to retire.

Soon after, the Turkish government launched a major case dubbed "Ergenekon" (named after a mythical site in the Altay Mountains, birthplace of the Turkic people), that investigated and sentenced many intellectuals and clerical staff allegedly belonging to extreme right-wing terrorist organizations. It was during the course of handling this investigation that cracks appeared in the relationship between Erdogan and Gülen, two Islamist activists who had formerly joined forces against the secularist elite.

In 2013, newspapers funded by the Gülenists published a report on corruption involving three cabinet ministers. After the three were indicted and pleaded guilty, in one fell swoop Erdogan replaced ten cabinet ministers, including the three, alleging that the Gülenists controlled a secretive "Parallel State" that comprised military personnel, police officers, judges and media professionals. Gülenist media responded by accusing Erdogan of dictatorial corruption and deviating from democracy.

As a distant observer acquainted with power struggles in the history of China, basically a non-religious country, what I see in Turkey is that as the Westernized secularists became marginalized, discord began to show between former Islamist allies. Regardless of whether the parties involved share the same religious beliefs, the pattern of competition in the political dimension is once again evident in twenty-first-century Turkey.

Erdogan was elected president of Turkey in 2014. He nominated his long-time aide, Ahmet Davutoglu, as prime minister, and announced that he aimed to be a substantive president rather than the traditional, symbolic head of state. In retrospect, by this announcement he altered the nature of governance and democratic practice in Turkey.

In fact, many Turks had already begun referring to him as "Sultan." The first act of this "Sultan" after he came to power was to turn the 999-room prime minister's residence, which he had built at great expense when he was prime minister, into the Presidential Palace—so that the current prime minister would not be able to enjoy this palatial complex.

In 2018, Erdogan was the first president to be directly elected by the Turkish people for a five-year term (renewable once), as per the 2017 constitutional amendment establishing the new executive system that concentrates immense power in the office, and abolishes the post of prime minister.

One hundred years after the fall of the Ottomans, and as more and more Turks feel nostalgic for the Ottoman Empire, Erdogan has gone some way to satisfying the yearning for its past greatness. Recently, when he greeted the visiting President of Palestine, the Turkish Presidential Guard of Honour procession turned out in 16 separate squads, each clothed in distinct attire that represented one of the sixteen historical regimes established by the Turkic peoples!

Erdogan's reign marked a new era of democratic political parties coming to power in Turkey and coincided with the international coalition against terrorism in the wake of the 9/11 terrorist attack on the United States, and this increased Turkey's importance in the Greater

Middle East. The launch of the Davutoglu's so-called "Zero-Problem with Neighbors" foreign policy, and the administration's moderate and tolerant treatment of the Kurdish community represented two promising beginnings. Unfortunately, Erdogan and his team, due to their own limitations and pressing desire to win votes among chauvinistic nationalists and those who opposed "appeasement" of the Kurds, were ultimately unsuccessful in both endeavors.

In December 2015, Turkey shot down a Russian Su-24 attack aircraft on the Turkey-Syrian border, causing Russia's ire over this incident and imposed sanctions on Turkey. However, after disagreements with the United States about the origins of the failed 2016 coup in Turkey, Erdogan soon made peace with Russia.

Evidently, the geopolitical map of the Middle East can alter at any time due to Turkey's vacillation; many Turkish people who have supported Erdogan relish Turkey's increasing geopolitical influence.

At the end of the nineteenth century, in order to perpetuate its waning rule, the Ottoman imperial government tightened its internal control while promoting the expansionist ideas of "Pan-Islamism" and "Pan-Turkism." If we look at the various policies launched by the Erdogan administration over the last decade, it appears that he is following in the footsteps of the late Ottoman Empire and consciously departing from Kemalism to advocate a twenty-first-century form of "Neo-Ottomanism."

The next presidential election in Turkey will be held in May 2023, coinciding with the centennial of the demise of the Ottoman Empire as well as the birth of the Republic of Turkey.

At this time, when Russia and Ukraine are fighting close to Turkish territories, when Kurdish guerillas (PKK) use Syria and Iraq as a sanctuary in their fight against the Turkish armed forces, when the renewed Serbia-Kosovo stand-off in the Balkans draws the attention of all of Europe, and last but not the least, when Armenia and Azerbaijan in South Caucasus are once again sparring with each other, a fair and smooth presidential election in 2023 can very well be a weathervane of where the majority of Turkish people want their country to go.

However, since the Erdogan government has managed Turkey's economy poorly, all Turkish people including ardent AKP supporters are suffering from the runaway inflation along with a drastic depreciation of the Turkish lira. Thus, Erdogan's chance of staying in the huge Presidential Palace should be lessened in the coming political contest. Yet, surprisingly or not, a Turkish court recently sentenced Ekrem Imamoglu, mayor of Istanbul and the most likely presidential candidate from the opposition, three years in prison and barred him from politics. Whether this severe punishment of a rival will enhance Erdogan's chance of re-election or prompt the opposition parties to unify is hard to predict.

At any rate, combining all the events and trends mentioned above, the likelihood of Recep Tayyip Erdogan continuing to be President of Turkey is still quite high. But, whether his re-election means an outright mandate for his brand of Neo-Ottomanism is far from clear.

PART IX

Conclusions

CHAPTER 38

The Ancient Silk Road: "Geography as Destiny"

Emerging from Africa, Surveying the World

The earth has a history of approximately 4.6 billion years. Plains and mountains, oceans and deserts and flora and fauna all boast a much longer history on our planet than mankind. Human survival and progress have never occurred independently of our "geography," i.e., the physical environment that we inhabit.

Primates appeared on earth about 7.5 million years ago. While the history of modern Homo sapiens goes back several tens of thousands of years, only during the last ten thousand have we arguably entered a "civilized" phase, and we have a recorded history of just five or six thousand years.

Approximately one hundred thousand years ago a group of modern Homo sapiens departed East Africa and entered West Asia, from where they gradually dispersed throughout the Eurasian landmass.

Forty thousand years ago, a small number of inhabitants on an island in Southeast Asia crossed what was then a fairly narrow strait, and arrived in Australia. Due to a bout of global warming, shortly thereafter the sea level rose, the strait widened and migration to Australia ended until European settlers came by boat from afar in the late 1700s. During the forty thousand years after the arrival of the first indigenous inhabitants, their descendants were only able to survive and develop within the existing environmental conditions.

About 13,000 years ago, some humans trekked from the northeast corner of Eurasia across the frozen Bering Strait and set foot in modern-day Alaska. Not long thereafter the earth entered the Ice Age (aka, Fourth Glacial Period), the Bering Strait widened and ceased freezing over. The indigenous peoples of North America continued their southeasterly migration, reaching the southern tip of South America near the Antarctic Circle about one thousand years later. From the time that humans first crossed the Bering Strait until Columbus' "discovery" of the New World, the inhabitants of North America had no contact with other peoples, and they independently created the Mayan and Inca civilizations of Central and South America, respectively.

Mankind first emerged in Africa, a huge continent whose area exceeds that of China, India and Greenland combined. But Africa's Sahara Desert (itself larger than the United States) and a belt of saline territory to its south separates North Africa, which borders on the Mediterranean, from central and southern Africa. Most rivers in central and southern Africa are unsuitable for navigation, while jungle and marshlands render passage on land difficult too. The great beauty of coastal regions notwithstanding, usable harbors are few. Thus the various regions of Africa are isolated and transport between them is hindered by naturally occurring obstacles.

Now let's take a look at the Eurasian continent. The terms "Europa" and "Asia" were coined by the ancient Greeks. Because Greece is considered as the cradle of European civilization, and the global impact of Europeans has been unmatched for nearly three hundred years, therefore people worldwide label this, the largest swathe of territory on the face of the earth, "Eurasia." In other words, as perceived by the ancient Greeks, the entire world now artificially divides the earth's largest landmass in two, i.e., Europe and Asia, when in fact there is no natural boundary between the two.

About 11,000 years ago, the inhabitants of Europe, Asia, Africa, the Americas and Oceania were all standing at the same starting line on the global timeline, since all were still in a "pre-civilized" state. However, certain factors specific to the physical environments of Europe and Asia meant that humans in the Americas, Africa and Oceania would find themselves lagging behind the instant they departed from their starting blocks. Firstly, the Eurasian landmass possessed several key east–west arteries that are located at similar latitudes and endowed with similar climates. Its abundant varieties of plants and animals were conducive to agricultural development and the dissemination of tools and know-how. Secondly,

Eurasia was home to many large animals that could be domesticated, such as cattle, horses, donkeys, camels and Asian elephants. This was very advantageous to long-distance transport and trade, which greatly increased opportunities for Eurasians to learn from one another.

By contrast, with their mountains and rivers, the terrains of Africa, the Americas and Australia did not facilitate east–west traffic. In comparison to their huge land areas, their coastlines were relatively short and natural harbors few, so they were not conducive to coastal traffic. Land transport was mainly north–south and required passing through regions that featured dissimilar temperatures, and this too was disadvantageous to the movements of people, trading agricultural goods and transplanting crops. Furthermore, Africa, the Americas and Australia lacked large animals that could be domesticated, and transport—on their backs or by pulling a carriage—heavy loads for their masters. Ironically, there was a surfeit of large animals disinclined to take orders from human beings, such as African elephants, zebras, giraffes, hippos, rhinos—not to mention lions and leopards!

Thus we can say with certainty: No people that seeks to make its mark in human history can do so in isolation from the environmental conditions in which it exists.

West Asia: Cradle of the Agricultural Revolution

Twelve thousand years ago, the earth's climate grew warmer. Some animal species acclimated to the cold, such as reindeer, gradually migrated north. In order to stick close to their prey, some hunting peoples moved north too and entered previously rarely inhabited frigid zones—namely the Eurasian Steppe and the coniferous forests further north (named Taiga zone), as well as inside the Arctic Circle.

Thanks to plenty of sunshine, rain, rivers and fertile soil, animals and plant species were abundant in West Asia, and this allowed people to hunt their prey, fish and harvest fruits and root vegetables within a small area. Therefore, it was in West Asia that agricultural cultivation and livestock rearing emerged earliest. Later, inhabitants consciously coordinated planting and rearing activities to maximize their harvest so that they not only had sufficient foodstuffs (meat, vegetables and grains) for the present, they could also store a portion of them. In order to store water and extra grain, pottery also made its appearance in West Asia. This mode of survival not only made sedentary life possible, it made fixed settlements a necessity.

Historians generally agree that the Agricultural Revolution marks the beginning of human civilization, and they place it at about ten thousand years ago. The preceding period is known as the Old Stone Age (Paleolithic Era), which was followed by the New Stone Age (Neolithic Era) that lasted until the advent of the Bronze Age some six thousand years ago.

With the development of agriculture, surplus food could sustain a larger population, and this allowed a portion of the workforce to engage in handicrafts, trade, management and other tasks, and towns began to appear. Written language was born about 5,500–6,000 years ago, and with it, recorded history. These phenomena all occurred in Mesopotamia ("[land] between rivers"), a reference to the Euphrates and Tigris in modern-day Iraq. Shortly thereafter, independent agricultural civilizations emerged in the Nile Valley (Northeast Africa), the Indus River Valley (South Asia) and the Yellow River Basin (East Asia).

The earliest known Neolithic community was Jericho on the West Bank of River Jordan, dating back some 9,000 years. Still extant are remains of clustered dwellings that covered a large area and lodged an estimated two thousand residents. Archaeologists reckon Jericho's main agricultural products were wheat and barley, and dwellers raised goats. Most significantly, among other items, obsidian originating in Anatolia (modern-day Turkey) and shells from the red sea have been excavated at the site.

In other words, with the emergence of civilization, where the geography of the environment permitted it, merchants traveled long distances to engage in trade, and this stimulated exchanges between peoples and their goods, know-how and thought.

In Mesopotamia and the Nile Basin, thanks to the availability of river water, a social order that could mobilize manpower to facilitate irrigation developed very early. It was in these two regions that first appeared "extra-tribal" forms of governance, and the worship of certain deities. The sovereign in these two regions gradually came to be recognized as the incarnation of the gods who possessed supreme authority. At this point, society began to refine the division of labor. In addition to the king, clerics and peasants, members of other professions emerged, such as soldiers, government administrators, vendors, artisans and handicraftsmen.

In fact, trade and agricultural production appeared on the scene almost simultaneously, so merchants and farmers were arguably co-creators of early human civilization.

Nomadic Commerce and the Spread of Civilization

In the northern part of Eurasia lies a relatively flat and arid swathe of grassland, lightly covered by trees and shrubbery, known as the Eurasian Steppe. It extends from the lower reaches of the Danube to the Dnieper, through Ukraine and southern Russia (the Black Sea and northern reaches of the Caspian) to the Volga River and eastward to the Kazakh Steppe, the Altai Mountains, the Dzungar Steppe and the Mongolian Plateau, and all the way to the Greater Khingan Range in northeast China. This 10,000-kilometer stretch of grassland is not suitable for farming, but neither is it a region of nearly uninhabitable permafrost.

A long time ago, various peoples and tribes speaking languages of various families were active on these steppes. About ten thousand years ago, just when certain inhabitants of the temperate zone in West Asia began to engage in farming, people living on the grasslands also started to purposefully raise livestock, leading their herds to graze in different pastures during the summer and winter. This marked the genesis of nomadic culture.

Mankind does not arbitrarily decide in favor of an agricultural or nomadic lifestyle; rather, these two cultures represent the outcome of attempts to adapt to distinct physical environments. However, both occurred at roughly the same period in human history.

Nomadic life requires many items that its practitioners cannot produce, so nomads are more dependent than farmers on interaction with populations that are active in distant locales. Because they often relocate to distant destinations, nomadic tribes and peoples are more adept at long-distance trade, and tend to marry partners whose language and bloodlines differ from theirs. This nomadic trait makes it difficult for historians of sedentary farming populations to track changes in language and lineage among nomads, and thus it has been difficult to determine what became of ancient nomads such as the Northern Huns.

The nature and radius of nomadic activities began to increase significantly six thousand years ago when horses were domesticated in the grasslands of southern Russia. Once man could raise horses in large numbers, the distances covered in overland traffic surged markedly. Then the horse-drawn carriage came on the scene, significantly raising both the ability to transport goods and to wage war. Thus the earliest people to travel along the Eurasian Steppe were those nomads who resided in the area north of the agricultural belt and south of the permafrost covered by coniferous forests.

Besides migrating from west to east, the nomadic population frequently journeyed southward into temperate regions inhabited by farming peoples. At times they traded and at times they looted, but both activities aimed primarily at obtaining from the sedentary farmers the foodstuffs, jewelry and textiles the nomads lacked. In exchange for these items, they typically provided livestock, furs and ores.

The earliest human civilization to emerge was that of West Asia's farming population. So when the northern nomads traded with West Asians, the fruits of the latter's civilization—the wheel, calendar and handicrafts—naturally passed to the nomads, who then took them to the easternmost portion of the Eurasian Steppe. The world-famous horses of Mongolia most certainly spread there from Europe. The chariots employed by King Wu of Zhou, manned by two warriors ("one driver and one archer"), were the principal weapon that sealed his victory over the Shang Dynasty. This vehicle was very similar to the two-man war chariot that had long been in use in West Asia, indicating that West Asian civilization had spread to western China prior to the Zhou Dynasty that was established in the eleventh century BCE.

Of course, in the process of interacting with the agriculturalists, the nomads also imparted their expertise in horse rearing, horseback archery, metallurgy and fabrication of bows and arrows. Interaction between the two populations was hardly "one-way," and the know-how exchanged by one party was not necessarily superior to the other's.

In summary, until the twentieth century, the conflicts between and integration of nomadic and agricultural peoples was a recurring theme, and one which strongly impacted the historical evolution of all of Eurasia.

Even before the Shang and Zhou Dynasties, there were contacts between the eastern and western portions of the Eurasian landmass. At the time silk fabric had already appeared in the Yangtse River Basin, but it is not clear if it had spread to the West. But it has been confirmed that four thousand years ago a group of Indo-European speakers migrated from the northern Black Sea area to the northern foot of the Altai Mountains. Some of their descendants went south and entered Xinjiang's Barkol Steppe and Gansu's Hexi Corridor. Chinese historical records refer to them as the Yuezhi, while Western scholars label them "Tocharians." Scientists have discovered that it was the Yuezhi who brought wheat from the West to the upper reaches of the Yellow River, thereby adding an important variety of grain to the millet-based civilization of the Yellow River Basin.

Silk, Spices and Empire Building

Between 3,000 and 1,500 years ago, that is from the early Western Zhou to the Northern and Southern Dynasties, the most active and powerful nomads on the Eurasian Steppe were dubbed "Scythians" by the Greeks. They spoke an Indo-European tongue, and were referred to as "Saka" by the Persians, or "Sai" according to Chinese records. The Scythians were closely related by blood and language to the Sogdians of Central Asia, but the former farmed and engaged in commerce, while the Scythians made their living from nomadic herding and waging war.

Since the nineteenth century, archaeologists have discovered many graves and royal tombs in western Kazakhstan and northwest Mongolia, and they have unearthed many exquisitely detailed gold adornments. The Scythians established the earliest steppe empire in human history, hundreds of years earlier than the Huns. After the rise of the latter, the two peoples did have contacts. Some of the Scythians later settled, establishing kingdoms in Central Asia and Xinjiang region, including Wusun in Chu Valley and Khotan (modern-day Hetian) in the Tarim Basin.

The Huns arose among the northern grasslands of the Mongolian Plateau. After conquering Central Asia, they also became a threat to the Han Dynasty. Emperor Wu of Han dispatched Zhang Qian to the "Western Regions" as an envoy to the kingdoms that lay further west of the Hexi Corridor in the hopes of forging alliances against the Huns. But in economic and cultural terms, the significance of Zhang Qian's mission was to bring Chinese silk to Wusun and other regions in Central Asia, thereby pioneering the aptly named "Silk Road."

The empires established by the Scythians and Huns were grassland-based, while those of the Qin and Han Dynasties and the Persians were agricultural. Regardless of place or time, a people's social organization and administrative structure are related to its economic activity, and—naturally—subject to its physical environment. When material conditions are underdeveloped, the radius of commercial activity and political influence of any population will not be extensive. Therefore, the earliest form of governance was a tribe of a few hundred individuals. Only later did alliances emerge among nomadic peoples, while agricultural groups formed small city-states. After that, feudal kingdoms came into existence. Nominally, a mutually agreed king was revered, but in fact members of the feudal aristocracy occupied land and each ruled as he pleased.

Starting with the Qin Dynasty in China and eventually in Europe—in seventeenth-century France—the phenomena of the autocratic king and a unitary state emerged. When some rulers strengthened their administrative ability (mainly via deterrence through force) and resource allocation (minting coinage, taxation and trade monopolies), a new form of governance and political structure was born. Termed "*diguo*" in Chinese, this signifies a single nation ruled by an all-powerful emperor. In European languages this is typically referred to as "empire." The latter did not necessarily denote a Chinese-style hereditary autocratic emperor, but the empire had to possess a very large administrative organization, vast territory and a large population comprising various peoples, languages and faiths.

About two thousand years ago, there existed four different but interconnected agricultural empires extending from West Europe to East Asia. Furthest west was the Roman Empire, which ruled most of Europe, the Middle East and North Africa; east of it was the Parthian Empire, which governed Mesopotamia, the Iranian Plateau and west Afghanistan; further east, the Kushan Empire, based in south Afghanistan and west Pakistan, exercised control over most of Central Asia, northwest India and even southwest Xinjiang of China and the easternmost was the Han Dynasty, whose realm stretched from the Tarim Basin and the Hexi Corridor all the way to the Pacific Ocean.

Thanks to these four empires, orderly commercial activities were facilitated over great distances. Each empire typically possessed an army to maintain security, a fixed currency and a set of reliable laws. This made long-distance trade throughout Eurasia a normal state of affairs, increasing interaction between various regions and peoples, and thereby promoting contact between different cultures. These exchanges stimulated progress in Europe and Asia, but left southern Africa, the Americas and Australia increasingly far behind.

During the century following Zhang Qian's mission to the Western Regions, the frequency of traffic on the grasslands increased markedly. The towns and settlements formed around water sources in the desert became linked like a string of pearls, forming the so-called "Oasis Silk Road."

It was along the transport arteries formed between the Eurasian Steppe and the interconnected agricultural towns that trade in luxury items first flourished. Given the era's limited transport capacity, trading large amounts of bulky goods over great distances wasn't feasible. But Chinese silk, Mediterranean glassware, gems from Central Asia and India, and spices sourced in India and Southeast Asia were welcomed by the affluent in many regions—not unlike today's LV handbags and Chanel's haute couture. Perhaps the most iconic item in this trade was Chinese silk.

Some two thousand years ago when this web of trade routes connecting Asia and Europe actually came into usage, the "Silk Road"—not so named until a German scholar employed the appellation "Seidenstraße" (lit., "Silk Road" in German) in 1877—Roman aristocrats were already smitten with Chinese silk. Just one or two bolts of silk fetched a tael of gold. The renowned Roman orator and writer Seneca is said to have warned that if everyone took to clothing themselves in silk, the empire would go bust!

In fact, the Chinese were merely silk suppliers, and were not responsible for its sale along the Silk Road or its transport to remote destinations. Silk sourced in eastern China changed hands between many a reseller before it ended up on the eastern coast of the Mediterranean. The global supply chain and the concept of added-value had apparently already been realized two millennia ago!

I'd like to mention here another luxury item adored by the Romans: Spices. They were largely produced in the Indonesian archipelago and southern India, typically exported from India's southern ports via the Indian Ocean to Yemen, and then transported on land commercial routes in western Yemen to various sites on the Mediterranean. The Romans fancied themselves in silk, and they also liked to cook with spices. In *Apicius*, a renowned Roman collection of over five hundred recipes, more than four hundred required spices from the Far East. China was the homeland of the ancient silk road, but India was unquestionably the center of the world's "Spice Route."

Linking Europe and Asia by Land and Sea

As mentioned above, there were two major east–west transport arteries in Eurasia: Pioneered by nomadic peoples, the Steppe Silk Road was located on the northern Eurasian grasslands (45–55 degrees North latitude), while the other, the Oasis Silk Road (30–40 degrees North latitude), was established by a sedentary population and linked various towns and desert oases throughout West, Central and East Asia.

However, there was also a sea route that skirted the southeast portion of the Eurasian landmass while transporting goods. Much of it passed through the tropics, but since wooden ships rot quickly in this climate, archaeologists have had a hard time finding remains of the vessels that plied the "Maritime Silk Road." It has been ascertained that the earliest known form of transport that qualifies as a "boat" dates back about ten thousand years: A raft comprising sewn animal skins has been discovered near northern Norway.

A key section of the Spice Road lies between southern India and southwest Yemen. This is a fairly long sailing distance. Approximately 2,300 years ago, when the Greeks ruled Egypt they set sail from the Red Sea and entered the Indian Ocean. Savvy navigators who also excelled at observation and deduction, the Greeks were the first to discover the pattern behind the monsoons (also known as "trade winds"): During the winter they blow from the north toward the south, and vice-versa in the summer. Thus traditional commerce in the Indian Ocean generally involved a one-way trip once in six months, and a full year for a round-trip voyage.

Ancient Persian and Egyptian goods dating back to the Zhou Dynasty have been found on land along the coastal areas of China's Guangdong Province. The Museum of the Nanyue King's Mausoleum in Guangzhou contains items unearthed from the palace of this early Han Dynasty ruler of Guangdong, including fine adornments such as beads and items made of lapis lazuli that originated in North Africa and West Asia. Giraffes have also been mentioned in Han Dynasty documents. This indicates that the Maritime Silk Road has a long history, but in its early stage it was not particularly significant in terms of cultural exchange because traders plying the sea route were relatively few and the goods they could transport were limited. This was the case until about five hundred years ago, when this situation changed in a big way.

Pax Mongolica: The Ultimate Land-based Power

At the outset of the thirteenth century in northern China, Genghis Khan forged a powerful alliance comprising a group of Altaic-speaking tribes. They used "Mongol," a little-known tribal name, to designate the alliance and set out to conquer territory to the south and the west, and in the process of these expeditions members of this rather broad alliance gradually formed a shared sense of identity, and began to call themselves "Mongols."

In fact, the languages and customs of this group were quite similar to those of the Huns, Xianbei and still-extant Turkic-speaking peoples in West and Central Asia as well as China's Xinjiang, and certainly to the Khitan people of north China and Central Asia. In particular, the Turkic-speaking and the Khitan peoples found it easy to identify with the Mongols led by Genghis Khan.

At the time, the Mongols had mastered the most powerful methods of war-making anywhere on the globe. They possessed their own high-speed cavalry, artillery (invented by the Chinese) and the Persian catapult ("trebuchet," a large-scale contraption that hurled stones, useful in sieges). In less than fifty years, they swept across Eurasia to form four khanates, whose dominion included the Eurasian Steppe and temperate regions within Eurasia that practiced agriculture—plus the territory of the Yuan Dynasty in Chinese history. All of this territory is what historians mean when they refer to the "Mongol Empire."

As noted earlier, mankind began long-distance trade in the earliest times, and the four empires of ancient history—Roman, Parthian, Kushan and the Han—created advantageous conditions to facilitate it. During the thirteenth–fourteenth-century reign of the Mongols, the regions they dominated included the two major east–west arteries established in Eurasia since ancient times (one passing through the steppe, the other passing through the temperate agricultural zone). This enabled them to create a new epoch in east–west traffic on the Eurasian landmass. They maintained peace and order on these arteries, invented a high-speed courier system and operated a large number of *caravanserai* (roadside inns for Silk Road merchants), all of which paved the way for globalization by later generations.

In recent years, many western scholars have reassessed the history of the Mongols as viewed by Persian and Central Asian Muslim historians, and European scholars too. Some Chinese and Japanese academics have also raised questions about history as documented by ancient Han scholars. Generally speaking, historical records in China have consistently featured a "Han-centric" point of departure delineated over many centuries: Northern peoples who swept south were incorporated into a framework in which Han culture dominated the known world, one in which the governance of China must conform to the existing Han political ethic wherein the ruler "governs by virtue of divine designation." This argument ignores the distinct identity of these northern peoples, as well as the history they inherited from their forebears.

Since a large number of historical materials about the non-Han peoples of north China have not yet been put in order and analyzed in detail, contacts and similarities between the Huns, Xianbei, Khitan and Turkic peoples have not been apparent. On the other hand, Muslim scholars in Persia and Central Asia have regarded the Mongols as invaders and enemies of Islam. When assessing the Mongols, these scholars did not judge them against the same standards as they applied to the long-term power struggles and massacres undertaken by indigenous Muslim rulers both before the Mongols invaded and after they withdrew. Meanwhile, the discourse in the West regarding the Mongols has been curiously positive; the man-in-the-street generally admires this bunch of able warriors capable of withstanding great hardship, and since they also defeated Europe's foes—the Muslims—the Mongols hardly qualify as demons!

On the other hand, the Mongols also brought with them the "Black Death" (Bubonic Plague) that ravaged fourteenth-century Europe, so they were hardly "good" for Europe. However, neither Muslim scholars nor European commentators have explained why the Mongolian nobility, who exterminated the Arab's Abbasid Empire and executed the Caliph, then converted to Islam less than a century after invading Central and West Asia. Like the Tatars and Ottomans who arrived several centuries before them, not a few Mongols became members of the political elite in East Europe and West Asia, socializing and intermarrying with the Slavs of Ukraine and Russia.

The Mongol Empire began its decline in the early fourteenth century, but rulers of many states were designated members of the "Golden Family"—descendants of Genghis Khan—and were thus able to maintain their exalted positions for several centuries after his death. The Emir of the Khanate of Bukhara in Uzbekistan reigned until he was forced to abdicate by the Soviets in 1920. The dynasty of the Muslim kings of Hami in Xinjiang, a title first conferred by Emperor Kangxi of Qing, was not terminated until Feng Yuxiang, a warlord in northwest China, chased the last Mongol ruler out of his huge palace in 1930.

Aside from members of the Golden Family by birth, during the fourteenth–fifteenth centuries a Mongol from the Barlas Confederation in Transoxiana ruled Central and West Asia masterfully. He was Timur, a soldier born near Samarkand. He was an adherent of Islam and spoke a Turkic tongue, and considered himself a member of the Golden Family. In his eyes, the greatest honor of his life was to take for his wife the Chagatai Khanate Princess, herself a member of the family; in recognition of this, he insisted that his underlings address him as Lord Fu-ma (fu-ma meaning "royal son-in-law"), a reference to his exalted status as a prince by marriage.

Even though he was not related by blood to Genghis Khan and the founder of the Timurid Empire that covered Central Asia, Afghanistan, North India, Iran, the Caucasus and eastern Turkey, Timur never dared to take the title of Khan. He referred to himself as the Emir (lit., regional military commander) and the tomb he prepared for himself in Samarkand was known as the "Emir's Mausoleum." Timur led war expeditions for forty years yet never tasted defeat, but he died in 1405 in modern-day Kazakhstan on the way to attack China.

After Timur's death, his territory in the temperate agricultural zone of Central Asia was invaded and occupied by authentic members of the Golden Family hailing from the Kipchak Steppe. These were descendants of Genghiz Khan's grandson Batu and his underlings, and they called themselves Uzbeks. Today's Central Asian Uzbeks originated in the grasslands of North Asia, but they have lived a sedentary life for five centuries. The indigenous inhabitants of this region throughout the last millennia were referred to as the Sarts (lit., "townspeople"), which refers mainly to Persian-speaking Sogdians. But now they call themselves Tajiks.

With the fall of the Timurid Empire, the situation in West Asia and Central Asia also altered. In the West, there arose the Ottoman Empire that occupied southeastern Europe, Anatolia (Asia Minor), the southern Caucasus and the Crimea, north of the Black Sea. To the east of the Ottoman Empire was the Persian Safavid Empire dominated by followers of Shia Islam. Further east was the Mughal Empire on the Indian subcontinent, founded by Babur, a sixth-generation descendant of Timur.

Not long after the Mughal Dynasty was founded, however, it was invaded and its territory gradually usurped by the arrival in the Indian Ocean of the Portuguese, Dutch, French and British. The emergence of

European maritime powers in India marked the end of the era of land-based power centered on the Silk Road. Henceforth, the ancient Silk Road that passed through Central and West Asia on its way to Europe recalls the forlorn ambience of Tang Dynasty Du Fu's verse:

> Sun sets on the general's great banner,
> As cold wind moans and war-steed neighs.

Chapter 39

The New Silk Road: Eurasia's Historical Destiny

The geography and climate of Eurasia are favorable to communications, and therefore very early on mankind was able to link, via a series of stopping points, the entire length of the landmass, and engage in "segmented trading," i.e., within a given segment of the route. By the fourteenth century AD, under the Mongol-ruled Yuan Dynasty, overland and maritime silk routes connected East Asia, Western Europe and the East African coast. The construction of this vast and complex and transport network can arguably be considered as the "geographic destiny" of that era of human history.

In the most recent five centuries, the economic, cultural and social development of each of the world's continents have been most uneven. Looking forward to the future, a resurgent China expects to play an important role. Each country in Eurasia, as well as some African ones, will participate in constructing a "New Silk Road" to promote mankind's further development, a collaboration that will be implemented based upon the principals of reciprocity and mutual benefit. Such is the historical destiny of twenty-first-century Eurasia.

Maritime Power and the Rise of Western Europe

Some three thousand five hundred years ago, under the dual influence of the Egyptian and Hebrew civilizations, the inhabitants of Crete in the eastern Mediterranean created Minoan civilization. Five hundred years later it spread north to the Greek peninsula, becoming the source of European civilization, and when Greek civilization spread to the Italian peninsula, it formed Roman civilization.

During the first and second centuries CE, the Roman Empire was at its apogee and controlled Europe south of the Rhine and west of the Danube, as well as areas bordering on the Mediterranean as far east as the Caucasus. In the fourth century, the capital of the Roman Empire moved eastward to Constantinople (now Istanbul), presaging the future Eastern Roman Empire. From then on, the western frontiers of the Roman Empire came under continuous attack and occupation by the Huns, who came from Asia, and by Germanic peoples hailing from northern Europe.

When the city of Rome fell to the Germanic "barbarians" in 476 CE, the erstwhile imperial order was laid to waste, and Western Europe lapsed into six or seven hundred years of social chaos and stagnation. During this period, the Eastern Roman Empire formed what later historians would label "Byzantine Civilization," based upon Eastern Orthodox Christianity that employed Greek as its liturgical language.

Islam arose in the Arabian Peninsula during the seventh century and within just a few decades, it had destroyed two great ancient kingdoms, Egypt and Persia, as well as badly damaging the Roman Empire. By the eighth century, the Arab Empire extended across three continents—Africa, Europe and Asia—and west to the Atlantic, and east to the Indus. The tenth–eleventh centuries were the "Golden Age" of Arabo-Islamic civilization: Over a period of two hundred years, Muslim scholars from Spain to Afghanistan studied and synthesized Greek, Persian and Indian civilizations, and created a brilliant medieval civilization of their own. Their knowledge of mathematics, astronomy and medicine was second to none.

In the eleventh century, European farmers began utilizing new iron blades that made deeper plowing possible. As a result, agricultural output rose and the human population count soared. Each locality constructed a self-sufficient "manor economy," with a social order whose political framework was based upon a hierarchical relationship between feudal lords, big and small. As agriculture developed, West Europe saw the widespread emergence of "bourg" (lit., medieval village near a castle) dominated by merchants and artisans, and with them the birth of a class of town dwellers—"bourgeois"—who no longer depended on the land for their livelihood.

This was an era of great dynamism and confidence among the inhabitants of Western Europe. In the Iberian Peninsula (modern-day Portugal and Spain), the Christian political authorities began their "Reconquista" (lit., reconquest) to gradually expel the Muslim Moors of North Africa who had governed Iberia since the eighth century. Meanwhile to the east, the emperor of the East Roman Empire based in Constantinople was under imminent threat from the Seljuk Turks, and he requested aid from the Pope in Rome. Pope Urban II initiated a call to Christians for the formation of the First Crusade (1095–1099), whose raison d'être was the recapture of the Holy City of Jerusalem, occupied by Muslims for more than four centuries.

Flush with religious fervor and prejudice, as well as greed for the wealth of the Orient, major and minor members of nobility from throughout Western Europe—mainly Franks, including France's canonized Louis IX—organized seven crusades to the east during the twelfth–thirteenth centuries, with participation by town-dwelling hoi polloi too. They occupied Jerusalem, and even established a number of Crusader kingdoms in Syria and Palestine that ruled for more than a century.

Nearly two hundred years later, the Crusaders gradually lost their zeal for their holy mission, and they were expelled by the Muslim army in mid-thirteenth century. Just at this time, the Mongol army arrived in Syria from the east. It attempted to join forces with the Crusaders and attack the Muslims, but the parties had not reached an agreement. In 1260, the Great Khan Möngke passed away, and his younger brother Hulagu, who had led the Mongol war expedition this far west, opted to return eastward and contest the election for designation as the Great Khan, while leaving a small portion of his troops behind in Syria. As a result, the latter were annihilated by the Egyptian Mamluks (slave soldiers), thus marking the complete loss of the Mongol's massive military momentum accumulated over several decades.

During the twelfth and thirteenth centuries, the Europeans were exposed to the advanced Arabo-Islamic civilization in Iberia as well as on the eastern Mediterranean coast, and translated a great number of scholarly works from the Arabic in domains such as mathematics, astronomy, medicine, navigation, geography, philosophy and religion. They even translated long-lost Greek classics that had been preserved in Arabic. This can be considered the embryonic period of the European Renaissance, one that provided the anemic West with much-needed supplementary cultural "nutrition."

Closely related to the Western European Renaissance was the fall of the Eastern Roman Empire. The Ottomans, a branch of the Seljuk Turks, got a foothold in the European territory of the Eastern Roman Empire in the late fourteenth century. In 1453, the Ottomans attacked and occupied Constantinople, and the 95th emperor of the Roman Empire died on the city ramparts. In the period of more than one hundred years that followed, many Greeks fled Ottoman rule to various places in Western Europe, often serving as tutors to nobles and affluent city dwellers. Greek artisans migrated there too, raising the level of craftsmanship. Most significantly, the injection of classical Greek humanism via migration stimulated European society's "rebirth," better known by its French term, the "Renaissance."

After the suffering inflicted by the Crusades in the twelfth century, Islamic societies—formerly quite tolerant toward Christians—turned conservative, treating the "Franks" (the Arab's collective term for West Europeans) with hostility, and resisting their civilization. In the wake of Western Europe's sixteenth-century resurgence, this unreceptive mindset proved very disadvantageous to the evolution of Islamic culture. Faced with the long-term obstacle to direct trade with the East posed by the Muslim Arabs and Turkic peoples, during the Renaissance the Europeans began searching for a new path to Asia.

On the Iberian Peninsula the victorious Christians implemented a series of Inquisitions. They initially expelled unrepentant Muslims and Jews, and then persecuted those who had ostensibly converted to Catholicism (*conversos*) by bringing them before tribunals to judge if they were guilty of heresy, a sin punishable by death.

Yet at the very same time, the Christians were eagerly absorbing the Arabs' knowledge of scientific and navigational techniques. For more than a century, the Portuguese monarchy rewarded Portuguese seafarers who were willing to descend Africa's western coastline and pioneer new southbound routes. Meanwhile, the Spanish court subsidized the Italian explorer Christopher Columbus (Cristoforo Colombo) in his search for Asia via the western portion of the Atlantic. Once the Hundred Years' War (1337–1453) between France and Great Britain ended, they too began to seek opportunities for overseas trade and colonization.

In 1492, Columbus arrived in what he believed to be Asia, but was in fact Central America. In 1497, the Genoese explorer John Cabot (Giovanni Caboto) led an English team of explorers across the northern Atlantic and set foot in northeast Canada. In 1498, Vasco da Gama arrived in southwest India by way of the southern tip of Africa, the Cape of Good Hope. In 1502, on his fourth and last voyage there, Columbus sailed into the Caribbean and—once again—mistook the islands he encountered for part of Asia. In 1522, after having completed the first-ever circumnavigation of the world, Ferdinand Magellan's expedition arrived back in Spain (minus Magellan, who died in a battle in the Philippines). In 1534, the French explorer Jacques Cartier sailed north along Canada's St. Lawrence River to Gaspé Bay, where he erected a towering cross and claimed the territory in the name of the French king.

By this time the Mongol empire had long since declined, and the great Timurid Empire built by Timur who believed himself to be the heir to Genghis Khan, had also broken apart. Thus the era when Eurasia's land-based power reigned supreme had come to an end. It was to be gradually replaced by maritime power, a critical foundation for what was to become Europe's future global dominance.

The Industrial Revolution and Colonial Empires

In the first half of the sixteenth century, three momentous movements arose in Western Europe. Portugal and Spain began their occupation and establishment of many overseas colonies. Meanwhile, the Renaissance that had originated in Italy spread throughout Western Europe. The third was the Protestant Reformation that took place in the area north of the Rhine ruled by Germanic nobility.

Although these three movements occurred in different parts of Europe, they were interrelated. One key factor was that the transport network put in place by the Mongols in the thirteenth–fourteenth centuries became the fastest and safest land-based passageways in the history of Eurasia, making commercial, scientific and intellectual interaction between both ends of the landmass rapid and convenient. During this period, gunpowder, papermaking and printing know-how—all imports from the East—began to disseminate throughout Western Europe, thereby lifting the cultural level of the common man, and markedly increasing military capability as well.

In 1517, Martin Luther, professor of moral theology at the University of Wittenberg, posted his *Ninety-Five Theses* on church doors to denounce and resist the Vatican's support for issuing *indulgentia*, thereby igniting the Reformation in Western Europe. He encouraged believers to read the Bible, and advocated that the individual could interact directly with God without the aid of a priest ordained by the church. This proposition was a manifestation of Renaissance-era humanism, and its material basis was the Bible printed on paper; it no longer needs be painstakingly hand-copied onto parchment. He even described printing as "God's highest and extremist act of grace, whereby the business of the gospel is driven forward."

It is evident that the widespread resurgence of Western Europe was not a sporadic event, but rather the accumulation of a number of factors. Human civilization has always progressed via mutual study and borrowing. In the case of the sixteenth century, this revival was stimulated in part by knowledge originating among the Chinese, Arabs and Greeks.

The rejuvenation of Western Europe can be summarized thusly: As a member of the animal world, man recognized that by applying his rational nature he could perceive objective reality. With their emphasis on rationality and their understanding of objective reality as a starting point, Western Europeans were able to make great leaps in science and technology. In terms of the humanities and society, the Reformation signified that the Europeans had transcended the superstitions and ignorance of medieval times.

During the Reformation, many new sects advocated that the individual should not only look forward to Heaven after death, but should also strive through diligence and thrift to attain a happy life here in this world. Therefore, most Europeans not only did not abandon their faith in God, in their humble pursuit of the latter ideal they also exhibited humanism, the basic spirit of the Renaissance.

As they evolved into more affluent societies, at first the Portuguese and the Spaniards, and then the Dutch, French and British all left their homelands to explore and seek personal realization and wealth. The main external manifestation of Western Europe's revival was the seizure of territory and establishment of overseas colonies. Colonization resulted in a large influx of gold and silver into Western Europe, where its circulation stimulated commercial activity and made foreign trade even more crucial. This influx of precious metals marked the origin of what economists have dubbed "mercantilism."

Meanwhile, European monarchs took note of the handsome profits generated by overseas colonies, and actively organized support for their nationals to go abroad and engage in trade, exploration and colonization. The Dutch East India Company is an early example, after which

France and the United Kingdom each also established a franchise for managing their colonies and trading. The British East India Company effectively ruled Britain's possessions in India, up until 1858 when Queen Victoria was formally installed as British India's head of state. The practice of granting royal concessions to trading companies to govern colonial possessions was essentially a creative "workaround" devised by Western European countries, where (at least the appearance of) rule of law was considered important: The mother country bequeathed these companies with a special legal status, while acquiescing to their undertaking activities, such as slave trafficking and trading opium, that were in fact illegal back home.

When trade and commercial activities develop to a certain point, demand for production of more and higher quality products inevitably increases, thus prompting makers to improve modes of production. At the end of the eighteenth century, Britain's Industrial Revolution—symbolized by the usage of steam power—took place. Then France, the Netherlands and neighboring countries underwent their own era of industrialization. Already having led the globe for some two centuries, several of these newly industrialized countries now possessed extensive colonial empires.

By the latter half of the nineteenth century, several countries in the Western Europe, themselves not large in terms of land or population, had succeeded in ruling most of the earth's territory and the vast majority of its inhabitants. The disparity in power between the colonizer and the colonized was spectacular!

WORLD WAR I AND THE AMERICAN SURGE

In the mid-nineteenth century, the American Civil War ended and Canada acquired British Dominion status. Henceforth, North America comprised two newly emerging big powers formed largely by European immigrants. Both built railways from the Atlantic to the Pacific Coast, and mined minerals and developed large-scale, efficient agriculture in areas where Europeans had rarely lived in the past.

While there are obvious differences between the United States and Canada—the former long operated a system of slavery, while one-quarter of the latter's population is Catholic and francophone—the great majority of inhabitants share a common language, religious beliefs and customs, as well as a similar level of economic development. Neither country stations troops along the 6,000 km border, and citizens can cross it without a passport; a driver's license suffices. The United States and Canada rank as the world's two most friendly neighbors and big powers.

By the early twentieth century, the veteran colonial powers Portugal and Spain were already in decline. At that time, the world's most powerful colonial empires were those of Great Britain, France and Russia, but Germany and Italy, newly unified countries, were in hot pursuit and industrializing at a rapid clip. Germany occupied two colonies of its own, one in East Africa and one in the southwest. Italy also grabbed two colonies for itself in the Horn of Africa.

In terms of industrial capacity, however, the United States and Canada began to exhibit exceptional creativity in the late nineteenth and early twentieth centuries. The phone, motion pictures, phonograph, electricity generator, refrigerator, AC grid and airplane were all invented on North American soil. In addition, the United States and Canada were the world's first countries to implement ten years of compulsory education.

World War I broke out in 1914. Britain, France and Russia joined forces to contend with the Germans. Supported only by the rapidly declining Austro-Hungarian and Ottoman Empires, Germany found itself in a position of strategic weakness. Initially, however, German morale was strong and performance on the battlefield glorious. The fruits of the Industrial Revolution were applied to great effect in this war. Only a decade after the airplane was invented, the warring parties had established their own air forces and extended the domain of warfare, formerly conducted solely on the earth's surface, into a new realm—the three dimensional air space.

Since this article revolves around the "New Silk Road," it's appropriate to mention the German pilot, Manfred von Richthofen, better known as the "Red Baron." Born into a prominent Prussian aristocratic family, he entered military school at eleven years of age. Upon the outbreak of World War I, he served in the cavalry on the eastern front, but in 1915 he was transferred to the western front where he learned how to fly. At the time, the main type of fighter aircraft was a small biplane (dual-level wings) that accommodated just the pilot. There were also two-seaters, with a space for a back seat observer-cum-machine-gunner. Richthofen first served as the latter, but soon switched to flying solo.

Both smart and gutsy, he painted his fighter a flamboyant red. The Red Baron was the most renowned hero of World War I, shooting down 80 enemy aircraft in all, according to German statistics. On April 21, 1918, the day after he had brought down his 80th adversary, Richthofen was struck by a machine-gun bullet fired from the ground, crashed and died. He was just twenty-five. In fact, the heroic pilot had a special connection with the Silk Road. Baron von *Richthofen*, the geographer who proposed the term "Seidenstraße" back in the nineteenth century—silk road in English—also happened to be the Red Baron's uncle.

When World War I broke out, the American military initially remained uninvolved, "observing the tiger fight from the safety of the mountains," as the Chinese adage goes. Eventually the United States declared war, however, and dispatched its troops to defeat the Germans. During the war, the Bolsheviks overthrew the czar and Lenin announced an armistice with the Central Powers, effectively withdrawing Russia from combat. French casualties were very heavy, but it remained a major global player. Britain too was seriously impacted, but preserved its status as the world's greatest power.

But the real victor was the United States. Before the war terminated the Americans launched the slogan of "National Determination," and after combat had ceased, they encouraged the European colonies to fight for independence. Despite this anti-imperialist stance, after the war the United States insisted on maintaining possession of colonies wrested from Spain in 1898, Puerto Rico, the Philippines and a part of Cuba.

WORLD WAR II AND AMERICAN HEGEMONY

It was the Ottoman Empire and Germany that suffered the most grievously from the disastrous first world war. The Ottoman Empire was entirely dismembered, with control of its territories in North Africa and West Asia formally transferred, some to the British and some to the French. Germany was forced to formulate the Weimar Constitution, pay a huge indemnity and passively accept manipulation at the hands of the victorious Allied Powers. Nationalism grew popular as a result of these humiliations, and this contributed to the Nazis winning the 1933 elections.

Italy was on the winning side in the war, but deeply regretted having missed the earlier colonialist "bandwagon." Obsessed with catching up with its European rivals, under the leadership of the National Fascist Party, in 1934 Italy invaded the territory of one of East Africa's most ancient civilizations, Ethiopia. This marked the last attempt by a European power to establish a colony on the continent.

On March 15, 1939, when German troops invaded Poland, Britain and France had little choice but to intervene, and this ignited World War II. This time around, Germany's allies were Fascist Italy, and Japan, whose militarist-dominated imperial government had long since invaded China. Despite the implementation of full-scale Chinese War of Resistance Against Japanese Aggression beginning in 1937, and the outbreak of World War II in Europe, the isolationist United States was still reluctant to directly intervene in what was perceived as "someone else's" war. It wasn't until Japan's "unprovoked and dastardly attack" (President Roosevelt's words) on Pearl Harbor that the Americans declared war on Japan on December 8, 1941, and three days later, on Germany as well. With the United States having thrown its towel in the ring, the early battlefield superiority of the key Axis Powers—Germany, Italy and Japan—progressively declined, and the military initiative gradually passed into the hands of the US-led Allies. The atomic bombs dropped on Hiroshima and Nagasaki utterly destroyed Japan's will to resist, and highlighted America's research achievements.

With the war now over, the United States dominated the new international order. The United Nations, International Monetary Fund and the World Bank—all founded in 1945—as well as the Marshall Plan (1948–1952), reflected America's global strategy. At this point in time, one-half of the GDP of the nations of the world was generated by the United States. During the latter half of the twentieth century, much of the planet's population engaged in pursuit of "The American Way of Life."

During the Cold War, the Soviet-led socialist camp posed a real threat to the United States and Western Europe. However, due to its overall economic weakness, backward agriculture and emphasis on its defense industry to the detriment of light industry, its eventual decline had long been evident. During the presidency of Ronald Reagan (1981–1989), some American scholars predicted the disintegration of the Soviet Union within 10–15 years, mainly due to agitation of independence among the constituent republics in the Baltic Sea region and Central Asia. The Berlin Wall collapsed in 1989, and just two years later, the Soviet Union officially disbanded, and world hegemony rested entirely in the hands of the United States, the sole surviving superpower.

The acquisition and consolidation of this hegemony, of course, depended upon military force and political measures. But economic and cultural power sustains military and political power, and the source of economic and cultural power is good governance and the full exercise of individual creativity. From World War II through today, the United States has indeed led the world in terms of the economy and cultural creativity.

During the 70–80 years following the outbreak of World War II, scientific and technical progress has proceeded more rapidly than ever before in human history. The atomic bomb, TV, semiconductors, lasers, computers, the Internet, mobile phones, nanotechnology, satellites, the space station, gene technology, therapeutic use of stem cells and artificial intelligence—have combined to transport mankind into an utterly new era, and all these innovations appeared first in the United States.

Beginning in the mid-twentieth century, American-style dress and music gained worldwide popularity, and Hollywood's films were welcomed and imitated in countries everywhere. Today, the sartorial and lifestyle preferences of China's emerging middle class are obviously influenced by American culture. Driven by globalization, the international use of English is increasingly common. Looking around the world, we can see that America's high-tech, cultural and military power remains dominant, with no competitor currently in sight.

Geographically speaking, the United States' "homeland security" benefits from the country's location between the Atlantic and the Pacific, but its relative isolation from Eurasia (and Africa) means that it cannot easily project its power worldwide, and must seek alliances and establish military bases across the globe.

The New Silk Road: Reliant Upon the East

During the second half of the twentieth century, American aviation power was unassailable, and constituted a firm foundation for both long-range projection of US military might and exercising cultural influence. In 1969, the United States landed on the moon, and then went to develop many space-related technologies and hardware, including the Space Shuttle, various satellites and the International Space Station (ISS). In the 70 s, the United States invented the Internet, and forty years later, the entire globe has effectively become the "World of the Internet." As a result, human understanding of Nature and society has become broader and deeper, as well as more finely detailed and subtle.

During the final two decades of the twentieth century, the most far-reaching development in the world was China's entry into the process of economic globalization, which has transformed it into the most prominent power in the Eurasian landmass today. Over the last forty years, over six hundred million Chinese—twice the population of the United States—have been lifted out of poverty and received a modern education. The ratio of rural to urban residents has changed dramatically, from 8:2 in the 70s to about 5:5 today.

The state-sponsored development of people's intellectual capacities on such a large scale has not previously occurred in any society. The basic driver behind this achievement has been the government's deployment of huge amounts of manpower and material resources to construct housing, roads, bridges and tunnels, as well as larger projects including optical fiber networks, canals, dams, power plants, power grids, harbors and airports. The construction of this infrastructure represents the crystallization of thousands of years of civilization, as well as its fastest and most large-scale implementation in history.

As we recall the interaction between peoples and the exchange of ideas and goods throughout Eurasia, it is clear that the ancient overland and maritime silk roads did indeed promote the progress of human civilization. To further develop the present world and ensure that the fruits of civilization can, via modern technology and management, benefit the overwhelming majority of people today, a new, large-scale traffic artery now needs to be built linking the two ends of the Eurasian land mass, as well as connecting it with some African countries.

No matter how well aircraft and the Internet facilitate communications, the transport of large amounts of goods and people still requires overland and sea passageways. China has recently put forward the concept of "Belt and Road," with a particular emphasis on developing the infrastructure of developing countries. This is based on China's own experiences during development, as well as the current practical needs of those countries.

When the initiative was announced, it generated international attention, and both praise and criticism. In my opinion, promotion of "Belt and Road" by China has several advantages. China is the homeland of silk, and the nation's history has been intimately tied to the Silk Road, so these factors make it quite natural for China to make such a proposal. Furthermore, China has a tradition of accommodating distant neighbors, as well as experience in providing aid to Asian and African countries in the modern era. This should enable China both to adopt a long-term frame of reference, and to avoid actions aimed at quick but short-term benefits; it should also help "Belt and Road" gain acceptance from potential participants.

China is a major land- and sea-based power that possesses geographical depth and historical experience. "Belt and Road" resembles a concerto, with voice and instrument complementing one another, while each continues to play its own distinct role. At the same time, China now has strong economic momentum, abundant financial resources and scientific and technological strength. These advantages are important for the actual physical construction of the New Silk Road, as well as for the extensive international cooperation necessary for the construction process.

Moreover, historically China has not had conflicts—religious or in terms of culture—with any of the "Belt and Road" countries. This is in contrast with the history of the Crusades and European colonialism, and contemporary "Eurocentric" and "Americentric" mindsets, as well as anti-Islamic sentiment in the West, all of which might generate psychological resistance among the citizens of a fair number of countries toward any attempt by the Europeans or Americans to initiate projects on their sovereign territory.

In 1935, Mao Zedong wrote his famous poem, *Kunlun Mountain*, which contains these lines:

> Towering Kunlun,
> I'd cleave you in three:
> One piece for Europe,
> One for America,
> One to keep in the East.

As we look around the world today, we see that it is precisely these three forces that are capable of transcontinental operations. For the great majority of developing countries, the ideal situation is one in which these three forces coordinate and cooperate. The United States is now the world's dominant power, but it can't possibly do everything and lead in all matters. The European Union is currently the world's largest unified economic body, strong in science and technology; but European cohesion is dissipating, and Europe is fading relative to the United States and China. Among these three players, the most dynamic and capable, and least liable to encounter resistance while engaging in construction of the twenty-first century's New Silk Road, should be the "East" cited by Mao Zedong. Yet without cooperation of Europe and the United States, the initiative of the East will be difficult to implement smoothly.

It is my hope that both developing and developed countries will, in a spirit of mutual aid, mutual trust and mutual benefit, engage jointly in commerce, construction and sharing of resources, in order to support the "Belt and Road" goal of collective prosperity for all participating countries. The ancient Silk Road will be rejuvenated, and Eurasia will realize its historical destiny of promoting the further development of human civilization.

INDEX

C
Civilization-related concepts
  Agriculture civilizations, 12
  Akkadian Kingdom, 279
  Arabo-Islamic civilization, 43, 45, 48, 303, 305, 474, 475
  artificial intelligence, 26, 483
  colonialism, 9, 73, 74, 100, 102, 105, 485
  Elamite civilization, 279
  four great inventions, 15, 41, 61, 87
  gene technology, 483
  Grassland Silk Road, 186
  humanism, 323, 476, 478
  Kassite culture, 279
  Lucy, 3, 4
  miniature painting, 311, 322, 325, 367
  Nile Valley Civilizations, 14
  nomadic civilization, 190
  Oasis Silk Road, 17, 104, 119, 121, 125, 128, 135, 467, 468
  Perso-Islamic civilization, 367
  quatrain, 316, 317

  Reformation, 50, 477, 478
  Renaissance, 44, 48, 49, 61, 100, 102, 105, 127, 161, 310, 311, 317, 322, 323, 367, 368, 380, 409, 439, 475–478
  Susa's culture, 279
  the Agricultural Revolution, 278, 461, 462
  the Belt and Road Initiative, 99, 101, 112, 113, 126, 179, 222, 270, 271, 273
  the Industrial Revolution, 13, 24, 105, 477, 480
  The Indus Valley civilization, 239
  the Maritime Silk Road, 17, 133, 142, 468
  The Wailing Wall, 94
  Yoga, 230, 250, 260

E
Ethnic groups and tribes
  Akkadians, 64, 158, 279
  Assyrians, 14, 64, 66, 103, 363
  Cossack, 168, 343, 369, 376, 377

Jews, 14, 16, 21, 36, 43, 45, 94, 102, 232, 282, 300, 301, 343, 344, 365, 388, 406, 407, 414, 445, 476
Jurchen, 39, 41, 81
Khitan, 39, 41, 84, 125, 198, 469, 470
Kumyks, 365, 369, 374
Maratha, 256
Neanderthal, 358
Roman, 16, 18, 19, 27, 43–45, 49, 65, 71, 72, 94, 151, 171, 172, 265, 291, 292, 300, 363, 405, 414, 467, 474
Scythians, 17, 119, 158, 188, 189, 191, 205, 217–219, 254, 280, 358, 465
the Aryans, 15, 16, 23, 104, 130, 188, 278, 280, 345, 358
the Babylonians, 14, 21, 65, 282
the Circassians, 360, 369, 375–377
the Hephthalites, 159, 190, 191, 293, 295, 296
the Hittites, 16, 166
the Kalmyks, 374
the Kurds, 149, 192, 421, 427, 454
the Manchu, 23, 41, 109, 110, 199, 222
the Mongols, 17, 22, 23, 41, 47, 65, 72, 81, 126, 151, 159, 166, 168, 193, 194, 199, 206, 213, 223, 267, 268, 299, 309, 319, 321, 329, 345, 363, 367, 404, 407, 445, 469, 470, 475, 477
the Oghuz, 134, 200, 307, 308, 334, 387, 402
the Pashtuns, 306
the Persians, 21, 43, 44, 65, 72, 89, 94, 127, 130, 133, 159, 170, 190, 191, 198, 201, 204, 267, 268, 339, 344, 345, 366, 369, 402, 407, 465, 469, 471
the Seljuk, 20, 65, 308, 309, 318, 366, 367, 402–404, 444–446, 475, 476
the Sogdians, 21–23, 130, 131, 189, 205, 212, 465
The Sumerians, 64, 158, 279
the Tangut, 39, 41, 124
the Tartars, 199, 368
the Tocharians (Yuezhi), 17, 187, 188, 190, 210, 211, 219, 358
the Turkic peoples, 17, 22, 72, 190, 191, 263, 268, 299, 334, 366, 401–403, 433, 452, 453
the Xianbei, 82, 469, 470
Turkoman, 334
Tuva, 181, 223

G

Geographical terms
Almaty, 207
Baghdad, 43–45, 65, 67, 73, 85, 86, 92, 150, 200, 202, 266, 302, 303, 305, 307, 308, 319, 330, 402, 403, 405, 431
Baku, 357, 387, 391
Bangalore, 228–232
Bering Strait, 5, 6, 460
Bukhara, 22, 94, 131, 194, 205, 304, 306, 307, 312, 313, 316, 333, 402, 470
Buryats, 198
Cairo, 45, 74, 76, 79, 85, 93, 330, 347
Calicut, 256, 268
Caucasus, 29, 71, 125, 165, 168, 169, 171, 174, 194, 277, 291, 335, 355–360, 362, 363, 365, 367–371, 374–381, 383, 390, 391, 393, 408, 409, 417, 432, 450, 452, 454, 471, 474

Chang'an, 17, 22, 130, 216, 267
Chechnya, 169, 174, 360, 376, 380, 381
Chennai, 229, 247, 253, 255, 271
Crimea, 163, 164, 166, 168, 175, 378, 394, 409, 413, 471
Ctesiphon, 302
Dagestan, 169, 174, 360, 368, 376, 381
Edirne, 405, 412, 419, 439, 440
Euphrates River, 64, 291
Fergana, 160, 220
Fez, 415
Gandhara, 130, 158, 159, 266, 288
Goa, 228, 231–233, 235, 269
Greater Khingan Mountains, 12, 17, 186
Hami, 124, 192, 210, 211, 470
Herat, 127, 160, 311, 313, 320, 334, 368
Hexi Corridor, 17, 104, 120, 130, 134, 166, 180–182, 187, 190, 193, 197–200, 210, 212, 215, 464–466
Hotan, 105, 123
Ingushetia, 169, 174, 360, 376, 380
Isfahan, 336, 337, 339, 369
Istanbul, 20, 72, 120, 323, 376, 393, 404, 411, 417, 420–426, 431, 433, 436–438, 440, 449, 455, 474
Jerusalem, 22, 92, 94, 101, 126, 282, 296, 362, 378, 475
Kaifeng, 86, 402
Karakoram Mountains, 161, 182
Karakorum, 310
Kashgar, 136, 142, 162, 182, 186, 189, 209, 210, 212, 218–221
Khorasan, 133, 302, 309, 316, 335
Khotan (modern-day Hetian), 185, 189, 212, 213, 217, 465

Khujand, 204
Khwarazm, 125, 304, 309
Kolkata (Calcutta), 229, 234, 235, 237, 247
Konya, 308, 403, 444–447
Kuban Steppe, 357
Kuqa (Kucha), 39, 211, 212
Kurdish, 68, 150, 393, 394, 421, 434, 451, 454
Lahore, 160, 197, 202, 203
Lake Baikal, 24, 197, 198
Levant, 101, 284, 300, 367
Loulan, 187, 188
Madrasas, 312, 313
Manzikert, 366, 403
Mesopotamia, 7, 13–15, 36, 63–67, 103, 147, 158, 265, 277–279, 281, 282, 291, 294, 462, 466
Mumbai (formerly Bombay), 229, 247, 250, 254, 264
Nagorno-Karabakh, 389
Nalanda, 43, 90, 92, 123, 124
New Delhi, 65, 235, 246, 254, 259, 271, 273
Petra, 288
Pondicherry, 253, 256–260
Qiuci, 39, 85, 121, 133, 193
Qom, 335
Samarkand, 44, 85, 90, 92, 94, 120, 126, 127, 133, 160, 193, 202, 205, 307, 310–313, 368, 405, 471
Shiraz, 319, 340
Sochi, 357, 373, 381
Sumatra, 264, 266, 267
Susa, 279, 281, 283, 284
Syr Darya, 180, 181, 189, 191, 198, 201, 204, 277, 294, 306, 307, 366, 402, 403
Tabriz, 73, 309, 313, 334–336, 367, 368
Talas, 44, 84, 85, 100, 133, 266

Tamil Nadu, 253, 256, 259
Teheran, 394
the Altai Mountains, 187, 210, 463, 464
the Amu Darya, 121, 180, 181, 201, 203, 215, 294, 306, 309, 366, 402
the Aral Sea, 197, 277, 304, 307, 366, 402
the Balkan Peninsula, 71, 291, 377, 405
the Black Sea, 20, 94, 164, 166–168, 174, 188, 189, 210, 355–358, 360, 373, 377, 378, 408, 413, 420, 421, 425, 443, 463, 471
the Bosphorus Strait, 376
the Danube, 12, 120, 125, 167, 186, 279, 402, 404, 463, 474
the Dnieper, 163, 166, 206, 463
The Dzungar, 211, 221, 463
the Indus River, 7, 125, 158, 277, 284, 294, 318, 462
the Iranian Plateau, 181, 188, 277–281, 315, 358, 363, 466
the Kazakh Steppe, 160, 463
the Mongolian Plateau, 17, 65, 72, 167, 180, 181, 189, 191, 198, 199, 210, 212, 307, 365, 463, 465
the Nile, 14, 37, 69, 102, 462
the Outer Khingan Range, 194
the Pamir Mountains, 190, 198
the Persian Gulf, 17, 42, 65, 72, 73, 101, 140, 145, 148, 150, 159, 264, 265, 277, 367, 405, 408
the Volga River, 125, 167, 168, 191, 194, 368, 373, 463
the Yellow River Basin, 7, 24, 462, 465
Thrace, 284, 421, 426
Tigris, 13, 64, 278, 302, 462
Trabzon, 20, 441–444
Turpan, 124, 182, 187, 211–213, 220
Ulaanbaatar, 197, 207
Ulan-Ude, 197, 198
Yenisei River, 191, 307, 401, 402, 404
Yining, 221, 222
Zagros Mountains, 277, 278

H

Historical events and others
al-Qaeda, 150, 204, 380
Arab Spring, 68, 69, 77, 79
Area Studies, 100, 106–110
a system of slavery, 479
Bharatiya Janata Party (BJP), 230, 232, 233, 244
Chechen War, 380
China-Pakistan Economic Corridor, 142
Heartland Theory, 111, 136
International Monetary Fund, 482
Iran-Iraq war, 150, 155
Islamic State, 43, 44, 68, 69, 146
Justice and Development Party (AKP), 432, 450
Neo-Ottomanism, 454, 455
Orientalism, 105, 106
Rose Revolution, 165, 170, 172, 356, 385
Shanghai Cooperation Organization (SCO), 183, 273
Tanzimat, 415–417
The 1919 Peace Treaties of Paris, 421
The 9.11 event in the U.S., 433
the Crimean War, 378, 379, 416
the Crusades, 37, 72, 100, 154, 331, 476, 485

the East India Company (Britain), 103, 234, 256, 479
the East India Company (France), 256, 258, 478
"The Great Game", 136, 204
The Influence of Sea Power upon History, 136
the *millet* system, 406, 427
the Organization of Petroleum Exporting Countries (OPEC), 149
the royal guardian brigade, 307
the Treaty of Carlowitz, 409
the United Nations, 25, 111, 350, 482
The White Revolution, 346, 348
the "Young Turks" (formerly the "Young Ottomans"), 418
Treaty of Lausanne, 427
Xinjiang Production and Construction Corps, 223

L
Linguistic families, linguistic groups, and languages
Afroasiatic, 359
Altaic languages, 189, 191, 293
Arabic, 17, 18, 21, 23, 36, 37, 45, 46, 48, 51, 70, 71, 75, 86, 93, 96, 102, 104, 145, 159, 200, 202, 203, 214, 219, 266, 300, 301, 303, 305, 306, 308, 311, 315, 319, 328, 349, 359, 360, 367, 403, 475
Aramaic, 21, 23
a Semitic tongue, 14
Caucasian languages, 358, 360, 361
Chagatai, 128, 160, 194, 202, 203, 219
cuneiform script, 15, 36, 66, 279, 282
Farsi, 306, 316, 355

Greek, 16, 18–21, 36, 37, 44, 45, 65, 71, 72, 84, 86, 94, 102, 104, 130, 132, 159, 166, 188, 189, 191, 192, 265, 283–285, 287, 288, 291, 292, 296, 303, 339, 378, 403, 407, 411, 414, 420, 425, 427, 439, 441, 442, 460, 465, 468, 474–476, 478
Greek alphabet, 23
Hebrew, 23, 36–38, 75, 86, 359, 473
hieroglyphs, 36, 102
Hindi, 203, 235, 240, 259
Indo-European languages, 23, 103, 104, 166, 173, 187, 188, 358
Latin, 8, 18, 23, 46, 48, 200, 202, 305
Latin letters, 128
Mongolian, 22, 125, 134, 137, 160, 191–193, 198–200, 206, 207, 213, 219, 221, 267, 309–311, 335, 345, 358, 374, 403, 470
oracle bone script, 36, 37
Ottoman, 18, 19, 47, 67, 71, 73, 102, 103, 126, 154, 168–170, 220, 318, 360, 375, 377, 405, 406, 409, 413–415, 417–419, 421, 424, 427, 436, 439, 441
Pahlavi, 296, 301, 344–346, 351
Phoenician alphabet, 21, 23
Russian, 16, 28, 30, 42, 125, 136, 137, 148, 151, 163–167, 169–172, 175, 176, 181, 192, 194, 197, 202, 206, 221, 223, 270, 272, 335, 343, 360, 362, 368, 369, 373, 376–380, 383, 385, 386, 389, 393, 396, 397, 417, 420, 424, 454
Sanskrit, 15, 23, 91, 92, 104, 123, 130, 216, 230, 254, 266, 280
Sino-Tibetan family, 240

Sogdian, 21–23, 89, 131, 132, 185, 189, 193, 205, 213, 219, 280, 294, 295, 306, 402, 403, 471
Syriac, 18, 19, 21, 23, 38, 132, 133, 296
Tamil, 246, 253–256
the Dravidian language, 240
the Indo-Iranian family of languages, 240
the Oghuz, 307, 308, 334, 387, 402
the Syriac script, 22
the Tibetan (Tubo), 133, 134, 198, 199, 212
Tibeto-Burman ethnic groups, 240
Tocharian, 187, 189, 210, 213, 216, 465
Uighur script, 203
Urdu, 203, 257
Literary works
Amitabha Sutra, 122
A Record of Buddhist Kingdoms, 91, 124
Bustan (The Orchard), 319
Canon of Medicine, 46, 202, 305
Code of Hammurabi, 14
Diamond Sutra, 122, 216
Divine Comedy, 48
Dream Pool Essays (Meng Xi Bi Tan), 87
Great Tang Records on the Western Regions, 91, 92, 123, 124, 185
Gulistan (The Rose Garden), 319
I Ching, 55, 56
Introduction (Muqaddimah, 1377), 48
Jami'al-tawarikh (Compendium of Chronicles), 310
Leyla and Majnun, 318
Masnavi, 445
One Thousand and One Nights, 86, 267, 303
Qutadğu Bilig (Kutadgu Bilig), 218
Tao Te Ching (Book of the Dao), 91
Tarikh-i Jahangushay (History of the World Conqueror), 310
The Analects of Confucius, 41
the Behistun Inscription, 282
the Bible, 21, 49, 54, 477, 478
the *Book of Kings*, 309, 319, 322
the *Book of Songs (Shi Jing)*, 83, 84
the *Heart Sutra*, 97, 122, 124, 216
the Quran, 46, 48, 406, 423
the *Tale of Genji*, 40
The Travels, 93, 94, 96

P
Personalities
Abbas the Great, 336, 338
Abraham, 14
Abu Bakr, 328
Abu Muslim, 302
Afghani, 341
Akbar, 161
Alexander, 36, 72, 130, 158, 189, 215, 284, 287, 339
al-Ghazali, 334
Ali, 328–330, 342
Ali ibn Abi Talib, 328
Ali ibn Buya, 307
al-Mulk, Nizam, 308
Aquinas, Thomas, 46
Ashoka, 92, 124, 189
Atatürk, Kemal, 344, 428, 429
Babur, 127, 128, 160, 161, 193, 202, 204, 232, 471
Ban Chao, 179, 209, 218
Battuta, Ibn, 92–94, 96, 268
Batu Khan, 167
Chen Cheng, 160
Cyrus the Great, 282
Darius, 72, 282, 283

Darwin, 9, 66
Emperor Kangxi of Qing, 470
Emperor Wu of Han, 120, 190, 465
Erdogan, Recep Tayyip, 393, 433, 450, 452–455
Faxian, 17, 90, 91, 123, 124, 265, 266
Ferdowsi, 308, 309, 319
Gandhi, Mahatma, 230, 245, 246
Ganjavi, Nizami, 318, 366
Gülen, Fethullah, 451
Hafez, 68, 319, 320
Hasan ibn Ali al-Askari, 327
Haydar Aliyev and his son Ilham, 387
Huxley, 54, 58
Ibn Sina (Avicenna), 46, 202, 304
Jalal al-Din Muhammad, 445
Jami, 127, 313, 320
Juvayni, Ata-Malek, 310
Khan, Genghis, 22, 65, 124–126, 128, 132, 160, 161, 167, 168, 193, 194, 199, 206, 309–311, 367, 403, 469–471, 477
Khan, Hulagu, 45, 309, 311, 367
Khan, Nusrat Fateh Ali, 157
Khomeini, Ruhollah, 347
Khosrow, 296, 367
Khwarazm, 200–202, 304, 309
King Kanishka I, 92
Kublai Khan, 22, 45, 268, 309
Kumarajiva, 90, 121, 122, 124, 215–217
Leibniz, Gottfried, 55, 56, 58, 339
Louis IX, 101, 154, 475
Luther, Martin, 49, 477
Mehmed II, 405, 407, 435
Modi, Narendra, 232, 233
Muhammad, 43, 45, 46, 67, 75, 76, 128, 220, 234, 299, 300, 302–304, 325, 327–329, 402, 406
Muhammad Ali Pasha, 413
Muhammad bin Saud, 413
Muhammad ibn ʿAbd al-Wahhab, 413
Muhammad ibn Hassan, 330
Muhammad ibn Musa al-Khwarizmi, 304
Nehru, Jawaharlal, 242, 245, 246, 270
Newton, Isaac, 55, 58, 66, 339
Reza Khan, 343, 344
Ricci, Matteo, 50, 54
Richthofen (geographer), 112, 138, 182, 481
Rumi, 317, 318, 320, 444, 445, 451
Saadi, 319
Shah, Muhammad Ali, 343, 344
Stalin, Joseph, 164, 170, 171, 194, 355, 370, 379, 385, 427
Sultan Selim III, 413
Sultan Suleiman I, 439
Timur, 126, 127, 160, 193, 202, 219, 256, 264, 310, 311, 368, 405, 471, 477
Ulugh Beg, 127, 202, 311, 312
Uthman, 328, 329, 367
Xuanzang, 17, 43, 90–92, 96, 123, 124, 183, 185, 266
Xu Guangqi, 54
Yelü Dashi, 213
Zhang, Qian, 17, 90, 101, 119–121, 135, 180, 186, 188, 218, 465, 466
Zheng He, 127, 148, 159, 256
Zoroaster, 130, 283, 289, 290

R
Religious terms
Ahura Mazda, 130, 290, 294

Akhund, 329
Armenian Church, 362
Ayatollah, 332, 347–350
Brahmanism, 90, 188, 231, 244, 254
Buddhism, 17, 19, 22, 39, 40, 83, 90–92, 121–124, 128–130, 134, 159, 189, 192, 198, 215, 216, 231, 234, 239, 242, 254, 266, 325
Catholicism, 19, 49, 50, 171, 232, 327, 331, 332, 378, 476
Christianity, 16, 18, 19, 42, 44, 109, 131, 132, 161, 167, 169, 194, 290, 327, 328, 330–332, 360, 362, 374, 474
Coptic Christian, 36, 45, 300
Gandhara art, 104, 130, 159, 203
Hinduism, 19, 90, 161, 188, 230, 233, 239, 242, 255, 264
Islam, 16, 29, 43–47, 51, 70–72, 74, 75, 77, 90, 94, 100, 109, 126, 127, 133, 134, 161, 167, 191, 211, 219, 255, 264, 299–302, 309, 328, 329, 332, 335, 341, 348, 349, 365, 406, 413, 427, 439, 470
Jainism, 231, 242
Khoja, 219
Manicheans, 21, 23, 38
Mithra, 291
Muslims, 18–20, 42, 44, 46, 51, 66, 71, 74–77, 79, 92, 100–102, 126, 133, 134, 148, 159, 161, 168, 199, 200, 203, 212, 220, 230–232, 240–244, 255, 256, 268, 300–302, 304, 309, 317, 327–329, 331–334, 344, 361, 375, 380, 388, 405, 407, 413, 416, 418, 419, 421, 426, 432–434, 442, 450, 451, 469, 470, 474–476

Nestorianism, 132, 133, 212
"new religion" (Protestantism), 49
Orthodox Church, 18, 19, 71, 132, 170, 197, 360, 362, 450
People of the Book, 301, 406
Shamanism, 47, 76, 133, 191, 192, 212, 307
Shia Islam, 327, 330, 331, 335, 343, 344, 348, 349, 471
Sufis, 76, 92, 133, 306, 307, 313, 316–321, 333–335, 349, 446
Sunni Islam, 76, 126, 304, 308, 331, 334, 360, 374, 403
the *Ashura*, 328, 342
"Taqiyya principle", 331
Twelve Imams, 342
Vedic scriptures, 230, 243
Wahhabism, 380, 413
Zoroastrianism, 21, 94, 130–132, 161, 188, 212, 242, 283, 289, 290, 292–294, 299, 301, 332

S

States, dynasties, and regimes
Abbasid dynasty, 86, 266
Achaemenid Empire, 281, 282, 299
Babylon, 21, 23, 64, 65, 189, 266, 282, 284, 287
Buyid Dynasty, 307, 403
Chagatai Khanate, 160, 210, 211, 219, 267, 310, 311, 471
Crimean Khanate, 164, 168
Delhi Sultanate, 19, 92, 203
Eastern Roman Empire, 16, 43, 86, 100–102, 293, 299, 300, 308, 445, 474, 476
Georgia, 71, 141, 163, 165, 169–171, 173, 175, 362, 363, 384–386, 391, 392, 396
Ghaznavid Dynasty, 308, 309, 316
Golden Horde, 92, 125, 168, 194, 221, 368

INDEX 495

Ilkhanate, 22, 23, 65, 92, 126, 127, 133, 309–311, 319, 321, 367, 368
Karakhanids, 213
Khazars, 167, 365
Kievan Rus, 166–168
Kushan Empire, 92, 130, 158, 190, 203, 215, 268, 466
Macedonia, 284, 418, 421, 423, 424
Mauryan Dynasty, 215
Medes, 280–282, 284, 363
Mughal Empire, 193, 202–204, 232, 257, 471
Ottoman Empire, 19, 25, 47, 65, 66, 71, 73, 103, 148, 154, 164, 168, 191, 335, 336, 340, 367, 368, 370, 374–378, 383, 385, 388, 404–414, 416, 417, 419–421, 425, 426, 454, 471, 480, 481
Parthia, 131, 291, 292
Persian Empire, 71, 72, 183, 205, 278, 280–283, 287, 293, 308, 310, 315, 318
Qajar Dynasty, 340, 344, 351

Roman Empire, 18, 42, 49, 72, 132, 151, 169, 215, 265, 268, 291–293, 339, 340, 344, 362, 405, 436, 466, 474, 476
Saffarid dynasty, 305
Seljuk Sultanate of Rum, 20, 318, 403
Tahirid Dynasty, 305
the Mamluk Dynasty, 93, 375
The Pahlavi Dynasty, 343, 344, 346
the Ptolemaic Dynasty, 89, 284, 288
the Safavid Dynasty, 73, 335, 338, 368, 369
the Sassanid Empire, 44, 72, 293–295, 299, 335
the Seleucid Kingdom, 284
the Seljuk dynasty, 65
the Shaybanid Dynasty, 128, 219
the Umayyad Caliphate, 43, 44, 302, 327
the Zand Dynasty, 340
Western Xia, 39, 41, 124, 125, 201
Wusun, 121, 188, 215, 221, 465
Xiongnu, 120, 121, 189, 190, 198, 215

Printed in the United States
by Baker & Taylor Publisher Services